**EMOTION**
**Theory, Research, and Experience**

*Volume 2*

Emotions in Early Development

# EMOTION

Theory, Research, and Experience

EDITED BY

**Robert Plutchik**
Albert Einstein College of Medicine
Bronx, New York

**Henry Kellerman**
Postgraduate Center for Mental Health
New York, New York

*Volume 1:* Theories of Emotion
*Volume 2:* Emotions in Early Development

In preparation
*Volume 3:* Biological Foundations of Emotion

# EMOTION
## Theory, Research, and Experience

## Volume 2
## Emotions in Early Development

EDITED BY

## Robert Plutchik
Albert Einstein College of Medicine
Bronx, New York

## Henry Kellerman
Postgraduate Center for Mental Health
New York, New York

 1983

**ACADEMIC PRESS**
*A Subsidiary of Harcourt Brace Jovanovich, Publishers*
New York   London
Paris   San Diego   San Francisco   São Paulo   Sydney   Tokyo   Toronto

ACADEMIC PRESS, INC.
111 Fifth Avenue, New York, New York 10003

*United Kingdom Edition published by*
ACADEMIC PRESS, INC. (LONDON) LTD.
24/28 Oval Road, London NW1 7DX

Library of Congress Cataloging in Publication Data
Main entry under title:

Emotions in early development.

(Emotion, theory, research, and experience ; v. 2)
Includes index.
1. Emotions in children. 2. Infant psychology.
I. Plutchik, Robert. II. Kellerman, Henry. III. Series.
[DNLM: 1. Emotions--In infancy and childhood. 2. child
development. WS 105.5.E5 E546]
BF561.E48 vol. 2 [BF720.E45] 155.4'22 82-18483
ISBN 0-12-558702-3

PRINTED IN THE UNITED STATES OF AMERICA

83 84 85 86     9 8 7 6 5 4 3 2 1

V. 2

# CONTENTS

## Chapter 1
## Issues in the Development of Emotion in Infancy 1
*LOIS BARCLAY MURPHY*

v

## Chapter 2
## Precursors for the Development of Emotions in
## Early Infancy                                                                       35
### T. BERRY BRAZELTON

## Chapter 3
## Emotions as Behavior Regulators:
## Social Referencing in Infancy                                                       57
### MARY D. KLINNERT, JOSEPH J. CAMPOS, JAMES F. SORCE,
### ROBERT N. EMDE, AND MARILYN SVEJDA

## Chapter 4
## Individual Differences in Dimensions of
## Socioemotional Development in Infancy                                               87
### ROSS A. THOMPSON AND MICHAEL E. LAMB

# Chapter 5
## Affect and Intellect: Piaget's Contributions to the Study of Infant Emotional Development    115
### DANTE CICCHETTI AND PETRA HESSE

# Chapter 6
## Emotional Sequences and Consequences    171
### HARRY F. HARLOW AND CLARA E. MEARS

# Chapter 7
## On the Relationship between Attachment and Separation Processes in Infancy    199
### MYRON A. HOFER

# Chapter 8
## Emotions in Early Development: A Psychoevolutionary Approach    221
### ROBERT PLUTCHIK

## Chapter 9
## Emotional Development and Emotional Education     259
### ROSS BUCK

## Chapter 10
## On the Emergence, Functions, and Regulation of Some Emotion Expressions in Infancy     293
### SANDRA BUECHLER AND CARROLL E. IZARD

## Chapter 11
## An Epigenetic Theory of Emotions in Early Development     315
### HENRY KELLERMAN

# LIST OF CONTRIBUTORS

Numbers in parentheses indicate the pages on which the authors' contributions begin.

T. BERRY BRAZELTON (35), Chief, Child Development Unit, The Childrens Hospital Medical Center, and Professor, Harvard Medical School, Boston, Massachusetts 02115

ROSS BUCK (259), Professor of Communication Sciences and Psychology, The University of Connecticut, Storrs, Connecticut 06268

SANDRA BUECHLER (293), William Alanson White Institute, New York, New York 10023

JOSEPH J. CAMPOS (57), Professor of Psychology, Department of Psychology, University of Denver, Denver, Colorado 80208

DANTE CICCHETTI (115), Associate Professor, Department of Psychology and Social Relations, Harvard University, and Associate Professor, Program in Human Development, Graduate School of Education, Cambridge, Massachusetts 02138

ROBERT N. EMDE (57), Professor of Psychiatry, Department of Psychiatry, University of Colorado Health Sciences Center, Denver, Colorado 80262

HARRY F. HARLOW[1] (171), Emeritus George Cary Comstock Professor, University of Wisconsin, Madison, Wisconsin, and Research and Visiting Pro-

[1]Deceased.

fessor, Department of Psychology, University of Arizona, Tucson, Arizona 85721

PETRA HESSE (115), Department of Psychology and Social Relations, Harvard University, Cambridge, Massachusetts 02138

MYRON A. HOFER (199), Professor of Psychiatry and Associate Professor of Neurosciences, Albert Einstein College of Medicine at Montefiore Hospital, Bronx, New York 10467

CARROLL E. IZARD (293), Unidel Professor of Psychology, Department of Psychology, University of Delaware, Newark, Delaware 19711

HENRY KELLERMAN (315), Associate Director of Psychology and, Director of Psychology Internship Training, Postgraduate Center for Mental Health, New York, New York 10016

MARY D. KLINNERT[1] (57), Research Associate, Department of Psychology, University of Denver, Denver, Colorado 80208

MICHAEL E. LAMB (87), Professor of Psychology, Psychiatry, and Pediatrics, Department of Psychology, University of Utah, Salt Lake City, Utah 84112

CLARA E. MEARS (171), Research Associate, University of Arizona, Department of Psychology, Tucson, Arizona 85721

LOIS BARCLAY MURPHY (1), 2810 Corbland Place, N.W., Washington, D.C. 20008

ROBERT PLUTCHIK (221), Professor of Psychiatry (Psychology), Albert Einstein College of Medicine, Bronx, New York 10461

JAMES F. SORCE (57), Research Fellow, Department of Psychiatry, University of Colorado, Health Sciences Center, Denver, Colorado 80208

MARILYN SVEJDA (57), Research Fellow, Department of Psychology, University of Denver, Denver, Colorado 80208

ROSS A. THOMPSON (87), Assistant Professor, Department of Psychology, University of Nebraska, Lincoln, Nebraska 68588

[1]PRESENT ADDRESS: Department of Pediatric Psychiatry, National Jewish Hospital/National Asthma Center, Denver, Colorado 80206.

# PREFACE

The first volume of the series *Emotion: Theory, Research, and Experience* was concerned with general, systematic approaches to emotion that have been proposed by contemporary theorists in the field. All major traditions were represented: the ethological–evolutionary, the psychophysiological, and the psychodynamic.

Other volumes in the series, beginning with the present one, will deal with specific areas of emotion where important theoretical advances are being made. One such area concerns emotions in infants. Research in this field has reflected the three traditions just mentioned but, in addition, has been strongly influenced by a behavioristic approach that is based on a detailed description of the stimulus conditions that elicit emotions in infants and the exact form of the emotional responses. Contemporary theories show an overlap of ideas from these different viewpoints.

In an effort to strengthen the synthesizing potential of the present volume, we presented each of the contributors with the same list of basic questions concerning emotions in young organisms. They were asked to comment on such issues as the extent to which infants are born with certain emotions; how one infers the existence of emotion in infants; the relations between emotions and cognitions; the relations between emotions and personality; and the role of parent–child interactions in the appearance and development of emotions. Authors were free to explore the domain of emotions in early development in any way they wished, but all dealt with at least some of these questions.

Because of the extensive overlap of ideas in the different chapters, there is no simple or obvious way to group them. However, in a very rough sense, the first few chapters tend to be in the descriptive, behavioral tradition, whereas the later chapters rely relatively more extensively on ethological and psychoanalytic ideas.

In the first chapter, Lois Murphy summarizes some of her insights based on over 50 years of research. She considers such basic questions as the function of emotions; the problem of labeling affects in infants; the control and expression of emotions; and the development of the smile, of stranger anxiety, and of the sense of self. She emphasizes the need for careful and detailed descriptions of infant behavior, and she stresses the need for longitudinal, naturalistic studies to reveal the dynamic ebb and flow of affects and personality traits.

Brazelton, in the second chapter, is concerned with the parent–infant communication system. He points out the two-way, primarily nonverbal, interaction that takes place between mother and infant and the nature of the learning processes that occur in both the infant and the mother. The feedback loop that characterizes this interaction helps establish a sense of mastery in the infant which provides the basis for the eventual development of a sense of self.

The third chapter, by Klinnert, Campos, Sorce, Emde, and Svejda, deals with three fundamental issues: the extent to which emotions may be conceptualized as dependent or independent variables; the extent to which emotions determine cognitive evaluations; and the mechanisms that provide the basis for emotional influences on social behavior. They introduce an important new idea that they refer to as "social referencing," by which they mean the use of emotional information gained from another person to help evaluate situations. They believe that social referencing occurs in infants and that it has a developmental history. The evidence they present leads to the hypothesis that feeling states are both elicited by the emotional expressions of others and are regulators of behavior.

In the fourth chapter, Thompson and Lamb examine the problem of wide individual differences in emotional expressions observed in 1-year-old infants. An attempt is made to relate such individual differences to variations in mothers' reactions to signs of infant distress and to variations in face-to-face play interactions between mother and infant. Examination of these variables reveals that infant–mother attachment indices are related to measures of infant emotions and coping styles.

In Chapter 5, Cicchetti and Hesse examine in detail the implications for a theory of emotions of Piaget's theory of cognitive development. These authors make the fundamental point that cognitive development is generally inferred on the basis of emotional indicators such as crying, smiling, laughing, and surprise. Such reactions signal advances in the development of concepts about objects, spatial relations, causality, and similarity. The point is made that Piaget's descriptions of emotions imply that virtually all emotions and expressions are present at birth and are thus innate. Emotional development consists, in part, of changes in social functions of emotion, in intercoordination of emotional expressions, and in the ability of increasingly abstract situations to elicit emotional reactions. The final section of their chapter compares a parallelist with an epiphenomenalist position on the relation between emotions and cognitions.

The next five chapters reflect a more ethological, evolutionary perspective. Harlow and Mears, in Chapter 6, present their ideas on the development and mixing of a number of basic emotions: love, fear, anger, play. They trace these emotions, conceptualized as complex systems, in monkeys and in human infants and describe the interactions that take place between them in terms of both temporal development and the factors that influence their mixtures. The power of play is emphasized as a remedial, survival-related activity.

In Chapter 7, by Hofer, evidence is presented to suggest that the stress response of infant and mother to separation is more than the disruption of a social bond. The hypothesis is defended that attachment is a development, through repeated stimulation, of primitive biological-approach tendencies that have homeostatic, regulatory functions. One of the important implications of this approach is that it enables distinctions to be made among different biological or neurological mechanisms for each effect of separation. Thus, rather than examine a global "emotional stress response," one considers the mechanisms involved in each aspect of stress.

In Chapter 8, Plutchik considers early emotional development within his psychoevolutionary framework. He points out that emotions in infants must be considered within an evolutionary framework as fundamentally related to survival; that emotions are not only subjective feeling states, but are rather complex chains of events; that emotions can be known only by inference from many sources of information; that emotions have certain structural relations to one another; and that many psychological states or activities, such as personality traits, can be considered as derivatives of emotion. In addition, Plutchik elaborates on the concept of schemata and epigenetic rules as the genetic basis for both the expression and recognition of emotional states.

In Chapter 9, Buck presents his view of emotions as a monitoring system for various states of the organism. This monitoring process provides information about the autonomic–endocrine system, about subcortical events through displays, and about cortical processes through subjective experience. Buck develops the concept of "accessibility" of emotional responses to the responder as well as to others, and then describes the relevance of Piaget's theory of cognitive development to a theory of emotion. He concludes by applying these ideas to the concept of emotion education.

Buechler and Izard, in Chapter 10, present their conception of emotion as part of a motivational–personality–evolutionary system. They examine the concept of aggression from three points of view: psychoanalytic theory, "differentiation" theory, and their own "discrete emotions" theory. They argue that there are separate innate neural programs for the expression of each of the fundamental emotions: interest, pleasure, startle, distress, rage, and disgust. They emphasize the idea that emotions are not disruptive behaviors that require controlling, but are organizing and mobilizing experiences. In addition, they propose that facial expressions are the only reliable measurable indicators that distinguish among the fundamental emotions.

The final chapter of the book, by Kellerman, is an attempt to integrate an epigenetic view of emotions with psychoanalytic concepts. Kellerman proposes that emotions contain a deep substrate composed of dispositional elements including mood imperatives, defense propensities, intrapsychic components, and cognitive proclivities. These hypothetical structures implied by each basic emotion may be reflected in certain diagnostic orientations. This proposed epigenetic system interacts with object experiences within a psychosexual context, leading ultimately to the formation of personality traits.

The present volume on emotions in the early development of organisms is a rich tapestry of facts, hypotheses, and theories. The image that emerges from this overview of the contributions is that emotions are a fundamental aspect of neonatal existence in both humans and animals, and they serve complex and subtle communication functions as well as biological regulatory functions. Emotions are also seen as essential precursors of complex interpersonal dispositions that eventuate in an individual's character structure. The ideas presented here can provide the basis for much research in infant development. The third volume of the series will examine the biological basis of emotions.

# CONTENTS OF VOLUME 1

# EMOTION
## Theory, Research, and Experience

*Volume 2*

Emotions in Early Development

Chapter 1

# ISSUES IN THE DEVELOPMENT OF EMOTION IN INFANCY

*LOIS BARCLAY MURPHY*

## ABSTRACT

A wide variety of issues are addressed in relation to the nature of emotions in human infants. These include the problem of how to label affects in infants; the functions of emotion; control and repression of emotion; and individual and sex differences in emotional expression and development. Factors related to the development of the smile, separation anxiety, wariness, and attachment are described. Affects are seen as the outcome of a maturational–developmental synthesis; the innate genetically determined potential for emotional expression and feelings may be realized in different ways and at different rates depending on the sequences of environmental circumstances. The need for both naturalistic and longitudinal studies is stressed.

## THE INFANT ORGANISM–ENVIRONMENT SYSTEM

The human organism is a wonderfully complex, flexible, dynamic system with a large number of semiindependent subsystems capable of interacting with each other. Individual differences among organisms, whether infants or adults, can be

1

documented in every structure, from sizes and shapes of noses, ears, eyes, mouth, feet, hands to all the internal organs—hearts, stomachs, livers, etc. (Williams, 1956). In addition, there are differences among individuals in thresholds for sensory stimulation in every sensory zone, in pace and coordination of motor responses, as well as in internal schema-formation. There are differences in expressiveness, its intensity and differentiation. All these and other differences contribute to highly individual patterns of strength and vulnerability and resources for coping, and to the affects or feelings that accompany all experiences.

This complexity and individuality of the equipment of each infant has to be recognized before we review some of the sequences in the development of infant emotions. The pace and visibility and even the sequences of affect development are affected by the patterning of these individual differences in different subsystems. Such differences are documented by Shirley's (1930) table of the interquartile dates of emergence of major responses, in Escalona and Heider's (1959) ratings of the success of Escalona's predictions of preschool functioning on the basis of infancy records, in Heider's (1966) study of vulnerability in infants, as well as Bayley's (1956) observations, and in Murphy and Moriarty's (1976) long-term study of child development. Thus, generalizations based on mean age of appearance of a given response must be considered in relation to the range over a wide sample. Although individual differences in observed behavior have been documented extensively, differences in autonomic nervous system reactivity have also been studied (Jones, 1930; Lacey, Kagan, Lacey, & Moss, 1963), and we have to infer similar ranges of differences in every aspect of the nervous system and of all zones of tissue, including those involving feeding, digestion, elimination, breathing, and metabolism. In addition to complexities contributed by the wide range of individual differences, reinforcement of different functions by affective accompaniments and social reinforcements add to the preferences and priorities of exercise of different functions by the infant.

Examples of interactions will easily come to mind: An infant's satisfaction in motor achievements, turning over, crawling, and pulling-up to standing, then walking, leads, with some babies, to a high affective investment in motor conquests at the expense of social and communication investment. Thus, some eagerly active babies do not develop language as rapidly as other babies less enamored of motor skills but more fascinated by evoking and sustaining verbal exchanges. "Arthur" had 200 words at 14 months but did not walk until the age of 16 months; his delighted response to music from earliest infancy along with his verbal interests led to his ability to identify 28 phonograph records by the age of 2. By contrast, "Alvin" had no words at 14 months but was expert and fascinated with manual operations, turning knobs, putting on lids, putting things in, onto, under objects, even turning pages of books. Whereas Arthur was intrigued by the discovery that everything had a word for it, Alvin was intrigued with the endless possibilities of what he could do with objects (unpublished data). I am emphasizing the variety of individual differences in different systems and their interaction in order to provide perspective and as a caution against generalizing with regard to emotional development.

But the infant is not developing in a vacuum—all of the individual differentiated capacities are evolving within an environment with its own individual, differentiated characteristics. Murphy's (1947) field-theory conceives of personality as the overlap of organism and environment; the personality is not simply inside of the individual. This field-theory approach is essential for understanding emotional development in infants in their widely varying environments. Although scarcely one-half the babies born today in the U.S.A. are cared for solely by their mothers, it is practicable within a limited space to discuss the infant in relation to the mother who is likewise a person with her own pattern of strengths and vulnerabilities, temperament, tempo, vigor, level of adaptability, affective intensity, sending power, and degree of experience and competence with infants, among other characteristics. Likewise, the home and neighborhood have individual qualities of quiet or noise, color or drabness, crowdedness or spaciousness, confusion or order, among other characteristics. More concretely, the baby may have a cozy bassinette or cradle, or a big crib that offers no skin contact. We have to think then of the *infant–environment system* and the development of emotion within the complexity of this infant–environment system, with the zones of fitting, nonfitting, need-gratifying and frustrating, stimulating and depriving experiences. Brazelton (1961) has documented the rhythms of mother–infant interplay as each responds to and retreats from the other. In a sensitively evocative as well as richly documented paper on emotional availability, Emde (1980) illustrates the processes of mutual emotional responsiveness that constitute a reciprocal reward system for infants and parents; infants rewarded by expressions of parents' love develop the trust important for further involvement in the environment, and parents rewarded by infants' expressions of pleasure are sustained in their efforts to meet the infants' needs.

Conclusions regarding emotional development of normal infants need to be drawn from observations of the infants in the normal home environment: Smiles, for instance, are documented at an earlier age in infants observed at home as contrasted with observations in the laboratory or other strange situations. A recognition of the effect of a strange place, strange people, strange apparatus is necessary whenever any aspect of infant development is studied outside of the familiar environment. We do not have even an effort toward a study of the development of an infant with all of its unique characteristics in its total, changing environment. Heider (1966) made the most differentiated analysis of characteristics of mothers in relation to a detailed study of infants. But the ecology, the characteristics of the environment as used by parents and infants, remains to be explored.

Before we continue with the early development of emotion, we also need to glance at the situation regarding the study of emotion generally. Scientific discussions sometimes seem to be written by people whose emotional experience is stingy or narrow; in psychology books, we encounter little reference to bliss, delight, ecstasy, passion, or even enthusiasm—and even less tenderness, love, adoration, devotion, trust, reverence, feelings of inspiration. Where is amusement, fun, whimsy? To be sure, self-esteem and respect, curiosity, interest, and recently, boredom, have had some attention, but triumph, pride—affects more complex than self-esteem—and competitiveness are seldom encountered by psychology books. Nor do we find much discussion of aesthetic feelings—emotional responses to music, design, and the arts generally, as well as nature—although infants do respond with pleasure to complex sensory stimulation, including music and colorful design.

Discussions of emotional development have been loaded with studies of fear, anxiety, anger, ambivalence, grief, depression, and sadness. Feelings of intimacy, closeness, mutuality, sympathy, empathy, caring, and feelings underlying attachment, cooperativeness, the desire to please a significant person, have only recently been subjects for discussion, along with the emergence of research concerned with prosocial behavior (Radke-Yarrow, Zahn-Waxler, & Chapman, in press). In psychoanalysis, sexual and aggressive drives, affects and conflicts have had much attention, but feelings underlying dependency have been given short shrift and are rarely related to realistic limitations in coping adequacy, although it seems obvious that if a child cannot cope alone, he or she feels realistically dependent.

These paragraphs have not reviewed a complete spectrum of feelings or affects, but perhaps they have illustrated a problem: The emotional life, even of babies, is far more colorful, varied, complex, and fluid than it seems in most scientific reports. Consequently, whatever we say about scientific study of the development of emotion can provide only a partial glimpse of the range of early emotional experience.

In addition to recognizing the flow of feelings accompanying, underlying, stimulating, supporting, or distorting the changing pattern of the day, we have to recognize great individual differences in the intensity, range, and qualities of the emotional experience of different babies. Some are irritable and quick to get angry, others are easily delighted, still others are prone to be anxious; some are affectionate and warm, others are indifferent. Some respond empathically to the crying of other babies, but this is not universal. Different people use their emotions in different ways in their management of life, and so it is with infants.

When we approach the question of the development of emotion, then, we are confronted with a multitude of issues, many of which are very controversial and have been inadequately studied. Some thinkers claim that we cannot speak of emotion until the infant or child is conscious of what he or she is feeling. Others generously allow emotion to be recognized from all expressions or arousal of distress or pleasurable feelings.

## DEFINITION OF EMOTION

As a step in defining *emotion*, English and English (1961) see it as including the internal visceral or autonomic response  the overt responses, and the whole gamut of emotional communication—facial expressions, gestures, postures, words. Finally, they insist emotion is the *whole* that is constituted by the parts. I would add that feelings, affects, emotions are qualitative aspects of functioning and can be usefully considered on a scale from covert levels of feelings—such as mild interest to overt exuberance, slight discomfort to a temper tantrum—or as degrees of pleasure and, as Freud (1917) put it, unpleasure. Evidence ranges from subtle degrees of arousal to vigorous, whole-body motor, facial, vocal responses.

In agreement with Freedman (1979) I see affects as the outcome of a maturational–developmental synthesis; the innate genetic potential may be realized in different ways and at different rates, depending on the sequences of environmental circumstances. The emerging range of affects develops in interaction with cognitive motor and social development with gradual modulation, refinement, mixture, and control resulting from interplay with the environment. Pine's (1977) belief that the expansion in the affect array is based in substantial degree on cognitive specification and on the linkage of feelings and ideas provides a basic clue to the process by which mixed, modulated, or new affects evolve in the child.

Observation of babies and young children support a complex view of emotion; hungry babies cry with puckered or woeful face; autonomic and visceral changes occur simultaneously. They selectively see their bottles and dive or reach for them. That is, the crying is a response to the inner need expressed vocally and facially, and it is paralleled by the selective visual and motor behavior. As part of all this, innate neural programs and motor responses are involved. Babies do not have to learn to cry when hungry. It seems to me unsound to limit the term *emotion* to any one inner or outer aspect of the complex emotional process. Emotion from birth is the whole physiological–neurological–motor (including facial expression and overt behavior) response.

## SOURCES OF A POINT OF VIEW

My view is shaped not only by the results of my own and others' research but also by extensive observations and photographic records of babies and young children who have interested me from my early baby-buggy-peeker and big sister days to my present age, of 81. These have included observations of my younger brothers and sisters, my children, grandchildren, nephews and nieces, the babies and children of my friends, infants in foundling hospitals, day nurseries, nursery schools, and other institutions in the United States, Greece, Japan, India, and Nigeria, as well as in supermarkets, airports, and on the street. Observations of infants and children through their growing years, both in longitudinal research, therapy, and in "real-life" contexts provide a unique view of development in emotional differentiation, range, intensity of expressiveness, modulation, variability, and control in relation to the physical, cognitive, social development of the infant and changes in the environment encountered by the child. We must look at a broad spectrum of feelings, then, from the most primitive pleasantness–unpleasantness level and from interested attention through moods and covert or subjective feelings to affects overtly displayed in facial expressions and bodily behavior.

## PROBLEMS IN LABELING AFFECTS

"Adultomorphising" is a scientific sin in the minds of many psychologists and psychiatrists. Yet there is no way of avoiding it, When a baby cries, we have to infer that he or she feels bad just as we feel bad when we cry; and when the baby smiles, coos, or crows we recognize the joy empathically. Empathy is the process that turns an observation into understanding, and empathy has roots in our own experience. It does involve risks of misinterpretation, which can be reduced by careful consideration of the context—the stimuli for the emotional response and the sequel. If we infer that a smile expresses pleasure, our conclusion is reinforced when the baby reaches for more of the stimulus that led to the smile. The smile was then an expression of pleasure, a message, and an instrumental gesture directed to repeating the satisfying experience. This was seen most clearly in our longitudinal study group, when "Teddy" smiled and bounced to let his mother know that he wanted her to bounce him on her lap. Crying can also be a message, and with an occasional baby, an apparently deliberate technique to get attention. But no one is likely to doubt that generally an infant's crying expresses feelings, even if we are not sure whether it is angry or hungry or hurting or lonely. More subtle reactions are harder to assess.

As children grow older, exposure to typical expressive patterns and to responses of others to one's expressions exerts selective effect, so that major emotions tend to be expressed in similar, recognizable ways. As a result, emotional nonverbal communications are understood. Young children gradually learn to report feelings verbally. But under the age of 3, when children have limited capacity to tell us what they feel, facial expressions and actions are sometimes hard for us to decode. Why is Billy upset—Is he disappointed about something, did he hurt himself, is he frustrated, or what? When we say he is *upset* we are using a weasel term that covers our ineptitude in appraising the reason for Billy's tears.

Although emotion in the neonate is not clearly differentiated, mixed emotions are more likely to appear in the latter part of the first year than in the early months: Schaffer (1963) notes both smiling and crying in reaction to a stranger. But I have seen no reports of such mixed reactions to pain or hunger in infancy— later a smile may express an attempt to bravely deny pain.

## THE FUNCTION OF EMOTIONS

Different views of the nature and function of emotions are related to the sample and the setting in which babies are studied. In contrast to the ''discharge of tension'' concept of affects passed on from early observations by psycho-analysts, empirical studies of infants emphasize the biological survival and adaptive value of emotion as communication, signal of need, and reinforcement of response by others. Moss (1967) suggests that the cry is often a painful stimulus that probably has biological utility for the infant, stimulating the mother to act for her own comfort as well as out of concern for the infant. Bowlby (1973) was impressed by the ethological view that the cry functions as a releaser of maternal behavior. I believe that both discharge of tension and communication values are involved.

Krystal (1977) suggests that there is an affective component to every mental event. I share this view, which implies that interest, attention, preference, and choice involve affect. This is probably most true of the infant and young child whose organized motor habits and coping techniques have not yet become automatized.

## ADAPTIVE VALUE OF EMOTION

It is thus widely appreciated that emotions are adaptive—emotional expressions become messages contributing to survival. Emde's (1980) discussion of the mutual reward value to parents and infants also describes in moving detail the way in which the baby's smiles and happy cooing give rewarding pleasure to parents, and parents' delighted smiles reward and reinforce the baby's expressiveness. Pleasurable emotions motivate the behaviors used in approaching and developing relations with caregivers, family members, and friends, which contribute to the evolution of trust and sense of ''the world is good.''

Optimism and pessimism are emotional orientations to life of enormous importance for actual outcomes of efforts to cope with dilemmas and challenges. Although we might expect that a positive response to either the cry or the crow of joy would reinforce the baby's pattern, some research has indicated that what is reinforced is the *confidence in communication*—the baby whose caregivers respond appropriately to early cries, communicates in more mature ways a year later; when speech is available to express a wish or a feeling, crying decreases. This research finding (Ainsworth *et al.*, 1971) needs to be supplemented by records of the babies with constitutional predispositions to anxiety, low thresholds for pain, or persistent gastrointestinal distress, who continue to cry.

## RESEARCH ON INFANT AFFECTS

Scientific attention has been unevenly distributed over various kinds of emotional experience and expression in infancy: smiling and laughing, anxiety, distress, depression, fear have received far more attention than reactions to pain, pride, or triumph at achievement. Anger and related aggression, discussed by clinicians in the 1930s, have rarely been integrated into a comprehensive view of emotional development in the early years. Even temper tantrums, familiar to parents of toddlers and "terrible twos," have not been considered in relation to the interaction between increasing cognitive and motor competence with their stimulus to new wishes nor in relation to the developmental history of reactions to frustrations. Empathy and sympathy, studied in the 1930s in relation to personality development (Murphy, 1937), have been gaining attention in recent years, but rarely in relation to the child's overall emotional style.

Child development has traditionally pursued its research topically; for instance, books about fears deal with the number of children at a given age who are afraid of strangers, dogs, or thunder. Similarly, we have studies of smiles and laughter; and investigations of frustration and aggression. Only rarely do we find studies of the child as a whole seen in terms of qualities such as intensity and expressiveness as reflected in different emotions (Escalona & Hieder, 1959). Consequently, we do not as yet have adequate empirical data for a balanced study of emotional development from birth through the early years. And we have only fragments of evidence relevant to emotional development during the prenatal months, so that we are driven to inferences or, indeed, speculation. Along with this state of the science, we have very little study of the processes of interplay between the infant and its *whole personal and impersonal* environment, processes that contribute to the multiple aspects of emotional development.

## COMPLEX VIEW

A comprehensive approach to the development of emotion is offered in Izard's (1977) volume, *Human Emotions*. His interdisciplinary approach recognizes the importance of understanding emotion for scientific fields such as physiology, neurology, ethology, as well as various branches of psychology; and for clinical fields including medicine, psychiatry, the clergy, nursing, and social work, as well as clinical psychology. His range of topics extends from "interest–excitement and intrinsic motivation" to joy; distress–anguish, grief and depression, anger, disgust, and contempt and their relation to hostility and aggression; fear and the forms of anxiety; shame and shyness; and finally, guilt and conscience. In each area, he gives attention to the origins and development of the emotional experience. Although Izard (1977) is more comprehensive in his discussion of emotions than most psychologists, he has no chapters devoted to love or affection or any other topic related to tender emotions except for sex, to which he gives short shrift in his chapter on "Emotions, Drives, and Behavior."

## THE COMPLEXITY OF FEELINGS

Mixed feelings, ambivalent feelings, and sequences of contrasting feelings are observed from early infancy on. These include the sequence of interest to boredom; pleasure in satisfying hunger to literally getting "fed up" and even irritably pushing away the bottle that was greeted so eagerly at first; laughing during a playful game, then crying when play grows overstimulating or fatiguing; enjoying being cuddled for a little while, then wanting freedom to move or to see more. The baby smiles at the mother or caregiver whose ministrations are relieving or pleasurable and gets angry when the same person takes away an object. Babies may grab the nose, the hair, or poke the eyes of an attentive adult or child and cry in frustration when the victim abruptly pulls or pushes away the baby's hand. Thus, emotions are simple and discrete only in the textbooks. The confusion that grows out of the complexity of mixed feelings creates difficulties in integration and in theory construction.

## APPROACHES TO COVERT AFFECT

When the investigator's focus is on affect as reflected in obvious facial expressions and physiological disturbances or high arousal, less overt, or more subtle, levels of feelings are not discussed—trust, interest, liking, preference, satisfaction, confidence, hope, desire, longing, are examples, all of which are related to cognitive assessments of stimuli. Frustration tolerance also has both affective and cognitive aspects.

Schmale (1964) sees affects as reflecting the total psychic awareness of the individual's psychobiological state at any moment. The specific affect may include a psychic awareness of the composite of sensations, ideas, and actions. But the concept of psychic awareness overlooks the extensive evidence of unconscious affects revealed in psychoanalysis and also in hypnosis. How can we judge the infant's level of awareness of his or her psychobiological state?

## EXPERIENCES CONTRIBUTING TO
## EMOTIONAL STYLE

There are families and day-care centers in which there is always joy, and there are others in which happy feelings are rare. In one 2-year-old group studied by Jersild and Markey (1935), there was a conflict every 5 minutes—angry hitting by competitive children—whereas in another group with more playground space, a wider age range, and less competition, conflicts were more rare and sympathetic responses were more frequent (Murphy, 1937).

Different families in our culture, different subculture areas, and different ethnic communities have different emotional orientations, thresholds, and habits. I have known families whose members yell or scream at each other, in contrast to others in which voices are never raised in anger. When I lived in the New York area, it was not unusual to see a tired or irritable mother yanking a small child by the arm or roughly sitting the toddler down hard or slapping him when he tried to kneel on a bus seat to see better out of the window. During the 1950s and 1960s in Kansas, I never saw that kind of irritable behavior with a small child in public, although a fraction of mothers in our research group stated that they used corporal punishment. Margaret Mead repeatedly (personal communication) commented that Eskimos and some Indian groups never hit, spank, or beat their children as other Americans do.

The importance of the environment–infant interaction is illustrated by Gewirtz's (1965) study of infant smiling in four different subculture settings in Israel. Infants in the more stimulating kibbutz and family settings reached a chronologically earlier peak of smiling than infants in institutional and day-nursery settings. And the stimulated babies continued their peak frequency of smiling while the other showed a decline. Other investigators found comparable evidence for the importance of support, reinforcement, or continued response to the infant's smile. If there is no response, why keep smiling?

## INDIVIDUAL DIFFERENCES IN INFANTS'
## EXPRESSIVE PATTERNS

There are very great individual differences in babies' expressiveness of emotion, as Washburn (1929) demonstrated. In our Topeka, Kansas study (Murphy & Moriarty, 1976), differences in emotional expressiveness were observed in children of the same family. Both the constitutional thresholds and the idiosyncratic experiences of each child contributed to evolved temperament. We found differences in thresholds for emotional response to different stimuli: Some babies are distressed by loud or scratchy sounds, whereas others appear to be distressed by vague, soft sounds (Heider, 1966). Babies also differ in their pleasurable responses to different colors and to different ways of being handled, to play patterns, or to vocalizations from adults. Differences in skin sensitivity, coordination, tempo of intake, assimilation, and accommodation contribute to differences in emotional responses.

## VARIABILITY IN EMOTIONAL REACTIVITY

Gesell's and Ilg's (1943) emphasis on the contribution of developmental disequilibria to emotional instability and related behavior problems needs more study. But differences in constitutional variability and interferences with integration through the first year also contribute to differences in thresholds for disintegrative reactions to stress with accompanying emotional disturbances. Changes in the balance of emotional expressions are seen over the course of 1 year and then through the growing-up years.

Other factors contributing to change in the child's emotional pattern include changes in the level of health; persistent painful illnesses may be reflected in irritability or depression, whereas improvement or cure may, as with "Helen" in our study (Murphy & Moriarty, 1976), lead to an optimistic outlook. On the negative side, we see some children who have had a happy start in life become frustrated and depressed when confronted with coping demands or with a decrease in maternal care for which they had little preparation. This was observed in certain first babies whose mothers had another child when the first baby was only 1 year old (unpublished data).

## CONTROL AND REPRESSION OF EMOTION

Psychoanalytic views of mixed feelings, conflicts about, and repression of anxiety, anger, guilty feelings, and emotionally charged wishes have not been integrated into child development concepts. At what point in development do emotional conflicts develop? When does repression begin? What empirical evidence can we look for to answer these questions? What relation is there between a parent's successful comforting measures and the infant's repression of the feelings of pain, frustration, or disappointment? We know too little about the interaction of these experiences. What relation is there between the mother's offer of a substitute toy for something the baby has been enjoying but which she considers dangerous, and the baby's development of control? Is this early training a foundation for later tolerance of frustration instead of angry reactions to removal of a pleasurable object? Is this possibly a foundation for sublimation?

## BEGINNINGS OR PRECURSORS OF AFFECT

Although it is difficult to obtain evidence at present for sequences of development of feelings *in utero,* we can make two assumptions: (*a*) *Differentiation of morphology, neurophysiological process, motility, sensory capacities, and* (*b*) *likewise feelings* (*which may later be described as emotions*), *are processes that evolve from conception.* When the heart rate of a fetus can be measured, changes in heart rate in reaction to stimulation can be measured, and these are at least precursors of later changes with psychological accompaniments. Efforts to connect specific affects have had variable results. The most consistent finding is that heart rate decreases with attentiveness (Lacey, Kagan, Lacey, & Moss, 1963). It seems reasonable to assume that *feeling* evolves from the beginning along with the development of all other functions of the organism.

Greenacre (1952) wrote about the baby who has come very slowly with extreme pressure and stress through the birth canal. That baby may tend to cry a great deal, to find the world overstimulating because of the extreme sensitivity acquired during the stressful experience. She speaks of the "predisposition to anxiety" characteristic of such babies. Shirley (1939) found that premature babies had lower thresholds for response to sensory stimulation than full-term babies; I assume that this sensitivity was also accompanied by feelings.

When we watch babies in the first 2 months of life, we find responses that can only be called *interest* versus *boredom*—they pay sustained attention to certain stimuli, patterned or moving, for a period of time, then grow inattentive until a new stimulus is offered (Lipsitt, 1977). More than this, I saw a 1-month-old baby given a bottle after 4 weeks of breast-feeding frown in displeasure (or merely puzzlement?). And many a 2-month-old baby has already developed preferences: My next-door neighbor's baby laughed and cooed at a colorful mobile, but not at a mobile with a monotone coloring.

## DEVELOPMENT OF THE SMILE

Wolff (1959), patiently recording observations on newborns in their homes, takes quite seriously the early transient smiles that (at different ages with different babies) evolve into "social smiles." Social smiles were recognized many years ago by observers who kept diaries of the responses of babies and also by psychologists reporting on infant development. The first, fleeting smiles evidently go through a process of cognitive–affective evolution that emerges into the smiling recognition of a person, a smile often accompanied by excited bicycling of limbs, or even whole-body movement. About the age of 4–6 months, again varying from one infant to another, the baby recognizes the mother and father with heightened eagerness. The whole-body expression of joy at the appearance of a beloved parent continues to be seen in the excited jumping up and down and hugging with which many an American preschool child delightedly greets Daddy or Mommy after return from a day's work or a short absence.

Haith (1972) has protested the lack of concern with the affective meaning of the infant's smile to the baby and feels that the smile indicates that seeing a face makes the baby feel good. The ebb and flow of infant smiling when mother and infant play in face-to-face contact may also tell us that smiling and laughing are overflow outlets of affect. Haith also emphasizes that babies smile at their cognitive achievements because these are pleasurable.

Eagerness and delight can also be seen in a hungry baby's reaching for the bottle or breast, or in certain babies' bouncing to get mother to bounce, or signaling for music (as our baby did at 8 months) by blowing while looking toward the record player (I had a habit of blowing the record to remove any dust). The range of stimuli for joy in babies is, however, a relatively neglected field, despite Washburn's (1929) study of smiling and laughter in infants. By playing a number of stimulating baby games, she was able to demonstrate wide individual differences in the babies' tendency to laugh. She also found differences in the tendency to cry, and she summarized the babies' differences in emotional reactivity into four groups: risor-expressive babies who tended to laugh much; depressor-expressives with low thresholds for crying; multi-expressives who tended to both laugh and cry, and parvi-expressives who neither laughed nor cried much.

## FEELINGS IMPLIED IN
## REJECTION AND OUTREACHING

Babies' feelings of satiety or their dislike of certain foods must be inferred from their ways of clamping their mouths shut, blowing, or spitting out of food or rejecting unwanted foods in other ways (Murphy & Moriarty, 1976). By contrast, feelings of pleasure in a feeding are implied in the cooing or smiling that follows a feeding. Some babies splash and smile in their baths, or even when being diapered and powdered, whereas others with different skin sensitivity do not show signs of enjoying the bath, but strain or fuss while being bathed. Many babies dislike nose-cleaning and shampooing (unpublished data).

Much motor activity goes on with little facial expression of affect. Can we assume that the baby reaches out to explore, touch, swipe at, and bang things because he likes the sensations of contact and making something happen? When

4-month-old babies struggle to turn over or later push up patiently until they get on all fours, can we assume feelings of achievement after they have succeeded? Does it make sense to think that these motor efforts are totally without accompanying feeling? It is not unusual to hear a crow of triumph when babies, at about 10 months, succeed in standing up, holding onto the railing of their playpens. Before this achievement, did they have feelings of wanting to do that?

## AGE OF EMERGENCE OF SPECIFIC EMOTIONS

Controversies about the infant age at which it is valid to speak of mood or affects such as fear, anger, joy, love, are in part fueled by assumptions and theories of development. The question as to when the baby is conscious of an emotional response is, of course, very difficult to answer. Mothers are not burdened by such distinctions. If a baby boy yells in protest when the nipple is taken out of his mouth when he is hungry, the mother says, cogently enough, "He is mad." Similarly, if a safety pin pricks him and he cries, she comments on his pain cry.

Among Izard's (1977) list of sequences of emotion, the following are observable in babies of 1–2 months of age: interest–excitement; joy; distress; perhaps anger; and anxiety contagiously reflecting a mother's anxiety or a precursor of anxiety when uncomfortable or startled. From 3 months on, pain, fear, grief at separation can be distinguished, along with more nuances of pleasure and delight in interplay with caregivers and, a little later, triumph in achievement. Anxious reactions to strangers have been reported as early as 2 and 3 months; they are not usually seen until 7–9 months of age. Depression after loss of the mother or chief caregiver may be observed in the last quarter of the first year and into the second year. Other emotions listed by Izard (1977) as not emerging until later in early childhood include disgust, contempt, shame, shyness, and guilt.

What can we say about these sequences of emotional development? Is a hierarchy or priority list of survival value involved? Are some emotions dependent on perceptual–cognitive development necessary for appraisal of the stimulus? Crying in hunger or pain brings the concerned caregiver to provide a needed feeding or soothing to the newborn. Fear, as of the visual cliff (Gibson & Walk, 1960), which is then avoided, brings the infant to a level of capacity for self-protection after he or she has begun to explore the environment and is no longer constantly protected. This fear does depend on a level of perceptual–cognitive development not required at the neonatal stage of total protection by the caregiver. Triumphant feelings of success emerge only after motor developments have made possible the practice of new skills. In other words, both priorities for survival and neurological development underlying perceptual-cognitive–motor maturity are involved in sequential development of affect.

## WHAT DOES A BABY'S SMILE MEAN?

Researchers interested in the social development of the infant have tended to assume that the baby's smile is entirely a social response. Not enough attention has been paid to the smile as an expression of pleasure or delight evoked by many a sensory or motor experience. I have seen each of two healthy 2-month-old babies smile, laugh, gurgle, and coo at colorful mobiles even when they did not activate the movement themselves. They reacted as we react to the movements of a colorful hummingbird balancing and fluttering above its tube of sugar-water.

If pleasure is the basic smile affect, social responses are one subcategory. We can then make sense out of the extensive reports of the baby's response to the mother's (or other stimulus person's) eyes. The eyes are the brightest, often the most colorful and mobile feature of the face. We need more studies of the relation to infant smiles of color, mobility, previous pleasure experience, and other qualities of stimuli. Among other qualities, we have to include the neonate's response to a high-pitched voice and, before long, his or her selective response to the mother's voice. Here we cannot exclude the factor of prenatal conditioning or canalization, since we know that sounds are heard by the unborn. And after the mother has cared for the baby a few days, additional conditioning has taken place as the mother's voice accompanies nursing, diaper-changing, and soothing. The comfort, relief, pleasure provided by the mothering figure contributes to an intensification of response to social stimuli and lowered thresholds for them. And by the age of 4 months, the baby becomes the initiator of social responses in order, we must assume, to obtain pleasure.

When babies greet us with broad smiles and outstretched arms and legs, perhaps also happy crows, they are behaving in a way not unlike the way we behave when we greet a long-lost friend, so we have no conflict about describing their emotion as joy. Similarly a baby's cry of pain or woe evokes our memories and conditioned responses to our own emotional expressions. This same process of recognition of emotional quality goes on at all levels down to whimpers and restless fussing and subtle, warm smiles or open-mouthed astonishment or surprise. I doubt that we could recognize an emotional expression alien to our own experience.

We do get into trouble with the earliest "reflex smiles" and partial smiles described in Wolff's (1959) sensitive reports of observations of newborns. Here it may be a matter of choice whether we decide that rudimentary affect is involved, or only a primitive behavior response that is subsequently developed into an expression of one or another positive affect—pleasure, delight, gratitude, hopeful anticipation, relief from stress.

The baby's experience of pleasure is no luxury or evolutionary side benefit. It is important for its adaptive and even survival value as a means to counteract stress. "Soothing" a distressed, crying baby involves one or another process of providing pleasure, by new visual stimuli when the baby is lifted to the shoulder, by tactual, or by auditory stimulation (talking or singing to the baby). Although it took Norman Cousins (1977) to demonstrate that laughter could be life-saving to an adult, skillful mothers have known for generations that keeping the baby happy is good for it.

Studies of babies' smiles in the context of caregivers' responses provide a limited view of the baby's total emotional range or relation to its overall emotional development. The ability to communicate discomfort, protest, dislikes, overstimulation, or uncomfortable handling; expressing wants; maintaining equilibrium and emotional balance, as well as a happy, appropriately trusting response to the environment are important aspects of emotional development. Babies whose needs have been entirely met by sensitive, always responsive mothers (Murphy & Moriarty, 1976; see Chester, p. 70) have lacked practice in finding pleasure through their own efforts and are demanding and frustrated when it is impossible for their mothers to continue meeting every wish. Balanced emotional development requires opportunities for independent use of the environment for satisfaction. In line with this, our Topeka study (Murphy & Moriarty, 1976, p. 60) found a curvilinear relation between maternal attention and the development of the infant. Overstimulation and extreme attentiveness, as well as inadequate responsiveness of the mother disturbs the infant (Murphy, 1973).

These findings do not conflict with the results of an elaborate factor analysis of characteristics of mothers and 1-year-old infants brought for care to a parental clinic in Syracuse (Stern, Caldwell, Hersher, Lipton, & Richmond, 1969). Items on 23 maternal needs scales and 19 infant global interpersonal scales were rated on the basis of interviews and observations. The mother–infant interaction factor summary included such interrelations as these: Involved mother with high visual contact and high play correlated with a loving baby highly involved with mother and shared emotional rapport; a vigilant mother enjoying her baby but distant, correlated with a good humored, advanced baby who was also fearless with high drive but avoided physical contact. This analysis turned up mother–infant combinations with differing patterns of affective relationship, infant achievement, social responsiveness, and happiness, as well as two patterns of problem behavior involving hostile and demanding behavior, and disorganized interactions.

Studies of laughter at any age might well take their departure from a comprehensive inventory of situations evoking a wide range of qualities and degrees of vigor of laughter. I can offer only a few examples here. A 2-month-old baby laughs at a colorful mobile; a 4-month-old baby laughs with delight at my (i.e., familiar grandmother's) approach, at the pat-a-cake game I play with her and, later, at her success in pulling up to a standing position.

We may distinguish sensory pleasure–laughter, or laughter in delight in movement, in triumph, at humor, in relief from threat. Surely the bland term *arousal* is hardly sufficient to explain widely different qualities of laughter. Arousal there is, and Rothbart's (1973) emphasis on safety as well as pleasantness of the stimulus is useful but not sufficient to explain all of the varieties of laughter we see in infants. The pleasantness of mastery seen when a child laughs following success probably contributes to a sense of self.

The usefulness of laughter, like smiling, as a reward to the caregiver (Emde, 1979), who is then stimulated to repeat the pleasant or fun-giving experience, is paralleled by its value in teaching the infant that other people are influenced by this response.

Extensive discussions of the role of surprising, discrepant, or incongruous stimuli cannot be reviewed here in detail (see Ames, 1949; Ding & Jersild, 1932; Kagan, 1971; Sroufe, 1979 for further information).What is important in the contribution of cognitive development to the infant and therefore to the changing range of stimuli for laughter, is appraisal.

We assume that crying generally reflects, or is a message conveying, distress (even if it is only the distress of loneliness and the wish for companionship). It seems fair to assume that an infant's trembling may be a precursor of fear if we insist that fear properly involves a level of ego development not yet characteristic of the very young baby. The most primitive disturbance is basically a disorganized reaction to an overwhelming stimulus that cannot be integrated into the available coping response system. Later, as a child develops the capacity to retreat effectively, to protest, protect itself, or to seek help, we see a more organized response. And when speech develops, the child acquires the notion of being afraid and communicates it. Such sequences in the development of fear are the concern of psychoanalysts as well as child psychologists. Among the latter, Bridges (1931) long ago outlined sequences of differentiation of affects from the earliest distress and delight.

The infant's expression of anger or rage was discussed by Watson (1925) in terms of slashing and defensive arm movements when head and legs are severely restricted. But other studies found wide individual differences, and swaddling has been found to be soothing to young infants. It has been suggested that Watson's handling may have been rough. In any case it is obvious that we need careful records of the quality, timing, and other aspects of any stimulus situation as well as the infant's state and thresholds of sensitivity.

## INTERNAL AND EXTERNAL FACTORS IN EMOTIONAL DEVELOPMENT

The emotional development of the infant needs to be understood (*a*) in terms of the baby's pleasure–pain experiences in response to external personal and impersonal objects; (*b*) the baby's internal experiences (of comfort, or distress based on hunger, "gas" pressures, pain from infections, etc.); (c) the baby's response to the emotional expressions of people or animals in his or her immediate environment.

It is the last of these areas of emotional development that has had the least attention and analysis. In my study of the development of sympathy (Murphy, 1937), I summarized factors such as warmth and identification, empathic responses that have roots in infancy and earliest childhood, along with a basic social sensitiveness that responds to both the joy and the pain of another. Following Humphrey (1922), I suggested that early conditioned responses underlie the earliest imitation of another baby's cry. A baby girl's own cry is associated with her feeling of discomfort from any source. The cry of another baby becomes associated with her own cry and the related discomfort. Babies in a hospital nursery cry when another baby cries, and observations of babies in their own homes document the baby's crying response to the cry of a sibling, as well as the young child's cry or intense protest when a sibling cries (unpublished data).

Some young children cry in response to a crying face, even when the sound of crying is not heard, and to a picture of a crying face; I believe that a circular response mechanism is involved here. Emotional responses to sad or joyous music involve the same mechanism in young children with low thresholds for resonant responses to music. Zahn-Waxler and Radke-Yarrow (1979) have documented young children's empathic responses to emotional expressions of others. I found that children's sympathetic responses were more likely to occur when a child had previously had a similar experience (Murphy, 1937). But we can assume that the vividness of the stimulating emotional expression in relation to the sensitivity of the onlooker contributes to the empathic response. Examples of the response of a sensitive toddler to the crying of a 3-year-old brother, followed by successive comments of "crying, crying" to pictures on the wall illustrate the diffusion of an emotional response from an appropriate distress stimulus to projective responses (Murphy, 1937). The example of sympathetic crying may be taken as a paradigm of emotional responses to emotions of others. To see the implications of this conditioned response process, we can recall observations of differences in the amount of emotional expressiveness in different cultures and subcultures. Any traveler is struck by differences between the taciturn Vermonter and the noisy, expressive New Yorker of certain areas; or the poker-faced Scot in contrast to the vividly expressive Italian.

But the pattern of emotional development is not a simple, linear process. In my study of sympathy (Murphy, 1937), I found that some young children had more intense sympathetic responses when their thresholds were lowered by physiological disequilibria such as being just awakened or recently hurt. The role of identification, growing out of participation, is also implied in the greater sympathetic response to family and friends. Affective responses to other children are also predisposed by strong maternal (and paternal) drives seen in preschool children, whereas insecurity due to newness in the group inhibits expression. Identification with mother seemed strong in some instances, whereas compensation for inadequate or recently reduced mothering appeared to be involved in other instances. Related effects include the influence of proximity as contrasted with distance.

## THE QUALITY AND RANGE OF ENVIRONMENTAL STIMULATION

The importance of early processes of conditioning and imitation as well as provision of direct gratifying responses to needs can be realized as we reflect on the impoverished experience of infants in immaculate, sterile, foundling hospitals (in both the United States and foreign countries). Woebegone faces in poorly developed, sometimes marasmic, bodies demonstrate that babies as well as man "cannot live by bread (or milk) alone." Nurses are typically responsible for feeding schedules, sanitation, and bodily care and have little or no time for play or social interaction when one nurse has to care for 10–12 babies.

## INDIVIDUAL DIFFERENCES IN REACTION TO PAIN

An illustration of individual differences in emotional pattern is seen in emotional reactions to pain in half-a-dozen 3–4-month-old hospitalized foundlings observed 2 hours after their immunization inoculations (Murphy, 1973). One baby girl screamed without interruption for 2 hours (until I arrived and soothed her), another infant refused to suck the bottle; still another was hyperactive and could not settle down to nap. And a little girl who had previously been outstanding in her smiling social responsiveness was depressed and remained depressed for 2 weeks, as if disillusioned. Levy (1960) also reported that infants who had previously had inoculations subsequently cried at the sight of a doctor in a white coat, although not until the age of 6 months did a baby cry only at the sight of the needle.

## THE DEVELOPMENT OF EMOTIONAL ATTACHMENTS

The history of psychoanalytic efforts to understand how the emotional attachment of the baby to the mother is formed is carefully and thoroughly reviewed by Bowlby (1958). Bowlby has emphasized biological or ethological origins. I have had many experiences of caring for babies 2-, 3-, or 4 months old in the absence of their parents; only a rare infant has protested when I picked it up. No attachment has been consolidated, and it generally does not get consolidated until after thousands of experiences of gratifying care, stimulation, and expressions of love have taught the baby that mother—or father, or a sibling—is special (Murphy, 1964). The development of attachments and the associated emotions is a gradual, complex process. Immediate imprinting, such as occurs with Lorenz's ducks or geese, does not occur with human babies; if it did, the baby would be imprinted to the first nurse in the hospital who cares for it, or to the doctor who delivered it.

The youngest baby cannot cling, it has to be carried; only after months of life does it develop the capacity to cling, and many babies cling only when frightened at strange situations or people, usually after the first 6 months. A very young baby often turns its attention to a toy or interesting visual spectacle when the mother replaces it in the crib. It cannot follow physically until the second half of the first year, and it may not follow the mother visually if something else that is interesting attracts its attention. After the baby achieves locomotion, it both follows and leaves the mother and explores interesting objects when in a familiar situation. As Brazelton (1974) says, the baby attaches and detaches. The baby integrates sensory and affective responses to all the stimuli provided by the family, with the comforting satisfaction of visceral needs and the social play and love received and evoked. These experiences include oral gratification and multiple kinds of relief of body tensions and skin irritation, along with pleasurable vestibular experiences and recognition of mother's or father's support for opportunities to "look all around" and to listen to interesting sounds.

The baby and young child's emotional attachment to the mother is generally not exclusive. Schaffer and Emerson (1964) looked at the infants' relationships to fathers, older siblings, grandparents, and neighbors; they found that by 18 months 87% of the babies had formed multiple attachments. Schaffer concludes that there is no biological need for an exclusive bond. What pattern the emotional attachments take depends on the social setting and the emotional interplay of the persons in that setting.

Steps leading to emotional attachment to family members include the neonate's preference for the mother's voice, his or her fixation on the mother's eyes while nursing, delight in seeing the parent's face, association of feelings of relief and comfort with the needed physical care, and pleasure in face-to-face talking, play, and exercising with other family members.


NEWNESS

For infants and young children exposed to a range of stimuli in and outside of the house, newness is a frequent experience. The resulting discoveries evoke affectively toned cognitive responses of interest, curiosity, surprise, puzzlement, wonder, even awe. The drive to understand, to achieve cognitive mastery, varies in intensity among different children and is probably important in determining the quality of the affective response as well as persistence of effort to assimilate the stimulus and/or to explore its possibilities for manipulation. Sustained interest can be seen very early, including preference for complex forms that presumably provide more challenge than unpatterned shapes. I have photographed vivid surprise at 5 months. Puzzlement expressed in a frown or furrowed brows may be seen as early as 1 month, as illustrated in the photograph of a baby receiving a bottle after having been nursed at the breast the previous 4 weeks.

## CONTRIBUTIONS OF STUDIES OF REACTIONS TO STRANGERS AND STRANGENESS

Psychoanalysts concerned with the infant's emotional responses to people have focused on reactions to strangers. The question of when an infant's tension or distress at approach of a stranger can legitimately be regarded as fear is discussed by Katan (1972), who feels that many adults cannot distinguish between undifferentiated distress feelings and the quality of fear. Only after object constancy is well established and the secondary process (conscious thought) prevails can it be assumed that the small child's anxiety, grief, sadness, and anger are differentiated and experienced in a way comparable to that of adults.

Paradise and Curcio (1974) elaborated on this theme on the basis of a study of fearful and nonfearful infants' reactions to strangers. They concluded that not only object and person permanence but other variables were important to consider: rate of visual habituation to familiarity and visual attention to novelty. Fearful infants had more mature person-permanence concepts and showed more overall visual attention than did nonfearful infants.

Affective responses of infants to health workers in a clinic in the course of weighing, measurement, physical examination, tests, and immunization were studied by Spicher (1976). She found that the workers' identity as strangers, their unfamiliar activities with the infant, the intrusive, body-boundary-penetrating quality of their behavior, as well as the pain- and discomfort-producing aspects of their handling of the infants were related to the babies' disturbed responses, as were fatigue and age. This sensitive, differentiated analysis of the details of infants' emotional responses to strangers is a model for study of infant– environment interactions.

## SEPARATION ANXIETY

We need to consider separation anxiety in relation to details of preceding experiences and the personal and impersonal context of the separation. Sustained anxiety, sadness, or grief is usually seen only after prolonged separation from an established relationship, without the presence of another familiar person with whom the baby has a bond. But I have seen precursors of anxiety in the whimpering or fussing as if disappointed of a 2- or 3-month-old baby boy put down alone in his crib after a period of happy play. That is, distress at loss of a satisfying relationship may have very early beginnings, and develop at a later age into the serious depression reported by Spitz (1946) and others. An extensive review of depression in children is available in Schultebrandt and Raskin's (1977) book on *Depression in Childhood*. But more study of infants, from birth on, is needed in order to develop a fuller understanding of the development of grief. Such a study should include the young infant's crying at loss of his or her bottle or of a favorite toy held by the baby; loss of impersonal, cathected objects sometimes evokes grief almost as intense as loss of the personal object. This implies that contentment requires a satisfying relation to the familiar or cathected environment, and that a rupture of this relationship causes distress.

Some Topeka toddlers whose fathers stayed at home, or whose familiar grandmother came when mother went to the hospital were not disturbed (Murphy & Moriarty, 1976). In many studies of separation anxiety, the experience of separation is compounded with removal of the toddler to a strange place to be cared for by a strange person after a developmental experience largely confined to mother and father. Situational differences in experiences of separation must always be analyzed in evaluating the infant or young child's reaction.

## STRANGENESS ANXIETY

In addition, individual differences in perceptual sensitivity, and the range of experiences a baby has had, need to be considered in relation to strangeness. I have seen sensitive 2- and 3-month-old babies, when visiting a relative *with* their mothers, restless and sleepless in strange cribs. These were both extremely bright babies who had spent their time in the same area with mother, without safe experiences with her in a variety of settings. We need studies of the individual qualities of the infant as they interact with individual aspects of the environment.

## WARINESS

The problems involved in use of the term *anxiety* are bypassed in several studies by experienced observers of infants who focus on the onset of, and early development of, wariness, with attention to both the qualities of the infant and of the external stimulus. Bronson (1971) repeatedly studied 32 male and female infants from the age of 3–9 months, recording on videotape their reactions to the approach of a strange person and to a variety of unfamiliar objects. The aversive reactions included distress reactions of early infancy, then wariness of the unfamiliar, then acquired fears. Parameters affecting reactions to the unfamiliar included temperament of the infant, qualities of the stimulus, nature of the encounter situation, and the baby's age and experiential history. Some reactions seemed to reflect a momentary balance between wariness or fear, on the one hand, and a tendency to explore the new object or to establish a relationship with the new person.

Schaffer (1977) followed 20 infants from the age of 6–12 months, thus covering a different range. Up to 8 months, there was a tendency to touch, whereas after the age of 8 months, wariness, in the form of hesitation to touch the unfamiliar stimulus, was observed. He concludes that this change reflects the growing influence of memory on expressive behavior.

## FACTORS IN THE STRANGER STIMULUS

Infants' responses to strangers vary with the size of the strangers: They respond more positively to strange children than to strange adults. Perhaps they feel less threatened by the smaller size, or perhaps there is even an intuitive sense that a child is more like themselves. Wolf (1952) long ago documented a 2-month-old baby's fear of a strange woman whose hair color contrasted sharply with the color of the mother's hair. This suggests that the degree of contrast or difference is another main factor in the infant's distress, in line with our earlier discussions of discrepancy from the familiar.

More study of ways in which strange adults approach a baby is also needed; we have records of babies under 4 months being upset by strange people who approach them abruptly and intrusively or even aggressively, chucking them under the chin, pulling on their toes, pinching their cheeks, etc. Most babies show no fear when I approach slowly, keeping my distance at first, not touching the baby. Under these conditions a smile to the baby often brings a responsive smile.

However, the baby's relation to the mother and the exact situation when the stranger approaches, the immediate antecedent conditions and the baby's mood, thresholds for alarm, extent of familiarity with others than its parents, and previous experiences with strangers all have to be considered if we are to understand the reaction of a given baby to a given stranger. In giving attention to the details of the infant's characteristics and previous experience and to the stimulus, we are illustrating the implications of the organism–environment system concept.

## EMOTIONAL RESPONSES TO DEPRIVATION

Although emotions involved with loss and separation in infancy have been studied extensively since the work of Bowlby (1973) and of Spitz (1946) and others, feelings developed from stimulus-deprivation have not been fully explored. Levy's (1937) discussion of affect-hunger could have led to a broader consideration of stimulus-hunger, longing for love, and loneliness in infants. Evidence of inadequacies of cognitive and even physical development in depriving conditions has not been paralleled by evidence of the effects of early lack of love on the development of the child's capacity to love. The work of Harlow and Harlow (1974) with infant monkeys, and records of psychiatrists, imply that lack of loving contact may cripple an individual's capacity to love. Ethical considerations prevent the systematic experimental study of emotional deprivation for different periods of time with different groups of human infants; clarification of the issue has to use whatever natural situations are available for study. Tizard and Rees (1975) have found that children institutionally reared during their early years and then adopted developed normal affection for their parents.

## FEELINGS AND THE SELF

Before the infant is born, the nearly uniform environment in the amniotic sac and the limitation of vision narrow the range of sensory experiences and feelings that, after birth, contribute to the gradual integration of an image and a sense of self. The sounds that reach the fetus from outside and from inside the mother's body (heart and bowel sounds), the feelings of movement as the fetus changes its position, vestibular feelings as the fetus rocks in the uterus when the mother moves, probably all contribute a beginning nucleus of self-feelings. The babies who suck their thumbs *in utero* show us that the oral drive is already at work. The pressured journey through the birth process provides the most intense experience the baby has had or may have for some time. Cries in the newborn nursery, where needs of wet, hungry, uncomfortable, or unpleasantly stimulated babies cannot be instantly cared for, testify to distress. In the same nursery, comfort is also felt.

It is widely said that the baby is not aware of itself as separate from the environment until many months have passed. But the baby moves through shifting states from sleep, drowsiness, wakeful alertness with comfort, or hunger or discomfort from within or from external impacts such as tight or rough textured clothing, bumps against the crib railing, bath water too cold or too warm, and irritating nose-cleaning or shampoos when the baby has sufficient hair. In other words, there are from birth a great many assaults from the outside that, I believe, steadily contribute to a sense of self versus "out there." In addition, the baby is looking intently at this outside world when alert, steadily becoming familiar with the available visual stimuli, looking for something new or more complex, fussing when the vista is boring, demanding change. The American baby who is in its crib, buggy, stroller, infant seat, or swing—moved from one vehicle to another, or one room to another—is exposed to changing environmental settings. These many interesting pleasant and unpleasant experiences of change and variety stimulate differentiating awareness of the outside.

Along with the pleasant, interesting, boring, or irritating environmental stimuli, the baby is hearing its own voice, looking at its hands, enjoying multiple taste, contact, and rhythm sensations from sucking its thumb, and feeling the comfort of good feeding or the discomfort of colic, along with other body sensations pleasant and unpleasant. More than this, the baby expresses its dislikes by rejecting unwanted food (pushing out, spitting out, tightly closing its lips, etc.) and its likes by accepting, paying attention to, smiling or laughing at what it enjoys. In other words, it asserts itself in the early months of life, and after reaching, pushing, and swiping at objects, achieves the ability to grab and to hold. All of this is contributing to an accumulation of body self-feelings and feelings of wanting and getting satisfaction from the environment.

Integrating the feeling, perceiving, selecting, demanding, acting selves is a gradual process, and we can only speculate about when the baby's felt, seen, heard, and initiating self is experienced as "I." The baby's triumphant yelp on achieving a standing position reflects a sense of "I did it!" This occurs at different ages from 8 to 12 months in most American babies, but this is a culmination of a sequence of experiences of success in efforts to manage the body and the environment, all reflecting from birth developing capacities to choose—in other words, beginning expressions of a directing, organizing, ego that has to be integrated with the emerging felt self.

Most difficult, probably, is the problem of including both good and bad, satisfying and frustrating, confident and doubtful, trusting and distrustful feelings into a coherent self. What helps in this process is the continuity of feelings of dependability—that the caregiver will meet one's needs, that one can increasingly cope with, use, and enjoy the environment. The baby's restlessness in the strange crib, the strange place, or with a strange person, noted earlier, suggests that the secure early self is a self-in-my-familiar-world. Gradually, as feelings of competence increase, the child's self can maintain a feeling of security in a new situation, with new people, as with those young children who are quickly happy in the new situation of a friendly day-care center. An adequate discussion of the relation of feelings to the evolving self would have to include a discussion of the developing ego and the sense of identity, which is beyond the scope of this paper.

## IMPLICATIONS FOR RESEARCH

There are problems in studying emotion in infants: Whereas agreement among observers may be easy to reach when emotional expressions are clear-cut, many babies are "quiet," inhibited, or subtle in their expressions. A 1-year-old baby in a far corner of a playpen in a foundling hospital in Nigeria looked at me with head and eyes partly downcast. Was he shy, fearful, or depressed, discouraged, and lonely? I could not be sure. If we limit ourselves to the most expressive babies whose emotions are obvious, we miss too much.

Whether the excitement of spontaneous unmonitored discovery could be duplicated in systematic laboratory studies, I do not know. To babies or young children, a laboratory is a strange place, with strange people, and this situation will affect them differently. We could try and, in the process, learn something about the relation of excitement in discovery to other emotional and cognitive patterns in the same children. Do spontaneous discoveries stimulate curiosity? Is there any generalization to different sorts of discoveries, and does the delight persist?

Although the importance of state has been recognized in studies of neonatal responses, there is all too little concern with state in studies of emotional responses (to strangers, to separation, to stimulating activities) in later months. A recent cold or infection, teething, hunger, being waked up, fatigue, and other factors affecting the state of the infant may lower thresholds for minor distress, fear, or pain.

Affective aspects of oral experience range from feelings of comfort and pleasant taste to discomfort if milk or food is too hot and dislike of certain tastes or textures. More than this, for the young infant nursed at the breast, varying degrees of pleasantness or frustration may accompany ease or difficulty of managing the nipple and breast. The oral zone offers a basic arena for repeated feelings of gratification or frustration, for early efforts to cope (with difficulties in managing the nipple), and thus for earliest foundations of trust (or distrust), confidence (I can manage) or lack of it, hope or discouragement. Although psychoanalytic theory since Freud's (1905) *Three Essays on the Theory of Sexuality* has dealt extensively with emotional and personality outcomes of oral experience, child development research has not dealt adequately with this basic area, or with drives generally.

Moreover, in view of the importance of early anxiety, depression, and other negative feelings for the personality, social, and even cognitive development of the child, it behooves us to make progress in recognizing early affects that are not fully exposed. We can hardly risk frightening sensitive infants when applying instruments to check cardiovascular functioning—that would confuse our judgment about their initial affect.

Similarly, it is difficult to interpret the feelings lying back of the uncompromising stare of an unsmiling toddler. As I walk about my neighborhood or in the National Zoo, I am bemused by the different responses my smiles evoke from the toddlers. Some of them smile broadly in return and even say "Hi!" Others stare, but cautiously or in curiosity? What is the difference in the orienting process, in the presence or lack of presence of trust in the previous experiences of these different young ones?

Jones (1933), Shirley (1930), and Washburn (1929) all found wide individual differences in expressiveness (that is, appearance of smiles and amount of smiling). To what extent are individual differences in expressiveness a temperamental, congenital given? Or do they develop in response to stimulation? Escalona and Heider (1959) found that expressiveness was correctly predicted from infancy to the preschool stage in 74% of the cases. But shyness in response to strangers was successfully predicted in only 47% of cases. We could well study this question further and pay close attention to the relation of environmental stimulation and reinforcement to the emergence and continuity of expressive behavior.

The effect on the people in the environment of babies' ready smiling, crying, enthusiastic or inhibited greeting, or excited response to sight of bottle or toy needs more study; Research on the effects of the child's responses on the mother is a good beginning. Nonverbal communication by the infant is apt to carry more emotional freight than matter-of-fact expressions of wants by adults or older children.

## PROBLEMS INVOLVED IN STUDYING EMOTION

Duffy (1934) has long challenged the usefulness of studying emotion as such—activation is a more dependable variable, she asserted. This seems sound if we are focusing on the physiological responses. But from the point of view of students of personality and social development, it is necessary to learn about the interrelations of specific emotions, behaviors, and cognitive developments. Even conditioning can be understood best if we consider what reinforcements are most effective in terms of their satisfaction or pleasure-giving reward potentialities, as well as in their pain-inducing aspects.

The birth cry, subsequent cries, fussing, cooing, and the earliest part-smiles of the neonate are expressing affect at some level, even if the neonate's awareness of feelings and their stimuli is dim and vague. Both the affects and consciousness of them and of their antecedents and consequences evolve rapidly in the early months, just as motor coordination, perception, and communication evolve. Babies are reinforced both for crying and for smiling, and they learn what expressions will bring the responses they want from adults.

At the same time, there are problems in identifying affects on the basis of subtle expressive patterns. Does that frown (which I photographed when a 1-month-old baby was changed from breast to bottle) express puzzlement or displeasure? Is that smile a response to inner comfort or the beginning of a social smile? Is our impression of a social smile actually an accurate perception that the baby recognizes a person, or do we simply interpret his or her progress in visual focus as contributing to a "more human" expression? Since all emotions evolve gradually and with some babies remain subtle, we cannot always feel secure in our interpretation of an expression. Wolff (1959), observing infants in the home, confirmed mothers' discriminations between pain and hunger cries, for instance. More collaborations between investigators and the caregiver who knows the baby best would probably facilitate progress in the study of infant emotions, especially at early stages and with babies whose expressions are not vigorous and clear. Yarrow (1979) commented that mechanisms of activation of joy and fear are often similar although stimuli are different, and he also notes that one emotion may alternate with another or be used in the service of another, as when a child gets angry in order to fend off fear. An infant may be both attracted to and apprehensive about a new object or person (Schaffer, 1977).

Duffy's (1934) focus on activation leaves us handicapped in developing awareness of the variety of nuances of emotional communication important for social and even cognitive development. But attention to degree of arousal can help us to bring together, on a scale or spectrum, the range of feelings from mild interest, satisfaction, or dissatisfaction through affects of pleasure and delight, fear and anger, to intense emotions of triumph, rage, or passionate love. All these have both cognitive and neurological aspects, as we discussed earlier. All involve some degree (but not necessarily in the same direction) of autonomic reaction. All have a place in personality development and adaptation or survival. Without interest in and pleasure from their environment, some babies fail to thrive or die. The range of feelings from mildest to most intense arousal does not imply uniform biological value: Overstimulation from even happily exciting experiences can lead to disorganization and loss of equilibrium.


## NEED FOR INTERDISCIPLINARY METHODS

Up to this point, I have sketched patterns of early emotional behavior. An adequate view of emotional development can best be obtained by collaborative study by participant observers of normal children in a given culture or in several cultures. Detailed clinical observations—medical, neurological, and psychodynamic—need to be coordinated with experimental studies of those affects that can validly be observed in laboratory or natural situations. Psychologists and other human behavior scientists who cling exclusively to laboratory studies of children generally miss the excitement, wonder, delight, humor, and other nuances of emotional expression seen in children in real-life situations.

Much of the research on emotional development ignores sex differences in infant emotional patterns. Moss (1967) is an important exception: Among 30 infants studied over the first 3 months of life, the baby boys were more irritable.

They cried and fussed more, slept less, vocalized less, and smiled slightly less. Mothers held the male infants longer (perhaps in an effort to soothe them). At 3-weeks, when baby girls vocalized more than the baby boys, mothers imitated vocalizations by girls more frequently. At 3 months, mothers tended to spend less time with the more irritable male babies, and Moss suggested that the mothers of the irritable boys may have learned that they could not be successful in quieting boys whereas the girls were more uniformly responsive to maternal handling. He notes that males are more subject to inconsolable states, have less-well-organized physiological reactions, and are more vulnerable to adverse conditions than are females—all relevant to the boys' greater irritability and the fact that they are less easily soothed; that is, brought from a disturbed emotional state to a positive state or equilibrium. Moss (1967) reasons that the irritable infants who can be soothed and whose mothers are responsive should show a higher degree of attachment behavior.

In our Topeka study (Murphy & Moriarty, 1976) we found some mothers who were more tense in nursing baby boys as well as an instance of a gentle mother who did not meet the needs of a very vigorous baby boy. We await in the future careful study of the deeper emotional interactions between mothers and male infants and their consequences for the emotional development of the boys; narcissistic and exhibitionistic patterns affecting emotional development of baby girls also await further study. Moreover, longitudinal naturalistic studies alone can provide valid records of the ebb and flow of confidence, self-esteem, happiness, and anxiety. The infant–environment system needs to be seen in dynamic perspective, integrating multidisciplinary findings.

TABLE 1.1

Illustrative Affective Experiences in Middle-Class American Infants

*Pleasure (Affects, Feelings, Emotions)*

Newborn (function pleasure)
1. Contact, vestibular comfort (canalized *in utero*)
2. Interest, excitement (auditory stimulation canalized *in utero;* visual stimulation at birth, especially light, patterns, bright colors)
3. Oral gratification (nutritive, and nonnutritive sucking: thumb, pacifier, eager feeding)
4. Motor, rhythmic movement, beginning control (making mobile move by sucking)
5. Gastrointestinal comfort

1–2 months (goal-reaching pleasure begins)
Continuation of the above, plus
1. Satisfaction in coping by exercising choice, rejecting unwanted food, turning away
2. Increase in intensity of pleasure, smiling, gurgling, cooing, laughing at colorful mobile, eye contact with caregiver, watching sunbeam on upraised hand

(*continued*)

TABLE 1.1—*Continued*

---

Illustrative Affective Experiences in Middle-Class American Infants

---

3. Beginning of function pleasure in goal-oriented effort, swiping at cradle gym, deliberate visual searching, touching side of crib, buggy
4. Interest in and attention to own hands, own sounds; doubtless all sensations

3–5 months (mastery pleasure develops)
Continuation of all above, plus
   1. Surprise at vivid new visual stimuli
   2. Pleasure in body-mastery, rolling over from supine to prone, pulling up to sit
   3. Reaching, grasping, manipulating cradle-gym toys, making things move by manual pressure
   4. Confident delighted recognition of familiar, loving caregivers: mother, father, sibling
   5. Smiling, vocalizing, laughing in parent–child play
Peak of ecstatic pleasure occurs at this stage

6–9 months (autonomous locomotion and initiation of play develops)
Modulation of intensity of delight, development of cheerful mood, warm greetings; more matter-of-fact satisfaction in feeding
   1. Interest in creeping, pulling-up to standing, autonomous locomotion
   2. Pleasure in mother–baby games, peek-a-boo, pat-a-cake, "I catch you," etc.
   3. Evoking pleasurable responses from mother and others: bouncing to be bounced, signaling for music (activity to gain pleasure)
   4. Pleasurable vocalizing syllables, use of word-precursors to stimulate caregivers
   5. Enjoying manipulation of squeeze toys to make sounds, combining small blocks, banging

9–12 months (exploration and manipulation of the environment, expansion of interest)
Continuation of the above, plus
   1. Enjoys dropping and retrieving
   2. Overcoming stranger-anxiety
   3. Eager walking with help, in some cases walking alone
   4. "Loving"
   5. Trust, confidence, hope

*Unpleasure (Affects, Feelings, Emotions)*
Newborn to 2 months
Moderate to severe distress expressed in varying qualities of crying.
   Pain
   Hunger; delay or interruption in feeding
   Colic, stomachaches
   Frustration: removal of nipple, difficulty of managing nipple
Mild to moderate distress expressed in fussing or soft crying.
   Uncomfortable position, or uncomfortable in crib (lack of soft, cozy surround, or vestibular, rhythmic, experiences)
   Skin irritation from wet or soiled diapers
   Overstimulation, e.g., loud noise, excessive handling
   Lack of contact
   Tension, anxiety in caregivers

---

*(continued)*

TABLE 1.1—*Continued*

Illustrative Affective Experiences in Middle-Class American Infants

2–5 months
Continuation of above, plus
    Sharp pain from inoculation (expressed by screaming, and disorganized functioning)
    Fright from aggressive approach by stranger
    Disappointment in some babies when approaching person is not mother (sobbing woeful cry), and
       when put down in crib after satisfying interplay
    Irritated by failure of goal-oriented efforts
    Distress when toy is lost or removed
    Colic, decreasing at about 5 months

6–9 months
    Teething
    Painful encounters, bumps, falls while exploring
    Interferences by adults in goal-oriented efforts (anger)
    Separation from caregiver, familiar home setting, or crib
    Stranger anxiety
    Exposure to others' painful emotions (babies, children, adults)

9–12 months
    All of the 6–9 months sources of distress
    Fear of dogs, thunder, sudden loud noises as the infant is exposed to a wider environment
    Wider range of frustration due to interference by adults (anger)
    More intense stranger-anxiety in some babies (mastery achieved by some)
    Separation-anxiety, sometimes depression if mother leaves home daily for work and the baby is
       left with an unfamiliar person
    Distrust as residue of unpleasant experiences
    Hopelessness when suffering endless deprivation (rare in middle-class homes)

# REFERENCES

Ainsworth, M. D. S., Bell, S. M., & Stayton, D. J. Individual differences in Strange-Situation behavior of one-year-olds. In Schaffer, *The origins of human social relations*. London and New York: Academic Press, 1971.

Ames, L. B. Development of interpersonal smiling responses in the preschool years. *Journal of Genetic Psychology*, 1949, *74*, 273–291.

Bayley, N. Individual patterns of development. *Child Development*, 1956, *57*, 45–74.

Bowlby, J. The nature of the child's tie to his mother. *International Journal of Psychoanalysis*, 1958, *34*(5), 1–23.

Bowlby, J. *Attachment and loss (Vol. 2). Separation: Anxiety and anger*. New York: Basic Books, 1973.

Brazelton, T. B. Psychophysiologic reaction in the neonate. *Journal of Pediatrics*, 1961, *58*, 513–518.

Brazelton, T. B. The early mother–infant adjustment. *Pediatrics*, 1974, *31*, 931–937.

Bridges, K. M. B. *The social and emotional development of the preschool child*. London: Routledge, 1931.

Bronson, G. W. Infants' reactions to an unfamiliar person. Abridged from paper read at the biennial meeting of the Society for Research in Child Development at Minneapolis, Minn. April 1971. In L. Joseph Stove, Smith, H. F., Murphy, L. B. (Eds.), *The competent infant*. New York: Basic Books, 1973, 1978.

Cousins, N. Anatomy of an illness (as perceived by the patient). *Saturday Review*, May 28, 1977.

Ding, G. F., & Jersild, A. T. A study of the laughing and smiling of preschool children. *Journal of Genetic Psychology*, 1932, *40*, 452–472.

Duffy, E. Emotion: An example of the need for reorientation in psychology. *Psychology Review*, 1934, *41*, 154–198.

Emde, R. N. Emotional availability: A reciprocal reward system for infants and parents with implications for prevention of psycho-social disorders. In P. M. Taylor (Ed.), *Parent–infant relationships*. New York: Grune and Stratton, 1980, pp. 87–115.

English, H. B., & English, A. C. *A student's dictionary of psychological terms*. New York: Longmans Green, 1961.

Escalona, S. K., & Heider, G. *Prediction and outcome*. New York: Basic Books, 1959.

Freedman, D. A. The sensory deprivations. *Bulletin of the Meaninger Clinic*, 1979, *43*(1), 29–68.

Freud, S. *Three essays on the theory of sexuality* (Vol. 7). London: Hogarth, 1905.

Freud, S. *Mourning and Melancholea*. In *Standard Edition*, 1912, *14*, 237–260.

Gesell, A. and Ilg, F. L. *Infant and child in the culture of today*. New York: Harper, 1943.

Gewirtz, J. L. The course of infant smiling in four child-rearing environments in Israel. In B. M. Foss (Ed.), *Determinants of infant behavior* (Vol. 3). New York: Wiley, 1965.

Gibson, E. J., & Walk, R. D. The "visual cliff." *Scientific American*, 1960, *202*(4), 64–71.

Greenacre, P. *Trauma, growth and personality*. New York: Norton, 1952.

Greenblatt, M. Discussion. In P. H. Kuapp (Ed.), *Expression of the emotions in man*. New York: International Universities Press, 1963. Pp. 199–205.

Haith, M. M. The forgotten message of the infant smile. *Merrill-Palmer Quarterly*, 1972, *18*(4), 321.

Harlow, H., & Harlow M. The young monkeys. In J. B. Maas (Ed.), *Readings in Psychology Today* (3rd ed.). Del Mar, California: CRM Books, 1974.

Heider, G. Vulnerability in infants and young children. *Genetic Psychology Monograph*, 1966, *73*(1), 1–216.

Humphrey, G. The conditioned reflex and the elementary social reaction. *Journal of Abnormal and Social Psychology*, 1922, *17*, 113–119.

Izard, C. *Human emotions*. New York: Plenum, 1977.

Jersild, A. T., & Holmes, F. B. *Children's fears*. New York: Teachers' College, Columbia University Bureau of Publications, 1935.

Jersild, A. T. & Markey, F. V. Conflicts between preschool children. (Child Development Monograph, No. 21.) New York Teachers' College Publications, 1935.

Jones, H. E. Galvanic skin reflex in infancy. *Child Development*, 1930, *1*, 106–110.

Jones, M. C. Emotional development. In C. Murchison (Ed.), *A handbook of child psychology* (2nd ed.). Worcester, Massachusetts: Clark Univ. Press, 1933.

Kagan, J. *Change and continuity in infancy*. New York: Wiley, 1971.

Katan, A. Children who were raped. *Psychoanalytical Study of the Child*, 1973, *28*, 208–224.

Krystal, H. Aspects of affect theory. *Bulletin of the Menninger Clinic*, 1977, *41*, 1–26.

Lacey, J. I., Kagan, J., Lacey, B. C., & Moss, H. A. The visceral level: Situational determinants and behavioral correlates of autonomic response patterns. In P. H. Knapp (Ed.), *Expressions of the emotions in man*. New York: International Universities Press, 1963.

Levy, D. M. Primary affect hunger. *American Journal of Psychiatry*, 1937, *94*, 643–652.

Levy, D. M. The infant's earliest memory of inoculation. *Journal of Genetic Psychology*, 1960, *96*, 3–48.

Lipsitt, L. R. The study of sensory and learning processes of the newborn. In S. Volpe (Ed.), *Clinics in perinatology* (Vol. 4, No. 1). Philadelphia, Pennsylvania: Saunders, 1977.

Moss, H. Sex, age and state as determinants of mother–infant interaction. *Merrill-Palmer Quarterly*, 1967, *13*, 19–36.

Murphy, G. *Personality: A biosocial approach*. New York: Basic Books, 1947.

Murphy, L. B. *Social behavior and child personality*. New York: Columbia University Press, 1937.

Murphy, L. B. Some aspects of the first relationship. *International Journal of Psychoanalysis*, 1964, *45*, 31–44.

Murphy, L. B. The variability of infants' reactions to pain. *Clinical Proceedings of Children's Hospital, National Medical Center*, 1973, *29*(1), 3–7.

Murphy, L. B., & Moriarty, A. E. *Vulnerability, coping and growth*. New Haven: Yale Univ. Press, 1976.

Paradise, E. B., & Curcio, F. Relationship of cognitive and affective behaviors to fear of strangers in male infants. *Developmental Psychology*, 1974, *10*(4), 476–483.

Pine, F. *On the expansion of the affect array*. Bulletin of the Menninger Clinic, *43*, No. 1. Jan. 1979, 79–95.

Radke-Yarrow, M., Zahn-Waxler, C., & Chapman, M. Children's prosocial dispositions and behavior. In I. H. Mussen (Ed.), *Carmichael's manual of Child Psychology* (Vol. 4, 4th ed.). New York: Wiley. (In press)

Rothbart, M. K. Laughter in young children. *Psychological Bulletin*, 1973, *80*, 247–256.

Schaffer, H. P. Some issues for research in the study of attachment behavior. In B. Foss (ed.), *Determinants of infant behavior* (Vol. II). London: Methuen, 1963.

Schaffer, H. R., & Emerson, P. E. The development of social attachments in infancy. *Monographs of the Society for Research in Child Development*, 1964, *29* (Whole No. 94). (a)

Schaffer, R. *Mothering*. Cambridge, Massachusetts: Harvard Univ. Press, 1977.

Schmale, A. H. A genetic view of affects with special reference to the genesis of hopelessness and helplessness. *Psychoanalytic Study of the Child*, 1964, *19*, 287–310.

Schultebrandt, J. G. and Raskin, A. *Depression in childhood: Diagnosis, treatment and conceptual models*. New York: Raven, 1977.

Shirley, M. M. *The first two years of life*. New York: John Day, 1930.

Shirley, M. M. A behavior syndrome characterizing prematurely-born children. *Child Development*, 1939, *X*, 2.

Spicher, C. M. Infant affective responses during interactions with health worker strangers in a child health conference. *Maternal–Child Nursing Journal*, 1976, *5*(3), 131–150.

Spitz, R. Anaclitic depression. *Psychoanalytic Study of the Child*, 1946, *2*, 313–342.

Sroufe, A. L. Emotional development in infancy. In J. Osofsky (Ed.), *Handbook of infant development*. New York: Wiley, 1979.

Stern, G. G., Caldwell, B. M., Hersher, L., Lipton, E. L., & Richmond, J. B. A factor analytic study of the mother–infant dyad. *Child Development*, 1969, *40*, 163–181.

Tizard, B. & Rees, J. The effect of early institutional rearing on the behavior procep and affectional relationships of four-year-old children. *Journal of Child Psychology and Psychiatry*, 1975, *16*, 61–73.

Washburn, R. W. A study of the smiling and laughing of infants in the first year of life. Genetic psychology. Monograph 6, No. 5, 397–535.

Watson, J. B. *Behaviorism*. New York: Norton, 1925.

Williams, R. J. *Biochemical individuality*. New York: Wiley, 1956.

Wolf, K. M. Observation of individual tendencies in the first year of life. In M. J. E. Senn (Ed.), *Problems of infancy and childhood*. New York: Josiah Macy, Sr. Foundation, 1952.

Wolff, P. H. Observations on newborn infants. *Psychosomatic Medicine,* 1959, *21,* 110–118.

Yarrow, L. J. Emotional development. *American Psychologist,* 1979, *34,* 951–957.

Zahn-Waxler, C., & Radke-Yarrow, M. *A developmental analysis of children's responses to emotions in others.* Paper presented at the meeting of the Society for Research in Child Development, San Francisco, California, March 1979.

Chapter 2

# PRECURSORS FOR THE DEVELOPMENT OF EMOTIONS IN EARLY INFANCY[1]

*T. BERRY BRAZELTON*

## ABSTRACT

*At least four levels of behavioral organization in the communication system between parents and their small infants develop over the first 5 months. Based on a rhythmic interaction of attention and nonattention that is critical to the homeostatic controls necessary to the immature organism, the parents and infant can learn to communicate more and more complex messages in clusters of behaviors. These behaviors do not demand verbal communication. The clusters of behaviors contain the important elements of affective and cognitive information and form the base for the infant's learning about the world. Thus, in an important period of intense communication between parent and the infant, he or she provides the infant with affective and cognitive information, and with the opportunity to learn his or her own controls over the internal homeostatic systems that are necessary in order to pay attention to his or her world. The four stages of learning about these controls provide infants with a source of learning about themselves and provide the mother or father with an important opportunity for learning the*

---

[1]The support of the Robert Wood Johnson Foundation (Grant No. 7585.9), the Carnagie Corporation (Grant No. 7595.9), the Harris Foundation, and the National Institute of Mental Health (Grant No. 7300.6) is gratefully acknowledged.

EMOTION
Theory, Research, and Experience
Volume 2

*ingredients of a nurturant role with their baby. These early experiences of learning about each other are the base for their shared emotional development in the future, and are critical as anlages for the infant's future ego.*

As the rapidly increasing evidence for complexity in the human newborn unfolds, we are able to attribute more and more complex experiences to the infant from the first. Psychoanalytic literature in the past has essentially neglected the early months of life. As an illustration of this oversight, Mahler's elegant descriptions of mother–infant attachment start with infants of 4–5 months of age (Mahler, Pine, & Bergman, 1975). Thomas, Chess, and Birch's (1968) famous longitudinal study of temperamental differences in infants was not concerned with the first 3 months of their subjects' lives. References to early ego development (even in the hands of such pioneering masters as Hartmann and Kris, 1945) implied that the conscious life or the ego development of the infant began after 3 months. This paralleled the neurological literature (Thomas, Chesni, & Saint Anne Dargassies, 1960), which implied, until recently, that cortical function was relatively unimportant in storing experience until the infant was 3 months of age. "Voluntary" neuromotor behavior could certainly not be attributed to an infant before this time.

Piaget (1953, 1955), the pioneer in conceptualizations of cognitive behavior, began his descriptions with infants of 4 and 5 months. Not until the 1960s did we begin to realize that a great deal of experience was being amassed and stored by infants in the first few months of life. Fetuses are now being studied in the last half of gestation for their ability to respond to auditory and visual stimulus. They prefer certain stimuli to others and they can shut out or "habituate" to unpleasant ones and become increasingly attentive to preferred stimuli (Brazelton, 1981). The fact that they can make such choices implies the presence of a mechanism in fetal life that differentiates and "prefers" certain kinds of experiences and responds differentially to them. If this can be confirmed, the opportunity for learning *in utero* exists. Thus, we must begin to reconceptualize our ideas of the beginning of the effects of early experience.

We can now begin to conceptualize how experience can be represented in the memory of infants and how it can shape them toward future responses. These early experiences, when they are repeated, and when they are accompanied by a behavioral representation of recognition in the infant, must be considered as potential anlage (or precursors) of future ego development or as precursors of cognitive patterns, shaping the infant toward preferred psychomotor patterns. These early reactions are likely to become, as Greenacre says (1941), the "precursors for future response patterns." If they are successful patterns in early infancy, the chances are that they will be repeated, learned, and will eventually become preferred patterns in the older infant. In this way, the behaviors that represents reactions of the infant become precursors for future development.

With this in mind, the study of prenatal and neonatal behavior becomes a way of predicting the baby's future style and preferred patterns of behavior.

Since a parent has invested in, and is likely to be deeply affected by, the newborn's behavioral reactions, an assessment of the infant's behavior becomes a window into the reactions of the parent's responses to him or her. Thus, an infant's early behavioral reactions become important in understanding the infant as well as the parent's reactions to the infant.

An understanding of the infant's development within any particular developmental line—such as that of affect or emotional development—must include the interaction between this and other developmental lines. The immaturity of cognitive neuromotor and psychophysiological equipment of the baby limit the infant's potential for developing clearly definable emotions in the early months. The responses of the infant's neurological and physical systems are at the core of any development of emotions. The immaturity of these systems place obvious restraints on development, but their experiential maturation forms the base for future emotional experience. As infants "learn" to cope with a stimulus from the outside world, they experience a sense of achievement, and the feedback system that is activated may give them an inner representation of mastery (cf. White, 1959). Although this terminology is "adultomorphic" and probably represents mechanisms that are more consciously experienced in an older child or adult, it seems to me that the concepts of mastery and learning do fit the anlage of experiences on which the infant begins to build.

The central nervous system (CNS), as it develops, drives the infant toward maturation and mastery of self and world. Any internal equilibrium is tested and upset by the imbalance that is created as the CNS matures. Hence, maturation and an increase in differentiation of infant skills and potential become a force that drives the infant to reorganize and "relearn" control systems. Each step is a new opportunity for mastery and for learning new feedback systems.

There are two sources fueling this maturation. Feedback loops that close on completion of an experience after an anticipated performance affect the baby from within. Our concept is that, as each step is mastered, anticipation has generated energy that becomes realized and is available as the step is completed. In this way, a sense of mastery (cf. White, 1959) is incorporated by the developing infant, and this freed-up energy drives the infant toward the next developmental achievement. Meanwhile, there is a second important source of energy that fuels infant development and enhances each experience. The environment around the infant, when it is nurturant, tends to entrain responsive behavior to the behavior of the infant. Not only do parents register recognition and approval of an infant's achievement, but they add a salient, more developed signal to their approval. This signal, coupled with the positive reinforcement, both fuels the infant and leads him or her to match the adult's expectation. For example, when an infant vocalizes with an "Ohh," a parent will add, "Oh yes!" to it. The

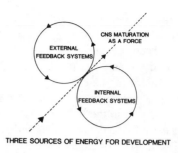

THREE SOURCES OF ENERGY FOR DEVELOPMENT

FIGURE 2.1. Three sources of energy for development.

parent couples an added experience with open approval of the infant's production. Thus parents offer the infant positive reinforcement and an added stimulus to reach for. They fuels the infant to go on (Als, 1979).

These two sources of energy—one from within, the other from without—are in balance under ideal conditions, and both provide the energy for future development. The infant's recognition of each of these sources, as he or she masters a developmental step, is often unconscious, but it adds to a preconscious recognition of mastery. This internal representation, coupled with the closure of feedback loops of mastery of steps in autonomic and CNS control, must become the precursors of emotional as well as of cognitive recognition and contribution toward the infant's developing ego.

When either of these are deficient, the infant's development of affective and cognitive stages can be impaired. This occurs when (a) an infant is at risk for CNS or autonomic deficits (such as one whose autonomic system is too labile or too sluggish, or one whose threshold for intake of stimuli is too low and is thus overwhelmed by each stimulus); or (b) when the environment is inappropriately responsive to the infant (either under or over). Thus, the internal and external feedback systems become intertwined from the first. Since each is dependent on the infant's endowment and on his or her capacity for overt and internalized reactions, the infant's genetic capacities determine the kind of internal and external feedback systems that are available. They both fuel the infant's development and place limits on it.

Thomas, Chess, and Birch (1968) first described a baby's developing style or temperament. Temperament certainly provides an observable, quantifiable matrix for accepting, utilizing, and discharging stimuli from the surrounding environment. This matrix then becomes a predictable way for an infant to react and sets up the expectation for his or her reactions for those who must nurture the infant. They can begin to see the infant as a person with a set of expectable reactions and they create a nurturing envelope around the infant, with reactions that are appropriate to that infant.

## INTRAUTERINE "LEARNING"

In the process of developing the Neonatal Behavioral Assessment Scale (NBAS) (Brazelton, 1973), I had the opportunity to learn, with wonder, the newborn infant's capacities for behavioral control and for expression of the newborn's reactions to inner and outer stimuli. I became aware of the matrix of states of consciousness that dominated infant reactivity to stimuli and that expressed his or her CNS responsiveness and control over incoming stimulation and outgoing responses. Indeed, I began to see infant regulation of state as an infant's most powerful control and response system. The diurnal regulation of an infant's states, the shaping of their sequence, and the diurnal expectancy for alert–sleep states throughout a 24-hour period not only demonstrates an economical refueling of the infant's systems but represents a homeostatic system at the base of self-regulation. Not only is it critical to infant survival and growth but it dominates the infant's ability to learn necessary regulation of him- or herself in order to attend and respond to the surrounding world. Cognitive and affective development are at the mercy of the proper regulation of this diurnally dominated cycling of states, as is the infant's physiological maintenance and growth. This was so predictable in the third trimester of pregnancy that a mother could begin to predict these cycles.

So important is the diurnal predictability of state cycling that mothers who accept these cycles without becoming aware of them can be made conscious of them if asked to keep a record of them. I have not found a mother who could not predict her baby's rest–activity cycle accurately after 2 or 3 days of conscious attention to it. This leads me to feel that such cycles are regular, organized, and predictable, and are a dominate base for other kinds of organization in the fetus. In addition, I am fairly certain that they are entrained to and responding to the rest–activity and diurnal cycle of the mother.

On this organizational base is overlaid more discrete responses to stimuli that reach the fetus either directly or indirectly via the mother. Rosen and Rosen (1975) described the EEG activity–rest cycling in the last trimester and postulated that there are discrete evoked responses of the fetal cortex that can be measured in the last trimester when noninvasive techniques become available. At present, fetal electroencephalography by electrodes applied directly to the fetal scalp after rupture of the membranes demonstrates rich responses; for example, evoked responses to sound, touch, and visual stimuli. Habituation of these becomes a way of measuring freedom from stress; evoked responses without change or habituation over time represents stress of the fetus (cf. the oxytocin stress test [Hon & Paul, 1970]). Using maternal reports and confirming them with fetal behavior during ultrasound techniques, we (Brazelton, 1981) have become convinced that the fetus in the last trimester responds reliably to visual, auditory, and kinesthetic stimulation. We have seen the fetus in the last trimester startle to a bright light presented in its line of vision, as well as to a loud sharp noise placed next to the abdominal wall. If a softer light is presented in the same position, the infant turns actively but smoothly toward it. If a soft noise is used, the baby will turn toward it. The behaviorally differentiated response to external stimuli suggests that fetal responses are present and can represent an early, unconscious system of behavioral signals to the mother. If these signals coincide with her own responses, they may be the base for an intrauterine synchrony between mother and child.

We have also noted that these responses are of a different nature and less predictable, more subdued, and more rapidly habituated to repeated stimuli if they are presented while the fetus is in a quiescent state resembling sleep. A mother can differentiate between at least three states in her fetus, an active "alert" state, a deep sleep with little or no movement, and an intermediate sleep state with irregular startle-like movements. The entrainment of fetal states to her states of consciousness, coupled with this responsiveness that is somewhat predictably tied to this matrix of states, resembles the richer response seen in the neonate. *In utero* experience then must be preconditioning the fetus to maternal sleep–wake rhythms and to the mother's style of reactivity. This kind of intrauterine entrainment would then set the rhythmic base for maternal cues with which the neonate could interact after birth. Not only would the neonate have experienced the maternal rhythms that entrained his or her rhythms, but auditory and kinesthetic cues from her would be "familiar." No wonder a newborn already prefers a female to a male voice at birth (Brazelton, 1979). The first opportunity for shaping of reaction patterns and the readying of them for "appropriate" cues after birth is provided *in utero*. In addition, the mother, in experiencing her unborn child's responses, learns about her baby.

## NEONATAL BEHAVIOR
## AS EVIDENCE OF "LEARNING"

Infancy in the human is relatively prolonged, as compared to other mammals. This period must serve an adaptive purpose in that it creates the opportunity for the infant to learn about the world as well as about him- or herself. The infant has the time to learn about cultural and individual family patterns and expectations. The infant has the opportunity, while within the protective envelope of nurturing adults, to learn complex coping and control systems and how they provide a base for alerting, for paying attention, for mastery of the rules of communication.

The remarkable capacities for attention and interactive behavior of the neonate when enclosed in the envelope of an adult interactant who is sensitive to the infant's need for regulation has led us to see the infant's dependency on a nurturing environment in a new light. No longer do we see the infant as insensitive, chaotic, or unpredictable, but equipped with highly predictable behavioral responses to both positive (appropriate to the infant) or negative (inappropriate or overloading) stimuli from the outside world. That these responses can in turn shape the responses of the adult interactant to set up a mutual feedback system is my thesis. Thus, nature and nurture become inseparable entwined by the need for reciprocal feedback in each of the interactions in a dyad such as the parent–infant dyad.

Kendon (1972) first alerted me to the patterning of nonverbal behaviors in a dyadic interaction between adults. The timing of cue behavior by a speaker so that it led the other participant to be "ready" to speak next seemed to represent a rhythmic sharing of temporal and behavioral expectations. Within this hypothesis, one could see that the power of the interaction enveloped interactants as they shaped their behavior to that of the other interactant. The opportunity for modeling on, and learning from the other, shaped them toward an infraverbal communication system. Watslawick, Beavin, and Jackson (1967) had the insight that there was never noninteraction as the members of a dyad participated with each other. One could speak of negative or of positive or even of neutral valences between them, but never of "noninteraction." This model for an understanding of the powerful communication system that must potentially exist between an infant, hungry for affective and cognitive signals, and a parent, hungry for an understanding of the inner working of his or her baby, led me to be alert to the reciprocity that can exist between a parent and an infant.

Communication is a system that demands mastery at all levels—control over neuromotor and psychophysiological systems, alerting, and prolonged attention in order to attend to cognitive and affective cues. In particular, it means learning enough about oneself in order to be available for adapting these systems to the "other" member. The ability to adjust to the goals and personality of others while retaining one's own identity is basic to reciprocity. This implies the ability to control or influence others with effective but nonviolating strategies and to be reasonably influenced by the other without being totally overcome or dominated (Gottman, 1979).

In working with a neonate, I was struck with the power of this kind of reciprocity as it formed an envelope of control within which the neonate could demonstrate his remarkable responsiveness. As an adult ready to follow the infant's behavioral cues, I found that they were clear and likely to be predictable when one used the concept of different states of consciousness as a matrix. If I maintained an awareness of the infants' use of state, I could then shape their behavioral responses by adapting my presentation of stimuli within a concept of positive to negative or "appropriate" to "inappropriate." This latter concept must be individualized to each neonate, based on the infant's threshold for sensory receptivity, on his or her capacity for control over motor and autonomic responses, and on the relative fragility or stability of his or her immature cardiorespiratory systems. As I shaped my own behavior to fit these requirements and attempted to utilize the infants' subtle behavioral and autonomic cues to shape myself to them in order to achieve their "best performances" on the responses in the neonatal assessment, I became aware of how powerfully the neonates were shaping me and my behavior. In other words, in order to produce their optimal responsiveness, I had to make myself available to them with a sensitivity to their need for control over motor activity and a sensitivity to their "states." I could feel, anticipate, and respond to subtle responses that allowed me to shape my behavior to them so that they could produce their optimal responses. Joint regulation of adult and infant, then, becomes the necessary base for such responsiveness (Als, 1978). That the neonate *and* the adult learn about each other and about themselves within such a system could hardly be questioned after experiencing it in such a way. The feeling of mutuality, of identification with "the other," must be at the base of successful interaction between parent and infant. In shaping him- or herself to learn the levels of appropriate and inappropriate stimuli to offer the newborn, the parent learns about the base from which the infant operates (Bullowa, 1979).

The NBAS is an interactive scale (Brazelton, 1973). In a 20-min assessment of the newborn baby, the examiner brings newborns from sleep to awake states and assesses their reactions to many kinds of stimuli within each state of consciousness. In performing an examination, we attempt to reproduce a mother's best efforts to communicate with her new baby as we elicit state changes and behavioral responses. The first part of the evaluation tests the infant's ability to protect him- or herself from disturbing, nonsocial stimuli such as a bright light, a bell, and a pinprick to the foot (Als, 1978). In order to attend to important social stimuli, the newborn must be able to shut out disturbing stimuli. The fact that newborns can shut off their responses to intrusive, negative stimuli is a proof of this strength.

## COMMUNICATION DURING
## NEONATAL ASSESSMENT

Let me describe how a neonate communicates with me as I examine him or her. One of the most remarkable performances that one can observe in neonates is seen as the infants change from a quiet state to a state in which they could become distressed if they were not able to control themselves. As they begin to rouse, they make real efforts to turn their heads to one side, then perform a cycle of hand-to-mouth movements (Babkin, 1959). When they are able to bring their fist up to their mouth and to hold it there, and even to suck on it, they quiet down, their agitated motor activity subsides and, as they relax, they begin to alert, looking around for auditory and visual stimuli. This active attempt to control disturbing motor activity and to maintain an alert state using the ability to bring the hand to the mouth seems to be a process designed to allow infants to attend to their environment. The observer who watches a neonate achieve this becomes struck with how "programmed" infants are for interaction with their environment.

When they are alerted, infants respond with periods of active fixation on an attractive visual stimulus such as a bright, shiny, red ball. They will quiet, maintain a quiet inactive state in order to follow the ball through complete 180° arcs of movement, and turn their heads as well as following it with their eyes. If, then, they are presented with a human face, infants will act "hungry" as they follow the face laterally and vertically. In this process of registering a preference for human stimuli, it is impossible for an adult interactant not to become "hooked" to the infant. The infant's ability to communicate this preference by facial and eye "softening" and their increasing attention is reflected in prolonged suppression of motor activity in the rest of their bodies, as well as in increased state control. The examiner or adult interactant becomes aware of his or her own involvement with the infant, as he or she, too, maintains an intense period of eye-to-eye and face-to-face communication.

In the same way, an infant can register auditory preferences. Infants can react to the sound of a bell or a loud rattle by turning away from it with startling, jerky movements that either propel the infant into a crying state or into an inactive state resembling sleep. In such a state, they shut out stimuli, hold their extremities and body tight, their eyes tightly closed, their faces masked, and their respirations deep, jagged, and regular (Brazelton, 1961). Thus, sleep can be a protective state. And in the same way, they can use crying as another way of regulating their environment as they attempt to control the input of stimulation from those around them. If in either of these shutting-out states, crying or sleep, they are offered a sound of a soft rattle or a soothing human voice, they are likely to quiet from agitation or rouse from light sleep and to become alert, gradually turning toward the attractive sound. If the stimulus is nonhuman, they will search for it while maintaining an alert facial expression and with all of their extremities is quietly inactive. When the stimulus is the human voice, the neonates not only searches for the observer's face but, when they find it, their face and eyes become wide, soft, and eager and they may even crane their necks, lifting the chin gently toward the source of the voice. As he does so, the infant's body tension gradually increases, but he remains quietly inactive. A nurturing adult feels impelled to respond to these signals by cuddling the baby.

As well-organized, alert neonates are held in a cuddled position, they mold into the adult's body, turning gently toward the chest. They may even grab hold of the adult's clothing with their free hand, and their legs may mold around the side of the adult's body. This molding response cannot help but become a reinforcing signal to the adult for more active cuddling, for looking down to engage the infant in face-to-face contact for rocking or singing.

When the infants are held upright at the adult's shoulder they first lift their heads to look around. As they do so, they actively hold on more tightly with all four extremities. After a period of alert scanning of the environment triggered by the vestibular stimulation of the upright position (Korner & Thoman, 1972), they are most likely to tire and to put their head against the adult's shoulder, nestled in the crook of the adult's neck. As the soft fuzz of the infant's head makes contact with the skin of the crook of the neck, mothers tell me that it causes a tightening sensation in their breasts, followed by a "let-down" reflex of milk. No adult is likely to resist the feeling of a soft head resting on the shoulder.

Another powerful set of communicative signals occurs as infants build up to crying. If an adult keeps on talking at one side of the infant's head, the baby will probably stop crying, quiet down, and gradually turn toward the voice. The adult can use the infant's capacity to alert to voices by changing his or her own vocal behavior. If an adult's voice softens, infants will maintain their focused searching and scanning. They will remain quietly alert and may "smile" or may soften their face into the precursor of a "smile face." As adult and infant continue to communicate, adults can bring infants up to a more active state by gradually increasing the pitch and timbre of their voices, or they may cause infants to "overload" and return to a crying state by changing their tempo to a staccato rhythm, *or* they may help infants maintain the quiet, alert state by speaking softly in a slow, rhythmic fashion.

## NURTURANT ENVELOPE AS A PRECONDITION

Joint regulation of these interactive systems in order to produce optimal performance in the neonate led us to see the powerful signaling systems, the regulatory systems of state control, and the nonverbal communicative systems that are available in the first few weeks in the human infant. By 4 weeks, Yogman, Dixon, Tronick, Adamson, Als, and Brazelton (1976) have demonstrated reliable, reproducible patterns of rhythmic behavioral responses that are already reserved for the mother and father. These responses are differentiated for each parent and are significantly different from the pattern or nonpatterns that already signal the baby's responses to a stranger (Dixon, Yogman, Tronick, Als, Adamson, & Brazelton, 1981). If these patterns are shaped so early, they must be predetermined *in utero,* to some extent, and shaped in the first few days and weeks by important messages and cues that are offered by each parent and quickly reorganized by the infant. These allow for (*a*) early patterning toward individual differences in both partners; (*b*) the importance of individual cues on the part of important adults and individual responses on the part of the infant; (c) rapid recognition of the important parameters of context, the parental envelope; and (d) physiological and psychological control.

The most basic control system that is necessary to the immature organism is the homeostatic regulation of the autonomic system. It determines what is within the limits of responsiveness and tells infants when to shut off their responses in order to protect themselves.

I first became aware of this regulatory system as it underlies attention to an object when I was working with Bower (1971) Bruner (1973), and Trevarthen (1977), as they were defining the behaviors involved in early reaching. Their work was demonstrating how early (in the first weeks) infants could pay attention to an object in "reach space" (10–12 in. in front of them in the midline) and, as they watched it, all of their behavior reflected their intense, rapt attention. Not only did they have an observable, predictable "hooked" state of attention as the object was brought into this space, but also the infants' entire bodies responded in an appropriate and predictable fashion as they attended to the object.

The infants stared at the object with wide eyes, fixating on it for as long as 2 min. without disruption of gaze of of attention (by 6 weeks of age). Their expressions were fixed, the muscles of their faces tense, with eyes staring and mouth and lips protruding toward the object. This static, fixed look of attention was interspersed with little jerks of facial muscles. Their tongues jerked out toward the object and then withdrew rapidly. Occasional short bursts of effortful vocalizing toward the object occurred. During these long periods of attention, the eyes blinked occasionally in single, isolated blinks. The body was set in a tense, immobilized sitting position, with the object at its midline. When the object was moved to one side or the other, the infants tended to shift their bodies so it was kept at their midline. Their shoulders were hunched as if the infants were about to "pounce." Extremities were fixed, flexed at elbow and knee, and fingers and toes were aimed toward the object. Hands were semiflexed or tightly flexed, but fingers and toes repeatedly jerked out to point at the object. Jerky swipes of an arm or leg in the direction of the object occurred from time to time as the period of intense attention was maintained. In this interaction with an object, the infant's attention seemed to be "hooked," and all his or her motor behavior alternated between the long, fixed periods of tense absorption and short bursts of jerky, excited movement in the direction of the object. The infant seemed to hold down any interfering behavior that might break into this prolonged state of attention.

Most striking in all of this was the intent, prolonged state of attention, during which tension gradually built up in all segments of the infant's body until abrupt disruption seemed to be an inevitable and necessary relief. This behavior was most striking by 12–16 weeks. It could also be observed as early as 4 weeks of age, long before a reach could be achieved.

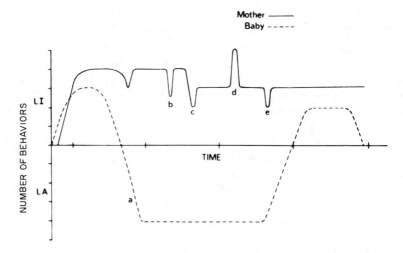

**Figure 2.2.** Three minutes of mother and infant interacting with each other. Baby is looking away for most of the interaction.

Additionally, I have observed the cardiorespiratory involvement of infants with congenital cardiac defects whose circulatory balance was precarious. As they get "hooked" on and interact with an object in reach space, their breathing becomes deeper and more labored, their cardiac balance more precarious, cyanosis deepens until attention to the object is decreased momentarily, and their color returns. The return of attention to the object brings on a repetition of the same cycle of "hooked" attention, increasing autonomic imbalance, and recovery as the baby turns away briefly. From these observations it is clear that an infant's attention to an object involves behavioral, neuromotor, and autonomic systems in a predictable, alternating increase and decrease in the deployment of attention and nonattention that is designed to protect an immature and easily overloaded cardiorespiratory balance.

The contrast between infant behavior and attention when interacting parents and when attending to an object was clear even as early as 4 weeks of age. Indeed, I felt I could see brief episodes of these two contrasting modes of behavior and attention as early as 2–3 weeks.

A striking way of illustrating the behaviors of the mother and the child, as well as the interaction of the two, is to present them in graphic form (Brazelton, Koslowski, & Main, 1974). Figures 2.2–2.3 are graphs drawn from mother–infant interaction periods. Time is measured along the horizontal axis; the number of behaviors, along the vertical axis. Curves drawn above the horizontal axis indicate that the person whose behavior the curve represents was looking *at* his or her partner. Curves drawn below the axis indicate that he or she was

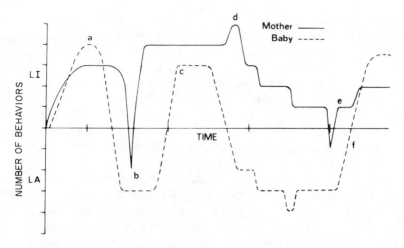

**FIGURE 2.3.** Three minutes of successful mother–infant interaction.

looking *away*. Solid lines represent the mother's behavior; broken lines, the baby's. Thus, a deep, broken line below the horizontal axis indicates that the baby was looking away while engaging in several behaviors.

As reflected by Figure 2.2, the mother looks at the baby after the baby turns to her. As they look at each other, she adds behaviors—smiling, vocalizing, touching baby's hand, holding baby's leg—to accelerate their interaction. Baby responds by increasing the number of his or her own behaviors (smiling, vocalizing, and cycling arms and legs) until the peak at point (*X*). At this point, baby begins to decrease his or her behaviors and gradually cuts down on them toward the end of their interaction. Mother follows baby's lead by decreasing her behaviors more rapidly, and she ends her part of the cycle by looking away just before baby does. Figure 2.2 shows a baby starting a cycle by looking at mother. She follows by looking at baby and adding four more behaviors in rapid succession—touching, smiling, talking, and nodding her head. Baby watches her, vocalizes, smiles back, cycles briefly, and then begins to decrease his or her responses and turns away at point (*a*). Mother stops smiling as baby begins to turn away, but rapidly adds facial gestures to try to recapture baby's interest. She continues to talk, touch, nod her head, and make facial gestures until point (*b*). At this point she stops the gestures but begins to pat baby. At point (*c*) she stops talking briefly and stops nodding. At point (*d*) she makes hand gestures in addition to her facial grimaces but stops them both thereafter. At point (*e*) she stops vocalizing, and baby begins to look at her again. He vocalizes briefly and then looks away again when her activity continues.

In Figure 2.3 the mother and baby are looking at each other, smiling, and vocalizing together. The baby begins to cycle and reach out to her. At point (a) baby begins to turn away from mother. She responds by looking down at her hands and she stops her activity briefly. This brings baby back to look at her at point (c). Her smiling, vocalizing, and leaning toward baby bring a smiling response. In addition, baby's arms and legs cycle, and baby coos contentedly while watching her. As baby turns away, mother first adds another behavior and gestures. Baby, however, adds activities—ignoring her reminders—and turns away from her. She gradually cuts out all her activity and by point (e) she looks away from him. Immediately afterward, baby begins to look back to her, and the cycle of looking at each other begins again at point (f).

Of course, the expectancy engendered in an interaction with a static object, as opposed to a responsive person, must be very different (Piaget, 1953, 1955). But what surprised me was how early this expectancy seemed to be reflected in the infant's behavior and use of attention. When the infant was interacting with its mother, there seemed to be a constant cycle of attention, (A), followed by withdrawal of attention (W)—the cycle used by each partner as he or she approached and then withdrew and waited for a response from the other participant. In each of these "states" (A and W), we found there were predicted behaviors, and clusters of behaviors were the stimuli that controlled the timing of each interactant's response to the other. Single behaviors were less predictive and were not reliable indicators of the quality of their interaction. A smile alone did not necessarily produce a smile, nor did a vocalization alone produce a vocalization. But if they were imbedded in several other behaviors, the likelihood of a matching response was markedly increased. In order to understand which cluster of behaviors will result in a set of responsive behaviors in the other member of the dyad, one must first understand the "state" of affective attention that has been captured and is expressed by each member of the dyad. Responses are largely dominated by the ongoing state of attention that exists between them. In other words, the strength of the dyadic interaction dominates the meaning of each member's behavior. If the mother responds in one way, their interactional energy builds up (A); if another, the infant may turn away (W). The same holds true of her responses to the infant's behavior. Clustering behaviors and sequencing them becomes critical in understanding the baby's use of particular behaviors as responses in an interaction.

The power of the interaction in shaping each participant's behavior can be seen at many levels. Using looking and not looking at the mothers as measures of attention–inattention, in a 1-min interaction there was an average of 4.4 cycles of such attention and apparent inattention. Not only were the spans of attention and of looking away of shorter duration than they had been with objects, but they were obviously smoother as the attention built up, reached its peak, and then diminished gradually with the mother. Both the build-up as well as the decrease in attention were gradual and were usually smoothly paced.

## MOTHER'S ROLE

In this setting, the most important role of the adult interactants seemed to be that of helping infants to form a regulatory base for their immature psychological and motor reactions.

The most important rule for maintaining an interaction seemed to be that a mother develop a sensitivity to her infant's capacity for attention and the infant's need for withdrawal—partial or complete—after a period of attending to her. Short cycles of attention and inattention seemed to underlie all periods of prolonged interaction. Although we thought we were observing continuous attention to the mother on the part of the infant, the stop-frame analysis uncovered the cyclical nature of the infant's looking and not-looking in our laboratory setting. Looking-away behavior reflects the need of infants to maintain some control over the amount of stimulation they can take in during such intense periods of interaction. This is a homeostatic model, similar to the type of model that underlies all the physiological reactions of the neonate, and it seems to apply to the immature organism's capacity to attend to messages in a communication system.

Basic to this regulatory system or reciprocal interaction between parent and infant is the basic rhythm of attention–inattention that is set up between them (Brazelton, Tronick, Adamson, Als, & Wise, 1975). A mother must respect her infant's needs for the regulation that this affords or she will overload the infant's immature psychophysiological system and the infant will need to protect him- or herself by turning her off completely. Thus, she learns the infant's capacity for attention–inattention early, in order to maintain her infant's attention. Within this rhythmic, coherent configuration, mother and infant can introduce the mutable elements of communication. Smiles, vocalizations, postures, and tactile signals all are such elements. They can be interchanged at will as long as they are based on the rhythmic structure. The individual differences of the baby's needs for such a structure sets the limits on it. The mother then has the opportunity to adapt her tempo within these limits. If she speeds up her tempo, she can reduce baby's level of communication. If she slows hers down, she can expect a higher level of engagement and communicative behavior from the infant (Stern, 1974). Her use of tempo as a means toward entraining the baby's response systems is probably the basis of the baby's learning about his or her own control systems. In the process of introducing variability, the baby learns the limits of its control systems. As he or she returns to a baseline, the baby learns about basic self-regulation. The feedback systems that are set up within this afford the baby a kind of richness of self-regulation or adaption.

Built on top of this base is the nonverbal message. By using a systems approach to understand this, we find that each behavioral message or cluster of behaviors from one member of the dyad acts as a disruption of the system, which must then be reorganized. The process of reorganization affords the infant and the parent a model for learning—learning about the other as well as learning about oneself within this regulatory system. An "appropriate" or attractive stimulus creates a disruption and reorganization that is of a different nature from those that are the result of an intrusive or "inappropriate" stimulus. Each serves a purpose in this learning model.

An inspection of the richness of such a homeostatic model, which provides each participant with an opportunity to turn off or on at any time in the interaction, demonstrates the fine-tuning available and necessary to each partner of the dyad for learning about "the other." The individual behaviors that may be introduced into the clusters of behaviors that dominate the interaction become of real secondary importance. A smile or a vocalization may be couched within several other behaviors to form a signaling cluster. But the individual behavior is not the necessary requirement for a response: The cluster is. The basic rhythm, the "fit" of clusters of behavior, and timing of appropriate clusters to produce responses in an expectable framework become the best prediction of real reciprocity in parent–infant interaction.

## VIOLATION OF
## THE EXPECTANCY FOR INTERACTION

With this regulatory model as a base, we (Tronick, Als, Adamson, Wise, & Brazelton, 1978) examined the powerful effects of the infant and mother of violating the expectancy they set up between them. To examine the infant's capacity for such regulation and the importance of interactional reciprocity to the infant, we experimentally distorted the feedback that the infant normally receives from the mother. The mother is asked to sit in front of her seated infant, remaining unresponsive and maintaining an expressionless face. The infant's intense reaction to this distortion demonstrates not only the importance of interactional reciprocity but also the baby's impressive ability to regulate his or her affective displays to achieve the goals of the interaction.

The sequence of initial greeting: realization of the distortion, wariness, checking, repeated attempts to bring the mother out of her immobility, and eventual withdrawal was observed in all babies from the earliest age studied, that is, from 1–4 months. The order of presentation did not affect the infants' reactions in the still-face condition. It did affect the normal interaction if the normal interaction followed a still-face condition. Under those circumstances, infants generally showed an initial period of wary monitoring of the mother when she came in. Occasionally, they would arch away from the mother as if they had not forgiven her the previous insult. Mothers generally would apologize to their infants and say things like, "I am real again. It's all right. You can trust me again. Come back to me." After less than 30 sec, all infants gave in to the normal interaction sequence (Tronick et al., 1978).

The differential observations made in the still-face and the normal face-to-face interaction support my conceptualization of mother–infant interaction as a goal-oriented, reciprocal system in which infants play a major, active role, constantly modifying their own communicative displays in response to the feedback provided by their partners. If the system is violated by a partner's nonreciprocity, infants will respond in an appropriate manner that indicates how powerfully they are affected by the disturbance.

Social interaction is a rule-governed, goal-oriented system in which both partners actively share from the very beginning. The still-face condition violates the rules of this system by simultaneously conveying contradictory information about one partner's goal or intent. The mother by her entrance and *en face* position is initiating and setting the stage for an interaction, but then her lack of response indicates a disengagement or withdrawal. She is communicating "hello" and "goodbye" simultaneously. Infants, because of their capacity to apprehend this display of intent, are trapped in the contradiction: They initiate and greet but then turn away and withdraw temporarily only to initiate again. If the infant's efforts fail to get the interaction back on track and to establish reciprocity, complete withdrawal eventually results.

## PREVERBAL COMMUNICATION

We see the emotional displays of the infant and adult as message-carrying displays (Als, 1979; Brazelton & Als, 1979). Language is not yet a part of the interaction, but there appears to be a lexicon of expression that conveys information to each about their partner's inner emotional state and serves to regulate the interaction. These messages have two aspects—a content aspect and a regulatory aspect. The content of the message may refer to any event or object. It is conveyed in interactions primarily by language. The regulatory aspect of a signal contains information about a communicant's acceptance, rejection, or modification of the current state of the interaction. It is expressed through the behavioral display of the communicants with their subtlety of emotional qualities. The content portion is similar to what Watzlawick, Beavin, and Jackson (1967) call the report aspect of a message, and the regulatory aspect of behavioral signals is a *metacommunication*, that is, a communication about a communication. In the still-face condition, the infant responds to the mother's contradictory messages by trying to signal that mutual regulation should be reestablished. I believe that this same process of mutual regulation occurs in the normal interaction. Moreover, the messages exchanged via behavioral displays are almost purely regulatory in character in that they refer only to the ongoing state of the interaction and not to objects or events, so that prior to the incorporation of language into the interaction the infant has developed and practiced the ability to regulate the pragmatic aspects of an interchange.

## STAGES OF REGULATION

We have identified four stages of regulation and of learning within this system over the first 4 months of life (Brazelton & Als, 1979).

1. Infants achieve homeostatic control over input and output systems (i.e., they can both shut out and reach out for single stimuli, but then achieve control over their physiological systems and states).
2. Within this controlled system, infants can begin to attend to and use the social cues to prolong their states of attention and to accept and incorporate more complex trains of messages.
3. Within such an entrained or mutual reciprocal feedback system, infants and parents begin to press the limits of (a) infant capacity to take in and respond to information, and (b) infant ability to withdraw to recover in a homeostatic system. Sensitive adults press infants to the limits of both of these and allows infants time and opportunity to realize that they have incorporated these abilities into their own repertoires. The mother–infant "games" described by Stern (1974) are elegant examples of the real value of this phase as a system for affective and cognitive experience at 3 and 4 months.
4. Within the dyad or triad, the baby is allowed to demonstrate and incorporate a sense of his own autonomy. (This phase is perhaps the real test of attachment.) At the point where the mother or nurturing parent can indeed permit the baby to be the leader or signal-giver, when the adult can recognize and encourage the baby's independent search for and response to environmental or social cues and games—to initiate them, to reach for and play with objects, etc.—the small infant's won feeling of competence and of voluntary control over his or her environment is strengthened. This sense of competence is at a more complex level of awareness and is constantly influenced by the baby's feedback systems. We see this at 4–5 months in normal infants during a feeding, when the infant stops to look around and to process the environment. When a mother can allow for this and even foster it, she and the infant become aware of his burgeoning autonomy. In psychoanalytic terms, the infant's ego development is well on its way!

In summary, this model of development is a powerful one for understanding the reciprocal bonds that are set up between parent and infant. The feedback model allows for flexibility, disruption, and reorganization. Within its envelope of reciprocal interaction, one can conceive of a rich matrix of different modalities for communication, individualized for each pair and critically dependent on the contribution of each member of the dyad or triad. There is no reason that each system cannot be shaped in different ways by the preferred modalities for interaction of each of its participants, but each *must* be sensitive and ready to adjust to the other member in the envelope. And at each stage of development, the envelope will be different; richer, we would hope.

I regard these observations as evidence for the first stages of emotional and cognitive awareness in the infant and in the nurturing "other." A baby is learning about itself, developing an ego base. The mother and the father who are attached to and intimately involved with this infant are both consciously and unconsciously aware of parallel stages of their own development as nurturers.

These four stages of learning about each other constitute a kind of entrainment of developmental processes for each participant with those of the other participant. Thus, they are learning as much about social communication as they are about themselves in the process. Learning about the internal control system becomes the experimental base for internalizing a kind of early ego function for the small infant. As infants achieve homeostasis and then go on to learn about a less-than-balanced state of expectation and excitement within a nurturant envelope, they learn about the control systems and the capacities for emotional experience with which they are endowed. They are experiencing emotion. As they learn to elicit and then to reply to the nurturant adults around them, they learn the importance of communication and even the experiencing of emotion in "the other." Thus, they are experiencing the ingredients of affect within themselves and learning to demonstrate and to enrich their responses to the external world in order to elicit affect in others.

As they do engage, respond to, and enlarge upon the adult's responses, infants learn from adults how to produce an appropriate affective environment—one that is appropriate and necessary for infant learning about themselves and about their world. Thus, infants are learning to fuel both sources of energy—that from within and that from without. They learn about causality within the emotional sphere. They begin to internalize controls that are necessary for experiencing emotion but also learn what is necessary for producing emotional responses from others. By the end of the fourth month, infants can "turn on" or "turn off" those around them with an actively controllable set of responses. They have begun to learn how to manipulate their own experience and their own world. The emotions that they are experiencing and registering unconsciously by this age can be consciously manipulated as well. They have been learning about their own emotions within the envelope of attachment (Bowlby, 1969, 1973). The anlage for detachment and autonomy are surfacing and the precursors for the infant's superego are already apparent.

In summary, the precursors for ego function, the anlages of emotional experience in an older child, are observable in the behavior of the fetus and infant. The experience of completing an anticipated act or social communication closes a feedback cycle, creating a sense of mastery that confirms children's sense of self and fuels them toward further development. By entraining the nurturant environment around them, infants add a further source of fuel as it provides an envelope within which they can learn more quickly a sense of "self" and the mastery of complex inner control mechanisms as well as social response systems that will assure them of future nurturance. Thus, early experience provides the base for precursors of future emotions.

## REFERENCES

Als, H. Assessing an assessment. In A. Sameroff (Ed.), *Organization and stability of newborn behavior: Commentary on the Brazelton neonatal behavioral assessment scale. Monographs of the Society for Research in Child Development,* 1978, *43*(No. 177), 14–29.

Als, H. Social interaction: Dynamic matrix for developing behavioral organization. In I. C. Uzgiris (Ed.), *Social interaction and communication in infancy: New directions for child development* (Vol. 4). San Francisco, California: Jossey Bass, 1979.

Babkin, P. S. The establishment of reflex activity in early postnatal life. In *Central nervous system and behavior*. Bethesda, Maryland: National Institute of Health, 1959.

Bower, T. G. R. The object in the world of the infant. *Scientific American,* 1971, *255*, 4–30.

Bowlby, J. *Attachment and loss* (Vol. 1). New York: Basic Books, 1969.

Bowlby, J. *Attachment and loss* (Vol. 2). New York: Basic Books, 1973.

Brazelton, T. B. Psychophysiologic reactions of the neonate. I. The value of observations. *Journal of Pediatrics,* 1961, *58*, 508–512.

Brazelton, T. B. Neonatal behavioral assessment scale. In *Clinics in developmental medicine* (No. 50). London: Heinemann, 1973.

Brazelton, T. B. Evidence of communication in neonatal behavioral assessment. In M. Bullowa (Ed.), *Before speech*. London and New York: Cambridge Univ. Press, 1979.

Brazelton, T. B. *Fetal responses*. Unpublished manuscript, 1981.

Brazelton, T. B., & Als, H. Four early stages in the development of mother–infant interaction. *Psychoanalytic Study of the Child,* 1979, *34*, 349–369.

Brazelton, T. B., Koslowski, B., & Main, M. The origins of reciprocity: The early mother–infant interaction. In M. Lewis and L. Rosenblum (Eds.), *The effect of the infant on its caregiver*. New York: Wiley, 1974.

Brazelton, T. B., Tronick, E., Adamson, L., Als, H., & Wise, S. *Early mother–infant reciprocity*. Parent–Infant Interaction, Ciba Foundation Symposium 33. Amsterdam: Elsevier, 1975.

Bruner, J. S. Organization of early skilled action. *Child Development,* 1973, *44*, 1–11.

Bullowa, M. (Ed.) *Before speech: The beginning of interpersonal communication*. London and New York: Cambridge Univ. Press, 1979.

Condon, N. S., & Sander, L. W. Neonate movement is synchronized with adult speech. *Science,* 1974 *183*, 99–101.

Dixon, S., Yogman, M. W., Tronick, E., Als, H., Adamson, L., & Brazelton, T. B. Early social interaction of infants with parents and strangers. *Journal of the American Academy of Child Psychiatry,* 20, 32, 1981.

Gottman, J. M. Detecting cyclicity in social interaction. *Psychological Bulletin,* 1979, *86*, 338–348.

Greenacre, P. *The predisposition to anxiety: Trauma growth and personality* (Parts I and II). New York: International University Press, 1941.

Hartmann, H. & Kris, E. The genetic approach in psychoanalysis. *The Psychoanalytic Study of the Child,* 1945, *1*, 11–30.

Hon, E. H., & Paul, R. H. *A primer of fetal heart rate patterns*. New Haven, Connecticut: Harty Press, 1970.

Kendon, A. Some relationships between body motion and speech. In A. N. Siegman & P. Pope (Eds.), *Studies in dyadic communications*. New York: Pergamon, 1972.

Korner, A. F. & Thoman, E. B. The relative efficacy of contact and vestibular propreoceptive stimuli in smoothing neonates. *Child Development*, 1972, *43*, 443–453.

Mahler, M. S., Pine, F., & Bergman, A. *The psychological birth of the human infant*. New York: Basic Books, 1975.

Piaget, J. *The origins of intelligence*. London: Routledge, 1953.

Piaget, J. *The child's construction of reality*. London: Routledge, 1955.

Rosen, M. G., & Rosen, L. *In the beginning: Your brain before birth*. New York: New American Library, 1975.

Stern, D. The goal and structure of mother–infant play. *Journal of the American Academy of Child Psychiatry*, 1974, *13*, 402–421.

Thomas, A., Chesni, Y., & Saint-Anne Dargassies, S. The neurological examination of the infant. In (Ed.), *Little Club Clinics in Developmental Medicine* (No. 1). London: National Spastics Society, 1960.

Trevarthen, D. Descriptive analyses of infant communicative behavior. In H. R. Schaffer (Ed.), *Studies in mother–infant interaction: Proceedings of the Loch Lomond Symposium*. New York: Academic Press, 1977.

Tronick, E., Als, H., Adamson, L., Wise, S., & Brazelton, T. B. The infant's responses to entrapment between contradictory messages in face to face interaction. *Journal of the American Academy of Child Psychiatry*, 1978, *16*, 1–13.

Watzlawick, P., Beavin, H. J., & Jackson, D. *The pragmatics of human communication*. New York: Norton, 1967.

White, R. Motivation reconsidered: The concept of competence. *Psychological Review*, 1959, *66*, 297–333.

Yogman, M. W., Dixon, S., Tronick, E., Adamson, L., Als, H., & Brazelton, T. B. *Father–infant interaction*. Paper presented at a meeting of the American Pediatric Society, Society for Pediatric Research, St. Louis, Missouri, April 1976.

Chapter 3

# EMOTIONS AS BEHAVIOR REGULATORS: SOCIAL REFERENCING IN INFANCY[1]

*MARY D. KLINNERT*
*JOSEPH J. CAMPOS*
*JAMES F. SORCE*
*ROBERT N. EMDE*
*MARILYN SVEJDA*

## ABSTRACT

*This chapter deals with three broad issues: Whether emotions are epi-phenomenal, how emotions play a crucial role in determining appraisal processes, and what the mechanisms are by which emotions may influence interpersonal behavior. We present evidence from studies indicating that emotions play a crucial role in the regulation of social behavior. Social regulation by emotion is particularly clear in a process we call* social referencing—*the active search by a person for emotional information from another person, and the subsequent use of that emotion to help appraise an uncertain situation. Social referencing has its roots in infancy, and we propose that it develops through a four-level sequence of capacities to process emotional information from facial expression. We discuss whether the social regulatory functions of emotion are*

[1]The preparation of this chapter was facilitated by several grants from the National Institute of Mental Health: MH-23556 to J. Campos and MH-22803 and Research Scientist Award No. 5K02MH36808 to R. Emde. M. Svejda was supported by NIH Nursing Fellowship No. 2F31NU05059-04. In addition, support was obtained from the Developmental Psychobiology Research Group of the Department of Psychiatry through an endowment created by the Grant Foundation.

57

*innate or socially learned, whether feeling plays an important role in mediating the effects of emotional expressions of one person on the behavior of another, and whether stimulus context is important in accounting for differences in reaction to the same emotional information.*

This chapter will deal with an important but neglected aspect of human emotions—their role in the regulation of the behavior of others and, particularly, their use in a process that we call *social referencing*. The neglect of the social regulatory aspects of emotion is easy to illustrate. Ask someone to describe what happens when a person is in an emotional state, and the resulting description will be predictable both in terms of what it includes and what it does not. It is almost certain, for instance, that there will be several allusions to *feeling states,* including physical sensations like a sinking feeling in the pit of the stomach, and more diffuse and pervasive feelings of *pleasantness and unpleasantness.* Mention of *autonomic reactions* will be prominent, as will the description of *expressive features* of the face, voice, and posture. *Instrumental behaviors* will be mentioned, including actions of withdrawal, attack, or stroking and cuddling, to name a few. Moreover, if the person describing the emotional state is scientifically inclined, he or she may mention the important *intraorganismic biological functions* served by these reactions, insofar as they redistribute energy within the body to prepare it for fight or flight, or their role as *evolutionary vestiges* of activities once useful for survival, like the opening of the eyes in fear and surprise, or the baring of the teeth in anger.

An important aspect of emotion that is less likely to be described is the effect that the emotional reaction has on those in the immediate surround. This seems curious, for these social consequences are both powerful and undeniable and may be more reliably present than some of the more customary reactions listed above. Ethologists have considered them central in animal studies of emotion, and clinicians have hinted at their importance in discussions of empathy. Still, they tend to be left out in most discussions of human emotion.

There are many ways in which the social regulatory functions of emotion are manifested. For instance, it is well known, though frequently not emphasized, that the emotional expression of one person can elicit contagious emotional reactions in another. This is particularly true for emotions such as sadness, joy, fear, and even anxiety. Emotional reactions are also the mediator of empathic responses in an observer—responses that can range from nurturance and soothing to anger and disgust at the perceived cause of another's distress. Empathic emotional responses may also be crucial determinants of prosocial behavior and conscience formation, suggesting that responsiveness to the emotions of others may have long-term consequences. Moreover, emotional reactions can affect the stream of social interchange in powerful ways. Consider that the same words or behaviors can be expressed in many different fashions: loving, frightened, sad, indifferent, or angry. Each of these modes of expression can lead to dramatically different responses on the part of the person to whom the words are directed. Indeed, this is the sense in which emotions "spice" interpersonal existence. Still another consequence of the emotional reaction of others is that they can mediate important types of social, observational learning. For instance, a child does not have to receive a painful shock in order to learn to avoid touching a dangerous object. It suffices for children to notice that when they reach for this object the result is a well-timed and emotionally arousing scream or gasp from their parents. Finally, the emotional reactions of others become a crucial resource for any person, especially infants and children, when they are in a state of uncertainty about how to appraise or evaluate an ambiguous circumstance. When faced with such a dilemma, people both seek out and use the emotional reactions of others to help guide their own behavior in that setting.

Emotional expressions are thus causal events in the sense that they influence the behavior of others and pervade almost all social interactions, whether they are between friends, strangers, or enemies. So the question arises, why, in psychological research, has there been such a neglect of the social regulatory functions of emotions? Why is it that psychological theorists so often center on the intrapersonal and intraorganismic factors associated with emotions, to the detriment of the study of emotions as social regulators? Indeed, why has there been such a longstanding bias to treat emotions solely as dependent variables, as "slaves" of some other, more basic, process?

One reason for the neglect of the regulatory role of emotions is the more general tendency to conceptualize emotions as epiphenomenal. Many theorists have argued that emotions are, at best, variables of secondary importance, reflecting more basic and more significant underlying processes of which they are noncausal spinoffs. Conceived of in this way, emotions are like the gauges on the dashboard of a car: They monitor the internal functions of the engine or other parts but do not directly affect the operation of the vehicle. The tendency to treat affect or emotion as epiphenomenal pervades the writings of many psychologists (e.g., Skinner, 1974) who otherwise do not spend much time studying it. But surprisingly, it also pervades the writings of some of the theorists who have been most influential in keeping the study of emotions alive. Bowlby (1969), for instance, is one who has argued for the epiphenomenal nature of feeling states. He draws an analogy: Feelings play a role in behavior much as the redness or whiteness of a metal plays a role in that metal's malleability. However, just as it is heat that produces malleability, not whiteness, so it is a cognitive appraisal process that determines behavior, not feeling states. Affects, then, are mere phases or outward manifestations of the operation of cognitive appraisal processes, just as color is a phase in the heating of a metal. However, neither affect nor color can or should be confused with true causes of the phenomena of interest.

Kagan (1978) is another theorist who treats emotional responses as epiphenomenal. He believes that reactions such as smiling and distress are important primarily because they are very sensitive indexes of the operation of important cognitive processes, in particular, the assimilation or lack of assimilation of new information into preexisting cognitive structures. So, for Kagan, smiling after solving a problem allows observers to infer that effortful but successful assimilation to a schema has taken place. Distress, on the other hand, permits observers to infer than an event has not been successfully assimilated even though the person has tried several hypotheses in an attempt to explain the phenomenon. Similar considerations may apply to fearfulness and laughter. McCall and McGhee (1977) propose that fear results from extreme, unresolved, subjective uncertainty, and laughter results from the resolution of such extreme uncertainty. The treatment of emotional reactions only as dependent variables is thus particularly evident in so-called discrepancy theories, within which there is scarcely any consideration of the possible intrapersonal or interpersonal functions of emotional behavior.

If one is persuaded that emotions are epiphenomenal, one is not likely to study their consequences. However, others go even farther and question whether "emotion" is a valid phenomenon in the first place. Duffy (1941, 1962) for example, has argued that there are no valid measures of emotional states, and she challenged researchers to provide an ostensive or operational definition of emotions that would distinguish presumptive emotional states from nonemotional ones such as exercise, drives, or physiological arousal. The apparent failure of researchers in the 1950s and 1960s to isolate facial expressions, behavioral reactions, or autonomic patterns that bore a reasonably close relationship to emotional states raised a difficult question: If the outward manifestations of emotions are unstable, idiosyncratic, and nonspecific, what can they possibly communicate to others? How can they possibly influence social reactions?

The dominance of psychology by behaviorism for so many years also impeded conceptions of emotions as socially regulatory. In the first place, behaviorists were generally committed to the principle that one first has to understand the simpler aspects of psychological phenomena before one proceeds to study the more complex ones. As a result, the study of all higher psychological processes languished. Among the neglected higher processes were problem solving, language, and nonverbal communication, the study of all of which was postponed until more fundamental processes, like conditioning, were understood. Accordingly, the study of emotion as a causal process was restricted to fairly circumscribed intraorganismic processes like fear-motivated avoidance learning (Miller, 1951; Mowrer, 1960). Second, the way in which behaviorists operationalized emotions was not conducive to thinking about them as communicative processes. Behaviorists acknowledged the difficulty of assessing responses that were uniquely emotional and tended to give operational definitions of emotions

3. EMOTIONS AS BEHAVIOR REGULATORS

in terms of stimulus circumstances. For instance, fear was studied by applying shock, anger by creating frustration, curiosity by generating novel stimuli, etc. Such an operational strategy seemed eminently reasonable: It was widely believed at the time that one could not infer the specific emotional reaction of a person unless one also knew the stimulus that the person was exposed to (Sherman, 1927). Given this approach to emotions, it was easy to maintain that the best information about emotions is given by knowledge of the stimulating circumstances, and not by knowledge of the emotional reaction.

For many reasons, then, it was difficult to consider the role of emotions as socially functional. However, since 1960, there has been a slow shift in attitudes among psychological researchers that has set the stage for one of the most exciting new developments in emotion theory: *The treatment of emotions as independent variables*. The basis for the shift was found in the rich theoretical tradition of Darwin (1872/1975), which had led to emotional signaling research among animals (e.g., see Chevalier-Skolnikoff, 1973), but which had been less influential in human studies. The shift began when important emotion theorists like Ekman, Friesen, and Ellsworth (1972), Izard (1971, 1977), Plutchik (1962, 1980), and Tomkins (1962, 1963) called into question many of the bases for skepticism about the measurement of emotional expression, particularly in the face. These theorists claimed that there was indeed information in the face (later extended to the voice by Scherer, 1979) that was decoded into emotion categories reliably (i.e., elicited agreement among sets of judges) and accurately (i.e., agreed with the self reports of the actor posing the expression or the person experiencing the emotion). These theorists also argued that emotional expressions communicated more than dimensional information such as level of activation or level of hedonic tone. They claimed that emotional patterning conveyed very specific messages, ranging from the seven to ten so-called basic emotions to the hundreds of blends possible from combinations of the primary emotions. These theorists thus sharply challenged Duffy and the others who believed that there were no responses unique to emotion. They emphasized the importance of patterning of expressions rather than single expressive behaviors and looked for patterning in response systems that have socially communicative value rather than in internal autonomic reactions.

These theoretical analyses were important, but not nearly so much as the cross-cultural work they generated. A number of studies by Eibl-Eibesfeldt (1979), Ekman and Friesen (1971), Izard (1971), and others (Ekman, Sorensen, & Friesen, 1969), showed that not only were facial expression patterns similar across widely differing Western cultures, but they were similar even among preliterate tribes with minimal exposure to Western civilization. The most remarkable aspect of the studies of preliterate tribes was not only that such tribes were able very reliably to recognize the emotional expression in a photograph of a Western subject but also that the tribesmen could reliably produce the facial expressions of several basic emotions. To account for these cross-cultural regularities, Ekman (1972) and Izard (1971) have postulated the existence of pre-wired neural programs that control emotional expression and that were believed to be innate and thus evident even in very young infants.

A considerable amount of research on the facial expressions of human infants has now been done, and the conclusion emerging from these studies is rather clear and consistent: Facial expression patterns can be judged by scorers who know nothing about the eliciting circumstances that the baby is exposed to; emotional expression patterns fit the templates suggested from the theoretical analyses of Izard, Tomkins, Ekman, and Plutchik and, to date, the emotional patterns identified in infants include those for surprise, happiness, fear, sadness, anger, disgust, and pain (Emde, Kligman, Reich, & Wade, 1978; Hiatt, Campos, & Emde, 1979; Izard, Huebner, Risser, McGinnes, & Dougherty, 1980; Stenberg & Campos, 1982; Stenberg, Campos, & Emde, in press).

Although these developments are still at the level of emotions conceptualized as dependent variables, the regularity of the patterning of expression recently discovered and the close relationship the emotions show to eliciting circumstances or intended pose give the researcher confidence that the variables being studied are not ephemeral, idiosyncratic, or untrustworthy, as was once believed. Three factors have combined, however, to lay the groundwork for a new wave of research on emotions as social regulators. First of all, in the 1970s, linear stimulus–response models of causation began to be replaced by new interactive or systems models of explanation. Systems approaches blur the distinction between independent and dependent variable, because, among other reasons, what is a consequent at one point in time can be an antecedent of something else at a later point. For every variable in a system, the researcher is led to ask: What is its feedback role? Its feedforward role? Its role as a moderator or as a catalyst? These are precisely the questions now being asked of human emotions. How does an emotional experience influence the process that may have generated it in the first place? How do emotions facilitate one's train of thought and make some psychological processes more likely and others less so? How does a preexisting emotion influence performance on a task? How does it energize behavior? In what way does it result in certain actions and not in others?

Second, we are in a functionalist age. We now constantly infer what the biological adaptive value of a process is, both for the individual and for the social group in which the individual lives. Some evolutionary biologists studying the origins of facial expressions (e.g., Andrew, 1963), have described how expressive reactions that once had an intrapersonal function slowly evolved to have a socially adaptive function, including functions for roles in dominance hierarchies, greeting behaviors, reproductive rituals, etc. Others have argued for the relatively independent evolutionary–adaptive origins of social signals themselves (Emde, 1979; Hamburg, 1963). In short, the interest in speculation about biological adaptive value has spread to social adaptation and to social regulations. As a result, we are increasingly inclined to ask questions about the socially regulatory role of affective expressions, particularly now that we know them to have such strong and consistent cross-cultural and developmental manifestations.

Finally, the field of infancy has been blessed with exciting studies of the nonverbal communication processes of human infants in interaction with their mothers. A number of researchers, among them Brazelton, Goldberg, Papousek, Schaffer, Stern, Trevarthen, Tronick and others, have pioneered in the study of dyadic interaction and variables affecting social regulation. They have focused on social signals that help to determine the reciprocity and interactional synchrony or smoothness of the parent–child interaction. These social signals were shown to serve rather discrete functions. Some, like eye-to-eye contact or smiling, serve to greet and to initiate social exchange. Others, like gaze aversion, serve to cut off interaction and to regulate the infant's level of arousal by modulating stimulus input. Still others, like cooing and gurgling, serve reinforcing functions, helping to maintain interaction. When first studied, these reactions were not necessarily related to affective states. However, with the increasing realization that the absence or distortion of these signals led to disappointment, puzzlement, or even grieving in the parents (Brazelton, Tronick, Adamson, Als, & Wise, 1975; Emde & Brown, 1978; Fraiberg, 1977) or to similar reactions in the infants themselves (Tronick, Als, Wise, & Brazelton, 1978), social signals increasingly have been linked to the affective functions that they serve for each participant in an interaction.

In summary, then, recent developments in psychological theory stress the importance of emotional variables as reliable and clearly patterned and raise the possibility that emotions play a causal role in the determination of social behaviors.

## SOCIAL REFERENCING

How does one proceed to investigate the social regulatory effects of emotions, and what are the advantages in beginning such a study of social regulatory effects from a developmental perspective? Following a tradition initiated by Cooley's concept of "the looking glass self" (Cooley, 1912) and George Herbert Mead's theory of the emerging social self (Mead, 1934), Klinnert (1978), and later, Campos and Stenberg (1981) and Feinman and Lewis (1981), have described a process called *social referencing,* which is an important and general way in which the emotional expressions of the nurturing parent can play a very significant role in the emotional development of the child. According to Campos and Stenberg (1981) social referencing concerns the tendency of a person of any age to seek out emotional information from a significant other person in the environment and to use that information to make sense of an event that is otherwise ambiguous or beyond the person's own intrinsic appraisal capabilities. The important implications of the social referencing concept for our purposes is that the behavior of the referencing individual is predicted to differ as a function of the emotional information provided by others in the environment.

From the standpoint of emotion, the process of social referencing is in certain respects a subset of the important cognitive process of evaluation and appraisal (e.g., Arnold, 1960; Bowlby, 1969; Lazarus, 1968). Appraisal refers to the evaluation—by either inferential means or by prior learning—of the beneficial or harmful impact of an event or person on oneself or another. Arnold (1960) and Lazarus (1968) distinguish two types of appraisal: Primary appraisal is the immediate, intuitive evaluation of an event resulting in emotional feelings and expressions. Secondary appraisals are the processes that augment or reduce the perceived intensity of the emotion elicited by the primary evaluation. As we conceive it, social referencing is in a sense a type of secondary appraisal because it is called into play most clearly when prior intrinsic appraisal processes fail to predict the impact of an event. Although appraisals based on social referencing may be termed *secondary*, they are nonetheless of central importance: contemporaneously, because referencing reduces uncertainty and leads to behavioral outcomes; prospectively, because they lay the foundation for future primary appraisals. Moreover, because the perceptual information that is sought out in social referencing is very often specifically emotional in nature, social referencing constitutes a prototypic example of how emotional expressions can no longer be treated as mere epiphenomena.

The most frequent and most influential manifestations of social referencing are likely to occur early in life, when primary appraisal capacities are unlikely to be well developed. Consider that infants are confronted daily with novel objects, people, or situations, the appraisal of which is likely to lead to uncertainty about the impact that such an environmental event has for their welfare or for the consequences of their own actions. At these times, infants predictably will seek *emotional* information from others to aid in their appraisal of uncertain situations. Furthermore, in infancy more than in other periods of life, the referencing individual is likely to have available a ready and trusted emotional resource—the child's caregiver. Although we feel, as do Feinman (in press) and Lewis and Feiring (1981), that social referencing takes place throughout the life span because uncertain evaluations of stimulus circumstances know no age limitations, our position is that social referencing is most likely to play a central role with human infants and toddlers. This is so because environmental demands are likely to create the highest incidence of uncertainty in that age group. As a result, we have chosen to initiate the study of social referencing from a developmental perspective that has its onset in human infancy.

## EMPIRICAL WORK ON
## INFANT SOCIAL REFERENCING

Is there any evidence that infants need to seek out emotional information from their caregivers? Or that they use this information in important ways to help them guide their own behavior in uncertain settings? One indication that they do comes from an intriguing study by Carr, Dabbs, and Carr (1975), the results of which sharply challenged widely prevailing beliefs that it is merely the mother's *physical* presence that provides the child with emotional security. Carr *et al.* placed 24-month-olds in the corner of a room with interesting toys and contrasted their behavior when the mothers were seated facing them and with their backs to them. Carr *et al.*, surprisingly, found that one-half the children abandoned the toys in order to place themselves in front of the mother! Surely, by 24 months of age, infants must have a good representation of their mother's spatial location in the room (Piaget, 1954). Why, then, would they want to place themselves in front of her? Is it possible that, in an uncertain setting like a laboratory, these infants needed to be within "eyeshot" of the mother's face so as to be able to seek out and read her emotional reaction to the unfamiliar setting they were in?

Consider another indication. Beginning at 5 months of age, infants approached by an adult stranger frequently shift their gaze alternately between the approaching stranger and the mother sitting nearby. Data from one longitudinal study documenting this effect with both normals and Down's syndrome infants were reported by Sorce, Emde, and Frank (1982). This type of alternate scrutiny of the face of mother and stranger has been interpreted, plausibly enough, as a facial comparison process that allows the infant to confirm that the stranger is indeed discrepant from mother, resulting in distress (Schaffer, 1971). However, Sorce *et al.* reported that with both Down's syndrome infants and with normals there is a sharp increase with age in the likelihood of maternal referencing—an increase that continues well past the age at which the infant can distinguish the mother from the stranger (a process that Barrera and Maurer [1978] place at 3 months, and others place even earlier [Carpenter, 1973]). Moreover, Feinman (1980) observes such referencing well into the second year of life. Given the numerous difficulties with the discrepancy and facial comparison hypothesis of infants' reactions to strangers (Campos & Stenberg, 1981), it appears necessary to postulate some other function for this phenomenon. Is it possible that the infant is looking to the mother in order to be able to read her affective reaction to the approach of the stranger? Perhaps the well-documented effect of mother's presence on diminishing infant stranger distress, even when mother is quiet and merely visible (Campos, Emde, Gaensbauer, & Henderson, 1975; Emde, Gaensbauer, & Harmon, 1976) is due to the referencing of maternal expressions that are reassuring.

Still a third indication of the potential importance of the mother's emotional availability comes from a recent study by Sorce and Emde (1981) in which infants showed a definite preference for emotionally responsive mothers. Fifteen-month-olds were placed in a playroom and presented with four successive situations designed to produce uncertainty in the infant. To control for the possibility that it is simply the option of having the mother's face visible that provides the child with security, the mother's face was always physically visible to the child. However, one-half the mothers were instructed to read a magazine and not respond to the infant's bids, whereas the other one-half were to watch their infants and respond to their initiatives in a natural manner. Results showed that the infants whose mothers were "available" to respond to their bids showed more exploration and more pleasure than did the infants whose mothers were reading. The infants with emotionally responsive mothers moved farther away from her but continued an active interest in her and made more bids for her attention. The infants of the responsive mother also referenced her far more frequently than did those of the unavailable mothers. Sorce and Emde noted that maternal responses to the infants' looks to her were primarily *emotional* signals, that is, smiles, eyebrow flashes, reassuring pats, etc. This study thus suggests that mother's facilitating effect on her infant's exploratory behavior is mediated by her emotional signals and that, even though her face is in view, infant referencing diminishes along with exploration when such signals are not forthcoming.

None of these studies, however, has directly manipulated the mother's expression of affect and observed whether the *nature* of the affective expression (i.e., whether the mother was happy, angry, or sad, etc.) influenced the baby's behavior. Only such a demonstration can provide convincing evidence for the importance of the social regulatory function of emotional expressions. There are several studies from our laboratories and those of others that indicate that emotional expressions of the mother do indeed serve a powerful regulatory role on her infant's behavior.

The first of these studies of facial expressions as a social regulator was a doctoral dissertation study by Klinnert (1981). The major objective was to manipulate mother's facial expression in order to assess the effect of those expressions on her infant's coping behavior. The following paradigm was used: To create uncertainty in the infants, three stimulus toys were specially designed to be novel and mobile but somewhat frightening in appearance: a spider, a dinosaur (both of which were remote-controlled), and a model of a human head (the "Incredible Hulk"). A triangular spatial arrangement of mother, infant, and toy enabled the infant, on noting the entrance of each object into the room, to check mother's facial expression, which in turn was experimentally manipulated by instructions to the mother to pose one of three different expressions. Three trials were given to each infant. For each trial, the mothers posed a different facial expression: joy, fear, or neutral. It was hypothesized that the infants would approach the toys when the mother smiled, avoid them and retreat to her when she posed fear, and show mixed reactions to the neutral expressions.

Infants were retained as subjects only if they referenced the mother's face following the emergence of the toy on all three trials. The final sample included 72 infants, 36 12-month-olds and 36 18-month-olds. The mothers were trained in posing peak facial expressions as described by Ekman and Friesen (1975); they displayed the expressions without accompanying sounds or gestures. They were instructed to look alternately from the toy to the infant while posing their expressions and were cued during the trial by means of a wireless device in the ear.

The results of Klinnert's (1981) study were quite clear. Referencing the mother in this situation not only proved to be a highly expectable occurrence at both ages, but the mother's posed facial expression indeed influenced the babies' subsequent behavior toward the toys. At both ages, babies moved closest to the mother when she posed fear, moved farthest from the mother when she posed joy, and maintained an intermediate distance from her when she appeared neutral. The data thus provided clear evidence that social referencing takes place in an ambiguous situation and that the maternal facial expressions serve to regulate the coping behavior of the infants.

A second, rather different paradigm was designed to test the same general issue of the socially regulatory role of facial expressions (e.g., Sorce, Emde, Klinnert, & Campos, 1981). Its aim was to determine whether infants can be nonverbally induced to cross or not to cross the deep side of a visual cliff depending on the mother's facial expression. The visual cliff has long been used to test depth perception in human infants (e.g., Walk & Gibson, 1961), as well as fear of heights (e.g., Campos, Hiatt, Ramsay, Henderson, & Svejda, 1978; Richards & Rader, 1981). The cliff table is made of clear, very hard glass and is divided into two sides. On one side (the shallow side) there is a checkered pattern immediately under the surface of the glass. On the other side, a similar checkered pattern is spaced some variable distance beneath the glass to create the illusion of a drop-off, which the solid glass prevents. One of the interesting features of the visual cliff performance of both infants and animals is that when the visual illusion of a drop-off on the deep side is great enough (e.g., 4 ft.), there is avoidance of crossing the deep side despite tactual evidence of a solid surface. Moreover, if the dropoff on the deep side is sufficiently shallow (e.g., 4–6 in.), most infants will readily cross the deep side to their mother. Through extensive pilot testing, it was found that for 12-month-old infants (the age targeted for initial testing with this paradigm), a drop-off of 12 in. was not so great as to elicit total avoidance nor so little as to produce no hesitation to cross the deep side to get to the mother. In this study, as in Klinnert's before it, mothers were pre-trained to pose facial expressions—in this case, fear and happiness—and were also cued by a wireless device to pose the appropriate expression when the infant reached the center of the cliff table. However, in contrast to Klinnert's study, the visual cliff study used a between-subjects design in which only one trial was given to each infant; this was done in order to eliminate the possibility of any carryover effects.

The specific testing procedure was as follows: The infant was held by a female experimenter on the shallow side of the cliff table, as far from the cliff edge as possible. The mother was instructed to wind up an attractive toy, place it on the glass surface covering the deep side (to give further evidence of tactual solidity there) and to induce the infant to cross to her by simply smiling at him or her. No words, sounds, or gestures were used by the mother. When the infant approached the center of the cliff, the experimenter, watching the infant on a video monitor in an adjacent room, instructed the mother to shift her facial expression. In one condition, mothers continued to smile, or smiled even more broadly ($N = 19$, 9 females and 10 males). In another condition, mothers shifted to a fearful expression ($N = 17$, 8 females and 9 males). In both conditions, mothers were cued to pose the facial expression only when the infant had first looked *down* at the deep side and then looked *up* to the mother; this was done in order to ensure that, as in Klinnert's study, the investigation tapped a social referencing process.

The results of this study were dramatic. For those infants who showed social referencing on reaching the drop-off point, the facial expression pose determined to a large extent whether infants crossed the deep side or not. Of the 19 infants whose mothers smiled, 14 infants crossed the deep side. Of the 17 infants tested with the shift from a smiling face to a fear face, *no infant crossed the deep side to the mother*. Thus, facial expressions were demonstrated to make a major difference in the tendency of infants to negotiate the cliff table! Whether the social regulatory effect is mediated by the pleasantness or unpleasantness of the mother's facial expression or by a more discrete emotion message cannot be determined from this study but can be tested quite readily and, indeed, is one of the important questions we are investigating in our laboratory at present.

In a somewhat different approach to social referencing, Feinman and Lewis (1981) provided affective information to infants whether or not it was sought out. They have shown how the mother's affective evaluation of the approach of a stranger can account for important individual differences in the reactions of infants to strangers in the first year of life (Feinman & Lewis, 1981). Feinman and Lewis instructed mothers of 10-month-olds to direct positive or neutral facial, vocal, and gestural messages about a female stranger either to the stranger herself or, in separate groups of infants, to the infants. Feinman and Lewis reported that when the mother's communication was positive and directed at the infant, the babies showed much more positive behavior toward the stranger—for example, smiling and approaching her more, and offering her more toys. These findings did not merely reflect a ''mood'' effect with the mother's positive behavior resulting in more general happiness in her infant: The positive behavior was directed quite specifically toward the stranger rather than, for example, to the mother or other objects in the environment. The effects of the affective signals were particularly evident for temperamentally "easy" babies, as determined by the Carey and McDevitt (1978) Infant Temperament Questionnaire. These results thus complement our earlier discussion of the Sorce et al. (1982) study: When a stranger approaches, infants may indeed look to the mother to a large extent to obtain emotional information about the stranger. Certainly, Feinman and Lewis have demonstrated that once the emotional information is imposed on the infant, at least some infants use the information differentially.

So far we have not differentiated among the various types of emotional channels that provide socially regulatory information. Although they are likely to be important in real life, little or nothing is known about the separate influences of the postural, gestural, or tactile modalities, and only a small amount of research has focused on the vocal channel. By far the greatest amount of research in this area has dealt with both the production and understanding of facial expressions. The following section, therefore, focuses primarily on the infant's ability to utilize the information conveyed by facial expressions.

## LEVELS OF UTILIZATION OF FACIAL EXPRESSION INFORMATION

What skills are necessary to enable infants to utilize the information they have gained from facial expressions to guide their subsequent behavior in an adaptive manner? The skills seem to us to be remarkably many and complex. The infant first needs to orient toward the source of this information, human faces. Second, the infant must be able to detect facial information that plays a role in the affective expression. Third, the infant must be able to detect the unique patterns of facial components since it is the configuration of features, rather than individual components, that best communicate emotion in the face (Hiatt et al., 1979). Fourth, the infant has to appreciate what emotional message this specific configuration displays. And finally, the infant has to be able to use the information gained through this facial display to select what behavior to carry out.

It is unlikely that the infant is born with this complex battery of skills. What little evidence exists suggests that there is an orderly sequence in the development of this ability. We propose a developmental progression involving four hierarchical levels in infancy.

## LEVEL 1: LACK OF FACIAL PERCEPTION

We believe the balance of evidence suggests that newborn infants can neither recognize facial expressions nor perceive whole faces. Two sets of findings cast doubt on earlier beliefs that neonates do perceive visual gestalts and prefer to look at facelike configurations. First of all, newborns scan edges, light–dark transitions, bars, and contours (Haith, 1981), but show no tendency to scan entire figures (Salapatek & Kessen, 1966). Since they also lack sufficient peripheral vision to note the extension of a form much beyond the point of fixation (Salapatek, 1975), they therefore give no indication that they can perceive whole figures of the visual angle typically projected by faces. Previous reports of neonatal discrimination of faces from nonfaces can thus be explained in terms of the face having many more of the physical features that powerfully attract newborns' attention, and not in terms of the perception of faces as such (Sherrod, 1979, 1981).

Moreover, the manner in which neonates scan faces makes it very doubtful that they have access to the patterned information that specifies emotional expression to a perceiver. Such information is inside the facial contours, yet when neonates look at a face, they tend to scan the external contours and not the interior (Hainline, 1978; Haith, Bergman, & Moore, 1977; Maurer & Salapatek, 1976).[2] It is not until 2 months of age that infants first begin reliably to scan the interior of the face (Haith et al., 1977). The visual field of the infant from birth to 2 months thus seems to us to be too impoverished to provide much in the way of facial affective information.[3]

[2]Parents and most of today's infancy researchers are convinced that newborn infants engage in eye-to-eye contact with adults and scan the eyes; this would seem to contradict the careful studies of Maurer and Salapatek (1976) and Haith et al. (1977). However, two related phenomena may account for this seeming discrepancy. First, what may be happening is that the infant is staring in the general direction of the eyes, but not necessarily at the eyes themselves. It is very difficult to measure the point of fixation of the infant's eyes, even when using precise corneal photography techniques (Slater & Findlay, 1975). Therefore, what appears to be eye-to-eye contact to the parent or observer may sometimes reflect an approximation. Second, social interactants (caregivers or observers) are likely to "synchronize" and "lock in" their looking with infant gaze behavior. It is an undeniable fact that a newborn's looking is a powerful and attractive stimulus for adults; subtle and complex adjustments are characteristic (Butterfield, Emde, Svejda, & Neiman, 1982).

[3]In light of current research, findings reported by Field and Walden (in press) are startling. These investigators used an habituation paradigm to assess 1-day-olds' discrimination of facial expressions of emotion. An examiner posed happy, sad, and surprised faces, repeating the pose until the infants reached an habituation criterion of looking at the experimenter's face for less than 1 sec. A dishabituation effect was suggested by increases in looking time from the last trial of one expression to the first trial of the next. These data were interpreted by the authors as showing that "neonates can discriminate among at least three basic expressions—happy, sad, and surprised [p. 189]." Longer looking time to the happy pose was considered to reflect preference, possibly because happy faces are more familiar. Furthermore, the authors reported that when observing happy and sad faces, the infants primarily scanned the mouth region, whereas they scanned both the eye and mouth region for the surprise expression.

Although specific methodological details are not available, these findings seem to be subject to a number of crucial methodological flaws. In using the habituation paradigm, Field and Walden failed to control for spontaneous recovery, which is pervasive among young infants. The increases in looking time reported "from the last trial of one expression to the first trial of the next [Field &

## LEVEL 2: FACIAL PERCEPTION WITHOUT
## APPRECIATION OF AFFECT

As systematic scanning of the face develops, the infant enters a second level of perceptual functioning that lasts from 2 to 5 months of age. At this level, the infant becomes capable of discriminating among displays that differ in facial expression. However, we have found no convincing evidence that infants at this level can yet process the affective meaning of the information in the face.

Many researchers have argued that infants at this age do, in fact, perceive emotion in the human face. They support their position by citing a number of articles: For instance, La Barbera, Izard, Vietze, and Parisi (1976) presented pictures of joyful, angry, and neutral facial expressions to 4- and 6-month-old infants and reported that joy was looked at longest, neutral expressions the least. Young-Browne, Rosenfeld, and Horowitz (1977) used a habituation– dishabituation paradigm with 3-month-olds to demonstrate that surprised-looking faces were discriminated from happy and sad ones. Happy and sad faces, however, were not discriminated from each other. Still other reports noted that 3-month-olds can discriminate smiling from frowning expressions (Barrera & Maurer, 1978).

Although these findings show that the pictorial stimuli were reliably discriminated by infants, it is a mistake to conclude from them that infants are perceiving emotional expressions. As has been pointed out before in other contexts (e.g., Appel & Campos, 1977), discrimination of two displays in no way specifies the basis for the discrimination unless all bases for discrimination but one are controlled for. This did not occur in any of the studies we mentioned, so the possibility remains that the discriminations were mediated by the detection of nonaffective informational differences. A study by Oster and Ewy (cited in Oster, 1981) clearly demonstrates how a discrimination between two expressions need not involve processing the affective quality that differed among the pictures. Oster and Ewy found that 4-month-olds discriminated sad faces from grinning faces only when the grin was toothy. A closed-mouth sad face was not discriminated from a closed-mouth smile. Something about the toothiness (e.g., greater contour density?) facilitated the discrimination. It is therefore possible that the differential fixation times and dishabituation effects shown for 3-month-olds may well result from discrimination of nonaffective features.

---

Walden, in press, p. 187]'' is to be expected, simply because one look of less than 1 sec is not sufficient evidence for habituation, and response recovery occurs on the next trial regardless of stimulus. Even if habituation had been demonstrated, it seems unlikely that the visual stimulus to which the infants became habituated was the configuration of facial features that comprise an affective expression since there is convincing evidence that neonates do not scan the interior of the face.

We have also failed to find evidence that infants show differential affective reactions (as opposed to discriminative responses) to positively versus negatively toned expressions before five months of age. Buhler and Hetzer (cited in Buhler, 1930) first provided evidence for this lack of differentiation, and their findings were subsequently corroborated by Ahrens (1954), and by Kreutzer and Charlesworth (1973). All of these authors reported that prior to four or five months of age, infants smiled as happily in response to scowls or frowns as they did to a smiling adult.[4]

Of course, infants at 2 or 3 months of age show negative as well as positive affective reactions to human beings in the context of social interactions. Even at this young age, infants seem to understand that in normal interactions their partner's behavior should conform to certain rules (i.e., engaging in eye contact, animated vocalizations, and bodily gestures). Tronick *et al.* (1978) and Cohn and Tronick (1981) have shown that when mothers remain either still-faced or simulate emotional depression, 3-month-olds initially greet the mother, then withdraw and become fussy when mothers fail to respond differently. These findings show the importance of contingency in social interaction even at this early age, but they need not imply an appreciation by the child of the mother's affective expression.

What may impede the appreciation of emotion displays at this time? Is it possible that the infant has not yet undergone sufficient perceptual development? Does the infant need much more skill in perceptual integration to be able to extract affect-specifying invariants from the forehead, eye, and mouth regions of the face? There is some evidence that infants of this age may not typically process information from the mouth region, either because they do not relate the mouth to the rest of the face or because they do not pay much attention to the mouth in the first place (Ahrens, 1954; Caron, Caron, Caldwell, & Weiss, 1973). Campos and Stenberg (1981) have noted that the failure of the Young-Browne *et al.* (1977) study to find discrimination of happy from sad faces may reflect the difficulties infants have in processing information from the mouth region, where the distinctive features of happy and sad facial expressions perhaps are clearest.

---

[4]The results of an investigation by Spitz and Wolf (1946) were also consistent with the lack of differential responsiveness by young infants to positive versus negative expressions. Moreover, perhaps because they studied institutionalized infants, they failed to find differentiation even beyond 5 months, in contrast to the reports of others. The interpretation of the Spitz and Wolf study, however, is marred because of the nature of the display they used. As has been pointed out separately by Klinnert (1978) and Oster (1981), Spitz's rendering of a so-called classic threat expression does not conform to current notions of either angry or sad expressions. Instead, it presents what Spitz described as the bared teeth of a wild animal, a facial display the infants may have confused with a smile.

In addition to deficiencies in perception, there may also be deficiencies in motor schemes that may be necessary for decoding of visual affective displays. Piaget (1960), for instance, has argued that environmental stimulation acquires meaning through its assimilation into motor information-processing structures. Is it possible that affective stimulation also may acquire meaning through intercoordination with the infant's own expressive reaction system? Perhaps it is the case that until infants can coherently express fear or anger in their face, they may not be able to interpret fear or anger expressions in others. If the infant is still in a period of undifferentiated emotional expression, as has been aruged by many (e.g., Bridges, 1932; Emde et al., 1976; Sroufe, 1979), and if behavioral expression is needed to clothe perception with emotional meaning, the infant in this age range would not yet be expected to appreciate emotional expressions of others.

There may also be a much simpler explanation for the lack of appreciation of emotion. Infants may not have had sufficient opportunities to note the action consequences of facial expressions. The deficit may reside in social learning opportunities. There is clearly much need for research in this area and age period.

## LEVEL 3: EMOTIONAL RESPONSIVENESS TO FACIAL EMOTIONAL EXPRESSIONS

The major characteristic of level 2 was that infants were capable of processing differences in facial stimuli but were not processing these displays in affectively meaningful ways. The advance at level 3 is that the infant who looks at an emotional expression now resonates emotionally to it: The infant can react with a positive or negative expression depending on the affective quality specified by the facial configuration.

Evidence for the development of appropriate emotional responses to different facial expressions comes from studies that used infants' facial and vocal emotional expressions and emotional behaviors to assess their responsiveness. Buhler and Hetzer (cited in Buhler, 1930) reported that at 3 months almost all of the infants responded positively to a face regardless of the affective expression the face possessed. Between 4 and 7 months of age, infants increasingly responded negatively to angry expressions. Interestingly, from the eighth month and beyond, the infants' reactions to the negative face became unsystematic, and Buhler and Hetzer suggested that the older infants who responded positively to the negative expressions seemed to treat the mock scolding as a joke or game. Kreutzer and Charlesworth (1973) also reported evidence for the emergence of emotional resonance by 6 months of age. Four-month-olds in their study responded indiscriminately to combined facial and vocal modeling of happy, sad, angry, and neutral expressions. However, 6-month-old and older infants showed more negative reactions to negative expressions modeled by the experimenter.

Infants thus appear to become emotionally responsive to positive versus negative facial expressions at about 5–7 months of age. This increased responsiveness to facial configurations may be related to dramatic improvements in the capabilities of the human infant to note the different regions of the face (Caron *et al.*, 1973), to better detect visual organization (Bertenthal, Campos, & Haith, 1980), and to extract invariances from sensory displays (Campos, Bertenthal, Benson, & Schmid, 1980; Cohen & Strauss, 1979; Fagan, 1976). In addition, this age period is associated with marked changes in the expression of emotions such as fear (Campos *et al.*, 1978; Emde *et al.*, 1976), anger (Sroufe, 1979), and sadness (Spitz, 1965). The improvement in ability to perceive gestalts must enhance the ability to perceive facial expression patterns. The ability to extract invariances from sensory displays may in turn permit the infant to extract invariant facial expressions from the same faces in different contexts, or from different individuals (Nelson, Morse, & Leavitt, 1979). In addition, the development of expressive emotional systems may either permit or facilitate the understanding of emotional displays in others, for reasons we elaborated on earlier. The additional time to experience the consequences of expressive behavior may also play a role in the developments that make level 3 possible.

## LEVEL 4: FACIAL EXPRESSIONS USED IN A REFERENCING CONTEXT

The developments at the third level are important insofar as they permit an emotional resonance between the perceiver and the encoder of an emotional expression. Once the infant appreciates the emotional expressions in the face of another, the groundwork is laid for such emotional expressions to serve three different functions: action consequence, situational reference, and the inference of emotional feeling states in another (Frijda, 1969). Each of these functions requires increasingly complex cognitive prerequisites. Hence, we are led to postulate a time lag between the emergence of emotional resonance and the beginning of use by the infant of emotional expressions by other persons to appraise environmental events.

Action anticipation means the prediction of the stimulus person's behavior, particularly as it impacts oneself. "Understanding a given reaction as anger," says Frijda (1969), "may consist of readying one's self to receive attack [p. 169]." This is the function of emotional expressions studied by Camras (1977) in her study of kindergarteners' reactions to anger expressions in playmates: The observation of a playmate's angry facial expression made children more hesitant to obtain a toy than they were after observing nondistressed and nonangry expressions. Note how the cognitive demands of the action anticipation function are relatively simple. Here all that is necessary is for the infant to understand that an environmental event (the expression of an emotion) may be related to the self. In the Piagetian theory of sensorimotor intelligence, this is the simplest of organism–environment understandings—one that requires only the criteria for Stage 3 of sensorimotor intelligence. Accordingly, we would not be surprised to find such appreciation of emotion consequences in infants as young as 5–9 months (i.e., in our level 3 of emotion understanding). The emergence of action anticipation may coincide with the emergence of emotion resonance, although it is just as possible that action anticipation may lag behind resonance.

Situational referencing, in contrast to action anticipation, implies that the perceiver gains information about an environmental event by noting the facial reaction of the person being observed. Frijda (1969) provided this example: "When we see someone become terrified, we expect also to see something with startling properties in the observed person's line of sight [p. 169]." Situational referencing and the related process of social referencing must involve a higher cognitive skill than action anticipation insofar as there is a third environmental event or object in the picture besides the emotion encoder and the perceiver. Furthermore, Piagetian theory postulates that the infant only slowly comes to understand that one environmental event is related to or predicts something about another environmental event (Piaget, 1952). This skill develops well after children appreciate the possible effect of an environmental variable on themselves. Indeed, the construction of such "objective relationships" is the hallmark of Stage 5 of sensorimotor intelligence (Lamb & Campos, 1982), and so is expectable quite late in the first year of life. There may thus be as much as a 2–5 month lag between the emergence of understanding of action consequences and the emergence of situational referencing.

*Social referencing* is, briefly put, a two-person communication about a third event. It must therefore share cognitive features with the child's understanding of the referent of the mother's pointing behavior. In social referencing, for instance, the child must relate the mother's emotional reaction to the uncertain event in question. In understanding pointing, the child must relate the gesture of the index finger to some third object in the world. It is not until the third or fourth quarter of the first year of life that infants reliably understand the referent of the mother's pointing gesture (Leung & Rheingold, 1981) or the direction of the mother's gaze (Butterworth & Jarrett, 1980; Scaife & Bruner, 1975). Before that, it is not uncommon to see infants of 8 months or so merely stare at the mother's index finger, totally oblivious of any referent to the pointing gesture. Moreover, given that social referencing involves not so much the gesture of pointing as much as it does the understanding of the target of another person's looking behavior or vocal or gestural expression,[5] it seems likely to us that behavior regulation following social referencing may not be evident until late in the first year of life.

Although no studies have yet been done with infants young enough to identify the age of emergence of social referencing, the studies done to date confirm that the capacity is present by 10–12 months of age. It will be recalled that Klinnert (1981) found that the affective quality of the mother's facial expression determined the direction of approach or avoidance of 12-month-olds to a toy. Sorce *et al.* (1981) similarly found that the mother's facial expression could determine whether a 12-month-old infant crossed the visual cliff or not. Feinman and Lewis (1981) also obtained effects of emotional communication with infants who were 10 months of age. The evidence that exists, then, although incomplete, is nevertheless consistent with the existence of a fourth level of affective information processing.

BEYOND LEVEL 4

Further developments in the complexity of reactions to emotional expressive displays continue well past the infancy period. The ability of infants to infer another's feeling state surely exceeds their sensorimotor information-processing capabilities, insofar as it involves the understanding of central representational processes in another person and not just an understanding of the here-and-now behavior of the expressive individual. Harter (1979) has described how children in the school years undergo an ordinal developmental sequence in their understanding of the expressions of emotions by others. At first, children do not understand that an individual can feel two emotions at the same time. Later, they understand that a person can experience two emotions, but sequentially. It is not until 9 or 10 years of age that children understand that a person can feel two quite opposite emotions simultaneously. Like cognition, emotional development does not stand still. Like cognition, also, behavioral regulation by emotion has its roots in infancy.

---

[5]We have not discussed levels of processing of nonfacial emotional information because there is not much literature on such topics. However, even if the first three levels of processing of emotional information take place sooner for the voice or for gesture than for the face, the *cognitive prerequisites* for social referencing would ensure that there would not be much of an age decalage between the emergence of social referencing for the different channels. Furthermore, vocal expressions of emotion are less likely to be used in social referencing, as we define it, independently of a visual component (e.g., looking at the object of the emotional expression). In real life situations, messages in more than one channel are probably typical. The integration of visual, vocal, and gestural expressive channels is a topic of major research importance that we intend to pursue.

## SOCIAL REFERENCING AND IMPLICATIONS
## FOR EMOTION THEORY

We have just described how social referencing is one way in which emotional expressions, specifically facial ones, influence the behavior of others. The empirical evidence we reviewed leaves no doubt that by 12 months of age infants actively seek out emotional information from caregivers and make use of others' emotional signals to guide their coping behavior with respect to a third event. Social referencing thus augments infants' appraisal capacities. We tentatively suggested a four-level developmental sequence in the ontogeny of social referencing because we feel that the sequence organizes the current research related to infants' abilities to use the facial expressions of other people, highlights gaps in our knowledge, and serves what we hope is an important heuristic purpose.

The notion of social referencing, however, raises several issues that we have not yet addressed. One that is of critical importance concerns the precise mechanism for its emergence: Is the infant's reaction to emotional displays the result of a learning process, or does it reflect a more innate or endogenous capacity? A second issue concerns the role of feeling states in accounting for the infant's behavior following the detection of the emotional expressions during referencing. Do emotional expressions serve merely as environmental cues or do they mediate behavior by directly eliciting a resonant emotional response on the part of the infant? In Zajonc's (1980) terminology, do the expressions of others elicit "cold" but meaningful perceptions or do they produce "hot" empathic reactions in the perceiver? A third question concerns factors that increase the probability that infants will utilize the emotional information provided by others. Does emotional information observed in another individual always influence the behavior of the perceiver, or does the context within which the referencing behavior occurs play a significant role in determining whether the information is not only detected but also used to influence one's behavior? We shall briefly discuss each issue in turn.

### THE ROLE OF LEARNING

The mechanism for the emergence of emotional responsiveness to the expressions of others is as yet unclear. Learning theories, of course, would state that facial expressions come to serve as discriminative stimuli for an infant's behavior as a result of the classical conditioning of such cues with the consequences of the caregiver's behavior for the child. A smile from another, for instance, might become the signal that food is coming or that a play episode is about to begin. A frown might indicate that punishment will ensue. A fearful expression might forecast the mother's prompt removal of the child from a particular situation, and so forth.

There is little doubt that learning must play some role in the development of the child's comprehension of the caregiver's nonverbal behavior. At the very least, as we have argued elsewhere (Campos & Stenberg, 1981), perceptual learning might be necessary to facilitate the child's detection of expressive invariances in the face, voice, or gesture of another. In addition, learning is probably crucial in determining the specific manner in which the child regulates his behavior following the perception of expressions.

However, there is also very suggestive evidence to indicate that social learning may not be necessary for the emergence of emotional reactions to the expressive behaviors of others in the environment. This evidence comes from a study by Sackett (1966) of eight rhesus monkeys reared in isolation from contact with humans or other monkeys except for a brief period of hand-feeding during the first 5–9 days of life. The isolate monkeys were presented with slides of monkeys in a variety of socially communicative displays, including threat, play, fear, exploration, and sexual activity. Slides of infant monkeys alone or with their mothers were also presented. Despite the lack of any opportunity for social learning, at 2½–3 months of age the monkeys began to react to threat displays with aversive reactions: They vocalized, climbed, and moved about more following presentations of such slides. These slides also led to an abrupt decline in lever press rate when they were made contingent with that response. On the other hand, positive reactions were shown by these monkeys when the slides were of infant monkeys. A more recent study by Kenney, Mason, and Hill (1979) also demonstrated the elicitation of positive reactions to positive expressions (lip smacking) and negative reactions to negative expressions (staring) in isolate-reared monkeys.

Both Sackett's (1966) and Kenney et al.'s (1979) studies demonstrated that experience was important, however. In Sackett's study, the emotional reactions to the threat displays decreased as the monkeys became older, suggesting to Sackett that experience with social expressions may be necessary at least for the maintenance of a maturationally determined sensitivity to at least some types of emotional displays. In Kenney et al.'s study, monkeys given some social experience produced emotional reactions to the positive and negative expressive displays at earlier ages and with higher levels of intensity than did social isolates. Experience may thus facilitate the development of sensitivity to emotional displays. So, as in other areas where the respective influences of maturation and experience are investigated (cf. Gottlieb, in press), endogenous and experiential factors interact in complex ways to determine a sensorimotor outcome.

## THE ROLE OF FEELING

An even thornier issue about how sensitivity to expressions comes about is that of the role of *feeling states* as mediators of the behavioral regulation produced by the perception of emotional expressions in others. Examples abound in everyday life of complex stimuli, such as traffic signals or road signs, that guide our behavior without the need for a special state of consciousness to account for their effects. Can we therefore explain the behavior-regulatory effects of emotional expressions of others as mere reactions to environmental cues and nothing more? Or does the emotional expression have to elicit a conscious, hedonic tinge in order to explain the effects of another's expression on one's behavior?

Although it is tempting to sidestep the issue we are raising on the grounds that psychology has never dealt adequately with the measurement of discrete states of consciousness, we prefer to take a stance on the matter and propose that the feeling state elicited by expressions in the perceiver must play an important role in the consequent behavior regulation. We take this position in part intuitively. When one observes a person writhing in pain and screaming in agony, one *feels* a corresponding negative state in oneself, and that feeling is sometimes so powerful that it motivates not only nurturant responses or help-seeking on one's part, but also avoidance behaviors such as turning away from the distressed person, or even leaving the scene. Furthermore, using the feelings generated by others is central to the empathic process. Such feelings provide day-to-day guides for parents in responding to their infants and children. Similarly, they provide guides for clinicians in diagnosing and treating patients. Indeed, a large part of the art of therapeutics consists in monitoring and making use of one's feelings in response to those who are seeking help (Emde, Gaensbauer, & Harmon, 1982).

There is a second reason why we believe that emotional expressions indeed elicit feelings in the perceiver. Many emotional expressions, particularly those in voice and gesture, but also, to some extent, those in the face, have physical elements very likely to elicit feeling directly. For instance, abrupt, angular movements, shrill, high-pitched voices, loud or otherwise intense vocalizations and movements, and the rise time and duration of an action are aspects of stimulation that, when independently manipulated, probably elicit emotional reactions even outside the context of emotional expressions. So even if one rejected the possibility of a "psychophysical correspondence," in Gibson's (1950) terms, between patterns of expressive movements and the direct elicitation of feeling, simpler and less patterned stimulus components like those just enumerated may accomplish the same end.

A third argument for the possible role of feeling states as mediators of reactions to another's emotional expression comes from Hoffman (1978). He argues that the sight of another's facial expression may lead the viewer to experience the other's feeling through "motor mimicry." Such micromomentary imitative behaviors may generate facial feedback that either elicits the feeling state directly (Izard, 1971) or at least lowers the threshold for subsequent elicitation of that feeling. Although there are difficulties with the facial feedback hypothesis as an explanation of the elicitation of feeling states (Buck, 1980), the motor mimicry process has not been adequately tested and is thus worth further consideration.

We propose, therefore, that feeling states are both elicited by the emotional expressions of others and that they are indispensable mediators of behavioral regulation. Although we are fully cognizant of the difficulties of measuring feeling states, researchers should not be prevented from attempting converging operations to tap what may be the most crucial variable of all in accounting for how emotion directs behavior.

## THE IMPORTANCE OF CONTEXT

The third question we raised earlier dealt with the factors that influenced behavioral regulation consequent to the detection of expressive reactions in another. We believe that it is critically important to consider the context of the perception of the emotional expression. In a social referencing situation, the context seems to be one of either uncertainty or ambiguity. The greater the uncertainty, the greater the likelihood that referencing will take place. Moreover, the more the individual's uncertainty, the more effective the emotional information from another will be in affecting the referencing person's coping behavior. This conclusion is supported by a follow-up to the visual cliff-referencing study that we cited earlier. If the deep side of the cliff is covered, in essence giving the table two shallow sides, few 12-month-olds reference, and those who do are not affected by the mother's fear expression: They cross the deep side of the cliff. This is in sharp contrast to the behavior of infants exposed to the context of a modest drop-off at the center of the cliff table. This finding suggests to us that emotional information may be most effective the more uncertain the child is, and that the increased effectiveness of that information is probably due to the active nature of the child's search for it.

However, the regulatory role of emotional expressions for behavior is not limited to situations involving referencing. A boy, for example, who is about to munch on a dangerous houseplant and who hears a piercing scream from his mother is very likely to regulate his behavior accordingly—that is, he will very likely stop what he is doing, look at the source of the scream, then take some coping action that might include crying, backing away from the plant, or initiating another activity. Nevertheless, even when emotional information is *imposed* on a person rather than sought out, we believe that context plays a profound role in the type and the probability of behavioral regulation that follows the perception of an emotional expression. Consider the cry of a child. In a situation in which the cry is perceived to take place in a relevant context (e.g., the loss of a toy, an injury, etc.), one type of behavior will predictably be elicited in the caregiver. On the other hand, the same cry coming from a context perceived to be irrelevant (i.e., not related to any real danger or distress on the part of the child) will elicit rather different consequences from the caregiver—consequences that may range from ignoring the child through annoyance to actual spanking or outright physical abuse of the child. In both examples, the feeling state will be negative but the quality of the negative state may differ according to context and so will the perceiver's behavioral regulation—what he or she chooses to do. One of the most pervasive contextual factors is the object of the expression. To be effective in behavioral regulation, the perception of the expression must be related to something in the environment—whether oneself or a third object. If the expression occurs in a context in which the object of the expression is unclear, the expression will merely result in confused or perplexed behavior.

Context has always been an equivocal concept within emotion theory. In part, this results from the use of context by those inimical to the notion to disprove that expressive behaviors have reliable and valid specifications. As a result, most psychologists working within the framework of discrete emotions theory try to *control for* context in order to rule out the possibility that what is communicated by an expression is actually mediated by the background information that is simultaneously available (e.g., Emde *et al.,* 1978; Hiatt *et al.,* 1979). But context is important for all perceptual processes, as the Gestaltists maintained many years ago. The temporal or spatial background within which a stimulus is presented affects one's perception of that stimulus. However, the importance of the background does not make the stimulus unimportant. We thus argue for the reintroduction of contextual factors as variables of measurable importance in understanding the mechanisms of behavior regulation.


## CONCLUSION

Before we close this chapter, we feel that a final word may be in order regarding cognition–emotion relationships. There has been considerable controversy recently about whether cognition must precede emotion, or whether emotion may precede, and indeed lay the basis for, cognition (see Zajonc, 1980). The social referencing function we have described in this chapter demonstrates the intricacy, and perhaps the impossibility, of ever being able to tell whether cognition or emotion is primary. What one chooses to be "primary" in our opinion reflects the slice of time one chooses in an ongoing social or nonsocial transaction. Thus, social referencing is most likely to take place by our hypothesis when intrinsic appraisal (a cognitive process) fails. However, the uncertainty generated by the primary appraisal, the appreciation of the stimulus patterns that are uniquely emotional (i.e., the expressions of another), the outcome of the social referencing process itself, and the motivation for the initial primary appraisal are all likely to be emotional processes.

It thus may be preferable at this point to abandon the pursuit of issues about temporal priority and to address instead issues about how cognitions and emotions interact to make possible important outcomes for human behavior and personality. In this regard, we propose that social referencing has both theoretical and practical implications. It may be one of the mechanisms par excellence of the growth of a child's emotional reactions, attitudes and deep-seated preferences. It may be important diagnostically in identifying types of interactional failures in parent–child dyads, in identifying defects in parental signaling characteristics, as well as infant receiving characteristics (Haith & Campos, 1977), and it may highlight the importance of being aware of a child's perceptual handicaps for emotional communication. Social referencing may also imply that observational learning mediated by the perception of emotions needs to be investigated in infancy. But above all, social referencing demonstrates the more general point that emotions must be considered as organizers and regulators in interpersonal behavior. The functions of emotion thus hardly "terminate in the subject's own body" as William James (1890) once argued and many have since assumed. Emotions have transmission properties that we have only begun to consider.


# REFERENCES

Ahrens, R. Beitrag zur Entwicklung des Physiognomie und Mimikerkennens, *Zeitschrift fur experimentelle und angewandte Psychologie*, 1954, *2*, 412–454.
Andrew, R. The origin and evolution of the calls and facial expressions of the primates. *Behavior*, 1963, *20*, 1–109.
Appel, M., & Campos, J. Binocular disparity as a discriminable stimulus parameter in early infancy. *Journal of Experimental Child Psychology*, 1977, *23*, 47–56.
Arnold, M. *Emotion and personality* (2 vols.). New York: Columbia Univ. Press, 1960.
Barrera, M., & Maurer, D. *Recognition of mother's photographed face by three month old infants.* Paper presented at the meeting of the International Conference on Infant Studies, Providence, Rhode Island, April, 1978.
Bertenthal, B., Campos, J. J., & Haith, M. Development of visual oranization: The perception of subjective contours. *Child Development*, 1980, *51*, 1072–1080.
Bowlby, J. *Attachment and loss* (Vol. 1). New York: Basic Books, 1969.
Brazelton, T. B., Tronick, E., Adamson, L., Als, H., & Wise, S. Early mother–infant reciprocity. *Parent–Infant Interaction*, Ciba Foundation Symposium 33. Amsterdam: Elsevier, 1975.
Bridges, K. M. Emotional development in early infancy. *Child Development*, 1932, *3*, 324–341.
Buck, R. Nonverbal behavior and the theory of emotion: The facial feedback hypothesis. *Journal of Personality and Social Psychology*, 1980, *38*, 811–824.
Buhler, C. *The first year of life.* New York: John Day, 1930.
Butterfield, P., Emde, R., Svejda, M., & Neiman, S. Silver nitrate and the eyes of the newborn: Effects on parental responsiveness during initial social interaction. In R. Emde & R. Harmon (Eds.), *Attachment and affiliative systems: Psychobiological aspects.* New York: Plenum, 1982.
Butterworth, G., & Jarrett, N. *The geometry of pre-verbal communication.* Paper presented to the annual conference of the developmental psychology section of the British Psychological Society, Edinburgh, September 1980.
Campos, J., Bertenthal, B., Benson, N., & Schmid, D. *Self-produced movement and the extraction*

*of form invariance*. Paper presented at a meeting of the International Conference on Infant Studies, New Haven, Connecticut, April, 1980.

Campos, J., Emde, R., Gaensbauer, T., & Henderson, C. Cardiac and behavioral interrelationships in the reactions of infants to strangers. *Developmental Psychology*, 1975, *11*, 589–601.

Campos, J., Hiatt, S., Ramsay, D., Henderson, C., & Svejda, M. The emergence of fear on the visual cliff. In M. Lewis & L. Rosenblum (Eds.), *The development of affect*. New York: Plenum, 1978.

Campos, J. J., & Stenberg, C. Perception, appraisal, and emotion: The onset of social referencing. In M. E. Lamb & L. R. Sherrod (Eds.), *Infant social cognition: Empirical and theoretical considerations*. Hillsdale, New Jersey: Erlbaum, 1981.

Camras, L. Facial expressions used by children in a conflict situation. *Child Development*, 1977, *48*, 1431–1435.

Carey, W., & McDevitt, S. Revision of the infant temperament questionnaire. *Pediatrics*, 1978, *61*, 735–739.

Caron, A., Caron, R., Caldwell, R., & Weiss, S. Infant perception of the structural properties of the face. *Developmental Psychology*, 1973, *9*, 385–399.

Carpenter, G. *Mother–stranger discrimination in early weeks of life*. Paper read at a meeting of the Society for Research and Child Development, Philadelphia, Pennsylvania, March 1973.

Carr, S., Dabbs, J., & Carr, T. Mother–infant attachment: The importance of the mother's visual field. *Child Development*, 1975, *46*, 331–338.

Chevalier-Skolnikoff, S. Facial expression of emotion in nonhuman primates. In P. Ekman (Ed.), *Darwin and facial expression: A century of research in review*. New York: Academic Press, 1973.

Cohen, L., & Strauss, M. Concept acquisition in the human infant. *Child Development*, 1979, *50*, 419–424.

Cohn, J. F., & Tronick, E. Z. Communicative rules and the sequential structure of infant behavior during normal and depressed interaction. In E. Tronick (Ed.), *The development of human communication and the joint regulation of behavior*. Baltimore, Maryland: University Park Press, 1981.

Cooley, C. H. *Human nature and the social order*. New York: Scribners, 1912.

Darwin, C. *The expression of the emotions in man and animals*. Chicago, Illinois: Univ. of Chicago Press, 1975. (Originally published, 1872.)

Duffy, E. An explanation of "emotional" phenomena without the use of the concept "emotion." *Journal of General Psychology*, 1941, *25*, 283–293.

Duffy, E. *Activation and behavior*. New York: Wiley, 1962.

Eibl-Eibesfeldt, I. Human ethology: Concepts and implications for the science of man. *The Behavioral and Brain Sciences*, 1979, *2*, 1–57.

Ekman, P. Universals and cultural differences in facial expressions of emotion. In J. Cole (Ed.), *Nebraska Symposium on Motivation* (Vol. 19). Lincoln: Univ. of Nebraska Press, 1972.

Ekman, P., & Friesen, W. Constants across cultures in the face and emotion. *Journal of Personality and Social Psychology*, 1971, *17*, 124–129.

Ekman, P., & Friesen, W. *Unmasking the face* . Englewood Cliffs, New Jersey: Prentice-Hall, 1975.

Ekman, P., Friesen, W., & Ellsworth, P. *Emotion in the human face: Guidelines for research and an integration of findings*. New York: Pergamon, 1972.

Ekman, P., Sorensen, E., & Friesen, W. Pan-cultural elements in facial displays of emotion. *Science*, 1969, *164*, 86–88.

Emde, R. N. Levels of meaning for infant emotions: A biosocial view. In W. A. Collins (Ed.), *Minnesota Symposium on Child Psychology* (Vol. 13). Minneapolis: Univ. of Minnesota Press, 1979.

Emde, R. N., & Brown, C. Adaptation to the birth of a Down's syndrome infant: Grieving and maternal attachment. *Journal of the American Academy of Child Psychiatry*, 1978, *17*, 299–323.

Emde, R. N., Gaensbauer, T. J., & Harmon, R. J. Emotional expression in infancy: A biobehavioral study. *Psychological Issues* (Vol. 10, No. 37). New York: International Universities Press, 1976.

Emde, R. N., Gaensbauer, T. J., & Harmon, R. J. Using our emotions: Some principles for appraising emotional development and intervention. In M. Lewis & L. Taft (Eds.), *Developmental disabilities: Theory, assessment, and intervention*. New York: S. P. Medical & Scientific Books, 1982.

Emde, R. N., Kligman, P., Reich, J., & Wade, T. Emotional expression in infancy: I. Initial studies of social signaling and an emergent model. In M. Lewis & L. Rosenblum (Eds.), *The development of affect*. New York: Plenum, 1978.

Fagan, J. Infants' recognition of the invariant features of faces. *Child Development*, 1976, *47*, 627–638.

Feinman, S. Infant response to race, size, proximity and movement of strangers. *Infant Behavior and Development*, 1980, *3*, 187–204.

Feinman, S. *Social referencing in infancy*. Merrill Palmer Quarterly, in press.

Feinman, S., & Lewis, M. *Social referencing and second-order effects in ten-month old infants*. Paper presented at a meeting of the Society for Research in Child Development, Boston, Massachusetts, April 1981.

Field, T., & Walden, T. Perception and production of facial expressions in infancy and early childhood. In H. Reese & L. Lipsitt (Eds.), *Advances in child development and behavior* (Vol. 16). New York: Academic Press, 1982.

Fraiberg, S. *Insights from the blind*. New York: Basic.Books, 1977.

Frijda, N. H. Recognition of emotion. In L. Berkowitz (Ed.), *Advances in experimental social psychology* (Vol. 4). New York: Academic Press, 1969.

Gibson, J. *The perception of the visual world*. Boston: Houghton Mifflin, 1950.

Gottlieb, G. The psychobiological approach to the study of human development. In M. Haith & J. Campos (Eds.), *Infancy and the biology of development. Carmichael's handbook of child psychology* (Vol. 2), P. Mussen, ed. New York: in press.

Hainline, L. Developmental changes in visual scanning of face and nonface patterns by infants. *Journal of Experimental Child Psychology*, 1978, *25*, 90–115.

Haith, M. *Rules that newborns look by*. Hillsdale, New Jersey: Erlbaum, 1981.

Haith, M., Bergman, T., & Moore, M. Eye contact and face scanning in early infancy. *Science*, 1977, *198*, 853–855.

Haith, M., & Campos, J. Human infancy. In M. Rosenzweig & L. Porter (Eds.), *Annual Review of Psychology*, 1977, *28*, 251–293.

Hamburg, D. Emotions in the perspective of human evolution. In P. Knapp (Ed.), *Expression of the emotions in man*. New York: International Universities Press, 1963.

Harter, S. Children's understanding of multiple emotions: A cognitive–developmental approach. Address presented to the Jean Piaget Society, Philadelphia, Pennsylvania, April, 1979.

Hiatt, S., Campos, J. J., & Emde, R. N. Facial patterning and infant emotional expression: Happiness, surprise, and fear. *Child Development*, 1979, *50*, 1020–1035.

Hoffman, M. L. Toward a theory of empathic arousal and development. In M. Lewis & L. Rosenblum (Eds.), *The development of affect*. New York: Plenum, 1978.

Izard, C. *The face of emotion*. New York: Appleton-Century-Crofts, 1971.

Izard, C. *Human emotions*. New York: Plenum, 1977.

Izard, C., Huebner, R., Risser, D., McGinnes, G., & Dougherty, L. The young infant's ability to produce discrete emotion expressions. *Developmental Psychology*, 1980, *16*, 132–140.

James, W. *Principles of psychology*. New York: Holt, 1890.

Kagan, J. On emotion and its development: A working paper. In M. Lewis & L. Rosenblum (Eds.), *The development of affect*. New York: Plenum, 1978.

Kenney, M., Mason, W., & Hill, S. Effects of age, objects, and visual experience on affective responses of rhesus monkeys to strangers. *Developmental Psychology*, 1979, *15*, 176–184.

Klinnert, M. D. *Facial expressions and social referencing*. Unpublished doctoral dissertation prospectus, University of Denver, Denver, Colorado, 1978.

Klinnert, M. D. *Infants' use of mothers' facial expressions for regulating their own behavior*. Paper presented at a meeting of the Society for Research in Child Development, Boston, Massachusetts, April 1981.

Kreutzer, M., & Charlesworth, W. *Infants' reactions to different expressions of emotions*. Paper presented at a meeting of the Society for Research in Child Development, Philadelphia, Pennsylvania, March 1973.

La Barbera, J., Izard, C., Vietze, P., & Parisi, S. Four- and six-month-old infants' visual responses to joy, anger, and neutral expressions. *Child Development*, 1976, *47*, 535–538.

Lamb, M., & Campos, J. *Development in infancy: An introduction*. New York: Random House, 1982.

Lazarus, R. Emotions and adaptation: Conceptual and empirical relations. In W. Arnold (Ed.), *Nebraska Symposium on Motivation* (Vol. 16). Lincoln: Univ. of Nebraska Press, 1968.

Leung, E., & Rheingold, H. Development of pointing as a social gesture. *Developmental Psychology*, 1981, *17*, 215–220.

Lewis, M., & Feiring, C. The child's social network: Social object, social functions, and their relationship. In M. Lewis & L. Rosenblum (Eds.), *The child and its family*. New York: Plenum, 1979.

Lewis, M., & Feiring, C. Direct and indirect interactions in social relationships. In L. Lipsitt & C. Rovee-Collier (Eds.), *Advances in infancy research*. Norwood, New Jersey: Ablex, 1981.

McCall, R., & McGhee, P. The discrepancy hypothesis of attention and affect in infants. In I. Uzgiris & F. Weizman (Eds.), *The structuring of experience*. New York: Plenum, 1977.

Maurer, D., & Salapatek, P. Developmental changes in the scanning of faces by young infants. *Child Development*, 1976, *47*, 523–527.

Mead, G. *Mind, self, and society: From the standpoint of a social behaviorist*. Chicago, Illinois: Univ. of Chicago Press, 1934.

Miller, N. E. Learning drives and rewards. In S. S. Stevens (Ed.), *Handbook of experimental psychology*. New York: Wiley, 1951.

Mowrer, O. H. *Learning theory and behavior*. New York: Wiley, 1960.

Nelson, C., Morse, P., & Leavitt, L. Recognition of facial expressions by seven-month-old infants. *Child Development*, 1979, *50*, 1239–1242.

Oster, H. "Recognition" of emotional expression in infancy? In M. Lamb & L. Sherrod (Eds.), *Infant social cognition: Empirical and theoretical considerations*. Hillsdale, New Jersey: Erlbaum, 1981.

Piaget, J. *The origin of intelligence in children*. New York: International Universities Press, 1952.

Piaget, J. *The construction of reality in the child*. New York: Basic Books, 1954.

Piaget, J. *Psychology of intelligence*. Paterson, New Jersey: Littlefield, Adams, 1960.

Plutchik, R. *The emotions: Facts, theories, and a new model*. New York: Random House, 1962.

Plutchik, R. *The emotions: A psychoevolutionary synthesis*. New York: Harper & Row, 1980.

Richards, J., & Rader, N. Crawling-onset age predicts visual cliff avoidance in infants. *Journal of Experimental Psychology: Human Perception and Performance*, 1981, *7*, 382–387.

Sackett, G. Monkeys reared in isolation with pictures as visual input: Evidence for an innate releasing mechanism. *Science*, 1966, *154*, 1468–1473.

Salapatek, P. Pattern perception in early infancy. In L. B. Cohen & P. Salapatek (Eds.), *Infant perception: From sensation to cognition* (Vol. 1). New York: Academic Press, 1975.

Salapatek, P., & Kessen, W. Visual scanning of triangles by human newborns. *Journal of Experimental Child Psychology*, 1966, *3*, 155–167.

Scaife, M., & Bruner, J. The capacity for joint visual attention in the infant. *Nature*, 1975, *253*, 265–266.

Schaffer, H. Cognitive structure and early social behavior. In H. Shaffer (Ed.), *The origins of human social relations*. New York: Academic Press, 1971.

Scherer, K. R. Non-linguistic vocal indicators of emotion and psychopathology. In C. Izard (Ed.), *Emotions in personality and psychopathology*. New York: Plenum, 1979.

Sherman, M. The differentiation of emotional response in infants. The ability of observers to judge the emotional characteristics of the crying of infants, and of the voice of an adult. *Comparative Psychology*, 1927, *7*, 335–351.

Sherrod, L. Social cognition in infants: Attention to the human face. *Infant Behavior and Development*, 1979, *2*, 279–294.

Sherrod, L. Issues in cognitive–perceptual development. In M. E. Lamb & L. R. Sherrod (Eds.), *Infant social cognition: Empirical and theoretical considerations*. Hillsdale, New Jersey: Erlbaum, 1981.

Skinner, B. F. *About behaviorism*. New York: Knopf, 1974.

Slater, A., & Findlay, J. The measurement of fixation position in the newborn baby. *Journal of Experimental Child Psychology*, 1975, *14*, 349–364.

Sorce, J. F., & Emde, R. N. Mother's presence is not enough: The effect of emotional availability on infant exploration. *Developmental Psychology*, 1981, *17*, 737–745.

Sorce, J. F., Emde, R. N., & Frank, M. Maternal referencing in normal and Down's syndrome infants: A longitudinal study. In R. N. Emde & R. Harmon (Eds.), *The development of attachment and affiliative systems*. New York: Plenum, 1982.

Sorce, J. F., Emde, R. N., Klinnert, M. D., & Campos, J. J. *Maternal emotional signaling: Its effect on the visual cliff behavior of one-year-olds*. Paper presented at a meeting of the Society for Research in Child Development, Boston, Massachusetts, April 1981.

Spitz, R. *The first year of life*. New York: International Universities Press, 1965.

Spitz, R., & Wolf, K. The smiling response: A contribution to the ontogenesis of social relations. *Genetic Psychology Monographs*, 1946, *34*, 57–125.

Sroufe, L. A. Emotional development in infancy. In J. Osofsky (Ed.), *Handbook of infant development*. New York: Wiley, 1979.

Stenberg, C., & Campos, J. *The development of the expression of anger in infancy*. Unpublished manuscript, University of Denver, Denver, Colorado, 1981.

Stenberg, C., Campos, J. J., & Emde, R. N. The facial expression of anger in seven-month-olds. *Child Development*, in press.

Tomkins, S. *Affect, imagery and consciousness: The positive affects* (Vol. 1). New York: Springer, 1962.

Tomkins, S. *Affect, imagery and consciousness: The negative affects* (Vol. 2). New York: Springer, 1963.

Tronick, E., Als, H., Wise, S., & Brazelton, T. The infant's response to entrapment between contradictory messages in face-to-face interaction. *Journal of the American Academy of Child Psychiatry*, 1978, *17*, 1–13.

Walk, R., & Gibson, E. A comparative and analytical study of visual depth perception. *Psychological Monographs*, 1961, *75*, (15, Whole No. 519).

Young-Browne, G., Rosenfeld, H., & Horowitz, F. Infant discrimination of facial expressions. *Child Development*, 1977, *48*, 555–562.

Zajonc, R. Feeling and thinking: Preferences need no inferences. *American Psychologist*, 1980, *35*, 151–175.

Chapter 4

# INDIVIDUAL DIFFERENCES IN DIMENSIONS OF SOCIOEMOTIONAL DEVELOPMENT IN INFANCY

*ROSS A. THOMPSON*
*MICHAEL E. LAMB*

## ABSTRACT

*Although emotional expressions have adaptive functions for infants from an early age, infants also exhibit striking individual differences in qualitative dimensions of emotionality (such as the range and lability of emotional expressions, their latency and rise time, peak intensity, and recovery) and their capacity to regulate or control the course of emotional arousal (i.e., coping). Our goal is to explore the origins of individual differences in emotionality and coping evident in 1-year-olds by examining the nature of mother–infant interaction during the early months. We explore early interaction primarily in two contexts: instances of infant distress soothed by a caretaker's ministrations (i.e., distress–relief sequences) and face-to-face play interaction between an infant and caretaker. We propose that in both cases, the caretaker's contingent and appropriate responsiveness to the infant's socioemotional cues, and the use of a bright and varied expressive repertoire, foster the infant's development of animated emotional responsiveness and adaptive coping capacities. These early interactive factors may contribute to important differences in socioemotional responsiveness exhibited by infants at 1 year of age. We explore these differences in the context of research employing the Strange Situation procedure, in which individual differences in the security of infant–mother attachment are paralleled*

EMOTION
Theory, Research, and Experience
Volume 2

*by individual differences in infant emotionality and coping and are related to facets of mother–infant interaction during the first year. These findings provide some support to our theoretical analysis, although further research is clearly needed. To this end, in the final section we outline important areas for further inquiry and suggest methods for addressing them.*

Human infants are born with a repertoire of emotional expressions that serve many adaptive functions. Primarily, emotional expressions mediate infant–environment interactions and are associated with either approach and further engagement in stimulus events or withdrawal and disengagement. Emotional expressions also have an important signaling function, particularly to caretakers. Yet in addition to their normative functions in all infants, there are also important differences among infants in the quality of their emotional expressions and in their apparent ability to regulate or control emotional arousal once it occurs. These differences constitute the theme of our discussion.

Even the casual observer of young infants is likely to be impressed by their diversity of emotional expressiveness and affective self-regulation. Some infants, for example, are characterized by bright, animated facial and vocal expressions, whereas others are typically more subdued. In some infants, emotional arousal reaches a climax after a prolonged and gradual build-up, whereas in others affective states begin and end more abruptly. Some infants seem capable of expressing a broad range of emotions varying in intensity, whereas others appear to have a more limited expressive repertoire. There is also variability in the rapidity of recovery; that is, in the amount of time that must pass before an infant is "ready for" another emotionally arousing experience.

Three broad analytical dimensions seem adequate to describe these individual differences. First, there is *hedonic tone* (positive or negative), which can refer both to the characteristic affective state of the individual as well as to the tone of any particular response. Characterization of individuals in terms of hedonic tone are common components of most descriptive accounts. Second, there are those qualitative features that constitute *emotionality*. These features include the range and lability of the emotional expressions observed, the intensity of these displays (expressed as either average or peak intensity), the latency between the eliciting stimulus and the onset of an emotional response, the rise time to attainment of peak intensity, and the time taken for return to the prestimulus baseline following the eliciting event (recovery). Third, there is the infant's capacity to *regulate or cope* with states of emotional arousal. Once an affective reaction has begun, what can the infant do to keep emotional arousal within tolerable limits? How successful are these efforts at self-regulation?

We are concerned in this chapter with experiential influences on the development of individual differences in these dimensions of emotional responsiveness. Developmental psychologists have characteristically regarded such individual differences as facets of infant temperament that are probably of constitutional origin (Rothbart & Derryberry, 1981; Thomas, Chess, Birch, Hertzig, & Korn, 1963), and we would not deny or understate the importance of biological influences. We believe, however, that experiential influences are also important, and we attempt here to describe some of the ways in which infant–caretaker interactions may shape the early development of emotional responsiveness in the baby. Of course, interactions with other persons—such as fathers, siblings, relatives, and babysitters—surely affect socioemotional development, but primary caretakers are likely to be most influential because the contexts in which they are involved are especially salient to the baby, and also because of the sheer amount of interaction they share. (For simplicity, we will refer to the baby's primary caretaker as the mother, since this is often the case.) Our goal is to explore the ways in which consistent patterns of social interaction between a mother and baby influence the development of emotional responsiveness in infancy. These issues have been investigated rather scantily, so our account is uncomfortably speculative. We hope that our analysis helps to guide future research, however, and to this end we include a number of suggestions regarding promising areas and methods of investigation.

Since we are concerned with the development of individual differences in emotional responsiveness, we devote the first section to a description of the individual differences discernible among 1-year-olds. The relevant research comes from Ainsworth's pioneering work on the security of attachment, as assessed using the "Strange Situation" procedure (Ainsworth, Blehar, Waters, & Wall, 1978). Individual differences in the security of infant–mother attachment are essentially socioemotional in nature, with several coherent patterns of behavior and affective expression evident in infants. After describing these patterns, we consider, in the second section, the experiences from which these individual differences are likely to arise. Here we review evidence concerning early social interaction in an attempt to illustrate how the quality of the caretaker's behavior is likely to influence the development of emotional responsiveness in the baby. We propose that the mother's use of a bright and varied expressive repertoire and her tendency to respond contingently and appropriately to the infant's cues foster the development of animated emotional responsiveness and adapative self-regulating or coping capacities in instances of heightened arousal. Since most of the research we review has been descriptive in nature, this section is highly speculative; the predictions seem plausible and logical, but direct empirical support is lacking. The plausibility of our reasoning is supported by Ainsworth's research on the origins and correlates of individual differences in the security of infant–mother attachment, however, and thus her research is reviewed in the third section. Security of attachment is especially relevant since it has been related to individual differences in emotionality (as noted previously), and also to facets of mother–infant interaction during the first year. In the fourth section, finally, we outline a methodology for future research on the origins and correlates of individual differences in emotional responsiveness.

## SECURITY OF ATTACHMENT AND ITS AFFECTIVE CORRELATES

The term *security of attachment* refers to the baby's "working model" of an attachment figure, an internal representation of the caretaker which is gradually built-up over the course of repeated interactions (Ainsworth, 1973; Ainsworth *et al.*, 1978; Bowlby, 1973; Lamb, 1981a, 1981b). The infant's perception of the mother's helpful responsiveness and psychological accessibility are especially important determinants of the security of attachment (Sroufe & Waters, 1977). According to attachment theorists, babies who are securely attached have developed, out of repeated experiences with the caretaker, a confident expectation that the mother will be available when needed and have learned to depend on her responsiveness and accessibility in future instances of distress or alarm. In contrast, infants who are insecurely attached are thought to have mothers who are less predictably or appropriately responsive to their signals, and this influences their expectations of her.

The infant's expectations are most clearly evident in a procedure known as the Strange Situation, which was originally developed by Ainsworth and her colleagues (Ainsworth & Wittig, 1969; Ainsworth *et al.*, 1978). The Strange Situation is a semistandardized paradigm designed to create gradually escalating stress so that the organization of the infant's attachment behaviors vis-à-vis the parent can be assessed. Stress is induced by the appearance of an unfamiliar adult and by two brief separations from the parent—once in the company of that adult and another when the baby is left alone (complete details are provided by Ainsworth *et al.*, 1978).

The baby's reunion responses following brief separations from the parent are especially pertinent in assessing the security of attachment, but there are also distinctive differences in patterns of exploratory play activity. Infants who are *securely attached* (Group B) are characteristically able to use the parent as a "secure base" from which to explore during the preseparation episodes, and most return to play again after their mothers' return. They also typically express positive emotion to their mothers during the preseparation episodes (Waters, Wippman, & Sroufe, 1979). Upon reunion, they greet their mothers, either with distal bids (smiling and/or proffering a toy), or by seeking proximity and/or contact. In short, they evince pleasure at their mothers' return.

In contrast, *insecure–avoidant* (Group A) babies tend not to seek interaction with the mother either before or after separation. Instead, they actively avoid the caretaker by gaze-avoidance, moving away from her, or ignoring the adult's initiatives. In addition, these infants engage in noninteractive exploratory play throughout the Strange Situation episodes, even during separations. Finally, babies who are deemed *insecure–resistant* (Group C) display a great deal of distress and contact-seeking activity during reunions, but these are accompanied by angry, resistant behaviors: pushing away, hitting or slapping the mother, tantrums, throwing toys, and the like. The play activity of these babies is sporadic and inconsistent, seldom persisting beyond the first separation episode.

Clearly, separations from mother are distressing to most babies, especially when they occur in unfamiliar settings. However, Group A, B, and C infants also differ in the quality and intensity of distress, their ability to cope adaptively with the separation, and their tendency to soothe after the parent returns (Ainsworth, Bell & Stayton, 1971; Ainsworth *et al.*, 1978). Securely attached infants exhibit well-regulated distress evoked by the caretaker's departure. Although the intensity of separation-related upset varies among the four Group B subgroups, distress regularly subsides on the parent's return. Securely attached babies also seem to cope adaptively with the distress engendered by separation. They often exhibit active searching behaviors such as going to the door, pounding on it, and calling to mother. In addition, they tend to display other self-comforting activities, such as going to mother's chair or purse, retrieving some familiar article, or returning to the toys. Furthermore, they typically recover from distress rapidly after reunion, returning to playful exploration as their distress subsides. In sum, their distress is well regulated and is adaptively reactive to changes in the eliciting conditions (i.e., the mother's departure and return).

Group C infants behave very differently. These babies exhibit distress even during the preseparation episodes, and they manifest other indications of pervasive fear and anxiety (Ainsworth & Wittig, 1969). During and after the first separation, resistant infants exhibit intense upset that does not subside easily and is subsequently accompanied by angry behavior directed toward the mother upon reunion. Moreover, these infants seem less capable of adaptive coping than the Group B infants. They search little and make few attempts at self-comforting. Exploratory play terminates during the first separation and is seldom resumed. In general, distress is not well regulated nor adaptively responsive to changes in the eliciting conditions; these infants seem to lose control of their distress and do not easily recover it.

The emotional reactions of Group A infants are more subdued than those of either B or C babies. Avoidant infants typically manifest less separation distress than most other infants and they maintain high levels of play and exploration even during separation. The most striking feature of these infants is their subdued, almost blunted affect, although their subdued emotional responses are somewhat paradoxically combined with searching during the mother's absence. In short, they actively seek mother's return but exhibit little upset in her absence.

By and large, the A, B, and C patterns of emotional responsiveness are evident both at home and in the laboratory. In their small but intensive longitudinal study, Ainsworth *et al.* (1978) found that those infants who were resistant in the

Strange Situation at 1 year cried more at home throughout the first year than did those who displayed secure behavior at age 1. Analyzing data from the same study, Blehar, Lieberman, and Ainsworth (1977) reported that the quality of face-to-face encounters between mothers and their 6–15-week-old infants significantly differentiated infants who were secure from those who were insecure in Strange Situation assessments at 1 year. Infants later deemed secure were earlier rated as affectively brighter and more positive, whereas insecure infants had been more likely to fuss, look impassive, or terminate their interactions.

The significance of these group differences is underscored by evidence concerning the predictive validity of attachment classifications. Main (1973), for example, found that infants deemed insecurely attached at 12 months displayed more anger toward their mothers and were less cooperative with unfamiliar adults at 20 months of age, whereas securely attached infants later exhibited greater cooperativeness and more "game-like spirit." Similarly, Matas, Arend, and Sroufe (1978) reported that, compared to secure infants, insecurely attached infants showed somewhat more frustration in a series of problem-solving tasks administered several months later. Compared with insecurely attached infants, securely attached babies are also more friendly and positive in initial encounters with peers (Pastor, 1981; Waters *et al.*, 1979) and unfamiliar adults (Owen, Chase-Lansdale, & Lamb, 1981; Thompson & Lamb, 1982).

In sum, individual differences in the quality of infant behavior in the Strange Situation tell us something about the general quality of the socioemotional responses of these babies: differences that can be seen more clearly in encounters with the primary attachment figure but that appear to generalize beyond the mother–infant relationship. Individual differences in the quality of infant reunion behaviors are paralleled by differences in the quality of separation-related distress and emotional self-control and coping. In contrast to the well-regulated upset and adaptive coping strategies of securely attached infants, insecurely attached infants exhibit either pervasive distress that inhibits both soothing and adaptive coping (Group C) or subdued emotional reactions coupled with searching (Group A). The differences in coping and reunion behaviors are not simply determined by differences in the intensity of distress since infants in the four securely-attached subgroups exhibit a range of distress reactions but all greet the mother positively upon reunion.

## MOTHER–INFANT INTERACTION AND THE DEVELOPMENT OF SOCIOEMOTIONAL RESPONSIVENESS

In this section, we review studies that help us determine why and how these group differences develop. We focus initially on two primary areas of social interaction: distress–relief sequences and face-to-face interaction. Later, we discuss the contribution of the mother's contingent responsiveness to infant cues.

## DISTRESS–RELIEF SEQUENCES

We are concerned here with attempts by adults to soothe distressed infants. Crying is the most potent, socially significant signal of which newborns are capable: It has an imperative quality that elicits responses from adults (Murray, 1979). Typically, caretakers respond to infant cries by picking up the distressed infant, and this is the most effective way of soothing infant distress (Bell & Ainsworth, 1972; Korner & Thoman, 1970, 1972). Furthermore, when an infant is soothed, it not only quiets but also moves into a state of perceptual alertness that fosters the association of caretaker cues with the relief of upset. Thus, *distress–relief sequences* involve interactions in which the quality of the mother's responding to the baby's socioemotional cues may be especially important. Each time the infant's distress is affected by the mother's ministrations, in other words, the baby is able to learn about the caretaker—both about her physical characteristics and also her behavioral predictability (Lamb, 1981a, 1981b).

Several reasons account for the special importance of distress–relief sequences (see Lamb, 1981b, for a fuller discussion). First, instances of infant crying and its relief constitute repetitive, highly predictable associations between an infant behavior and an environmental response in a context that is highly salient to the baby because of the states of heightened arousal that are involved. Second, the association between distress and its relief is relatively easy and adaptive for the baby to learn. Third, the relief of infant distress is typically followed by a state of quiet alertness (Korner & Thoman, 1970, 1972) that ensures optimal receptiveness to the visual, auditory, tactile, and olfactory stimuli that identify the caretaker.

The repeated relief of distress by the mother may thus provide opportunities to learn about not only her physical attributes but also the predictability of her responses—in other words, whether mother can be counted on to provide assistance promptly and appropriately (Lamb, 1981a). This may influence, in turn, the development of the infant's socioemotional responding. When the baby's cry elicits a prompt and appropriate response, the infant's capacity to obtain help from others through crying is reinforced. Consequently, trust in the caretaker and confidence in one's own effectance may develop out of early distress–relief sequences (Lamb, 1981b). In addition, the infant's confidence in the mother's helpful responsiveness should make states of heightened arousal somewhat easier to tolerate since assistance is anticipated. Such expectations may facilitate the development of a broader range of affective expressions in the infant as well as the capacity to maintain behavioral organization when distressed or alarmed. In contrast, infants who have little confidence in the mother's responsiveness are less likely to perceive their socioemotional signals to be functionally effective. They may thus exhibit muted emotional expressions (when the mother is consistently insensitive or unhelpful) or persistent, uncontrolled crying (when the quality of the caretaker's response is unpredictable). Distress may be more disruptive or disorganizing in either case because there is little expectation of a helpful response from the parent.

In longitudinal analysis of infant crying during the first year, Bell and Ainsworth (1972) obtained some support for our formulations. They found a significant correlation between the promptness of maternal responses in each quarter-year and the amount of crying in later quarters. The more prompt the responses, the less frequent and briefer were the episodes of crying in subsequent months. Moreover, by the end of the first year, the amount of infant crying was inversely related to the usage of alternative forms of communication, such as words, gestures, and facial expressions. In other words, crying had become a discriminating signal that was complemented in the infant's communicative repertoire by a variety of other cues.

## FACE-TO-FACE INTERACTION

As noted earlier, the relief of infant distress is usually followed by a period of heightened alertness. Parents often take advantage of this by initiating sequences of face-to-face interaction with the baby. These interactions are fleeting at first because neonates are unable to maintain alertness for long and their repertoire of social behaviors is limited. By the second month of life, however, infants begin to smile socially and develop an increasingly differentiated array of facial and vocal expressions that can be employed in social encounters—especially those that involve face-to-face interaction, since this takes place close enough to the infant that its somewhat limited visual capacities are entirely adequate (Schoetzau & Papoušek, 1977).

There are several reasons to view face-to-face interactions as important influences on the early development of emotional responsiveness. Over the early months, mother and baby repeatedly exchange emotional signals during caretaking routines and play. These exchanges are important to both partners: For the mother, they provide assurances that the infant appreciates her ministrations; for the infant, they provide a context within which to learn the roles of reciprocal social interaction. Moreover, these interactive encounters are typically characterized by heightened emotion, and thus they provide the infant repeated opportunities to monitor and regulate the emotional arousal engendered by interactions with mother. As a result, individual differences in emotional responses may develop, in part, from the quality of early face-to-face interactions; they can foster the baby's pleasure and tolerance for heightened emotion or they can inhibit the infant's capacity to cope adaptively.

Consistent patterns of face-to-face interaction are especially likely to influence the development of emotional responsiveness since interaction during the early months is a mutually regulated process, the harmony of which is affected by each partner's responsiveness to the socioemotional cues of the other. The reciprocal quality of social exchanges can be observed in mother–infant play interactions from the first trimester of the infant's life. During these interactions, both mother and baby engage each other with a variety of socioemotional signals that elicit predictable responses from the partner (Stern, 1974, 1977). The infant's interactive repertoire is initially rather limited: Smiles serve to maintain the partner's interest and attention, whereas crying causes interaction to cease altogether. In addition, the baby is capable of regulating the course of social exchange through visual orientation. When the infant looks at the partner's face, social interaction begins (particularly since mothers often maintain a "frame" of sustained visual regard during play), whereas looking away terminates interactive exchanges, at least momentarily (Fogel, 1977; Stern, 1974). The baby can also promote social exchanges by looking and smiling simultaneously; reduce or modulate engagement by momentarily redirecting attention; or turn-off encounters by means of gaze-avoidance.

The infant's behaviors are complemented by a repertoire of "infant-elicited social behaviors" in the adult (Stern, 1977). These include the melodic pitch and rhythm of the mother's voice, syllabic extension characteristic of "baby talk," facial expressions that are exaggerated in morphology and duration, sustained gazing, behavioral rhythmicity, repetitiveness, slowed tempo, and approach-withdrawal movements of the head. The adult's behaviors predictably capture the infant's attention and, quite often, provoke smiling and cooing as well. This is because infant-elicited social behaviors involve the sensory qualities that are most engaging to young infants—high-pitched sounds and movements of the head, eyes–eyebrows, and mouth—occurring at a tempo that is appropriate for the baby's information-processing capabilities (Sherrod, 1981). They also involve the repetition (with minor modification in morphology or timing) of familiar behaviors, and this, too, tends to engage the baby attentionally and affectively (Stern, Beebe, Jaffe, & Bennett, 1977). Behavioral repetition also helps to create interactive expectations that often elicit smiling and cooing when they are later confirmed (Sroufe & Wunsch, 1972).

In short, while offering her baby an animated expressive demeanor, a mother performs those behaviors that young infants tend to find interesting and pleasureable. Of course, caretakers differ greatly in the breadth of their repertoire and the relative ease with which they perform creatively for the baby. From the infant's standpoint, these differences are likely to have an important influence on the quality of interaction. When mothers employ a rich variety of facial and vocal behaviors, their infants are likely to experience a variety of positive arousal states during the course of social interaction. The baby is likely to keep attending to the caretaker, positively responding to her overtures, and behaving in such a way as to maintain the interactive encounter. By contrast, when mothers are more subdued, their infants are likely to exhibit less pleasure and interest in interaction; at times, they may even fuss or turn away (Blehar et al., 1977). Field (1979a, 1979b, 1981), for example, found that infants looked less frequently at mothers who played in a subdued, inexpressive manner compared to when mothers were naturally animated. Moreover, the adult's bright, animated behaviors typically elicit from infants reactions that adults find rewarding (e.g., smiling and cooing, sustained gazing, behavioral excitement), so a broad expressive repertoire in the mother prolongs interactions in this way also. In contrast, few features of perfunctory encounters motivate either partner to sustain the interaction. In sum, the consistent quality of early face-to-face encounters may foster either a broad range of bright, animated emotional expressions in the baby or a more subdued and, at times, negative expressive demeanor.

The mother's expressive behaviors also serve as models for the child's own emotional expressions. There is growing evidence that facial expressions of emotion are not communicatively coherent during the early months (Emde, Kligman, Reich, & Wade, 1978), even though facial displays may include preadapted components (Ekman, 1972, 1973, 1977; Izard, 1977). The mother's discriminating use of exaggerated facial expressions and vocal bids may foster the infant's conformity to socially accepted expressive patterns, thus increasing their communicative usefulness. This may account for a common tendency to feel that older children show more emotions than infants: Their expressive behaviors become more communicatively coherent with age. This socialization process may also contribute to the fine-tuning of mother–infant exchanges, making socioemotional messages easier to convey and to be "read" by both partners. This socialization process is unlikely to proceed so successfully when the caretaker's facial and vocal displays are muted or bland.

## CONTINGENT RESPONDING TO INFANT CUES

To summarize, we propose that the vitality and animation of the mother's emotional expressions may affect the range, communicativeness, and coherence of the infant's positive emotional expressions. Even more important than the mother's expressiveness, however, may be the extent to which she is "tuned in" to the infant's cues, coordinating her socioemotional bids with the baby's ongoing activity. Her sensitivity to respond appropriately to the baby's cues may substantially influence the infant's emotional responsiveness, use of emotional signals, and ability to regulate states of emotional arousal adaptively.

Several researchers (e.g., Brazelton, Koslowski & Main, 1974; Kaye, 1977; Stern, 1974, 1977) have commented on the efforts mothers make to maintain their child's arousal within a moderate range that is sufficiently high to foster positive interactive exchanges yet not so intense as to yield distress and avoidance. According to Stern (1974), infants are most likely to manifest the behaviors that adults find attractive when they are moderately aroused, so one incentive for keeping the infant so aroused, from the parent's standpoint, is to foster mutual pleasure during the social encounter. Kaye (1977) has suggested another incentive:

> Maternal responses can be classified along a continuum from "turning on" to "turning off" the infant. Mothers serve as buffers to keep their infants at moderate levels of arousal, neither too high nor too low. They do this partly for their own convenience and pleasure; but they also do it, I believe, for the same reason an animal trainer maintains his animals at a moderate level of hunger. Performance and learning depend upon the infant's state, and mothers devote a great deal of energy and vigilance to the maintenance of an optimal state. Whether this is instinctive or a conscious purpose need not concern us here; I present it as a descriptive fact [p. 198].

In other words, Kaye suggests that mothers maintain the infant's arousal within the desired range by employing their infant-elicited social behaviors discriminatively in response to changes in the baby's level of attention and affect. When the infant briefly turns away for "time out" from focused interaction, the sensitive mother pauses or reduces the intensity of her bids. When the infant resumes gazing again, the mother perceives this as a signal to resume the exchange, and responds appropriately with an increase in the intensity and animation of her bids. Mothers also attempt, as a general rule, to monitor their infants' ongoing state: They look for signs of disinterest (to which they may respond by moving to a new game), fatigue (which may mean it is time for winding-down the social encounter), or heightened interest in further interaction.

The mother's sensitive, contingent responsiveness to the baby's cues permits both mother and baby to synchronize their interactions around the baby's attentional and affective state. Interactions of this kind may influence the infant's developing capacity to monitor and regulate the emotional arousal engendered by these exchanges in several ways. First, well-synchronized interactions ensure that the infant's level of arousal changes in a manner that is gradual, well modulated, and appropriate to the infant's tolerance of stimulation. This is likely to influence two aspects of emotional arousal: rise time (i.e., the latency until attainment of peak intensity of arousal) and recovery (i.e., how long it takes to return from peak intensity to baseline). In other words, when the mother coordinates her interactive bids with the infant's cues, escalations and declines in arousal are likely to occur at a rate that is most pleasurable for the baby.

Second, the experience of well-synchronized interaction may lead the infant to enjoy arousing play for its own sake, and this may enhance the delight experienced in interactive exchanges. Berlyne's (1960, 1969) notion that an "arousal jag" results in smiling or laughing suggests that increases in arousal or excitement become pleasurable in their own right because the individual comes to anticipate a decline in arousal once the peak intensity has been achieved. Anticipatory pleasure may occur in infants whose sensitively responsive mothers have provided prior interactions involving pleasurable escalations and declines of arousal.

Third, well-synchronized interactions reinforce the functional efficacy of the infant's strategies for regulating interaction (e.g., gazing and gaze-avoidance, smiling and crying) and thus the likelihood that they will be used effectively when regulation is necessary in the future. Since the majority of these strategies—particularly those that are functional in the early months—involve social signals, their efficacy depends upon the mother's contingent and appropriate response to them. When the sensitive mother allows these cues to help direct the course of interaction, their efficacy as regulatory signals is reinforced. Further, since these regulatory cues influence the infant's own arousal by altering the course of mother–infant interaction, the infant's developing coping capacities may be shaped by the quality of maternal responsiveness. Finally, by permitting the infant to regulate socioemotional exchanges, the parent may also foster a generalized sense of personal effectance in the child as well, and this may make the infant more likely to use these and other signals discriminatively in the future (Lamb, 1981b).

In sum, when a mother acts as a co-participant with the infant in the regulation of social interaction, she fosters the infant's confidence in his or her signaling capacities, makes pleasant exchanges more enjoyable for the baby, and also contributes to the development of competent coping capacities. Of course, no human caretaker is always appropriately responsive to her child; variability in the sensitivity of any mother can be due to her situation, mood, and personality, as well as to the nature of the infant's demands (Lamb & Easterbrooks, 1981). On the other hand, there seems to be some stability over time in individual differences in maternal sensitivity (Ainsworth, Bell, and Stayton, 1974), which suggests that infants experience a reasonably consistent history of maternal responsiveness in early social encounters. For this reason, it seems valuable to consider how significant deviations from the more optimal patterns of socioemotional exchange just described are also likely to affect the infant's emotional responsiveness.

## ALTERNATIVE INTERACTION PATTERNS

Several alternative interaction patterns can be envisioned. Some caretakers dominate the course of social exchange, apparently disregarding the infant's cues and desires. They seem to follow an implicit agenda for social interaction which they carry out regardless of the infant's responses or initiatives. Conversely, some caretakers are much more passive in their interactions, employing a very limited range of infant-elicited social behaviors and often displaying them inappropriately. They fail to initiate emotionally arousing playful exchanges, and they often fail to respond to the infant's overtures.

When the caretaker behaves insensitively in these ways, the baby's socioemotional signals have little influence on the course of interaction because the mother is predictably unresponsive to them. Thus, the baby's signals are rendered functionally ineffective by the parent's failure to respond appropriately. In such instances, we might expect a flattened range of affect, with emotional expressions being neutral in tone or subdued in intensity because of the lack of coordination between maternal bids and the infant's readiness to respond. Since the parent seldom coordinates the course of socioemotional exchanges sensitively, the infant may develop precocious self-regulatory or coping capacities that do not depend on the parent's responsiveness to social signals. These coping behaviors may be autonomous or automanipulative in nature (e.g., oral activities, rocking or banging, and self-soothing activities) and would be accompanied by little clear-cut socioemotional signaling.

Other caretakers behave in a markedly inconsistent manner, at times responding sensitively to their infants' attentional and affective cues and at other times ignoring them. Inconsistent responsiveness of this sort is likely to influence the baby's socioemotional responding rather differently than does maternal insensitivity. We might expect to see the mother's irregularity mirrored in her infant's behavior, at times engaging the parent in positive encounters, at other times withdrawing from or resisting interaction. When positive emotions are expressed, they are likely to occur as irregular bursts of affect (involving very brief rise times and rapid recoveries) that are the result of momentary synchronies between the behaviors of infant and parent. The irregularity and unpredictability of these episodes may render them disconcerting rather than pleasant to the baby. Furthermore, since past encounters have met with inconsistent maternal responses, the baby's socioemotional signals may be characterized by high intensity in order to evoke more appropriate responses from the caretaker. Thus, where consistent insensitivity to infant cues may lead to flattened and subdued emotional expressions, inconsistent responding may result in persistent, unmodulated demands by the baby. In both cases, the infant's behavior is shaped by the diminished capacity of its signals to elicit appropriate parental responses.

Even if inconsistent responding by the parent leads to more intense, imperative signaling by the infant, the baby's capacity to cope adaptively with heightened arousal may suffer for at least two reasons. First, although intense arousal can be tolerated when a pleasurable drop-off is anticipated (cf. Berlyne's [1960] "arousal jag"), states of heightened excitement may be difficult to tolerate when this drop-off cannot be confidently expected. Consequently, greater disruption should accompany states of heightened emotion in infants who have unpredictable mothers, with the arousal assuming an uncontrolled or unmodulated form. Play encounters may be abruptly terminated when the baby gets too "wound up;" states of distress may be difficult to soothe. Second, maternal unpredictability may inhibit infants from learning to count on the mother's regulation of arousal or to depend on their own self-regulatory capacities. As a result, the coping ability of these infants is likely to be diminished.

We have described maternal responsiveness here in terms of alternative extremes for the purposes of discussion. Most mothers, of course, fall somewhere in-between, and thus the effects of their interactive behaviors on their infants are likely to lie somewhere between the broad parameters described. On the other hand, when mothers are clearly abusive or neglectful, infants' emotional expressions assume more aberrant forms. Gaensbauer and his colleagues (Gaensbauer, 1982; Gaensbauer & Mrazek, 1981; Gaensbauer & Sands, 1979) have documented some of the patterns of socioemotional responsiveness that are characteristic of infants and toddlers who have experienced maternal abuse or neglect: Some are affectively shallow or depressed, others show a persistently angry mood, and others exhibit markedly inconsistent emotional responding. The life histories of these children strongly suggest that these affective patterns reflect the quality of caretaker responsiveness experienced in the home.

## THE GENERALIZATION OF SOCIOEMOTIONAL RESPONDING

Although we have described face-to-face interaction and distress–relief sequences as the arenas in which to explore the effects of maternal responsiveness on the baby's emotionality and self-regulatory capacities, the influences surely extend beyond these social contexts. Indeed, most caretaking tasks demand a capacity to accurately read and appropriately respond to infant signals, and thus individual differences in the effects of caretaker responsiveness are likely to extend cross-situationally.

During the second half of the first year, the quality of mother–infant interaction is influenced by the baby's nascent awareness that mother is a person who consistently exists in time and space (cf. Piaget, 1952/1936). Out of this concept of object (or person) permanence develops the baby's "working model" of the mother; that is, an integrated set of expectations derived from a history of interactions with her. Since many of their early encounters are affectively toned, it is likely that the baby's working model of the mother has important affective components that influence subsequent encounters with her. These expectations may bias the baby to respond in a positive, cooperative way to the mother, avoid or ignore her, or to be angry or rejecting.

Indeed, this may be the origin of the distinctive patterns of emotional responsiveness that differentiate securely attached from insecurely attached infants which opened our discussion. A history of encounters that are frequently unsatisfying or aversive may account for the anger and uncooperativeness exhibited by some insecure babies to the caretaker. In contrast, the more positive friendliness of securely attached infants perhaps occurs because their cognitive representations of the mother bias them to respond more sociably.

## SECURITY OF ATTACHMENT AND MOTHER–INFANT INTERACTION

Ainsworth's reports concerning the antecedents of behavior in the Strange Situation add credence to the formulations discussed in the previous section. In her work, broad ratings of maternal behavior in the home during the last 3 months of the baby's first year have been related to observations of mother and infant in the Strange Situation at 12 months (Ainsworth & Bell, 1969; Ainsworth et al., 1971, 1974). Of the many rating scales employed, Ainsworth and her colleagues found that four significantly differentiated the mothers of securely attached infants from the mothers of insecurely attached babies. Compared with the mothers of insecure infants, mothers of secure babies were deemed more *sensitive* to the baby's signals and needs, more *accepting* (versus rejecting) of the caretaking role, more *cooperative* (versus interfering) with the infant's self-initiated activity, and exhibited greater *accessibility* to the baby's desires (rather than ignoring them when inconvenient). Blehar et al. (1977) found similar differences during the first 3 months of these infants' lives. The mothers of infants who were later deemed securely attached were more lively and playful in early interactions with their infants, they paced social exchanges contingently upon the baby's behaviors, and they encouraged interaction more than did the mothers of infants later deemed insecure. Mothers of insecurely attached infants, on the other hand, were more routine, abrupt, or impassive in early social interactions. In this sample, moreover, individual differences in the sensitivity and contingency of maternal responsiveness seemed to be stable over the first year (see Ainsworth et al., 1974; Bell & Ainsworth, 1972).

Although these analyses refer to a single longitudinal study of 23 infants and their mothers, other studies provide support for Ainsworth's findings. Matas et al. (1978), for example, found that global ratings of the mother's "supportive presence" and "quality of assistance" in a problem-solving task at 24 months significantly differentiated the mothers of infants deemed secure and insecure at 18 months. Main et al. (Main, Tomasini, & Tolan, 1979; Tolan & Tomasini, 1977) tested infants in the Strange Situation at 12 months and then examined maternal behavior in a follow-up assessment at 21 months. The mothers of securely attached infants were rated more sensitive and accepting and were judged to be more facially expressive than the mothers of insecurely attached infants. The mothers of insecurely attached infants displayed more anger and had less animated facial displays.

Estes, Lamb, Thompson, and Dickstein (1981) reported a strong relationship between maternal affective quality and the security of attachment of 19½-month-olds. The mothers of securely attached infants displayed more positive emotional involvement than did the mothers of insecurely attached infants. Maternal ratings at 12½ months also predicted infant behavior at 19½ months, but not vice versa, suggesting a direction of influence from mother to infant. Finally, Owen, Chase-Lansdale, and Lamb (1981) reported that subjective impressions of the importance of parenthood (assessed prenatally as well as 3 and 6 months postnatally) were related to the security of infant–mother attachment in the Strange Situation at 11–13 months. Parents who gave parenthood high value and work lower value were more likely to have secure attachments with their infants. Owen and her colleagues proposed that the attitudinal and motivational differences in the parents were translated into behavioral differences that, in turn, affected the infant–parent relationship.

Taken together, these studies indicate that the mothers of securely attached infants enjoy more harmonious and less conflicted exchanges with their babies than do the mothers of insecurely attached infants. Their affective expressions tend to be brighter and more positive, they are more lively and playful with their infants, and they take into account more often the baby's desires and social initiatives when interacting with them. By contrast, the mothers of insecurely attached infants exhibit less animated and more negative affective displays, their caretaking and playful encounters are more routine and abrupt, and they seem to be less sensitive to the infant's signals and cues.

Moreover, mothers of babies within the insecurely attached groups also seem to differ among themselves in important ways. Ainsworth et al. (1971, 1978) reported that the mothers of Group A (avoidant) infants consistently found interaction and contact with their babies aversive; they responded to their infants' cues inappropriately or after long delays. The mothers of Group C (resistant) infants, on the other hand, responded inconsistently and in an unpredictable fashion to infant cues.

These data suggest that the caretaking experiences of securely and insecurely attached infants could contribute to the patterns of reunion behavior in the Strange Situation described earlier, and also to the differences in emotionality and coping capacities noted earlier. In short, the mothers of securely attached infants seem to foster animated emotional responsiveness by means of their own affective vitality in interactive encounters. They also contribute to the development of adaptive self-regulatory capacities by responding promptly and appropriately to their infants' socioemotional cues. In contrast, the mothers of insecurely attached infants seem to foster less adaptive emotional and coping styles, and we have identified two different interactional patterns within this group. On one hand, mothers who are consistently insensitive or unhelpful have infants who are characterized by muted emotional expressiveness and relatively autonomous coping capacities that may include, at times, avoiding interaction with the caretaker altogether. On the other hand, mothers who are inconsistent in their responsiveness tend to have infants whose emotional expressions are intense and not well-modulated and whose coping under stress is deficient compared with that of other babies.

In this discussion, then, we have sought to explore the origins of individual differences in emotionality and coping that can be observed in 1-year-olds by examining the nature of mother–infant interaction during the early months. Although there is a sizable gap in the ages of the infants described in these research literatures, we are impressed with the consistency in observations and in patterns of influence. Our goal, therefore, has been to offer a conceptual framework for exploring the experiential origins of individual differences in emotional responsiveness as a way of stimulating further research in this area. To this end, in the next section we describe research methods that may prove useful to future investigators.

## RESEARCH STRATEGIES AND METHODS

Having drawn primarily upon descriptive studies in this chapter, we are well aware of the need for systematic research on infant emotional responsiveness and its relationship to consistent patterns of infant–mother interaction. Progress in this area depends on the development and utilization of sophisticated research techniques: coding procedures that attend to the intensity and lability of emotional responses as well as to hedonic tone; temporally based measures that permit analysis of dimensions such as latency, rise time, and recovery; and methods of appraising maternal behaviors that rely on discrete behavioral assessments rather than summary judgments. Since we are presently conducting research focused on these dimensions of infant and maternal responsiveness, in this section we outline some research strategies and their applications.

## INFANT EMOTIONALITY AND COPING

As noted in the introduction, *emotionality* encompasses a variety of interrelated qualitative features of emotional responsiveness. These include the *range* and *lability* of expressions, the *latency* between the eliciting stimulus and the onset of an emotional reaction, the *rise time* to peak intensity, and *recovery*—the time taken for return to the prestimulus baseline after the eliciting event. Each of these dimensions can be used to describe emotional reactions regardless of their hedonic tone. In order to assess these dimensions, however, a research strategy must include measures that are sensitive to the intensity and quality of emotional reactions and are temporally based in order to provide data concerning changes in emotion over time.

## The Multimethod Approach

In our current research, we are employing multiple measures—tapping facial expressions, vocalizations, and the overall quality of behavioral activity—because each modality is likely to yield different sorts of information and to be sensitive to different dimensions of emotional response. Facial expressions, for example, provide cues whose meaning is easily appraised by observers. Whether or not facial displays of emotion have universal features of evolutionary origin (e.g., Ekman, 1972, 1973, 1977; Izard, 1977), they certainly provide information on which we frequently rely in daily life. However, in research contexts, the informational value of facial expressions is limited in several important ways. If one is observing infants in freely-mobile settings, a great deal of information is lost simply because the infant's face is turned away from the camera or observer. To avoid this, one has to immobilize the infant or employ multiple cameras, each of which has attendant disadvantages: the loss of ecological validity in the former case; prohibitively expensive equipment costs in the latter.

Furthermore, even when the infant's face can be observed, the information conveyed facially is often unclear or ambiguous for two reasons. First, the quality of the observational record (due to the distance from camera or observer to baby, the varying angle of the baby's head, etc.) often handicaps attempts to perform sophisticated analyses of facial expressions. Those who have succeeded in doing so (e.g., Hiatt, Campos, & Emde, 1979; Oster, 1978, Oster & Ekman, 1977) have had to employ highly structured laboratory situations. Second, facial cues of emotion are themselves often ambiguous, entail "blends" of different affective signals, and are otherwise limited in their communicative quality during the first year of life (Emde et al., 1978; Hiatt et al., 1979). Like others, therefore, we have been able to differentiate among facial expressions only on a bipolar (positive–negative) dimension, with simple gradations of intensity at each end.

The quality of the baby's vocalizations may be more informative, in part because they are easier to record than are facial expressions. With an appropriate recording system, the problem of missing data is virtually eliminated. More important, infant vocalizations are much more differentiated than are facial expressions. Spectrographic analyses have shown that infant vocalizations can be differentiated according to their pitch, intensity, rhythmicity, continuity, and speed of onset (Truby & Lind, 1965; Wasz-Hockert, Lind, Vuorenkoski, Partenen, & Valanne, 1968; Wolff, 1969). Significantly, these stimulus dimensions are communicatively meaningful: caretakers take them to convey differences in the quality of arousal experienced by a baby (Murray, 1979; Wolff, 1969).

Consider infant crying as an example. Researchers have typically combined mild whimpering, fussing, angry protests, sobbing, and hyperventilated crying or screaming into a single analytical category and have simply asked whether or not a distress response occurred (e.g., Ainsworth et al., 1978; Schaffer & Emerson, 1964). However, distinctions among various kinds of crying can be informative if one is exploring differences in the intensity of distress, or in its quality (e.g., Does the infant sound angry? Anxious?). In our own work, we are able to differentiate reliably among 9 different kinds of infant crying (see Appendix). The same underlying heuristics—pitch, intensity, rhythmicity—can also be used to differentiate among positive vocalizations.

In addition to facial and vocal expressions, one can assess individual differences in emotionality by appraising the impact of affective arousal on the infant's ongoing behavioral activity. As with adults, heightened emotions frequently disrupt the activity of infants: Disorganized movements of the arms and legs occur when infants are positively aroused (e.g., Kistiakovskaia's [1965] "animation complex"), whereas organized activity breaks down when infants are distressed. Thus the quality of activity relative to a prestimulus baseline can also serve as a useful index of emotionality in infants. For example, one might observe an infant playing with toys when the mother is present and then note how the play changes when an unfamiliar adult enters the room or when mother leaves briefly. Is the exploratory quality sustained? Does the play become more distracted, degenerating into gross motor manipulation without sustained visual regard? Or does the child cease playing altogether?

Behavioral quality is likely to be more sensitive to certain dimensions of emotional arousal than are facial expressions and vocalizations. In particular, this kind of measure provides important information concerning the escalation of and recovery from heightened emotion. Concerning the former, an emotional reaction may build up slowly before it is overtly manifested in a whimper or a laugh. Although this gradual build-up would go unnoticed if facial or vocal cues alone were used, it may be indexed behaviorally by a change in the quality or tempo of activity. Similarly, once the unfamiliar adult has left the room, the baby's recovery can be indexed by observing how long it takes before the infant returns to exploratory play.

Clearly, one strength of a multimethod research strategy lies in the differential sensitivity of each measure to various aspects of emotional responsiveness. In addition, one can examine the convergence of these measures and identify the contexts in which they provide redundant information (e.g., high versus low stress; escalation versus recovery). In our observations of infants in the Strange Situation, for example, we find that our measures of facial and vocal expression and of the quality of toy play provide different kinds of information during recovery from separation distress (i.e., following reunion with the mother), whereas these measures tend to provide redundant information during separations. Moreover, there appear to be individual differences in the cross-modality consistency of emotional cues provided by 12½-month-old infants.

## The Temporal Dimension

As noted earlier, measures of infant affect should be temporally based in order that many dimensions—such as the latency to onset, rise time and recovery—can be assessed. In our research, consequently, we employ a strategy involving summary ratings on each affect scale (i.e., facial expressions, vocalizations, quality of activity) in consecutive 15-sec scoring intervals. Thus for each 3-min episode of the Strange Situation, 12 summary judgments are made on each rating scale.

Clearly, several considerations guide the selection of such a scoring strategy. When summary judgments are made in consecutive scoring intervals, the stream of behavior is "chunked" for analytical purposes into discrete units. While a continuous scoring strategy (such as recording the duration of each behavioral act) would ensure greater fidelity to the observed behavior, it would present enormous difficulties in data retrieval and reduction. Furthermore, if the size of the temporal unit is appropriate, the chunking strategy is both valid and readily amenable to reliable scoring and analysis. The scoring unit should be long enough that the trained observer has sufficient material on which to base judgments, but not so long that many different events must be encompassed within a single summary judgment. The choice of a time unit thus depends on the lability and duration of the behavioral acts, the age of the infant, and the specific goal of the investigation.

Once the ratings have been made, a variety of summary variables can be created for further analysis. For example, the quality or intensity of an emotional response can be appraised by calculating the modal rating obtained over the relevant scoring intervals; peak intensity is, of course, a function of the highest rating achieved; and lability can be examined by counting the number of transitions between rating categories denoting positive and negative emotions. Finally, variables such as latency to onset, rise time, and recovery are functions of the number of scoring intervals in which a particular rating (or range of ratings) is obtained (e.g., latency: number of intervals from mother's departure to an initial distress rating). Clearly, one advantage of a fine-grained, temporally based approach is that it enables the researcher to create a variety of summary variables for further analysis.

We are currently relating these measures of emotional reactions in the Strange Situation to other socioemotional dimensions such as temperament and attachment classification. We wish to determine how securely attached infants differ from insecure babies in emotionality and temperament, and how these aspects of emotional responsiveness change between 12½ and 19½ months. In companion studies, we are comparing the reactions of these normal infants with a sample of babies who are cognitively retarded (i.e., Down's syndrome infants), and with a group of infants who have been abused and neglected by their mothers. These studies underscore the importance we attribute to these ways of examining emotional responsiveness in infants, and to their relevance for comparative analysis.

## Coping Strategies

The strategies employed by infants to regulate, control, and cope with heightened emotion merit further attention because their study may elucidate both developmental and individual differences issues. As suggested earlier, individual differences in coping and self-regulatory strategies develop early in infancy, and may be influenced by the quality of the caretaker's responsiveness. Thus we would expect to uncover formative relationships between maternal sensitivity and age-appropriate dimensions of the infant's coping capacities.

Of course, coping strategies vary greatly with age. As Stern (1977) and other researchers have shown, young infants regulate face-to-face interactions with adults by maintaining or terminating mutual gazes. An important research task is to trace the temporal course of gazing in relation to other dimensions of the baby's emotional responsiveness, particularly the escalation and decline of arousal. Moreover, by employing a temporally based strategy like that just described, one could assess the effectiveness of gazing and gaze-avoidance in regulating emotional arousal.

As the infant's behavioral repertoire develops, its range of coping capacities increases, and by the end of the first year there are important individual differences in the extent to which such capacities are utilized in instances of stress. In our study involving the Strange Situation, for example, we are recording those behaviors that occur when the mother is out of the room. Thus we examine the intensity of searching activity—for example, some infants go quickly to the door and remain there calling for mother until her return, while others simply watch mother leave the room. We also investigate other, more discrete questions. Does the baby go to the mother's chair, purse or coat? Is there an increase in oral behavior compared to preseparation episodes? Does the baby return to the toys and, if so, does it choose familiar or unfamiliar toys?

Furthermore, during two of the three separation episodes, an unfamiliar adult is with the infant. By observing initiatives to the stranger and responsiveness to her overtures, we hope to assess the degree to which infants can be soothed and otherwise helped by an unfamiliar adult. When the stranger offers a toy, for example, does the infant ignore or resist the bid, watch passively, or accept the toy and perhaps begin to play interactively? How does the child respond when the stranger offers to pick up the baby? Does the infant make any initiatives to the stranger?

We have also observed unusual behaviors that seem to have a self-comforting function. Most are automanipulative in nature (e.g., pulling on an ear, rocking back and forth, or waving a hand when distressed), but others involve the rhythmic manipulation of toys or other objects.

Coping strategies are of interest to us for several reasons. First, defining the relationship between infant coping and the quality of infant–mother attachment may help us to extend the suggestive findings reported by Ainsworth and her colleagues (1978). Does the more harmonious interaction that securely attached infants enjoy equip them to cope more adaptively than insecure infants with brief separations from mother? Do they respond more positively to the stranger's ministrations? Do we see in secure infants greater reliance on certain coping strategies (such as active searching and calling to the mother) rather than others (such as automanipulative or oral behaviors)? Second, there is the issue of within-individual consistency over time in the range and quality of coping behavior. To address this issue, we have observed the same infants in the Strange Situation at both 12½ and 19½ months of age. Preliminary analyses suggest that the infants employ much more sophisticated strategies at 19½ months: they tend to employ language more, to use the stranger more adaptively, and to exhibit a good deal of anticipatory behavior (such as indicating a desire to leave the room with mother following the first reunion).

Finally, we are interested in the relationships between various dimensions of emotionality and the baby's self-regulatory capacities. Does a slower rise time facilitate the baby's efforts to monitor and regulate affect as it escalates, for example, or does a momentum develop which is difficult to control? Does greater emotional lability inhibit or promote adaptive coping? What is the relationship between the intensity of arousal and its regulation?

## MATERNAL RESPONSIVENESS

Most attempts to study maternal influences on socioemotional development have involved broad summary ratings of caretaking style. In many studies, mothers have been rated on general qualities such as their sensitivity to infant cues or their psychological accessibility to the baby (e.g., Ainsworth *et al.*, 1971). A major strength of summary ratings is that they capitalize on the capacity of trained observers to integrate information and to make sophisticated judgments regarding qualities that are not amenable to a more objective, quantitative, behavioral analysis (Lamb, 1982). However, when the rating criteria are not fully explicit, summary judgments rapidly degenerate into judgments of good or bad mothering. Such judgments are likely to be so idiosyncratic and historically time-bound that they are not useful components of empirical research. There remains a clear need for objective but sophisticated techniques for assessing individual differences in maternal behavior.

As part of the study described earlier in this section, David Estes and Susan Dickstein have joined us in exploring ways of assessing maternal responsiveness through analysis of maternal behavior during both the Strange Situation and an assessment of an infant's stranger sociability. Our goal is to describe the quality of the mothers' emotional cues and the ways in which they attempt to soothe their infants before relating individual differences therein to the infants' attachment classification. All of the scales are defined behaviorally, but they differ in the degree to which sophisticated judgments must be made by trained raters.

The first set of measures tap the quality of the mother's expressions. Here Estes and Dickstein have developed an inclusive scale to assess the mother's emotional expressiveness and involvement (i.e., does she seem interested in the infant's performance and is this communicated facially and/or vocally?) during the 5-min assessment of stranger sociability. They have also developed several more discrete assessments. These include separate ratings of the hedonic tone and semantic content of the mother's utterances, and tabulations of the frequency of social bids (such as smiles). By describing the mother's behavior at various levels of analysis, therefore, we hope to determine the convergent validity of these measures.

Another set of measures appraise the mother's style of departure, reunion and soothing. Estes and Dickstein wish to determine whether differences in these aspects of maternal behavior are more strongly related to the infant's attachment classification than are differences in maternal behavior occurring earlier in our assessment. If so, it would suggest that individual differences in the infant's reunion behavior are, in part, reactions to the mother's current behavior in the situation.

## CONCLUSION

In this chapter, we have speculated about the origins of individual differences in the emotional responsiveness of infants, focusing much of our discussion on individual differences in socioemotional style related to behavior in the Strange Situation. Our own research convinces us that reliable and valid individual differences indeed exist, and that the Strange Situation provides an effective means of tapping and highlighting these differences. Surprisingly little is known about the origins of these distinctive patterns of socioemotional behavior, however. Ainsworth's pioneering research emphasized the formative importance of maternal behavior and focused attention on maternal sensitivity as a critical variable. In our discussion, Ainsworth's influence is clearly evident, although we remain uncomfortable about the empirical support on which her conclusions are founded. Ainsworth's longitudinal study (see Ainsworth *et al.*, 1978) involved only 23 infants, and most of the relevant findings were obtained using very broad rating scales that involved substantial inferences on the part of the raters. Since we find the tenor of Ainsworth's conclusions appealing, however, we have spent most of the preceding pages attempting to understand *how* maternal behavior might influence socioemotional development. In the course of so doing, we have defined critical aspects of infant and maternal behavior very specifically, and we hope that this exercise will prove heuristically useful.

## APPENDIX: SCALE FOR ASSESSING INFANT DISTRESS VOCALIZATIONS

This rating scale is designed to assess the characteristic quality of an infant's distress vocalizations over 15-sec scoring intervals. These vocalizations differ from each other in a number of important ways. The *intensity*, or loudness, of the baby's cry is one dimension; it primarily reflects how hard air is being forced from the lungs through the vocal cords. The *rhythmicity* of the cry has to do with the alternation of crying and inhalation: Is it regular or irregular? Generally speaking, milder forms of distress are arrythmic or irregular, whereas the more intense forms of crying are characterized by a rhythmic alternation of crying and inhalation. A third dimension concerns whether crying is *continuous* or intermittent: Does it occur in short bursts or longer episodes? The *pitch* of a baby's cry is a fourth dimension: Is it high or low? Finally, there is the assessment of the *sound quality* of a baby's cry: Does the infant sound angry? Distressed? Anxious? Is the cry imperative or demanding?

    0  *No vocalization* was heard at any time during the scoring interval.

    1  *Pleasure vocalization* includes squeals or shrieks of delight, cooing, laughing, or other vocalizations denoting excitement or positive engagement in some activity. These are characteristically intermittent, of brief duration, and discontinuous in quality. Pitch varies, but is usually high. Sometimes the baby uses words that have a positive tone; in these instances, use the notation 1(W).

    2  *Neutral vocalization* includes babbling and other vocalizations that have neither a distressed nor a positive quality. Like pleasure vocalizations, these are also characteristically intermittent, of brief duration, and discontinuous in quality. Whereas the pitch of pleasure vocalizations is usually high and varies a great deal, the pitch of most neutral vocalizations is characteristically lower and is less variable. Sometimes the baby uses words that have neither a distinctively distressed nor positive tone; in these instances, use the notation 2(W).

    3  *Mild distress* includes brief, mild whines, squeals of frustration or anguish, mild wails or sobs, fretting and other vocalizations that have a distinctly negative quality. These are characteristically intermittent, discontinuous, and of brief duration. Although they are not full-fledged crying or calling as such, they nevertheless indicate mild or low-level distress in the infant. Sometimes the baby uses words that have a distressed quality; in these instances, use the notation 3(W).

    4  *Calling* includes vocalizations that seem intended to signal or summon the caretaker and have a distinctly negative or distressed quality. Like protest crying, there is an imperative tone to this kind of vocalization. In contrast to protest, however, calling is of brief and intermittent

duration, is more discontinuous, and conveys much milder distress. Sometimes words are used in this capacity (such as *Ma! Ma!*); in these instances, use the notation 4(W).

5 *Distress gasps* occur when the infant's breathing has become audible and the rate has increased; the baby is taking breaths in short, quick gasps. What has become audible is the breathing; there is no cry accompanying this. Often, but not always, gasping of this kind occurs as a prelude to a full-fledged cry or immediately follows a long bout of sobbing.

6 *Fussing or whimpering* occurs when the cry is partial or intermittent rather than continuous over the scoring interval, conveying the impression of moderate distress. In particular, the pattern of breathing and crying is arrythmic, in contrast to the more rhythmic alternation of cry and inhalation that is more characteristic of sobbing. In fussing, the cry is more intermittent and discontinuous; crying is interrupted frequently. The cry also has a distressed rather than an angry or anxious tone. Pitch may vary widely, but generally is moderate or low.

7 *Whining* conveys the kind of moderate distress that is also characteristic of fussing; in contrast to fussing, however, whining denotes anxiety or frustration rather than clear-cut distress. This is conveyed especially by the tone and pitch of the cry: Whining characteristically has a moderate to high pitch and a strident quality; it is intermittent and discontinuous. Whining also has a demanding or insistent quality, due largely to its persistence over time; in contrast, fussing either tends to cease over the short run or develops into a kind of crying denoting more intense distress (such as sobbing). Fussing and whining are also distinguished by their characteristic pitches, with whining usually somewhat higher in pitch than fussing/whimpering.

8 *Protest* is a hard cry that sounds as much like shouting as it does like crying and conveys an angry, imperative quality. The cry is typically of strong intensity; the pitch is characteristically low or moderate. The cry is usually continuous, with the pattern of cry and inhalation somewhat rhythmic, but not always. An imperative, demanding cry.

9 *Sobbing* is a full-fledged cry denoting clear-cut distress. It lacks the angry, imperative quality of protest. Sobbing is continuous and of moderate to long duration; its rhythmicity is revealed in the regular alternation of crying and inhalation. Sobbing may occur at either moderate or very high intensity, depending on the intensity of distress. Pitch is usually medium to low.

10 *Screaming* is an intense, abrasive cry of high pitch and intensity; the infant sounds almost in pain. This is characteristically a hard cry, and its abrasiveness derives from the high pitch. The cry is usually continuous, and the pattern of cry and inhalation characteristically somewhat rhythmic. Usually there are longer bursts of crying than is usually the case with sobbing, with similarly lengthened breathing pauses. The infant sounds distressed rather than angry.

11 *Panic cry* characteristically comes in three distinct stages: First a long sob that is of greater than usual duration; then a long (almost interminable) pause in which the infant is continuing to exhale but no sound can be heard; and finally, an audible inhalation before the next sob. Crying is intense, continuous, and rhythmic.

12 *Hyperventilated cry* denotes very intense distress, largely due to the rapid alternation of cry and inhalation at a rate that is faster than normal sobbing. The cry is also very intense, continuous, and rhythmic.

# REFERENCES

Ainsworth, M. D. S. The development of infant–mother attachment. In B. Caldwell & H. Ricciuti (Eds.), *Review of child development research* (Vol. 3). Chicago, Illinois: Univ. of Chicago Press, 1973.

Ainsworth, M. D. S., & Bell, S. M. Some contemporary patterns of mother–infant interaction in the feeding situation. In A. Ambrose (Ed.), *Stimulation in early infancy*. New York: Academic Press, 1969.

Ainsworth, M. D. S., Bell, S. M., & Stayton, D. J. Individual differences in strange situation behavior of one-year-olds. In H. R. Schaffer (Ed.), *The origins of human social relations*. New York: Academic Press, 1971.

Ainsworth, M. D. S., Bell, S. M., & Stayton, D. J. Infant–mother attachment and social development: Socialisation as a product of reciprocal responsiveness to signals. In M. P. M. Richards (Ed.), *The integration of the child into a social world*. London and New York: Cambridge Univ. Press, 1974.

Ainsworth, M. D. S., Blehar, M. C., Waters, E., & Wall, S. *Patterns of attachment*. Hillsdale, New Jersey: Erlbaum, 1978.

Ainsworth, M. D. S., & Wittig, B. A. Attachment and exploratory behavior of one-year-olds in a strange situation. In B. M. Foss (Ed.), *Determinants of infant behavior IV*. London: Methuen, 1969.

Bell, S. M., & Ainsworth, M. D. S. Infant crying and maternal responsiveness. *Child Development*, 1972, *43*, 1171–1190.

Berlyne, D. E. *Conflict, arousal and curiosity*. New York: McGraw-Hill, 1960.

Berlyne, D. E. Laughter, humor and play. In G. Lindzey & E. Aronson (Eds.), *Handbook of social psychology* (Vol. 3, 2nd ed.). Reading, Massachusetts: Addison-Wesley, 1969.

Blehar, M. C., Lieberman, A. F., & Ainsworth, M. D. S. Early face-to-face interaction and its relation to later infant–mother attachment. *Child Development*, 1977, *48*, 182–194.

Bowlby, J. *Attachment and loss* (Vol. 2). *Separation: Anxiety and anger*. New York: Basic Books, 1973.

Brazelton, T. B., Koslowski, B., & Main, M. The origins of reciprocity: The early mother–infant interaction. In M. Lewis & L. Rosenblum (Eds.), *The effect of the infant on its caregiver*. New York: Wiley, 1974.

Ekman, P. Universals and cultural differences in facial expressions of emotion. In J. B. Cole (Ed.), *Nebraska Symposium on Motivation* (Vol. 19). Lincoln: Univ. of Nebraska Press, 1972.

Ekman, P. Cross-cultural studies of facial expression. In P. Ekman (Ed.), *Darwin and facial expression*. New York: Academic Press, 1973.

Ekman, P. Biological and cultural contributions to body and facial movement. In J. Blacking (Ed.), *Anthropology of the body*. New York: Academic Press, 1977.

Emde, R. N., Kligman, D. H., Reich, J. H., & Wade, T. D. Emotional expression in infancy. I. Initial studies of social signaling and an emergent model. In M. Lewis & L. Rosenblum (Eds.), *The development of affect*. New York: Plenum, 1978.

Estes, D., Lamb, M. E., Thompson, R. A., & Dickstein, S. *Maternal affective quality and security of attachment at 12 and 19 months*. Paper presented to the biennial meeting of the Society for Research in Child Development, Boston, Massachusetts, April 1981.

Field, T. M. Interaction patterns of pre-term and term infants. In Field, T. M., Sostek, A. M., Goldberg, S., and Shuman, H. H. (Eds.), *Infants born at risk*. New York: Spectrum, 1979 (a).

Field, T. M. Visual and cardiac responses to animate and inanimate faces by young term and preterm infants. *Child Development*, 1979, *50*, 188–194 (b).

Field, T. M. Infant gaze aversion and heart rate during face-to-face interactions. *Infant Behavior and Development*, 1981, *4*, 307–315.

Fogel, A. Temporal organization in mother–infant face-to-face interaction. In H. R. Schaffer (Ed.), *Studies in mother–infant interaction*. New York: Academic Press, 1977.

Gaensbauer, T. J. Regulation of emotional expression in infants from two contrasting caretaking environments. *Journal of the American Academy of Child Psychiatry*, 1982, *21*, 163–171.

Gaensbauer, T. J., & Mrazek, D. Differences in the patterning of affective expression in infants. *Journal of the American Academy of Child Psychiatry*, 1981, *20*, 673–691.

Gaensbauer, T. J., & Sands, K. Distorted affective communications in abused/neglected infants and their potential impact on caretakers. *Journal of the American Academy of Child Psychiatry,* 1979, *18,* 236–250.

Hiatt, S. W., Campos, J. J., & Emde, R. N. Facial patterning and infant emotional expression: Happiness, surprise and fear. *Child Development,* 1979, *50,* 1020–1035.

Izard, C. E. *Human emotions.* New York: Plenum, 1977.

Kaye, K. Thickening thin data: The maternal role in developing communication and language. In M. Bullowa (Ed.), *Before speech.* London and New York: Cambridge Univ. Press, 1977.

Kistiakovskaia, M. I. Stimuli evoking positive emotions in infants in the first months of life. *Soviet Psychology and Psychiatry,* 1965, *3,* 39–48.

Korner, A. F., & Thoman, E. B. The relative efficacy of contact and vestibular–proprioceptive stimulation in soothing neonates. *Child Development,* 1972, *43,* 443–453.

Lamb, M. E. The development of social expectations in the first year of life. In M. E. Lamb & L. Sherrod (Eds.), *Infant social cognition.* Hillsdale, New Jersey: Erlbaum, 1981. (a)

Lamb, M. E. Developing trust and perceived effectance in infancy. In L. P. Lipsitt (Ed.), *Advances in infancy research* (Vol. 2). Norwood, New Jersey: Ablex, 1981. (b)

Lamb, M. E. On the familial origins of personality and social style. In L. Laosa & I. Siegel (Eds.), *Families—Research and practice* (Vol. 1). *Families as learning environments for children.* New York: Plenum, 1982.

Lamb, M. E., & Easterbrooks, M. A. Individual differences in parental sensitivity: Some thoughts about origins, components, and consequences. In M. E. Lamb & L. Sherrod (Eds.), *Infant social cognition.* Hillsdale, New Jersey: Erlbaum, 1981.

Main, M. *Exploration, play, and cognitive functioning as related to child–mother attachment.* Unpublished doctoral dissertation, Johns Hopkins University, Maryland, 1973.

Main, M. Tomasini, L., & Tolan, W. Differences among mothers of infants judged to differ in security. *Developmental Psychology,* 1979, *15,* 472–473.

Matas, L., Arend, R., & Sroufe, L. A. Continuity of adaptation in the second year: The relationship between quality of attachment and later competence. *Child Development,* 1978, *49,* 547–556.

Murray, A. D. Infant crying as an elicitor of parental behavior: An examination of two models. *Psychological Bulletin,* 1979, *86,* 191–215.

Oster, H. Facial expression and affect development. In M. Lewis & L. Rosenblum (Eds.), *The development of affect.* New York: Plenum, 1978.

Oster, H., & Ekman, P. Facial behavior in child development. In W. A. Collins (Ed.), *Minnesota Symposia on Child Psychology* (Vol. 11). New York: Crowell, 1977.

Owen, M. T., Chase-Lansdale, L., & Lamb, M. E. Mothers' and fathers' attitudes, maternal employment, and the security of infant–parent attachment. Unpublished manuscript, Univ. of Michigan, 1981.

Pastor, D. L. The quality of mother–infant attachment and its relationship to toddler's initial sociability with peers. *Developmental Psychology,* 1981, *17,* 326–335.

Piaget, J. *The origins of intelligence in children.* New York: International Universities Press, 1952. (Originally published, 1936)

Rothbart, M. K., & Derryberry, R. The development of individual differences in temperament. In M. E. Lamb & A. L. Brown (Eds.), *Advances in developmental psychology* (Vol. 1). Hillsdale, New Jersey: Erlbaum, 1981.

Schaffer, H. R., & Emerson, P. E. The development of social attachments in infancy. *Monographs of the Society for Research in Child Development,* 1964, *29* (No. 3, Serial No. 94).

Schoetzau, A., & Papoušek, H. Mütterliches Verhalten bei der Aufnahme von Blickkontakt mit dem Neugeborenen [Mothers' behavior in making eye contact with newborn infants]. *Zeitschrift für Entwicklungspsychologie und Pädagogische Psychologie,* 1977, *9,* 231–239.

Sherrod, L. Issues of cognitive–perceptual development: The special case of social stimuli. In M. E. Lamb & L. Sherrod (Eds.), *Infant social cognition.* Hillsdale, New Jersey: Erlbaum, 1981.

Sroufe, L. A., & Waters, E. Attachment as an organizational construct. *Child Development*, 1977, *48*, 1184–1199.

Sroufe, L. A., & Wunsch, J. P. The development of laughter in the first year of life. *Child Development*, 1972, *43*, 1326–1344.

Stern, D. N. The goal and structure of mother–infant play. *Journal of the American Academy of Child Psychiatry*, 1974, *13*, 402–421.

Stern, D. N. *The first relationship*. Cambridge, Massachusetts: Harvard Univ. Press, 1977.

Stern, D. N., Beebe, B., Jaffe, J., & Bennett, S. L. The infant's stimulus world during social interaction: A study of caregiver behaviours with particular reference to repetition and timing. In H. R. Schaffer (Ed.), *Studies in mother–infant interaction*. New York: Academic Press, 1977.

Thomas, A., Chess, S., Birch, H. G., Hertzig, M. E., & Korn, S. *Behavioral individuality in early childhood*. New York: New York Univ. Press, 1963.

Thompson, R. A., & Lamb, M. E. Security of attachment and stranger sociability in infancy. *Developmental Psychology*, 1983, *19*, in press.

Tolan, W. J., & Tomasini, L. *Mothers of "secure" vs. "insecure" babies differ themselves nine months later*. Paper presented at the biennial meeting of the Society for Research in Child Development, New Orleans, Louisiana, March 1977.

Truby, H., & Lind, J. Cry sounds of the newborn infant. *Acta Paediatrica Scandinavica*, 1965, *163*, 7–59.

Wasz-Hockert, O., Lind, J., Vuorenkoski, V., Partenen, T., & Valanne, E. The infant cry: A spectrographic and auditory analysis. *Clinics in Developmental Medicine* (Rep. No. 29). London: Spastics International Medical Publications, 1968.

Waters, E., Wippman, J., & Sroufe, L. A. Attachment, positive affect, and competence in the peer group: Two studies in construct validation. *Child Development*, 1979, *50*, 821–829.

Wolff, P. The natural history of crying and other vocalizations in early infancy. In B. M. Foss (Ed.), *Determinants of infant behavior IV*. London: Methuen, 1969.

Chapter 5

# AFFECT AND INTELLECT: PIAGET'S CONTRIBUTIONS TO THE STUDY OF INFANT EMOTIONAL DEVELOPMENT

*DANTE CICCHETTI*
*PETRA HESSE*

## ABSTRACT

*Piaget's contribution to a theory of emotional development is discussed in this chapter. Although he has frequently been criticized for neglecting the emotional aspects of children's development, it can be demonstrated that Piaget has contributed substantially to a discussion of infants' and children's emotions. An extensive, descriptive presentation of Piaget's database of infants' emotions is provided here. Based on this descriptive account, a classification of the contexts in which infants' emotional expressions occur in Piaget's work is derived. It is shown how the theoretical language Piaget developed to refer to infants' cognitive development can be inferred based on this classification of their emotions. Furthermore, the implications of this presentation for a theory of emotional development are discussed, and issues such as the conceptualization of the origins and goals of emotional development and the ways in which "change" and the sequences and stages or organizations can be conceived in the emotional domain are addressed. Epiphenomenalism and parallelism are considered as two possible formulations of the relationship between cognitive and emotional development within a Piagetian perspective. Finally, based on some of the methodological and theoretical problems of Piaget's approach, suggestions are*

EMOTION
Theory, Research, and Experience
Volume 2

*made for future theory and research of the interface between cognitive and emotional development.*

This chapter addresses Piaget's implicit and explicit contributions to a theory of the relation between emotional and cognitive development. Previously, we have attempted to provide a justification for studying emotional development, particularly as it relates to other developmental domains such as cognition and language (Cicchetti & Pogge-Hesse, 1981). In this chapter, we would like to discuss Piaget's viewpoint on emotional development.[1] He has often been accused of having shifted developmental psychologists' interests exclusively toward cognitive development. However, as shall be seen in this chapter, Piaget has discussed the emotions extensively, using them to infer cognitive competence.

There is a systematic reason for the implicitness of the emotions in Piaget's work. Whereas theorizing about intellectual development appears to be "self-reflexive," at least in the sense that it is expressible in cognitive–linguistic terms, the emotions can be discussed and conceptualized only in cognitive or cognitive–linguistic rather than emotional terms. Hence, the cross-mapping between the cognitive and emotional domains is intrinsic to research and theory on emotional development. Consequently, the problems associated with cross-mapping cannot be avoided in the study of emotions. For example, it is very hard—if not impossible—to control the changes in ·meaning that emotional phenomena may undergo when being interpreted in terms of cognition/language. These changes may lead to differences in meaning between a merely felt and nonverbally expressed emotion and its cognitive representation; or they may just involve losses in information in the process of interpreting cognitively the nonverbally expressed and felt emotion. Thus, the cognitive interpretation may not represent the emotion in its entire complexity, and it may therefore lead again to changes in meaning.

It may be suggested that Piaget is in some respects the most advanced theorist of emotional development because he addresses all of the issues that are relevant with respect to a developmental theory of the emotions and its integration within a general theory of development (see Cicchetti & Pogge-Hesse, 1981). Piaget's observations of his own three children, Jaqueline, Laurent, and Lucienne, presented in his three books on infant development (Piaget, 1952, 1954a, 1962a), provide a rich description of the emotions that exist at different points of infants' development and of the types of situations in which these emotions emerge. Moreover, Piaget deals with the question of the sequences and stages characteris-

---

[1]This chapter will focus exclusively on Piaget's contribution to a theory of emotional development. Consequently, we mention the work of other investigators only when its parallels with the Piagetian framework are absolutely striking.

tic of emotional development. As far as the integration of different domains of development is concerned, Piaget provides the only existing, even though speculative, attempt at specifying the relationships among cognition, emotion, and morality (Piaget, 1962b, 1972). Piaget assumes parallelism to be characteristic of the relationship between cognition and emotion and considers morality, or at least one specific aspect of morality, the will, to be a later stage of emotional development (Piaget, 1954b, 1962b; Piaget & Inhelder, 1969).

In order to achieve the goals of this chapter, we shall proceed in the following manner. Drawing from Piaget's three books on sensorimotor development, *The Origins of Intelligence in Children* (1952), *The Construction of Reality in the Child* (1954a), and *Play, Dreams and Imitation in Childhood* (1962a), we shall present the "data" on the relationship between emotional and cognitive development, gleaned from the descriptions of Piaget's three children. On the basis of these observations, we shall provide a classification of the emotions mentioned by Piaget as well as the contexts in which they emerge during the course of infant development. Moreover, we shall discuss some of the issues that a developmental theory of the emotions must address. Guided in part by Piaget's observations, we will suggest some possible conceptualizations for the stages and structures of emotional development, the type of sequence characteristic of emotional development, the transitions between different stages of the emotions, and the relationships among the various developmental domains.

Piaget's theoretical position with respect to emotional development is derived from several sources in which Piaget has more or less explicitly outlined a theory of emotional development (see, for example, Piaget 1954b, 1962b, 1967, 1973; Piaget & Inhelder, 1969). In this regard, our focus is on Piaget's attempts to sketch the sequence and the stages of emotional development and on his formulation of the relationship between cognitive and emotional development. In a final section we outline some perspectives for future work on the interface between cognition and emotion within a Piagetian framework.

## PROBLEMS WITH PIAGET'S "DATA" ON EMOTIONAL DEVELOPMENT

Piaget's presentation of infants' emotions is biased. Since he is chiefly interested in the infant's development of cognitive categories, he mentions emotions almost exclusively in cognitive contexts. Thus, the more "social" emotions such as love, affection, shame, guilt, and embarrassment do not appear in Piaget's work on infancy. Therefore, the view of infant emotional development suggested by Piaget's work should be considered to underrepresent the complexity of the infant's emotional repertoire and its development across the first 2 years of life.

Kagan (1978) suggests that psychological events, and thus their definition, should incorporate at least some of the following components: (a) an overt action; (b) a change in feeling state; (c) cognitive representations of past, present, or future events; (d) an incentive event; (e) a historical or genetic component; (f) a physiological component; (g) a context (social as well as nonsocial) (p. 14). Because Piaget's primary focus is cognition, he mentions emotions mostly in the context of describing cognitive events and never attempts strict definitions of emotional states. Nor does Piaget provide us with descriptions of the physiological aspect of observable behavior. Furthermore, he is seldom detailed in his account of the other dimensions that Kagan and other psychologists (for example, Sroufe, 1977, 1979a; Sroufe, Waters, & Matas, 1974) consider to be necessary components of each psychological event.

Usually, Piaget provides some description of the overt action, change in feeling state, representation of past, present, or future time perspective, incentive event, and contextual determinants of the infants' response. Frequently, however, he reports only the most salient features of the infant's behavior, their context, and their prior history. Consequently, we do not know exactly how Piaget's infants express the same emotions at different points in their development. Neither do we know how the incentive events change with time, nor what the infant's different cognitive representations of the same event may be. A given incentive event might elicit the same or different emotions at different points in development. Or, different incentive events could conceivably elicit identical emotional expressions at the same or different points of development. Since Piaget rarely presents trial-by-trial data, and since he changes the stimuli and contexts he presents to his children, it is impossible to trace the ontogenesis of his infants' reactions to one and the same context.

This methodological limitation may be relatively unproblematic as long as Piaget discusses the emotional behaviors of crying, smiling, and laughter, but it is a far more serious objection when applied to his inferred emotional categories. For example, how does Piaget distinguish among astonishment, surprise, and amazement; amusement, delight, and joy; anger and rage; and fear, fright, and anxiety? Given the methodological shortcomings in the data, it seems pointless to distinguish between such close emotional concepts. Rather, we think that they should be considered as equivalent, because the results of our research on people's labeling of emotion-displaying photos and definition of emotional concepts indicate that people use the mentioned labels interchangeably (Hesse, unpublished manuscript).

Piaget does not base his inference of cognitive competence exclusively on his infants' emotional behaviors. For example, he frequently uses additional sensorimotor activities such as search behaviors to draw conclusions about his children's cognitive capabilities. To the extent that these other sensorimotor skills and symbolic capacities become increasingly clear and differentiated with development, Piaget no longer needs to rely as much on emotion to infer cognitive competence. Hence, there is a decrease in reported emotional behaviors in Piaget's observations of the second year of life, but this implies no more than that infants' emotions are no longer the major source of information on which Piaget bases his inference of infants' cognitive capacities.

Thus, there are gaps in Piaget's description of his infants' emotional behaviors and the contexts in which these occur. However, Izard's (1971, 1977) and Ekman's (1972) work on the universality and reliable identification of a set of basic emotions permit us to weaken some of our objections to the lack of detail in Piaget's observations. Adults' high reliability in labeling many emotions (especially fear, anger, surprise, happiness, sadness, and disgust) enables us to assume that at least a large percentage of Piaget's descriptions of emotional behaviors and his inferred emotional categories are likely to be used by other observers as well. Although his work on infancy does not enable us to give an exhaustive account of the developmental changes in emotional expressions and their contexts, Piaget's observations do provide us with very rich information about the *kinds* of emotions that tend to occur in the context of cognitive development in the first 2 years of life.

Furthermore, Piaget's longitudinal database is still among the most extensive available, at least in terms of its descriptive richness. Thus, although his work may not satisfy our conventional standards for detail, control of independent and dependent variables, and reliability, it at least allows us to form impressions about the ontogenesis of the kinds of emotions characterizing infancy and of the types of contexts eliciting them. Thus, despite its methodological limitations, we believe that Piaget's database provides a meaningful source for a reconstruction of infant emotional development.

## PIAGET'S DATABASE ON
## INFANT EMOTIONAL DEVELOPMENT

In order to present Piaget's data on infants' emotions in a manner as undistorted by our interpretations as possible, we developed a table that provides an exhaustive chronological summary of all of the emotional behaviors and inferred emotions characteristic of Piaget's six stages of sensorimotor development.[2]

[2]Due to space limitations, we have not included the table in this chapter. Interested readers may write us for a copy. We are currently working on a monograph that will provide more detailed information about the stimuli that elicit emotions at different developmental periods and about Piaget's descriptions of emotional behaviors and inferred emotions from infancy throughout adolescence. An analysis of Piaget's works for their emotional content provides the data-base for this monograph. In addition, this monograph will integrate Piaget's theoretical and empirical contributions on emotional development with those of the post-Piagetian researchers.

After a close examination of this database, and with the post-Piagetian research and theoretical perspectives in mind, we felt that four broad categories best captured the observational data contained in Piaget's books (see Table 5.1). We decided that a systematization of the situations that elicit emotions in Piaget's children in terms of *proprioceptive–kinesthetic reaction, recognition of similarity, competence,* and *recognition of discrepancy* would be the most accurate classification scheme.

*Competence* and *recognition of discrepancy* are the most plausible categories in view of Piaget's frequent descriptions of his infants' emotional reactions to their own accomplishments with and without objects (*competence*) and to unfamiliar objects, actions and events (*discrepancy*). Moreover, these two categories have been widely addressed by post-Piagetian approaches to infant development in terms of *competence motivation* (Goldberg, 1977; Harter, 1977; Shultz & Zigler, 1970; Watson, 1972; White, 1959), and the *discrepancy hypothesis,* respectively (Kagan, 1971; McCall & McGhee, 1977).

*Proprioceptive–kinesthetic reactions* refer to cases in which the infants display emotions in a reflex-like manner; that is, without apparent mediation of cognitive processes (Cicchetti & Sroufe, 1976, 1978; Darwin, 1872; Sroufe & Wunsch, 1972). As we will illustrate in our discussion of such reactions, the older and more cognitively sophisticated the infant becomes, the harder it is to decide whether cognitive factors are involved in the infants' emotional reactions.

*Recognition of similarity* refers to the infants' emotional reactions upon identification of physical objects, people, events, and so on, as similar to objects, people, and events encountered at an earlier occasion in their development. We think that this category is necessary in our discussion of Piaget's work because of its longitudinal nature. Since his observations cover the entire span of infant development, Piaget can identify situations as familiar or known to the infants.

## THE RELATION BETWEEN EMOTION AND COGNITION DURING THE SENSORIMOTOR PERIOD

In this section, we discuss the sequence of emotional development in its relation to cognitive development during infancy under the four categories presented in Table 5.1: proprioceptive–kinesthetic reaction, recognition of similarity, competence, and recognition of discrepancy.[3]

[3]Due to space constraints, we were unable to include our complete description of all of Piaget's examples. Consequently, we can provide only summaries of each emotional category for each of the six sensorimotor substages. We ask the reader to pay careful attention to Table 1 when noting our summary statements. Interested readers may obtain the original full-length description of each category by writing to the authors.

## PROPRIOCEPTIVE–KINESTHETIC REACTIONS

The proprioceptive–kinesthetic reactions category of emotional responses differs from other Piagetian affective reactions in the following respects. First, some of the stimuli seem to bring about the emotional responses directly. That is, there does not appear to be any mediation via cognitive interpretations, as exemplified by the case of an infant who begins to laugh as it leans its head backward. Second, other stimulus conditions eliciting these emotional reactions are internal to the organism, as in the case of the crying response to hunger. These are especially crucial to the infants' development of physiological homeostatic regulation—a task generally considered to be the first developmental issue an infant and its caregiver must resolve (Sander, 1962; Sroufe, 1979a, 1979b). Third, in some situations, the external stimuli eliciting the emotional responses possess certain intrinsic properties that bring about either positive affect, as in the case of high-pitched voices and certain soft noises (such as *pa, bzz, pff,* and so on); or may cause negative affect, as in the case of loud noises (such as *BOOM, BOOM, BOOM* sounds) or stimuli resulting in a loss of balance (Butterworth & Cicchetti, 1978; Cicchetti & Sroufe, 1976; Sroufe & Wunsch, 1972; Wolff, 1963) in the infant. Finally, perhaps the chief characteristic of these proprioceptive–kinesthetic emotions is that at least some of them do not develop; that is, they are not expressed phenotypically differently at different ages, and they are expressed in the same stimulus conditions. Thus, most of the responses to proprioceptive—kinesthetic stimuli (for example, being kissed on the stomach; tickling) do not seem to habituate. That is, the sequence of development of these responses essentially consists of a compilation or summation of responses to an increasingly broad array of stimuli because new stimulus conditions are added but no old ones are dropped. However, there is some indication that these proprioceptive–kinesthetic reactions can become related to more complex cognitive capacities of the infant. An example of a proprioceptive–kinesthetic emotion undergoing such a transformation is provided by the case of an infant crying with hunger upon hearing its mother's bed creaking in the morning.

To summarize the examples of proprioceptive–kinesthetic reactions provided in Table 5.1, during the first 3 months, the infant primarily reacts emotionally to physiological states of disequilibrium and to certain intrinsic properties of stimuli. We do not think it is necessary to interpolate a cognitive interpretation between the emotion-eliciting situation and the emotional reaction in any of the examples Piaget has provided. The only exception may be the infant's cries of hunger when in the mother's arms, since by this age the infant knows (that is, has formed a representation of) the mother as a food source.

Between 4 and 7 months, the infant still displays proprioceptive–kinesthetic emotional reactions to states of physiological distress (for example, hunger) and to various intrinsic properties of stimuli (for example, sounds, degree of intru-

# TABLE 5.1

## Classification of the Contexts in Which Piaget Uses Emotions to Infer Cognitive Competence in Infancy

| Infant's age in months | Stage of sensorimotor development | Proprioceptive–kinesthetic reaction | Recognition of similarity | Competence | Recognition of discrepancy |
|---|---|---|---|---|---|
| | | | _Classification of situations, and the emotional characteristics of them at different levels of development_ | | |
| 0–3 | I reflexes<br>II primary circular reactions | 0,1 crying when hungry, when other infants cry<br>1 smiling when hearing voices and *pa* and *bzz* sounds<br>1 excitement when sucking (expressed by panting)<br>2 joy when throwing head back repeatedly<br>2 laughter when leaning head back<br>2 anger when hunger becomes persistent<br>2 desire when hungry<br>3 crying when hungry and in mother's arms | 1 satisfaction when infant localizes father (even if immobile)<br>1,2 smiling when others imitate infant's sounds<br>2 laughter when recognizing father who is uncombed | 1 smiling accompanying own production of sounds<br>1 contentment when playing with tongue<br>1 satisfaction when playing with tongue, lip<br>1–3 smiling about imitations of Piaget's *tatata* sounds; about own hand movements with and without objects; when successfully grasping for familiar objects and causing crib roof to move<br>2 (function) pleasure when touching own body (nose, hands); and about play with own voice<br>3 laughter when successfully causing noisy objects to move<br>3 joy about own hand movements and their increasing coordination<br>3 interest in playing with own voice<br>3 pleasure about looking at moving toys, but no connection made between infant's movement and spectacle seen<br>3 laughter when playing with own voice<br>3 delight when shaking chain which affects movement of toys | 0,1 crying when losing nipple or finger out of mouth<br>1 rage when feeding is interrupted<br>1 anger when infant loses its thumb out of mouth; or is prevented by bandage from sucking thumb<br>1 interest in sounds leading to an attempt at localizing<br>1–3 curiosity about unusual movements of objects<br>1–3 surprise about new sounds and new objects<br>2 fright when failing to recognize uncombed father<br>2 excitement when watching mosquito net<br>2,3 interest in various objects, persons, actions, movements of objects and own hands<br>2,3 astonishment when causing dolls on crib-roof and rattle to move<br>3 fear of neighbor<br>3 anxiety when infant confronted with new objects it would like to grasp<br>3 joy about own hand movements |
| 4–7 | III secondary circular reactions | 4 crying when hungry and in mother's arms<br>4 fear when producing a sudden noise<br>7 smiling when father makes or causes | 4 rage when napkin is put under infant's chin indicating upcoming medication<br>4,6 smiling when Piaget imitates infant's | 4 excitement when movement of foot causes movement of doll on crib-roof<br>4–7 laughter when own actions bring about effects in people or objects or own imitations meet standards of adequacy<br>4,7 pleasure when making noise with rattle; | 4 surprise about moving letter opener with string (means–end relation)<br>4 fright about unknown objects & too loud noise<br>4 disappointment about father's disappearance from a place he was expected to be in |

122

| | | | | |
|---|---|---|---|---|
| 8-11 | IV coordination of secondary schemata | sounds (*ba*, finger snapping, shaking rattle)<br>7 laughter in reaction to father's production of new sounds (some involving intrusive interactions)<br>7,8 crying when hungry and hearing the mother's bed creaking or the mother's entering of the room<br>8 laughter when being tickled<br>9 laughter when father says *cou-cou* into infant's ear<br>10 amusement when pressing gums against each other<br>10-12 laughter when being tickled | thumb movements and vocalizations<br>4,6,7 smiling when recognizing father in various situations<br>5 interest when father imitates tongue protrusion<br>6 delight about exchange of reciprocal imitations with mother<br>6 smiling when father imitates the infant's vocalizations of the day before<br>6,7 laughter when recognizing father<br>7 pleasure when mother opens her mouth together with the infant during feeding<br>8 desire to make father imitate coughing<br>8-11 laughter in various contexts in which Piaget imitates the infants or causes dolls on crib-roof to move as done previously<br>9 smiling about Piaget's imitation of tongue protrusion and *baba* sounds; when realizing that mirror image displays the same movements as the infant<br>10 delight when father | when accurately imitating parents' vocalizations<br>4-8 joy, about own motor capacities<br>6 contentment about successful turning of matchbox<br>6 delight when feet reach doll and kick it<br>6,7 amusement about new effects caused by own hand movements with and without objects<br>7 crying when failing to get hold of bottle<br>7 laughter when finding hidden father<br>8 pleasure when establishing link between own arching up and movement of crib-roof<br>8 smiling when bouncing up and down and trying to get father to open and close the crib-roof<br>8 crying when not hungry and bib is put around neck<br>8 anxiety when own actions fail to bring about movement of bottle<br>8 contentment when bouncing up and down is regularly followed by father's moving of a saucer<br>8,9,11 laughter about successful handling of means—end relations<br>8,10 disappointment when realizing that own arching up does not cause father's moving of a saucer | 4 desire to get objects to suck on them<br>4 interest when stick strikes toy unexpectedly<br>4,5,7 astonishment when encountering new objects, hidden objects, new effects and displaced objects<br>5,6 anger when infant fails to get hold of objects that are too far away<br>6 curiosity when father is hiding objects<br>6,7 crying when infant fails to get hold of its bottle<br>6,7 interest in new effects, distant and partially covered objects<br>7 desire when father does not snap fingers anymore<br>7 disappointment when losing box out of hand<br>8 fear when Piaget, unseen, causes crib-roof to move; when Piaget moves bell although infant is holding it<br>8 amusement when putting finger into mouth making noise<br>8,9 desire for new objects (e.g., moon at evening)<br>8,9 curiosity when Piaget creates interesting effects; about partially covered objects; when encountering new objects<br>8,9 laughter when playing peek-a-boo-like games<br>8,9,10 interest when Piaget opens his mouth without making sounds<br>8,10 disappointment about objects out of sight; about A-not B error<br>9 anxiety when noise is too loud (when infant is decreasing then increasing noise of rattle); |

(continued)

TABLE 5.1—*Continued*

Classification of the Contexts in Which Piaget Uses Emotions to Infer Cognitive Competence in Infancy

Classification of situations, and the emotional characteristics of them at different levels of development

| Infant's age in months | Stage of sensorimotor development | Proprioceptive–kinesthetic reaction | Recognition of similarity | competence | Recognition of discrepancy |
|---|---|---|---|---|---|
| | | | imitates tongue protrusion | 8,10 pleasure about production of new sounds (snapping of index finger; blowing, breathing noisily) | when father is pulling watch from infant's hands |
| | | | 11 interest when Piaget, imitating the infant, sticks his finger into his ear | 9 pleasure about lifting itself up, repeating action several times | 9 laughter when father hides objects |
| | | | | 9 smiling when playing tug, pulling forcefully on watch chain | 9 anger at Piaget when he has hidden a doll |
| | | | | 9 laughter when imitating father successfully | 9,11 crying in contexts of separation from persons, objects |
| | | | | 9,10 interest in own hand movements | 9,12 astonishment about empty hands after dropping something; about a partially covered doll |
| | | | | 9,10 amusement about effecting spatial displacements of objects | 10 laughter when father makes his lower lip shake with his finger |
| | | | | 11 resentment when not searching thoroughly enough for an object displaced by father | 11 interest in new locations of objects |
| | | | | | 12 amazement when seeing father's face in the mirror |
| | | | | | 12 delight as father opens and closes match box |
| | | | | | 12 surprise when recognizing the spatial relations of objects (e.g., two ends of a cane) |
| 12–18 | V tertiary circular reactions | 13 fear when scratch is disinfected with alcohol | 12 smiling when Piaget makes a doll cry (behind his back) | 12 satisfaction after having reproduced father's movement of window with foot | 13–16,18 interest in new objects, unexpected effects, movements of objects with respect to one another |
| | | 13 crying when seeing the alcohol bottle with | 13 satisfaction when infant realizes move- | 13,14,16 pleasure about producing familiar actions in modified contexts | 15,16,18 surprise when failing to take into account the spatial relations of objects with respect to |
| | | | | 13,15,18 laughter about finding objects under various | |

124

which the wound has been treated
13 laughter when father rubs thighs

ment in its carriage (father's foot is pushing wheel)
14 satisfaction when playing tug with necktie ("game" has been played on previous occasions)
15,16 smiling when recognizing Piaget in garden; when imitating own call of two days earlier
15–18 laughter in various contexts of symbolic activity
16 laughter when infant imitates child's temper tantrum of previous day
18 laughter when Piaget imitates infant's crying

conditions of spatial displacement
14,15 delight about comprehension of means–end relations and other spatial relations of objects
15 satisfaction when succeeding in imitating father's touching of his forehead
15,18 amusement about finding objects in or putting them into various objects or places
16 desire when hitting flask to draw it closer
16 anger when unsuccessful at making a long series of blocks stand

one another; about the spatial relations of objects; and about strange behaviors in other people
15,18 astonishment when failing to take into account the spatial relations of objects with respect to one another; about unexpected displacements of objects and people

VI invention of new means through mental combination
19–24

19 saying *cry,cry* to dog, imitating the sound of crying
20 delight when putting shell on table, saying *sitting*
21–22 laughter when pretending to be Piaget and to see a seagull fly

19 pleasure about drinking out of empty glasses
24 laughter when opening window, yelling *hi boy* at boy in garden

20 laughter about creating an unexpected effect
21 smiling about unexpected movements of Piaget's legs that are covered with a blanket

sion). Thus, we see that the emotional reactions to some situations persist, whereas emotional reactions to new situations emerge. The fact that the infant's crying when hungry is displayed in increasingly more distant and cognitively complex situations may indicate a tendency for earlier emotional reactions to become hierarchically integrated into more complex cognitive interpretations of the emotion-eliciting situation. Cicchetti and Sroufe (1978) and Emde and Harmon (1972) discuss examples of the advantages of viewing emotional reactions as evolving systems that specify the relationships between early subcortical reactions (crying, blinking, endogenous smiling) and later psychological reactions (fear, exogenous smiling).

Between 8 months and 1 year, the proprioceptive–kinesthetic emotional reactions again occur in response to physiological states (for example, vestibular stimulation) and to the different intrinsic properties of the stimuli presented to the babies (sounds). Since Piaget did not present the same set of stimuli consistently to his infants from the very first day of life, it is impossible to determine to which stimuli the infants tend to react emotionally from birth and to which they only reacted later. Thus, it is not clear whether the infants would have laughed much earlier at being tickled or at their father making popping sounds with his lips. For example, Sroufe and Wunsch's (1972) work on the development of laughter in normal infants demonstrates that babies laugh to these stumulus events between 4 and 7 months.

The situations in which proprioceptive–kinesthetic reactions are elicited between 12 and 18 months of age do not presuppose many new capacities on the infant's part. The occasion on which laughter is elicited in the infant seems to be intrinsically enjoyable—that is, it does not require anything outside or prior to the situation to explain why the infant finds the situation pleasurable. The crying response to the alcohol bottle is comparable to the situations in the first year as soon as the mother entered the room. Both of these situations require only recognition memory of an event at Time 1 $(T_1)$ and the recognition of a similarity between another event at Time 2 $(T_2)$ and the event at $T_1$ that reminds the infant of a certain emotional quality of the event at $T_1$ and elicits a similar emotional reaction at $T_2$. We have included the infant's crying reaction upon seeing the alcohol bottle again as an example of a response reflecting or related to the proprioceptive–kinesthetic category because the infant cries upon remembering its own proprioceptive–kinesthetic reaction.

Between 18 and 24 months, we could not find any clear cases of proprioceptive–kinesthetic reactions. This may be due to the fact that it becomes increasingly difficult to find proprioceptive–kinesthetic reactions that are not embedded in more salient contexts of social interaction, competence, recognition of similarity or discrepancy. This trend does not necessarily reflect a genuine development on the infant's part away from proprioceptive–kinesthetic reactions toward reactions characterized by increasing cognitive complexity. Rather, it may merely be the consequence of Piaget's cognitive focus. To the extent that Piaget is interested in inferring infants' cognitive competence, emotional reactions in proprioceptive–kinesthetic contexts may be of only secondary importance to him, since they offer little insight into the cognitive complexities of the developing organism.

## RECOGNITION OF SIMILARITY

Another context in which infants display emotional reactions is in situations requiring the recognition of similarity. The identification of similarity calls for the existence of certain cognitive functions that are necessary in order to perceive two instances as alike. Like the case of recognition of discrepancy, it requires the following processing capabilities on the part of the infant:

1. The encoding of information acquired at $T_1$.
2. A cognitive interpretation of situation $T_2$.
3. The comparison between situations $T_1$ and $T_2$.
4. The recognition or judgment that $T_1$ and $T_2$ are alike.

Summarizing the examples of *recognition of similarity* during the first 3 months provided in Table 5.1, the infants' smiles indicate that they recognize the objects with which they are confronted as familiar, whereas they react indifferently or with fear when meeting strangers (unknown woman, uncombed father). Thus, smiling at this early age expresses a certain amount of recognition memory for objects (people) other than the child. Furthermore, the infant seems to require increasingly fewer nonvisual clues in order to recognize familiar people.

Laughter appears to be elicited in more highly arousing situations. The infant's failure to recognize its father must be fairly stressful and thereby quite arousing, hence leading to laughter as soon as the cognitive "imbalance" is resolved (see Sroufe & Waters, 1976, for an elaboration of this interpretation). Furthermore, this example casts some light on the infant's cognitive limitations. At this point in development, the infant needs certain facial clues in order to recognize people. Height, posture, and other characteristics of peoples' bodies do not seem to be sufficient to recognize them.

Between 4 and 7 months, the infants' emotional reactions indicate the infant's increased memory capacity. The infant is definitely able to remember events that happened a day earlier, as in the case of the *bva* and *bve* sounds, and it is obviously capable of remembering people on the basis of their visual characteristics and various sounds. Furthermore, the infant's memory capacity consists of more than just recognition, as indicated by the rage reaction when a towel is put under the infant's chin. This situation shows that the infant is increasingly in a position to reconstruct prior events on the basis of a few clues (or *indices,* as Piaget calls them), rather than needing the complete situation in order to recognize the similarity.

Moreover, the infants' emotional reactions indicate their ability to recognize a similarity between actions and sounds produced by others and their own behavior. This capacity is more complex than the one displayed during the prior period because it is more difficult to be aware of one's own behaviors, others' behaviors *and* a similarity between them, than to just recognize similarities between the various behaviors displayed by others.

The infants' emotions in the context of recognition of similarity do not only express cognitive changes during this period but also undergo changes themselves. Piaget no longer talks about infants' emotional behaviors only in terms of smiling, laughing and crying but also in terms of rage, interest, delight, and pleasure. Although he does not explicitly introduce the behavioral distinctions on the basis of which he infers the new emotions, his use of an increased repertoire of emotions suggests a differentiation of the emotional domain as well.

Between 8 months and 1 year, the infants' cries provide another example of an affective scheme—this time in the context of recognition of similarity. The infant seems to remember prior occasions on which the mother left after putting on her hat. The negative affect suggests that the scheme to which the infant has assimilated this experience is negatively toned ("this is one of those and I don't like it") (cf. Cicchetti & Sroufe, 1978).

The infants' smiling and laughter responses during this period indicate that they can recognize the similarity between their own sound productions and movements and their father's and can recognize the reflections of their own movements in the mirror. It is not clear, though, to what extent the infants are aware of the similarity between their own and their father's behaviors and the reflections of the mirror. Do they realize that their father is doing exactly what they are doing, or do they just perceive a similarity in the dimension of expressions—for example, that the father produces sounds in return to their production of sounds? It is not clear on which basis laughter and smiling reactions can be distinguished. The laughter-eliciting stimuli do not seem to differ from the smiling-eliciting stimuli as far as their intensity is concerned. It may be that they are more unfamiliar than the smiling stimuli, and thus that laughter expresses the reaction to novelty whereas smiling to already known stimuli expresses a certain degree of habituation to the stimuli. One indication that the latter interpretation is true can be found in the fact that one of the infants laughs when Piaget imitates its tongue protrusion at 8;14[4] but smiles in similar situations at 9;2. One of the girls' display of interest at 11;8 in reaction to Piaget's imitation of her sticking her

---

[4]This notation refers to 8 months, 14 days. A similar logic should be applied elsewhere in the text.

finger into her ear further buttresses this interpretation. It suggests the following possible sequence of reactions to one and the same set of stimuli: Interest at 11;8 when the infant's recognition of similarity between its own actions and somebody else's imitations of these actions occurs for the first time or is a recent discovery; laughter at 11;25 when the infant's recognition of such a similarity between its own and somebody else's actions has become well established; and smiling as soon as the infant becomes habituated to and thus less interested in recognizing this similarity. Sroufe and Waters (1976) also offer a compatible interpretation for this kind of behavior.

Two further cognitive accomplishments may be inferred on the basis of the infant's emotional reactions: First, the infant's smiling response to its own mirror image at 12;10 may be considered if not an indication of the complete development of the infant's self-awareness, at least as a precursor to it (see Lewis & Brooks-Gunn, 1979). Since it is impossible to infer on the basis of Piaget's interpretation whether the infant only detects the similarity between its own movements and the movements of the mirror image or whether it actually realizes that the movements of the mirror image are *its* movements, it is equally impossible to decide to what extent the infant has developed its self-awareness. Second, the infant's laughter at 12;0 in anticipation of its falling backward in the crib may be taken as an indication of its capacity to *predict* the outcome of its actions on the basis of its memory of prior outcomes of a similar situation. Thus, this situation indicates that the infant is not only capable of remembering previous events but also of predicting future events. Research conducted by Sroufe and Wunsch (1972) and by Cicchetti and Sroufe (1976, 1978) with normal and Down syndrome infants likewise found an increase in anticipatory laughter and smiling during this period.

The smiling responses between 12 and 18 months of age signal an increase in the infant's memory capacity, in its concept of object permanence, and in its self-imitation. The infant's smiling in response to recognizing its father in the garden indicates that it is capable of recognizing Piaget in different places, and thus has a context-independent object concept (at least of its father). The infant's smiling upon imitation of its own call indicates that it can remember events that happened 2 days earlier and that it is capable not only of recognition but also of recall memory. In order to repeat its own call of 2 days earlier, the infant has to be capable of actively retrieving the characteristics of its previous call. Furthermore, the fact that the infant is capable of self-imitation suggests that it has a conception of its own vocal and other productions, if not as *its* own, at least as another aspect of its environment.

The infant's laughter responses during this period express that it is capable of detecting abstract as well as concrete similarities. Whereas prior to this age the infant could recognize similarities only between concrete events at $T_1$ and their fairly exact replications at $T_2$, it is now capable of abstracting dimensions from concrete events and of recognizing similarities between dimensions instead of the concrete replicas of events. Even during this period, there seems to be a trend toward increasing abstraction. The instance of pretend sleep at 15;12 still expresses a fair amount of reliance on concrete similarities, whereas the instances of pretend behavior at 18 months are indicative of a fairly abstract notion of movement (spoon rocking) and of the properties of a doll's body (wrapping doll's dress around the arm).

The laughter reaction to Piaget's imitation of one of his daughter's cry-sounds is interesting because it may not only indicate the infant's capacity to recognize the father's response as similar to her own but also a conception on the infant's part of the appropriateness of the father's sounds. On the basis of this example, it is impossible to infer such a sophisticated person perception and precursors of reactions to humor on the infant's part. Nonetheless, this is an interpretation that is worth pursuing.

The infant's expression of satisfaction at 13;4 may indicate a certain progression in its conception of causality because it clearly establishes a link between a cause (the father's foot moving its carriage) and an effect (the movement of the carriage).

The infant's smiling and laughter responses between 19 and 24 months are not indicative of any new cognitive accomplishments. The laughter responses express the infant's symbolic capacities. However, the examples mentioned require only more primitive symbolic representations than the ones discussed during the 12–18-month period. The imitation of the father's looks presupposes only a concrete representation of his hairstyle abstracted from the rest of his facial and other characteristics. The example of the sea gull requires only a concrete conception of a sea gull and its activities as a bird and the realization that part of what a sea gull is like is missing in the picture in order to elicit the infant's addition of the missing aspect (flying). The only example that is somewhat more abstract is the one in which the infant refers to the shell's lying on the table as *sitting*. This instance requires a greater amount of abstraction from the usual context of sitting, namely, the replacement of a person as the agent of sitting by the object (shell).

COMPETENCE

In order for the infant to show function pleasure or pleasure about being the cause of something, it has to be able to do one or more of the following:

1. The infant must be actively engaged in an activity.
2. It must have a feeling of control over its own body.
3. In some cases, it must even perceive a relationship between its own actions and some results of these actions external to its own body.

4. The infant must compare the results of its actions to its internalized standards for a successful action. Depending on whether these standards are met or not, the infant will display positive or negative emotional reactions.

As can be seen from our descriptions in Table 5.1 of emotional behaviors in the context of competence, during the first 3 months, the infants' emotional reactions reflect two trends. As far as the infants' motor development is concerned, the emotional responses express an increasing sensorimotor coordination. As to the infants' cognitive development, the emotional reactions reflect the increasing capacity to establish causal relationships between the infant's own actions and the environment. Thus, the infants smile, are content, and display pleasure during their second and third months of life about their own vocalizations and their tongue and hand movements. To the extent that the infants display a tendency to react emotionally first to mouth movements, then to hand and coordinated hand movements, their emotional reactions can be said to reflect their motor development.

By the end of the third and the beginning of the fourth month of life, the infants start to smile in situations in which they do not just display motor reactions but also handle objects. Increasingly during the fourth month, the infants smile and laugh in situations in which they cause effects on objects in their environment. Smile- and laughter-eliciting situations can be distinguished on the basis of the familiarity of the stimulus, the vigor of the effect, and the kinesthetic pleasure brought about by the effect. The more familiar an object the infant is handling, the more likely it is that it will elicit smiles rather than laughter. The more vigorous the effect on an object and the stronger the kinesthetic pleasure derived from it, the more likely it is that the infant will laugh about its accomplishment.

It is important to note that one cannot yet attribute a complete concept of causality to the infant because, in the situations Piaget describes, the infants' actions causing the effects in objects cannot be separated from the objects. That is, no inference can be made as to whether the infants are aware that *their* actions *cause* the effects in the objects or whether they only conceive of the effects as pleasurable aspects of their actions.

Not much seems to be new about the situations in which emotional reactions are elicited between 4 and 7 months of age. The infants display joy over an increasingly larger number of their own behavioral capacities and their effects. The most interesting of the reported situations seems to be Laurent's laughter reaction at 4;18, when he tries to get (cause) his father to move his feet, and the laughter reactions at 7;17 to the successful imitation of sounds or actions produced by the parents. The instance during the fifth month is interesting, because the infant seems to believe that its own actions can cause its father to cause its feet to move. However, to the extent that the infant's own movements may just be an expression of general excitement, it is not clear whether such a complex thought process—involving the memory of the father's previous actions and a prediction of the father's future actions independent of the infant's own behaviors—can be attributed to the infant.

The infants' laughter and pleasure reactions when successfully imitating their parents are revealing because they suggest that the infants can match their own and their parents' actions with respect to a standard of perfection. In case of success in meeting the standard, the infants will display laughter or pleasure. In case of failure, they will display negative emotional reactions—that is, crying, as exemplified in the situation at 7;0 and 7;4, when the infant tries to get hold of the right side of its bottle (the standard or goal) but does not succeed.

During the 8–12-month period, the infants' emotional behaviors indicate advances in the development of the object concept, spatial relations, and causality. The infants obviously have a fairly well-established conception of the permanence of objects, as demonstrated by anticipatory smiling during the search for the father behind the chair, which presupposes the ability to represent objects out of sight. Furthermore, the infant's reaction of resentment at 11;30 when failing to find an object at place B indicates that the infant somehow knows that the object should be under B. However, more salient during this period is the infant's acquisition of means–end relations, as exemplified in various contexts by the infant's capacity to pull on strings in order to get hold of objects. In this connection Laurent's anxiety at 8;8 when he realizes that he has established the wrong means–end relationship between his pulling on a string and his father's moving of a bottle is very interesting. Other emotional reactions (for example, the infant's amusement at 9 and 10 months) express the infant's general pleasure during this period in exploring objects and their relations in space.

In this regard, it is interesting to note the correlation between the grasp of means–end relations and the development of a first clear distinction between cause and effect as far as causality is concerned. Thus, the infants' arching up—which has been regularly followed by the father's moving of a saucer—in order to get the father to move the saucer or to open and close the roof of the crib, express the infants' awareness of the distinction between cause and effect. However, at times, the infant seems to confuse "social" and "physical" causation as exemplified by the wrong inference that the pulling of a string is causing the movement of a bottle in front of the crib. As far as causality is concerned, the infants' emotional reactions do not indicate so much the infants' cognitive awareness of the distinction between cause and effect but rather their sense of accomplishment about actually bringing about effects in the environment.

Laughter reactions seem to be distinguished from less-intense positive emotional reactions on the basis of the infants' active involvement in the production of interesting effects in the environment. All the laughter-eliciting situations share the fact that the infants' own actions produce interesting spectacles in the environment.

Between 12 and 18 months, emotional behaviors are again an expression of the infants' cognitive advances. In the first half of the second year, the infants show progress in their development of the object concept, spatial relations, and imitation, which in turn are also related to their development of memory. For example, the infant's smile at 18;17 when imitating its own call of 2 days earlier reflects that it has a recall memory of at least 2 days.

In the context of the development of object permanence, the infants' laughter reactions indicate their awareness of the fact that objects can be found in different places. Necessarily involved in this notion of the permanence of objects over multiple displacements is the infant's advanced understanding of spatial relations. Objects can be on, in, and under other objects; one can put objects into other objects, and can take them out again. One can use one object as a means to handle another object as an end, and one may have to change the position of one object with respect to another in order to be able to put it or pull it into the other.

As far as the development of imitation is concerned, the infants' amusement at 18;17 when imitating animal voices seems to indicate an awareness on the infant's part that its own imitations can meet certain standards of adequacy set by the animals' sound productions. Alternatively, however, the infant may just find imitating animal voices to be a very pleasurable activity. That is, perhaps the degree to which an infant meets its own standards of accuracy are much less important than assumed by our first interpretation. The instance at 15;30 indicates that the infant has become increasingly capable of imitating actions that involve parts of its body that it cannot see (such as its own forehead).

The infants' pleasure in producing all sorts of slightly modified actions with or without effects on objects reflects a capacity that is essential to all symbolic productions to the extent that the latter presuppose the transformation of an action to an unusual context. It is therefore not surprising that the infants' first symbolic productions can be found during this period.

Between 18 and 24 months, the pleasure displayed by the infant in contexts of pretend behavior is indicative of fairly concrete symbolic behavior. That is, the infant's symbolic behavior does not change very much of the situation to which it is referring. The instance at 24 months is harder to interpret. It may mean that the infant enjoys its new capacity to greet people, but it may also have to do with something else that is not immediately obvious from the context Piaget presents.


## RECOGNITION OF DISCREPANCY

The emotional reactions displayed in contexts of discrepant stimulation all require that the following conditions be met:

1. The encoding of information acquired at $T_1$
2. A cognitive interpretation of situation $T_2$

3. The comparison between situations $T_1$ and $T_2$
4. The awareness that $T_1$ and $T_2$ are different
5. Depending on the complexity of the infant's cognitive structure, the information acquired at $T_2$ can be interpreted as moderately or highly discrepant from $T_1$. Moderately discrepant events tend to lead to positive emotional reactions; highly discrepant ones to negative ones (see, for example, McCall & McGhee, 1977).

As can be seen in Table 5.1, during the first 3 months the infants' emotional reactions in contexts of discrepancy express a cognitive development from the mere awareness of the negation of an ongoing activity (due to, for example, the loss of an object), to the infants' capacity to process the novelty of unfamiliar objects as discrepant. Whereas the former awareness requires only the matching of the representation of an activity or event at $T_1$ and its nonexistence or negation at $T_2$ (losing the nipple, a finger, and so on), the latter presupposes the representation of an activity, object, or event at $T_1$, $T_2$ and the comparison between the two with respect to a standard of similarity or identity.

Depending on how discrepant the stimuli are that the infant is confronted with at $T_2$, it will express either negative or positive emotional reactions. Sometimes the negative reactions will be transformed into positive ones if the infant manages to assimilate an initially highly discrepant event fairly easily. Thus, the infant laughs when finally recognizing the uncombed father, and it displays curiosity at a rattle after its first percussion has caused a fear reaction. Changes in emotional behaviors in the other direction (that is, from positive to negative), are possible as well, as in the case of the infant's reaction of astonishment to the noise of a rattle, which is replaced by uneasiness when the noise becomes louder and louder.

During the 4–7 month period, the infants' emotional reactions indicate their level of cognitive development as far as their concepts of object permanence, causality, and spatial relations are concerned. The infants' object concept is only partially developed, as indicated by the fact that the infant stops crying at 6;19 when the bottle disappears under the table and is curious, but does not display any signs of recognition, when Piaget has caused a pencil to disappear behind a screen at 6;17. However, some representation of objects seems to be present already at 4;26 when the infant reacts with disappointment to the father's disappearing from a place where it had expected him to be.

The concept of causality is not very advanced either, as expressed by the infant's surprise at 4;3 when it caused a letter opener to move with the aid of a string. The infant's concept of causality still seems to be restricted to the relationship between its own actions of hitting and bouncing up and down when it tries to get the father to continue his finger-snapping. However, by this time, the infant seems to have at least some notion of means–end and cause–effect relations, as expressed by its expectation of causing its father to snap his fingers by hitting a pillow.

The infant's spatial relations seem to be lacking an exact estimation of distance, as expressed by the infant's interest in grasping for distant objects at 6;23.

The period from 8 months to 1 year is rich with emotional behaviors that indicate changes in cognitive development (see also Emde, Gaensbauer, & Harmon, 1976; Sroufe, 1979a). As far as the development of object permanence is concerned, the infants show for the first time some form of separation anxiety when the mother is leaving or trying to leave the room. Furthermore, they are interested in objects of which they can see parts sticking out from under a diaper, and they are disappointed when committing the A-not-B error that indicates that they definitely expect the object to appear under A. Several interpretations of these findings are possible. The A-not-B error and the emerging separation anxiety can be considered as expressions of the infants' capacity to attribute some permanence to objects, but not across more than one spatial displacement. However, the infant's interest in partially covered objects cannot be accounted for by this interpretation, because it seems to be symptomatic for even an earlier level of object permanence, during which objects completely out of sight are also out of mind. One could argue either that infants can be at different levels of object permanence at the same time or that the infants are still interested in partially covered objects for other than solely cognitive reasons. Perhaps they reenact behaviors of previous levels of object permanence in a playful fashion.

As to the development of spatial relations, the infants' interest expresses a concern for the movements of objects. One of the important discoveries the infant makes while exploring the trajectories and other spatial properties of objects is that objects disappear from one place (for example, the father's hand) and appear in another one. This may be an important or perhaps necessary discovery for the development of object permanence across spatial displacements. Furthermore, the infants' estimates of distance tend to be wrong in the case of distant objects. The infants' expression of disappointment in contexts in which they reach for objects that are too far away indicates their awareness of the discrepancy between their expectation and the result of their (grasping) action.

The infants' notions of causality are questioned as well during this period. The infants have to realize that their arching up in the crib and pulling on strings are not the immediate causes of the (father's) moving of the saucer and bottle in front of the crib. These new discoveries may coerce the infant in the long run to become aware of the distinction between its own actions and their effects versus other people's actions (or the movements of objects) and their effects.

The infants' reactions to their own and their father's mirror image are of interest. As we have noted, infants' reactions to their own mirror image may indicate precursors of their self-awareness. The situation in which the father's image appears in the mirror is extremely interesting. Although the infant may not have a clear image of itself, it definitely recognizes the father as its father when seeing him in the mirror because the father's mirror image does not differ at all from his appearance in other contexts. Thus, the discovery that image and father are the same may even facilitate the infant's identification of itself and its mirror image.

Between 12 and 18 months, the infant's emotions reflect the increasing awareness that objects can move, act, and entertain relationships independent of the infant. Thus, the infant is interested in the movements objects make with respect to one another. Furthermore, the infant finds out about the more complicated relationships between objects (in particular their extension in space) when trying to pull sticks and toys into the playpen. Finally, the infant learns about strange behaviors in other people (for example, tantrums) and has to realize that known situations, events, or states of people—although they have been going on for a while—do not have to last forever. That is, the infant finds out about the hazards of induction at a very early age (for example, Lucienne when expecting to find Jaqueline sick in bed).

Between 18 and 24 months, the infant *laughs*—at 20;30 when a pencil gets stuck vertically in the hole of an ivory plate—and *smiles*—at 21;28 when putting its head on the father's knees that are covered with a blanket as the father moves his knees; in other words, their emotional reactions do not reflect any changes in their cognitive development.

## PIAGET'S CONCEPTUAL FRAMEWORK, AS INFERRED FROM INFANTS' EMOTIONAL REACTIONS[5]

In this section, using Piaget's own terminology, we will elaborate on the cognitive capacities we inferred from our analysis of infants' emotional reactions (see Table 5.2 for a summary of the cognitive abilities that we have inferred from infants' emotional behaviors and expressions).

To the extent that they become linked to infants' cognitive capabilities, *proprioceptive–kinesthetic* reactions are indicative of the infants' underlying recognitory assimilation capacities—that is, their ability to recognize objects, events, and so on, by comparing them with prior developed schemata. Furthermore, these reactions enable us to infer which kinds of schemata the infants have developed (for example, a schema of the mother as food source or a schema of an alcohol bottle as causing pain). Moreover, the infants seem to have partial, or subschemata, that enable them to recognize objects or events by virtue of encountering parts of them.

---

[5]To avoid redundancy the reader is referred back to Table 1 for detailed illustrations of our claims in this section.

The infants' emotional reactions in the context of recognition of similarity permit us to derive Piaget's concepts of secondary and tertiary circular reactions, generalizing and reproductive assimilation, as well as recognitory assimilation. Infants are capable of secondary circular reactions to the extent that they can recognize objects (as indicated by their smiling reactions at 4, 6, and 7 months when recognizing their father) and events external to them as similar (revealed by their expression of interest when their father imitates their tongue protrusion). Furthermore, the infants' humor reactions, and primarily their symbolic activities, express what Piaget has called *tertiary circular reactions,* since both of these activities presuppose the capacity to reinterpret the function of objects or to perceive new relationships between objects and their respective environments. The latter capacity also requires *generalizing assimilation*—the ability to assimilate new objects, contexts, or properties of objects to already available schemata.

Furthermore, the development of infants' imitative capacities can be traced on the basis of their reactions to similar actions, objects, and events. Piaget (1962a) claims that infants display the first sporadic imitations during the second substage of sensorimotor development. Only during the third substage do infants start to imitate sounds and movements that are already in their repertoire. Our account of infants' cognitive competence based on their emotional behaviors confirms Piaget's claims with respect to the periods between 4 and 7 months of life as well as 8–11 months. During the latter period, Piaget claims that infants become capable of imitating new visual models and nonvisible actions that are already in their repertoire.

The infants' competence in expressing emotions can also be interpreted in terms of Piaget's concept of circular reaction. In contexts of competence, not only can secondary and tertiary circular reactions but also primary circular reactions be inferred, insofar as infants react emotionally (for example with smiling, contentment, satisfaction, etc.) to exercising their own physical capacities without the use of external objects during the first 3 months of life. Secondary circular reactions can be inferred as soon as the infants become aware of the more remote effects of their own actions that presuppose a distinction between their own actions and the external environment (as revealed by their reactions of contentment, excitement, and pleasure about causing objects to make noises and movements, and so on, between 4 and 7 months of age. Tertiary circular reactions are required when the infants produce slightly modified effects on objects and demonstrate object permanence across several spatial displacements of objects. The coordination of secondary schemata (the fourth substage of sensorimotor development) enables infants to utilize means in order to obtain certain ends.

Furthermore, the infants' emotional behaviors that are displayed in contexts of competence enable us to infer the terminology Piaget has elaborated with respect to infants' development of play and their concepts of causality and time. The six sensorimotor substages of play are derivable from infants' emotional behaviors in contexts of competence. The first two substages, the exercise of reflexes and

TABLE 5.2

Infant's Cognitive Competence Inferred on the Basis of Their Emotional Behaviors

| Infant's age in months | Stage of sensorimotor development (including its cognitive characteristics) | Cognitive competence inferred from emotion(s) | | | |
|---|---|---|---|---|---|
| | | Proprioceptive–kinesthetic reaction | Recognition of similarity | Competence | Recognition of discrepancy |
| 0–3 | I reflexes<br>II primary circular reactions | beginning of object concept: representation of mother as food source | recognition memory: recognition of familiar versus unfamiliar people; facial clues necessary for recognition of people | awareness of exercise of own capacities: vocalizations, tongue; and hand movements, hand coordination<br>conception of effects brought about by the infant's actions on the environment; however, no clear distinctions made between own actions and their effects distinctions can be made between the degree of vigor of the effects | awareness of the negation, and nonexistence of objects or events |

138

| | | | | |
|---|---|---|---|---|
| 4–7 | III secondary circular reactions | representation (memory) of mother and her activities in various situations that are related to the provision of food | increased memory capacity: recognition of events that occurred 1 day earlier, and of sounds; partial development of recall memory first establishment of awareness of correspondences or similarities between own and others' behaviors | increasing awareness of remote effects of own actions standards of perfection developed with respect to the infant's own imitations | partial development of the object concept (out of sight still sometimes out of mind) partial development of means–end relations concept of causality still restricted to infant's own actions of hitting and bouncing lack of correct estimate of distance |
| 8–11 | IV coordination of secondary schemata | generalization of capacity to detect correspondences between own and others' behaviors emergence of the infant's self-concept beginning capacity to predict events that will take place in the near future | well established object permanence establishment of means–end relations between own actions on objects and the latters' effects on third objects no clear distinction between social and physical causation attempts to control own emotional behaviors | concept of object permanence developed, however, not across spatial displacements awareness of discrepancy between own expectations and actual events in case of the A-not-B error arising awareness of spatial displacements arising notion of different distances growing awareness of the difference between self and other as center of causality |

*(continued)*

TABLE 5.2—Continued

|  | | Cognitive competence inferred from emotion(s) | | |
| Stage of sensorimotor development (including its cognitive characteristics) | Proprioceptive–kinesthetic reaction | Recognition of similarity | Competence | Recognition of discrepancy |
| --- | --- | --- | --- | --- |
| Infant's age in months | | | | |
| 12–18   V tertiary circular reactions | evidence for recall memory: recognition of an event on the basis of its partial replication | increase in memory capacity: context-independent capacity to recognize people; recall memory for events that occurred 2 days earlier ability to detect abstract similarities, and to use them in the context of symbolic activities precursors of humor precursors of the role concept | concept of object permanence across several spatial displacements developed ability to produce slightly modified effects on objects with or without the help of third objects | awareness that objects can move and influence one another independent of the infant awareness of spatial relationships of objects with respect to one another |
| 19–24   VI invention of new means through mental combinations | | | awareness of new symbolic capacity to name objects/people and emotional behaviors | |

function pleasure, seem to be characteristic of the emotional reactions to competence in the first 3 months. *Pleasure to be the cause of something,* Piaget's
(1962a) third substage of sensorimotor play, adequately describes the contexts of
competence between the fourth and seventh months of life. During this period,
the infants distinguish more and more between their own actions and their external effects. That is, they become increasingly aware that they are the cause of
something outside of themselves. Piaget's fourth sensorimotor substage of play,
the *ritualization of schemata,* is due to the generalization of familiar schemata to
new situations. This substage of play is correlated with the utilization of the
possible means–ends relations of objects. As soon as means–ends relations are
repeated on the basis of the process of reproductive assimilation, and thus used
competently, they can be called *play.* The ritualization can be conceived as a
subordinated aspect of means–ends relations. Tertiary circular reactions allow
for the first time the playful new combination of familiar schemata and thus
enable the infant to produce new effects and to use means—end relations between
objects freely. Thus, the infants' emotional behaviors displayed in contexts of
competence reflect the changes in their play behavior.

   As to the development of causality, during the first two substages of sensorimotor development infants do not appear to be capable of distinguishing
between their own actions and their effects on the environment. That is, they do
not differentiate between the internal and external environment. The infants'
emotional reactions during the third substage permit us to infer what Piaget
(1954a) has called *magico-phenomenalistic* causality. In this substage, infants
attempt to bring about effects external to them by means of a set of action
schemata available to them that are not necessarily appropriate causes of the
desired effects. To the extent that infants become increasingly aware of the
inadequacy of some of their own action schemata in bringing about effects in the
environment (as inferred, for example, by their reactions of disappointment), one
can conclude that what Piaget has called *externalization and objectification of
causality* is taking place. During the fifth substage of sensorimotor development,
the infants' increasing reaction to the distinction between physical and social
causation and to their new ability to produce modified effects on objects with or
without the help of third objects, enable us to infer further objectification and
specialization of the infants' concept of causality.

   The development of the infants' concept of time is positively correlated with
the development of their conceptions of causality. Infants capable only of magico-phenomenalistic causality cannot have more than a very subjective sense of
time, centered on their own actions (what Piaget [1954a] called a *subjective
series*). To the degree to which infants externalize and objectify their concept of
causality, they also objectify their concept of time (*objective series*) in the sense
that they become increasingly capable of perceiving temporal relationships between objects and events external to or even independent of their own actions.

Infants' emotional reactions in the context of recognition of discrepancy, besides enabling us to infer most of Piaget's basic terminology (for example, the various types of assimilation and of circular reactions), also permits us to infer the steps that Piaget has assumed with respect to the infants' development of the concepts of object permanence, space and, to some extent, causality.

As to the concept of object permanence, between 4 and 7 months of age, the infants' emotional reactions (for example surprise, astonishment, and disappointment) to the disappearance of objects indicate the beginning of object permanence. Between 8 months and 1 year, the infants' emotional behaviors (for example, interest, curiosity, and desire) reflect that infants actively search for hidden objects although they do not yet have a notion of object permanence across several spatial displacements of objects. According to Piaget, it is not before the fifth substage of sensorimotor development that the infants' emotions allow for an inference of a concept of object permanence across several spatial displacements.

According to Piaget, the infants' concept of space is highly correlated with the development of the concept of object permanence. Every single step in the development of object permanence also presupposes an advancement as far as the infants' concept of space is concerned. Piaget (1954a) conceives of spatial development in terms of changes in infants' concept of a group that is "the expression of the processes of identification and reversibility which pertain to the fundamental phenomena of intellectual assimilation [p. 100]." Thus, so-called practical groups characterize the first two substages of sensorimotor development, allowing the infant to reverse its own actions. To the extent that the infant's space is centered on its own activities, the object concept cannot be developed very much. That is, Piaget believes that during these first two substages, objects are at most the extensions of the infant's actions rather than independent entities. During the third substage of sensorimotor development, infants develop what Piaget calls *subjective groups*. Even though infants' conceptions of space are still largely centered on their own activities, the concept of subjective groups allows for the integration of object-related, reversible activities in the child's repertoire. Concomitant with this advancement in the concept of space are corresponding developments in the concepts of object permanence and causality, the latter being restricted to the infant's activities as causes of effects (magico-phenomenalistic causality). The transition from subjective to objective groups, the latter being characterized by simple reversible operations that are no longer centered on the infant's activities, enable the infant to conceive of spatial relations of objects independent of its own actions for the first time. The development of active search for vanished objects would not be possible without this advance in the infant's concept of space. However, it is only with the complete development of objective groups in the fifth substage of sensorimotor development that the infant becomes capable of conserving objects as identical across several spatial displacements.

Similar to the changes in the three other categories, the infants' emotional reactions to the encounter of discrepant events and objects reflect some of the cognitive developments postulated by Piaget for the period of children's sensorimotor development (see Table 5.2). Thus, once again, infant's emotions can be demonstrated to be a window through which one can infer cognitive competence.

## THE CONTRIBUTION OF PIAGET'S DATA TO A DEVELOPMENTAL THEORY OF THE EMOTIONS

In this section, we discuss some of the implications that Piaget's database has for a theory of emotional development. Historically, a number of issues have been addressed in theoretical discussions of the concept of development and in the formulation of tasks that an integrative developmental theory must solve (Feldman & Toulmin, 1975; Flavell, 1971, 1972; Kessen, 1971). The most salient topics that have been raised are: the specification of the innate characteristics of development; the determination of the goal-state of development; and the description and explanation of periods of transition between initial and final developmental states. Moreover, attempts have been made to outline the types of sequences and the organization or structures of the various developmental domains.

## ORIGINS, CHANGES, AND GOALS OF EMOTIONAL DEVELOPMENT

According to Piaget's descriptions of the emotions present during the substages of sensorimotor development, it appears that virtually all emotions and emotional expressions are present at birth. Thus, Piaget's work on infant cognitive development lends at least some indirect support to the post-Piagetian claim that the majority of the emotional expressions are innate (Ekman & Oster, 1979; Izard, 1977, 1978, 1979; Oster & Ekman, 1978). Accordingly, one might ask whether it even makes sense to talk about emotional *development*.

Similarly, we must account for the goal-state of development. If all emotional expressions are present at birth, then is the final state of emotional development identical to its origins? If not, how do they differ from each other? Likewise, we think that the best way of addressing the issue of the transition from the initial- to the end-state of emotional development is to discuss the sequences characteristic of emotional ontogenesis. If we can specify the affective changes that take place throughout the process of development, then we also possess a reasonably clear conception of the origin and the goal-state of emotional development.

Since we were not able to detect any emotions or emotional expressions in Piaget's work that were characteristic of specific substages of infants' cognitive development, our task is to specify in which respects infants' emotions and emotional expressions stay the same and in what ways they change during the course of the sensorimotor period. First we shall discuss the ways in which Piaget's database suggests that infant emotions and emotional expressions remain the same.

## Type of Emotion

Although Table 5.3 suggests that the majority of the emotional expressions are innate, it is impossible to decide which emotions are present at birth and which develop or emerge. Piaget did not record his observations from the day of birth of his infants; however, virtually all the emotions and emotional behaviors listed in Table 5.1 are either present at birth or develop during the first month of life. Thus, with few exceptions (see our earlier discussions on disappointment, pretend anger, and pretend crying), the types of emotions characteristic of the different levels of sensorimotor development do not seem to change. Accordingly, Piaget's account of infant emotions, based exclusively on the discrete types of emotions that appear, suggests that there is no such thing as emotional development.

## Phenotypical Expression of the Emotions

Since Piaget almost never reports on changes in the expression of a given emotion nor on phenotypic differences between infants' and adults' emotions, it appears likely that phenotypic expressions of infants' emotions do not undergo transformations at all. If infants' emotional expressions were radically different from adults', then one would expect that Piaget would have mentioned the critical differences. However, to the extent that Piaget's primary focus is on cognitive development, it is conceivable that he may have overlooked subtle changes and differences between infant and adult emotional expression. Piaget's behavioral observations do suggest that he at least noticed some changes in the expression of emotions. For example, he claims that at approximately 6 weeks, infants' crying becomes more differentiated. However, due to the unsystematic nature of his observations, it is impossible to decide whether it is only the infants' crying that becomes more differentiated with development or whether other emotional expressions undergo similar differentiations that Piaget neglected to mention.

## Function of the Emotions

Based on our knowledge of the post-Piagetian literature on affective development, we think that our categorization of infants' emotional behaviors in terms of their various functions (that is, proprioceptive–kinesthetic, similarity, competence, and discrepancy—see Table 5.2) is a valid and fairly exhaustive description of infants' emotions throughout the sensorimotor period. That is, it appears that the functions that the emotions fulfill during the first 2 years of life remain constant. The only additional function that becomes more salient in the course of infancy is what we would call the *social function* of infants' emotions. As such, the older the infant, the more difficult it is to decide, for example, whether its smiling in reaction to the father's shaking of the dolls on the crib-roof is indicative of recognition of the similarity between this instance and earlier instances of the same event or, rather, whether the infant is responding to the social element of this interaction and its smiling is reflective of the increasing social function of emotion with development. Nonetheless, we decided to consider the social function of the emotions as secondary within Piaget's framework of cognitive development, largely because we felt that the infants' social reactions could be further subdivided into one of the four other categories of our classification system.[6]

A further change that occurs consists in the intercoordination of the various functions of the emotions. In other words, even though the functions of the emotions appear to remain constant, throughout the first 2 years of life it is progressively more difficult to distinguish among situations of competence, recognition of discrepancy, and so on. We think that this is the case precisely because the situations in which infants express their emotions become increasingly complex; hence, since these situations involve elements of a variety of emotional functions (that is, competence, recognition of similarity, discrepancy, and proprioceptive–kinesthetic reactions), it is more difficult to assign priority to a given function. This is consistent with a basic proposition of organismic-developmental theory (Werner, 1948); namely, that a given behavior can serve multiple functions or have multiple meanings. Now, we will present the ways in which Piaget's data suggests that there are clear developments in infant emotional ontogenesis.

[6]For a more detailed account of the social function of emotions, the reader should consult Campos and Stenberg (1981), Ekman and Oster (1979), Emde (1980), Izard (1977), Sroufe (1979a) and Stern (1977).

TABLE 5.3

Developmental Sequence of Emotional Behaviors and Inferred Emotions

| Infant's age in months | Stage of sensorimotor development | Proprioceptive–kinesthetic reaction | | Recognition of similarity | | Competence | | Recognition of discrepancy | |
|---|---|---|---|---|---|---|---|---|---|
| | | Reported for the first time | Reported as continuing to be displayed | Reported for the first time | Reported as continuing to be displayed | Reported for the first time | Reported as continuing to be displayed | Reported for the first time | Reported as continuing to be displayed |
| 0–3 | I reflexes II primary circular reactions | crying, 0(1) excitement, 1(1) smiling, 1(2) desire, 2(15) anger, 2(15) joy, 2(20) laughter, 2(21) | crying smiling laughter | smiling, 1(22) satisfaction, 1(22) laughter, 2(26) | | contentment, 1(5) satisfaction, 1(6) smiling, 1(30) interest, 2(. . .) (function) pleasure, 2(17) laughter, 3(0) joy, 3(13) delight, 3(14) | | crying, 0(12) anger, 1(2) curiosity, 1(7) interest, 1(8) surprise, 1(8) rage, 1(15) astonishment, 2(17) excitement, 2(18) fright, 2(26) anxiety, 3(7) fear, 3(7) joy, 3(13) | |
| 4–7 | III secondary circular reactions | fear, 4(15) | crying smiling laughter | rage, 4(12) interest, 5(9) delight, 6(25) pleasure, 7(1) | smiling laughter | excitement, 4(27) amusement, 6(1) crying, 7(0) | contentment pleasure laughter joy | desire, 4(10) disappointment, 4(26) | crying anger curiosity surprise |

| | | | | | | | | |
|---|---|---|---|---|---|---|---|---|
| | | | | | | | | interest<br>astonishment<br>fright<br>anxiety |
| 8–11 | IV coordination of secondary schemata | amusement, 10(12) | laughter | desire, 8(10) | smiling<br>laughter<br>delight<br>interest | anxiety, 8(8)<br>resentment, 11(30) | contentment<br>pleasure<br>laughter<br>smiling<br>crying<br>amusement | amusement, 8(14)<br>smiling, 9(27)<br>laughter, 10(7) | crying<br>anger<br>curiosity<br>surprise<br>interest<br>astonishment<br>fear<br>desire<br>disappointment |
| 12–18 | V tertiary circular reactions | | crying<br>laughter<br>fear | pretend crying, 18(30) | smiling<br>laughter | desire, 16(0)<br>anger, 16(0) | smiling<br>pleasure<br>laughter<br>amusement<br>delight<br>satisfaction | delight, 12(10) | surprise<br>interest<br>astonishment<br>laughter<br>anger |
| 19–24 | VI invention of new means through mental combinations | | | | smiling<br>laughter<br>delight | | pleasure<br>laughter | | smiling<br>laughter |

## Situational Changes

As can be gleaned from Table 5.1 and the additional sections describing Piaget's database, over the course of the first 2 years of life, infants' emotional reactions tend to occur in the context of more and more spatially distant and increasingly complex and abstract situations (see also Sroufe & Wunsch, 1972). For example, whereas during the first 3 months most of the infants' emotional expressions are related to activities and functions centered about their bodies (for example, hunger, vocalizations, movements, and so on), with development they occur more often to spatially distant stimuli (for example, father's thumb, spatial displacements of objects, and so on), complex social interactions (for example, reciprocal imitations), and cognitively abstract or symbolic contexts (for example, pretend sleep, use of own arm as a baby doll, and so on). Viewed another way, an examination of the changes in the situations in which infants' emotions occur reveals a trend that coincides with Piaget's descriptions of infancy in terms of primary, secondary, and tertiary circular reactions. In the early months, infants are centered on activities involving their own bodies (primary circular reactions). At around 3 months of age, the infants react to more distant stimuli and become capable of interactions with objects and persons (secondary circular reactions). At approximately 13–15 months, infants begin to extend their capacities to new, more abstract contexts (a necessary requirement for tertiary circular reactions).

## Cognitive and Motor Changes

Concomitant with the situational changes in infants' expressions of emotions, there occur parallel changes in the motor and cognitive domains. For example, the infants' more sophisticated motor capacities may contribute to their more frequent emotional reactions to distal stimuli. Likewise, their growing memory capacities and cognitive complexity allow for the processing of more abstract or symbolic information. Furthermore, over the course of the sensorimotor period, some interesting trends are revealed within the various categories of infants' emotions. For example, the emotions expressing infants' competence or competence motivation become increasingly negative in the course of infant development. This may be due to the fact that the infants become increasingly aware of obstacles hindering their activities, of the limitations on their control over the environment, and of their inability to meet their own internalized standards of mastery. For instance, as soon as the infants are capable of secondary circular reactions, they must realize that some objects are out of reach or are beyond their control. In contrast, the emotions that indicate infants' recognition of discrepancy become more positive in the course of infancy. This may be due to the fact that infants get to know their environment better and thus consider it to be more familiar and less discrepant. Moreover, due to their general motor and cognitive advancements, the infants' coping skills improve. That is, they learn how to avoid dangerous objects (for example, by crawling away) or they figure out how to solve difficult situations because they have encountered similar situations in the past and have been taught how to deal with them.

## Increasing Approximation of Adult Meanings of the Various Emotions

We assume that adults would more or less universally agree with the definitions we proposed for each of the four categories in our classificatory scheme. We would like to propose that the emotional reactions expressed by infants, if considered in terms of our classification system, gradually approximate the meaning adults tend to give to them. That is, if we go back, for example, to competence, we defined it in terms of the infant's (a) active engagement in an activity; (b) feeling of control; (c) awareness of the relationship between its own actions and some external effect; and (d) comparison of the results of its actions and its internalized standards. If we look at the examples of infants' competence provided in Table 5.1, we can see that points (a) through (d) of our definition of competence reflect the order in which infants tend to acquire them. That is, directly after birth infants show emotional behaviors expressing competence only in reaction to activities of their own bodies. A feeling of control is probably already inherent in those activities. At around 3 months of age, infants become capable of establishing a relationship between their own activities and external objects. In other words, only at this age do they become *competent* to handle and to recognize external objects. Not until the infants have developed internalized schemata or standards as to *how* to manipulate objects (which requires a great deal of practice with objects), do they express positive or negative emotions when meeting or failing to meet these standards.

This recapitulation of the definition of competence in terms of the infant's ontogenesis indicates that infants acquire behaviors and knowledge meeting our adult definitions of competence over the course of infancy. At the same time, this recapitulation provides us with a nice demonstration of the hierarchical organization of infant's capacities. Whereas at birth infants display only activities related to their body, they become increasingly capable of expressing all the other more complex aspects of our definition of competence as well as activities of their own bodies. In other words, the early features of infants' competence are hierarchically conserved in their later competence-related activities.

In the case of emotional reactions in the context of recognition of similarity and discrepancy, comparable developments are found. Infants become increasingly capable of recall rather than recognition memory of events. This suggests that, whereas initially infants are only capable of comparing two virtually identical events ($T_1$ and $T_1'$) that really do not require a judgment of their similarity or discrepancy but rather a "perceptual" or subcortical comparison, with development they learn to relate more clearly distinct events ($T_1$ and $T_2$), to compare them remembering both simultaneously, and to *judge* them rather than to *perceive* them as similar or discrepant (a case of cortical processing). Bronson's (1974) work on the development of the two visual systems and on the hierarchical organization of the central nervous system (Bronson, 1965) provides a possible explanatory neurophysiological framework for this phenomenon.

Here again we note that the infants gradually meet the adult requirement for the judgment of similarity and of discrepancy. Once more, their development provides an example of hierarchical integration because perception and recognition are still significant aspects of the basis of these judgments at later points in time. It is only in the case of the proprioceptive–kinesthetic emotional reactions that infants seem to move away from rather than to meet more fully the adult meaning of the category. This appears to occur primarily because these proprioceptive–kinesthetic reactions, though somewhat reflex-like, become linked to cognitive interpretations throughout the course of infants' development.

## Sequences of Emotional Development

Flavell (1972) has delineated five possible conceptualizations of the sequence characteristic of cognitive development that we feel may be extended to other domains as well: *Addition, Substitution, Modification, Mediation,* and *Inclusion.* Flavell (1972) posits an Addition sequence to refer to an accumulation of behaviors in the course of development, with early and later emerging behaviors coexisting throughout ontogenesis. A Substitution model is used to describe cases in which later emerging behaviors replace earlier ones. The Modification sequence describes behaviors occurring in early infancy that undergo developmental transformations to behaviors characteristic of a later point in development. Mediation is very similar to Modification because both postulate that early developing behaviors undergo transformations leading to the emergence of new behaviors and organizations of behavior. Contrary to Modification, however, a Mediation sequence is conceptualized as involving transformations that are only necessary but not sufficient for the emergence of new behaviors. Additional factors are required to make the transition to new, more articulated and integrated levels of organization sufficient. An Inclusion sequence suggests the possibility that earlier and later emerging behaviors become progressively coordinated into larger wholes, with the earlier behaviors becoming elements of the later-developing organizations.

When viewed in light of Flavell's model, it is evident that Piaget's portrayal of emotional development in infancy does not follow an Addition or Substitution sequence. Most of the emotions Piaget describes are present at birth and throughout the first 2 years of life. Thus, to the extent that neither new emotions nor emotional expressions emerge nor old ones disappear during infancy, the Addition and Substitution sequences are not applicable. However, if future research shows that various emotional behaviors and inferred emotions as such do undergo phenotypical changes, the Addition and Substitution sequences will have to be reconsidered.

The only possibility of conceiving of emotional development in terms of an Addition sequence is given by the changes in the *contexts* in which emotions tend to be displayed in the course of the first 2 years. To the degree to which the infants' emotional behaviors become generalized to more contexts, one could conceive of emotional development in terms of an Addition of contexts. However, this does not reveal anything with respect to the development of emotional expression as such.

Modification and Mediation sequences as characteristic of emotional development cannot be addressed on the basis of Piaget's data for the same reasons. Unless we find out more about possible changes in the phenotypical expression of the emotions or potentially emerging emotions in the course of infancy overlooked or not cited by Piaget, it will be impossible to argue for either of these sequences because they require some form of phenotypic transformation as the characteristic mechanism of emotional development.

On the other hand, an Inclusion sequence seems to describe Piaget's data on emotional development best, largely because Piaget is concerned with emotions only in cognitive contexts. That is, proprioceptive–kinesthetic reactions become increasingly embedded in complex cognitive contexts, and competence and recognition of similarity and discrepancy, as we argued before, seem to be hierarchically organized as well. The early characteristics of competence and of recognition of similarity and discrepancy are increasingly organized into larger behavioral units and conserved in them over the course of infancy. The increasing complexity of the infants' activities is a threefold one: The infants show improvements in social and physical object-related perspective-taking; the contexts in which emotions are displayed become more complex; and the infants become more capable of actively rearranging objects and contexts on the basis of abstract features as in the course of their symbolic activities. However, until more research is done on changes in emotional expressions per se, including blends of emotions that may characterize transitions in the development of emotional expression, we cannot make any further distinctions among the five possible types of sequences as possible descriptions of emotional development.

Future work will show how emotional development takes place: whether it is characterized by phenotypical changes in emotional expression as well as by corresponding changes in cognitive and motor development and in the types of situations that elicit emotions at different points in time during infancy. In addition, all of these changes could follow the same or different kinds of sequences of development. Thus, the development of emotional expressions could follow a Mediation sequence, cognitive development an Inclusion sequence, and motor development a Substitution sequence. It would be interesting to see whether the different domains of development are distinguishable in terms of the type of sequence they follow. Such differences in type of developmental sequence could provide us with a valuable tool in defining the differential characteristics of the various domains of development.

Moreover, we could specify whether we are talking about emotional development in terms of its concomitant cognitive changes (as we did earlier, when suggesting an Inclusion sequence as characteristic of emotional development) or in terms of its expressive or behavioral changes per se. Such a clarification would probably solve some of the problems arising in comparisons of different theories or models of infant emotional development because some psychologists talk about the sequence of emotional development in terms of cognitive changes (for example, Sroufe, 1979a) whereas others do so in terms of changes in emotional expression (Izard, 1978, 1979; Zajonc, 1980).

Furthermore, when we look at development beyond infancy, our perspective may change. Different types of sequences of emotional, cognitive, or motor development may be characteristic of different periods of children's development. Thus, for example, the development of emotional expressions could follow a Modification sequence during infancy, an Addition sequence during early childhood, and an Inclusion sequence during later childhood. Similarly, the types of changes characteristic of cognitive development and other developmental domains could undergo changes in the course of childhood.

Perhaps we have not found many obvious nonverbal expressive emotional developments in Piaget's work on infancy because they occur only at the transition from infancy to early childhood and at the transition from early to later childhood. Thus, it is conceivable that it may be useless to look for changes in emotional development *during* infancy or *during* early childhood because emotional changes signal the transition from infancy to early childhood as such. Therefore, we may have to address the issue of the type of sequence of emotional development by looking not only at the expressive and cognitive changes *during* a period of development, but also by relating the kinds of emotions that are characteristic of different periods of development (for example, shame, guilt, feelings of justice, and so on). Such an approach would be more complete and closer to that adopted by Piaget (1972), Kohlberg (1969, 1971), and Flavell (1971, 1972). These psychologists have addressed the issue of the sequence of development with respect to the relationship between whole levels or stages of development rather than solely with regard to changes within those stages.

## Organization of Emotional Development

The consideration of the organization and structure of infants' emotions is important for two reasons. First, in Piaget's cognitive-developmental or structuralist tradition of developmental psychology, the question of the organization of development has played an important role. It is the behavioral organizations characterizing children's performance at different points of their development that have been used to distinguish between the various levels or stages of children's development. Therefore, it would be interesting to see whether emotional development as such can be described in terms of organizations comparable to the ones characteristic of cognitive (Piaget, 1971), moral (Kohlberg, 1971), and social–cognitive development (Selman, 1980). Second, since no new discrete emotions or emotional behaviors emerge during the first 2 years of life, according to Piaget's database, it would be interesting to observe whether the organization of infants' emotions undergoes transformations.

This question is addressed in Table 5.4. It is difficult to separate the emotional and cognitive aspects of infant behavior, especially if one takes into account the context in which the emotions are displayed. That is, the combination of context and type of emotional behavior exhibited in that context can allow either for inferences about the cognitive capacities underlying the emotional expression or about the reason that particular emotion was expressed. Accordingly, we decided to examine the patterns of emotional expression per se in order to make a somewhat more definitive statement about whether the organization of infants' emotional behaviors change or remain the same.

The only patterns of emotions we could find in Piaget's reports were either essentially two or more emotional expressions sequentially displayed by the infants or blends of emotions (see Table 5.4). We could not find any blends or sequentially expressed emotions characteristic of specific substages of infancy. The only obvious trend is one toward an increase in complexity of both emotional blends and sequentially expressed emotions. As can be seen in Table 5.4, the first pattern of emotional behaviors involving more than two emotions is reported at 7 months of age, and the only instance consisting of five different emotional expressions is observed at 18 months. Although we are aware that Piaget reported very few situations consisting of more than one emotion and thus has not been concerned with changes in blends and the sequential expression of emotions in infancy, the few situations that were reported seem to suggest the possibility of increasingly sophisticated emotional expressions. Most of the time, the infants express no more than two emotions throughout infancy. The fact that more and more situations occur in which the infants display more than two emotional behaviors allows us to conclude that the infants at least acquire the capacity to express more than two emotions either at the same time (blend) or consecutively.

TABLE 5.4

Combinations ("Structures") of Emotional Behaviors and Inferred Emotions

| Infant's age in months | Stage of sensorimotor development | Combinations of emotional behaviors and inferred emotions | Contexts in which emotional behaviors and inferred emotions occur |
|---|---|---|---|
| 0–3 | I reflexes | surprise →ᵃ disturbance (1 month) | about deep tones |
| | II primary circular reactions | fright → smile (2 months) | fright when seeing father uncombed; smile when suddenly recognizing him |
| | | desire → anger (2 months) | when hunger becomes persistent |
| | | interest → smile (3 months) | interest in making dolls move; smile at success of making dolls move |
| | | astonishment → anxiety (3 months) | in the presence of new objects the infant would like to grasp |
| 4–7 | III secondary circular reactions | astonishment → fright (4 months) | when given new rubber monkey |
| | | fear → pleasure (4 months) | fear when producing a sudden violent noise; pleasure when moving to make it last |
| | | fright → vague smile (4 months) | when striking rattle violently by chance |
| | | motor pleasure → visual interest (6 months) | motor pleasure when turning box over; visual interest in modifications of an object's appearance |
| | | anger → intense desire (6 months) | anger when Piaget hides bottle in his hand; desire when infant stares at Piaget's hand, but does not try to move it |
| | | surprise → disappointment (7 months) | surprise when the infant loses a box it was holding; disappointment while looking at its empty hand for a long time |

154

| | | |
|---|---|---|
| | looking attentively → smiling delightedly (7 months) | when father drums with his fingers on a tin box |
| | howling → crying → stopping to cry → interest (7 months) | howling as soon as nipple disappears from view, when Piaget turns the infant's bottle in all directions; crying when pushing bottle away; stopping to cry when bottle is moved further away; interest when infant extends its hands, when Piaget brings bottle closer |
| 8–11 IV coordination of secondary schemata | great interest → laughter → contentment (8 months) | interest when Piaget gives watch to infant; laughter when Piaget pulls watchchain away, and infant feels resistance; content when exploring place watch disappeared from |
| | interest +[b] pleasure → smiling → disappointment → satisfaction (8 months) | interest + pleasure when father brings saucer in front of infant; smiling when saucer passes in front of infant again; disappointment when infant's movement not followed by movement of saucer; satisfaction when infant's movement is followed by movement of saucer |
| | curiosity → disappointment (8 months) | curiosity when exploring nail of Piaget's thumb; disappointment when looking at other thumb that is too far away |
| | fear → interest → pleasure (8 months) | fear—interest when Piaget makes crib-roof shake without infant's knowing that he is there; pleasure about success (when infant's arching movements make the crib-roof shake) |
| | smile → anxiety → fear → pleasure (9 months) | smile–anxiety–fear when noise is slight, then too loud; pleasure when intentionally grading the noise |
| | interest → resentment (11 months) | interest in father's watch; resentment when looking for watch in place B, but not thoroughly enough |

(continued)

TABLE 5.4—Continued

| Infant's age in months | Stage of sensorimotor development | Combinations of emotional behaviors and inferred emotions | Contexts in which emotional behaviors and inferred emotions occur |
|---|---|---|---|
| 12–18 | V tertiary circular reactions | interest → wailing → stopping to cry (12 months) | interest when trying to reach a cork with a stick; wailing when unsuccessful; stopping to cry when understanding how to use the stick |
| | | surprise + pleasure → smiling (12 months) | when put in front of mirror and seeing double gesture reflection |
| | | surprise → satisfaction (12 months) | surprise when father moves window with his foot; satisfaction when exactly reproducing the phenomenon |
| | | interest → pleasure (16 months) | interest when putting leg through handle of basket; pleasure about repetition and variation of action |
| | | laughter → astonishment → great pleasure → laughter → surprise (18 months) | laughter about own success in finding a ring; astonishment when not finding the ring; great pleasure about finding ring after unfolding father's fingers; laughter when by chance finding the ring; surprise about finding father's hands empty |
| | | astonishment → laughter (18 months) | astonishment about finding father's hand empty after he has withdrawn it from under a garment; laughter about finding object under garment where father left it |
| | | weeping → laughter (18 months) | weeping while calling mother; laughter when Piaget imitates infant in a tearful tone |

a → means "is followed by."
b + means "is displayed at the same time as."

156

However, it is problematic to portray this increasing complexity as emotional complexity. One could argue that the infants display more complex sequences of emotional behaviors *because* they become cognitively more sophisticated. A situation reported at 9 months of age (under "Competence" in Table 5.1) lends support to the latter interpretation. In this situation, the infant repeatedly shakes a rattle as if trying to control the different degrees of noise the rattle makes depending on the vigorousness of its own shaking. The infant obviously not only controls the noise the rattle makes but also—more indirectly—its own emotional expressions. Much closer scrutiny of the patterns of emotions infants display and of the cognitive contexts in which they occur is necessary before we will be able to say more about the relationship of cognition and emotion in infant development.

Furthermore, future research will have to show whether emotional blends or sequentially expressed emotions are a significant characteristic of emotional development. If the number of emotional blends and sequential expressions Piaget cites is representative of infants' emotional development—which we believe is unlikely—then their role in emotional development is questionable. It is plausible to argue that infants become increasingly capable of expressing and tolerating the expression of more than one emotion at the same time. If we can confirm the increase in blends and sequentially displayed emotions over the course of infancy found in Piaget's work, we will at least be able to conclude that cognitive and emotional development correlate as far as their degree of behavioral complexity is concerned. In order to infer more about the relationship *between* emotional and cognitive development, we need further analysis of the exact temporal relationship between new cognitive and new emotional capacities.

## THE RELATIONSHIP BETWEEN COGNITIVE AND EMOTIONAL DEVELOPMENT

Our presentation here of infant's emotions as outward manifestations of their underlying cognitive competence provides an added slant to our previous discussion on the role of affect in Piaget's theory (Cicchetti & Pogge-Hesse, 1981). In our earlier paper, following the widely held viewpoint that Piaget neglects or ignores the emotions in his work because of his exclusive interest in the development of cognitive categories, we claimed that Piaget discusses emotional development only with regard to and in terms of cognition, rather than as a domain in its own right. However, as revealed by our analyses of Piaget's database, it appears that cognitive and emotional development are interdependent, at least in infancy. It seems that infants' cognitive capacities cannot be thoroughly comprehended unless one studies their emotions as well. Our finding that affect and cognition are inextricably intertwined compels us once again to ponder the nature of this intricate relationship. As we noted in our earlier paper (Cicchetti & Pogge-Hesse, 1981), Piaget suggests two possible ways that the relationship between cognition and emotion may be conceived on the basis of his work: parallelism and epiphenomenalism. Piaget's officially stated position, detailed in his Sorbonne lectures (Piaget, 1954b), is parallelism; however, as we demonstrated previously, he also adopts, more or less explicitly, an epiphenomenalist viewpoint. In this section, we will outline briefly the major features of these two positions.

## Parallelism

According to Piaget's (1954b) parallelist viewpoint, emotion and cognition are complementary domains of the human mind, cognition providing the structure, emotion contributing the energetic aspects of behavior. These two domains are considered as entertaining noncausal relationships and as being irreducible because, although emotions may have an accelerating effect on cognition, they never change the cognitive structures.

As stated in our earlier account, there are several criticisms that can be leveled against Piaget's parallelist position (see Cicchetti & Pogge-Hesse, 1981). The parallelism notion implies that both cognitive and emotional development follow their own, independent developmental paths. Piaget devotes much of his theoretical and empirical work to explicating the development of cognitive constructs such as object permanence, space, means–ends relations, causality, and time and says comparatively little about the emotions that are developing during the sensorimotor stage, either in terms of their behavioral expressions or their environmental and stimulus characteristics. He considers pain, joy, and the basic distinction between pleasurable and unpleasurable effects of stimuli to arise in connection with infants' perceptions and to have either activating or terminating effects on actions. However, he does not specify the exact conditions under which joy, pain, and pleasant–unpleasant distinctions occur, nor does he detail precisely how they are expressed. At approximately 6 months of age, needs and interests supposedly become differentiated, concomitant with the infants' general decentration in the cognitive domain (for example, the differentiation of means and ends). Interests involve a qualitative or value aspect in addition to their quantitative or energy aspect. Piaget claims that the intensity of the interest is its energetic regulation, and that the content of the interest constitutes its value. Values are the expression of the infants' capacity to make judgments that enable them to prefer certain objects and experiences over others. This capacity ultimately leads to the infants' internalization of a hierarchy of values.

Piaget not only fails to specify the surface or phenotypic characteristics of infants' emotions but also does not specify their deeper or structural aspects. Partly due to this deficit, he does not detail either the type of sequence characteristic of cognitive and emotional development or their respective structures. Accordingly, it is unclear what sort of developmental model Piaget would suggest with respect to the domain of affect. A further problem is that the structures characteristic of the developmental stages are poorly defined, especially if we want to decide whether they are identical in the cognitive and affective domains. On the one hand, he states that the cognitive domain is structured and the affective domain is energetic. On the other hand, when introducing interests in terms of values and with respect to later stages in terms of the concepts of reversibility and the logic of sentiments, it seems likely that Piaget wants to ascribe structural properties, at least to some of the later-developing emotions.

Faced with this apparent contradiction, we asked ourselves what it might mean for emotions to become structuralized (Cicchetti & Pogge-Hesse, 1981). We believed that the following interpretations were the most plausible:

1. Piaget wants to claim that cognitive development evolves in stages and that a specific set of emotions corresponds to the cognitive capacities at every stage. Assuming a tendency toward greater structural complexity in the cognitive domain, one might argue that the emotions characteristic of later stages of cognitive development are more structured insofar as they correspond to more complex cognitive structures. However, this does not say anything with respect to the structure of the emotions themselves and is thus irreconcilable with Piaget's claim that increasingly complex structures organize the emotions with respect to one another, unless one suggests a second interpretation.

2. The emotions actually undergo a transformation and become cognitive to the extent to which they develop structures or organizations. This interpretation is in agreement with quite a few of Piaget's statements in which he tries to apply transitivity to the emotions in the sense that one can say that a goal $(G_1)$ is more interesting than another goal $(G_2)$, $G_2$ more interesting than a third goal $(G_3)$ and, therefore $G_1$ is more interesting than $G_3$. However, there is a problem with this position because there seems to be a difference between "feeling" emotions and "comparing" them, the latter not being an emotion itself. In other words, the fact that we can make transitive judgments does not imply that we feel "transitively," but rather that we have feelings of different intensities toward objects or persons and rank them by means of judgment that is cognitive. This implies not that the emotions themselves become cognitive in the course of development, but that they become increasingly embedded in structured cognitive contexts.

3. The problem mentioned in (2) suggests an additional construal of Piaget's position on this matter. Insofar as infants cannot reflect on their own emotions, one may conclude that their emotions are neither intellectualized nor structured, but rather just discrete energetic states. One can therefore state that the more

children interpret their emotions or reflect on them propositionally in the course of their cognitive development, the more structured their judgments about emotions become, but not their emotions themselves. This position seems to be most similar to Piaget's official statements because it reduces emotions to different intensities or energies and attributes the interpretation of these intensities to cognition. Accordingly, we can conclude that our interpretations of these energies become more structured, but not necessarily the energies themselves. The main problem with this position lies in the fact that it contradicts the whole post-Piagetian literature dealing with the universal existence of basic discrete emotions (Ekman, 1972; Izard, 1977, 1979; Tomkins, 1962, 1963), including Piaget's own use of infants' discrete emotions to infer their cognitive competence. This tradition of theorizing about emotions suggests that they are not just energies, or mere undifferentiated states of arousal, but have certain very distinct qualitative characteristics as well. Unless one wants to argue that these qualitative aspects are cognitive in nature, one has to grant more than energetic features to the emotional domain.

## Epiphenomenalism

Piaget's (1952) other position on the relationship between cognitive and emotional development suggests that emotions are epiphenomena of cognition, with states of need indicative of various types of cognitive disequilibria: "Desirability is the indication of a rupture in equilibrium or of an uncompleted totality to whose formation some element is lacking [pp. 10–11]." Piaget (1977) distinguishes among three different types of disequilibria and their corresponding forms of equilibration. Due to the interaction between subject and object from the very beginning of a newborn's life, one possible disequilibrium is between the assimilation of objects to schemata of action and the accommodation of these action schemata to object schemata. The corresponding type of equilibration is external insofar as it refers to the infant's relation to its physical and social environment.

The two other types of disequilibrium and equilibration refer to the internal organization of the organism. The second one focuses on the relations of subsystems (for example, different schemata like sucking, grasping, and so on) to the degree to which they are combined with one another due to reciprocal assimilation. The third type of disequilibrium and equilibration refers to the relationship of subschemata to the whole organization or structure of a developmental level. The equilibration of the disequilibria of subschemata and the whole structure is achieved by means of reciprocal assimilation and accommodation not only of juxtaposed subsystems as in the second type of equilibration but also of subsystems and the whole organization.

In order for the child to experience disequilibria at all, he/she must be capable of distinguishing among certain schemata, subschemata, or structures A, B, and C and corresponding objects or schemas A', B', and C', and certain properties a', b', and c' that the infant can distinguish from certain other properties, non-a', non-b', and non-c', that are not characteristic of these objects or schemata. Only if the latter properties can be considered as not belonging to certain assimilated objects or subschemata A', B', and C' does it make sense to talk about discrepancies or imbalances between schemata and nonassimilated objects or subschemata, because only then does a malproportion of negative and positive properties become obvious (Cicchetti & Pogge-Hesse, 1981).

Piaget distinguishes among three different attempts at equilibration, depending on the infant's level of development: one in which interferences or nonassimilated objects or subschemata are completely ignored and not integrated into the system; a second in which interferences can be partially integrated into the system; and a third in which minimal interferences can occur because virtually all possible intrusions are anticipated by the system.

Piaget's epiphenomenalist approach provides us with a careful analysis of the different possible types of cognitive disequilibria. However, there are several problems with this position. Piaget fails to specify what kind of need-states correspond to the different types of disequilibria and whether the states of need change in the course of development. As he did with the parallelist approach to the relationship between emotion and cognition, Piaget deals with emotions only in terms of an analysis of the cognitive states and structures corresponding to them and thus neglects the qualitative, quantitative, and structural analysis of the various emotions and emotional changes characteristic of the respective stages of development.

## Parallelism or Epiphenomenalism?

This chapter adds to Piaget's two accounts for emotional development not only by criticizing them but also by attempting to resolve some of the problems thus identified. For parallelism, we have addressed the supposedly neglected emotional aspects of infants' development and have demonstrated that Piaget has provided a very detailed, though implicit, account for the emotions emerging parallel to cognition throughout the course of infant development. On the basis of Piaget's data, it is impossible to specify the sequences and structures of infants' emotions conclusively. Stated differently, we still do not have more than tentative evidence that emotional development follows its own, independent developmental course.

Concerning Piaget's conception of emotions as energy, our presentation of Piaget's database suggests that it is both adequate and inadequate. It is appropriate to the extent that infants' emotional reactions always involve varying degrees of intensity or arousal. As has been shown, depending on their degree of arousal and other contextual determinants, infants react with either negative or positive affect to a given situation (McCall & McGhee, 1977; Sroufe & Waters, 1976; Sroufe et al., 1974). Since the intensity of infants' emotional reactions depends largely on the degree of cognitive sophistication that increasingly allows them to consider new information as intrusive or disequilibrating, both Piaget's parallelist and epiphenomenalist accounts seem to be appropriate interpretations: the epiphenomenalist position because it provides us with reasons for the existence of emotions in the first place, and the parallelist position because it attempts to deal with the changes the relationship between emotion and cognition undergoes in the course of development.

Piaget's conception of emotions in terms of energy is inadequate insofar as we could identify various basic discrete emotions as characteristic of infants' development. Thus, there seems to be more to emotions than merely their quantitative aspects. And the qualitative aspects of the different emotions that we can distinguish do not seem to be reducible to different forms of cognitive awareness. The best support for this argument can be derived by reference to the category of proprioceptive–kinesthetic emotional reactions that apparently are not cognitively mediated but involve nonetheless the display of the discrete emotions reported by Izard (1977), Ekman (1972), and Tomkins (1962, 1963).

In other words, the approach we have taken in this chapter suggests that infants' emotions are not just different energetic or quantitative states of infants' cognitive capacities but are qualitatively distinct from infant cognition. However, this does not resolve the conflict between the two competing positions of epiphenomenalism and parallelism, although it makes a parallelist account seem more appropriate. Nonetheless, we think that this chapter provides several additional contributions relevant to a resolution of the parallelist–epiphenomenalist debate.

This chapter lends support to epiphenomenalism because even though emotion and cognition tend to co-occur, emotions are indicative of cognitive capacities rather than vice versa. That is, emotions are the language in terms of which infants' cognitive development is expressed rather than mere reflections of children's emotional capacities.

When infants begin to make attempts at consciously controlling their emotional reactions (for instance, at 9 months when the infant consciously tries to reproduce the conditions under which certain emotional reactions tend to be elicited), this relationship between emotion and cognition starts to change. The relationship changes even more when infants' language capacities develop, for language can express both infants' cognitive and their emotional capacities.

Epiphenomenalism has been conclusively refuted in this chapter if interpreted as implying that infants' emotional reactions are no more than the subjective awareness of cognitive disequilibria. Although three of the categories of our classification system—namely, *proprioceptive–kinesthetic reactions, recognition of discrepancy,* and *competence*—can be reconciled with an attempt to define emotional reactions as expressions of different types of disequilibria (kinesthetic, "internally cognitive" between schemes and whole structures, or "externally cognitive" between standards or schemes of success and the result of actions respectively), this interpretation seems to be impossible in the case of *recognition of similarity,* in which no discrepancy or disequilibrium is involved.

Parallelism of emotion and cognition during infant development is supported by the fact that both infants' emotional states as well as their cognitive capacities seem to be of a qualitatively different nature. Emotions appear to have their own nature and meaning rather than just being the by-products of cognitive states (see also Zajonc [1980] in this regard). Emotions are identifiable as discrete states rather than as of varying intensity, and infants' cognitive capacities cannot be exclusively reduced to their emotional reactions, as they can also be inferred (at least to some extent) from infants' nonemotional sensorimotor behaviors. Furthermore, as has been demonstrated, infants' emotions seem to follow their own sequences and organizations of development that may presuppose certain necessary cognitive components without being reducible to them. Thus, fear seems to presuppose Substage 4 of sensorimotor development, and shame and guilt require Substage 5 or 6 as cognitive prerequisites. However, to the extent to which the cognitive capacities of the aforementioned substages do not only account for the development of fear and shame and guilt but also elicit emotionally neutral reactions, one might want to argue that they are necessary but not sufficient for these emotions to emerge.

Finally, Piaget's chapter in *Play, Dreams and Imitation in Childhood* (1962a) on affective schemata suggests that infants do not develop just cognitive representations or schemata but also emotional ones. Combining this interpretation with Piaget's account of different types of disequilibria and corresponding forms of reequilibration, we may conclude that not only cognitive but also intrinsically emotional disequilibria have to be equilibrated. Perhaps by allowing for both cognitive as well as emotional disequilibria (and possibly combinations of both), we will come closer to an adequate integration of Piaget's and Freud's work with respect to unconsciously represented emotional problems. This interpretation follows Piaget's in the chapter in *Play, Dreams and Imitation in Childhood* in which he tries to account for Freud's system of defense mechanisms in terms of conflicts between affective schemes leading to repression of some of the affective representations. This repression in turn leads to a preponderance of assimilation to dominant affective schemes rather than to new accommodations, the consequence being a fixation at immature levels of emotional development. That chapter epitomizes Piaget's problematic approach. Even in its course, one can see how Piaget vacillates in his point of view. He wavers back and forth among postulating emotional schemes as *parallel* to cognitive ones, as the *energy* of cognitive structures, and as forming a *necessary part* of every single cognitive scheme.

In sum, although this chapter has added additional arguments both in favor and against epiphenomenalism and parallelism, future work will have to provide further elaborations of these arguments and attempts to decide in favor of one or the other of these positions or their integration.

## CONCLUSIONS

Based on our discussions of Piaget's data on emotional development, we think that future research and theorizing in the domain, particularly as it relates to cognition,should focus on the following issues: specification of the beginnings and the goal-state of emotional development; an account of the sequences characteristic of emotional development throughout ontogenesis; a characterization of the respective structures or organizations of the various phases of emotional development; and a delineation both of the relationship between nonverbal and verbal emotional development and of how these two aspects of the emotions relate to cognition.

As to the origins of emotional development, we should describe with more precision which emotions are present at birth and which develop only later. We should specify whether development consists of only phenotypic changes of various types of emotions (such as happiness, sadness, surprise, fear, and so on) that are already present at birth, or whether it involves changes in the type of emotion, with fear and surprise emerging later than happiness and sadness due to their more sophisticated cognitive prerequisites (as suggested by most of the post-Piagetian literature on emotions: Charlesworth & Kreutzer, 1973; Izard, 1978, 1979; Sroufe, 1979a). Also needing to be monitored are the changes in types of situations that tend to elicit emotions. Reactions to new situations may or may not involve a differentiation of the emotional expression as well. Emotional reactions to new situations may either be derived from a repertoire of already available emotions, perhaps involving slight changes in expression, or they may be correlated with the emergence of completely new types of emotions.

As far as the goal-state of emotional development is concerned, the main issue seems to be whether it should be conceived of as emotional or as moral or as a stage of personality development. The latter two possibilities have both been suggested by Piaget (1962b, 1967), who considers the later phases of emotional development as identical to moral and personality development. He proposes that the will be considered an operation in the emotional domain that emerges at about the same time as children's concrete operations. And he considers more-organized personality characteristics during adolescence as an even later phase of emotional development (Piaget, 1967). Since there seem to be other than emotional aspects to moral and personality development (Kohlberg, 1969; Selman, 1980), it remains to be seen whether there are other than cognitive, moral, and personality characteristics to later emotional development.

Concerning the structures or organizations of emotional development, we have to explore whether it makes sense to consider structural aspects of emotional ontogenesis solely in terms of cognitive or intrinsically emotional structures. As we discussed, the latter could be conceptualized either as increasingly complex organizations or as blends of various emotions that are in children's expressive repertoires. Children either could become more capable of expressing sequences of several emotions (for example, surprise → interest → curiosity → happiness) or they could develop completely new types of emotions at certain points in their development that would be organizations of prior developed emotions. Love–attachment, aggression, shame–guilt, and jealousy are examples of emotional reactions favoring the latter suggestion because all of them involve several of the basic discrete emotions as their constituents.

With regard to the possible types of sequences of emotional development, it should be clarified which aspects of emotional development (for example, nonverbal, verbal, motor, and so on) display what kind of a sequence. Thus, as we noted, each of these aspects could be conceived to follow either an Addition, Substitution, Modification, Mediation, or Inclusion sequence. Different aspects of the emotions could follow differing sequential patterns, and one and the same aspect could follow different types of sequences at varying periods of development.

One of the most difficult and crucial issues is to specify the nature of the relationship between emotional and cognitive development. Parallelism is the weakest relationship because it assumes only that emotional and cognitive phenomena tend to co-occur. Epiphenomenalism and interactionism are more problematic in that they claim to specify *how* cognition and emotion are related.

In order to make a case for parallelism it would be sufficient to demonstrate that emotional and cognitive phenomena tend to co-occur and that changes in each respective domain emerge at approximately the same time. Furthermore, it would have to be demonstrated how cognitive and emotional development differ to prove their irreducibility. As we have indicated, the most likely candidates for the demonstration of differences between cognitive and emotional development are their characteristic sequences and organizations of development.

Whereas parallelism requires unique and irreducible features of emotional and cognitive development, epiphenomenalism requires the demonstration of structural and sequential commonalities in addition to very specific temporal characteristics of the relationship between emotional and cognitive phenomena. A fairly strong case in favor of epiphenomenalism would be made if we did not succeed in demonstrating distinct organizational patterns or a distinct sequence of development for the emotional domain—that is, if we could conceive of emotional development only in terms of the structures and sequences elaborated by Piaget with respect to cognitive development. An even stronger case for epiphenomenalism could be made if—in addition to a lack of specific sequences and structures of the emotional domain—changes in emotional development always came about *after* changes in the cognitive domain. Such a pattern would provide strong support for the argument that emotional developments presuppose changes in the cognitive domain.

Interactionism would describe the relationship between emotional and cognitive development if we found cognitive developments preceding emotional ones and vice versa, regardless of whether the cognitive and emotional domains had distinct sequential and structural characteristics. Such a framework would be compatible with everything we have said about the sequences and structures of cognitive and emotional development as well as the relationship between cognition and emotion. The post-Piagetian formulations of wariness and coyness as precursors to fear and shame (Sroufe, 1979) and our attempt to conceive of children's emotional development as a gradual approximation of adults' meanings of emotions would also fit this proposal.

The following example may serve as evidence for this approach. Let us assume we consistently found certain nonverbal emotional expressions (for example, coyness and wariness) that did not fully meet our adult definitions of emotions as far as their expressive characteristics and contexts of occurrence are concerned (that is, as shame and fear). Let us further assume that the cognitive capacities that form the necessary requirements of our definition of shame and fear, namely at least Stage 4 object permanence, always developed after the first emergence of the nonverbal emotional expressions that resemble shame and fear. Let us finally stipulate that the full-fledged expressions of shame and fear and other emotions consistently emerged after the development of the indicated cognitive capacities. If all or many of the cognitive and emotional developments in children came about in such a three-step sequence, we would be able to conclude that certain emotional developments are necessary for certain cognitive changes to emerge. These cognitive changes in turn would be necessary for the completion of the emotional developments that were the requisite conditions for the cognitive changes to come about.

In summary, we think that future investigations in the area of emotional development should address the theoretical and practical issues that we have raised in this chapter. As we have demonstrated, Piaget's framework allows us to discuss all of the theoretical questions relevant to the formulation of a comprehensive developmental theory. Thus, researchers and theorists of infants' and children's emotions should follow Piaget's lead and conduct as careful longitudinal research on emotional development as Piaget has done with respect to cognitive development.

## ACKNOWLEDGMENT

Dante Cicchetti would like to acknowledge the support he received from The Foundation for Child Development Young Scholars in Social and Affective Development Program. Dante Cicchetti also expresses his appreciation and gratitude to Dr. Sanford Gifford. Petra Hesse would like to acknowledge the support that she has received from the P.E.O. International Peace Scholarship Fund.

## REFERENCES

Bronson, G. The hierarchical organization of the central nervous system. *Behavioral Science,* 1965, *10,* 7–25.

Bronson, G. The postnatal growth of visual capacity. *Child Development,* 1974, *45,* 873–890.

Butterworth, G., & Cicchetti, D. Visual calibration of posture in normal and motor retarded Down's syndrome infants. *Perception,* 1978, *7,* 313–325.

Campos, J., & Stenberg, C. Perception, appraisal, and emotion: The onset of social referencing. In M. Lamb & L. Sherrod (Eds.), *Infant social cognition.* Hillsdale, New Jersey: Erlbaum, 1981.

Charlesworth, W. R., & Kreutzer, M. Facial expressions of infants and children. In P. Ekman (Ed.), *Darwin and facial expression.* New York: Academic Press, 1973.

Cicchetti, D., & Pogge-Hesse, P. The relation between emotion and cognition in infant development. In M. Lamb & L. Sherrod (Eds.), *Infant social cognition.* Hillsdale, New Jersey: Erlbaum, 1981.

Cicchetti, D., & Pogge-Hesse, P. Possible contributions of the study of organically retarded persons to developmental theory. In E. Zigler & D. Balla (Eds.), *Mental retardation: The developmental–difference controversy.* Hillsdale, New Jersey: Erlbaum. 1982.

Cicchetti, D., & Sroufe, L. A. The relationship between affective and cognitive development in Down's syndrome infants. *Child Development,* 1976, *47,* 920–929.

Cicchetti, D., & Sroufe, L. A. An organizational view of affect: Illustration from the study of Down's syndrome infants. In M. Lewis & L. Rosenblum (Eds.), *The development of affect.* New York: Plenum, 1978.

Darwin, C. *The expression of the emotions in man and animals.* London: Murray, 1872.

Ekman, P. Universals and cultural differences in facial expressions of emotion. *Nebraska Symposium on Motivation.* J. Cole and D. Jensen (Eds.) Volume 20. Lincoln: Univ. of Nebraska Press, 1972.

Ekman, P., & Oster, H. Facial expressions of emotion. *Annual Review of Psychology,* 1979, *30,* 527–554.

Emde, R. Levels of meaning for infant emotions: A biosocial view. In W. A. Collins (Ed.), *Minnesota Symposia on Child Psychology.* (Vol. 13). Hillsdale, New Jersey: Erlbaum, 1980.

Emde, R., Gaensbauer, T., & Harmon, R. *Emotional expression in infancy: A biobehavioral study.* New York: International Universities Press, 1976.

Emde, R., & Harmon, R. Endogenous and exogenous smiling systems in early infancy. *Journal of the American Academy of Child Psychiatry,* 1972, *11,* 177–200.

Feldman, C., & Toulmin, S. Logic and the theory of mind. In D. Levine (Ed.), *Nebraska Symposium on Motivation.* J. Cole (Ed.) Volume 23. Lincoln: Univ. of Nebraska Press, 1975.

Flavell, J. H. Stage-related properties of cognitive development. *Cognitive Psychology,* 1971, *2,* 421–453.

Flavell, J. H. An analysis of cognitive–developmental sequences. *Genetic Psychology Monographs,* 1972, *86,* 279–350.

Goldberg, S. Social competence in infancy: A model of parent–infant interaction. *Merrill Palmer Quarterly,* 1977, *23,* 164–177.

Harter, S. Effectance motivation reconsidered. *Human Development,* 1978, *21,* 34–64.

Hesse, P. The acquisition and development of emotional language: The ontogenesis of our emotional category system. Unpublished manuscript, Harvard University, 1982.

Izard, C. *The face of emotion.* New York: Appleton-Century-Crofts, 1971.

Izard, C. *Human emotions.* New York: Plenum, 1977.

Izard, C. On the development of emotions and emotion–cognition relationships in infancy. In M. Lewis & L. Rosenblum (Eds.), *The development of affect.* New York: Plenum, 1978.

Izard, C. Emotions as motivations: An evolutionary–developmental perspective. *Nebraska Symposium on Motivation.* H. Howe (Ed.) Volume 27. Lincoln: Univ. of Nebraska Press, 1979.

Kagan, J. *Change and continuity in infancy.* New York: Wiley, 1971.

Kagan, J. On emotion and its development: A working paper. In M. Lewis & L. Rosenblum (Eds.), *The development of affect.* New York: Plenum, 1978.

Kessen, W. Early cognitive development: Hot or cold? In T. Mischel (Ed.), *Cognitive development and epistemology.* New York: Academic Press, 1971.

Kohlberg, L. Stage and sequence: The cognitive–developmental approach to socialization. In D. A. Goslin (Ed.), *Handbook of socialization theory and research.* Chicago, Illinois: Rand-McNally, 1969.

Kohlberg, L. From is to ought: How to commit the naturalistic fallacy and get away with it in the study of moral development. In T. Mischel (Ed.), *Cognitive development and epistemology.* New York: Academic Press, 1971.

Lewis, M. & Brooks-Gunn, J. *Social cognition and the acquisition of self.* New York: Plenum Press, 1979.

McCall, R., & McGhee, P. The discrepancy hypothesis of attention and affect. In F. Weizmann & I. Uzgiris (Eds.), *The structuring of experience.* New York: Plenum, 1977.

Oster, H., & Ekman, P. Facial behavior in child development. In W. A. Collins (Ed.), *Minnesota Symposia on Child Psychology* (Vol. 2). Hillsdale, New Jersey: Erlbaum, 1978.

Piaget, J. *The origins of intelligence in children.* New York: International Universities Press, 1952.

Piaget, J. *The construction of reality in the child.* New York: Basic Books, 1954. (a)

Piaget, J. *Les relations entre l'affectivite et l'intelligence dans le developpment mental de l'enfant.* Paris: Centre de Documentation Universitaire, 1954. (b)

Piaget, J. *Play, dreams, and imitation in childhood.* New York: Norton, 1962. (a)

Piaget, J. Will and action. *Bulletin of the Menninger Clinic,* 1962, *26,* 138–145. (b)

Piaget, J. *Six psychological studies.* New York: Random House, 1967.

Piaget, J. *Biology and knowledge.* Chicago: University of Chicago Press, 1971.

Piaget, J. The relation of affectivity to intelligence in the mental development of the child. In S. Harrison & J. McDermott (Eds.), *Childhood psychopathology.* New York: International Universities Press, 1972.

Piaget, J. The affective unconscious and the cognitive unconscious. *Journal of the American Psychoanalytic Association,* 1973, *21,* 249–261.

Piaget, J. *The development of thought: Equilibration of cognitive structures.* New York: Viking Press, 1977.

Piaget, J., & Inhelder, B. *The psychology of the child.* New York: Basic Books, 1969.

Sander, L. Issues in early mother–child interaction. *Journal of the American Adademy of Child Psychiatry,* 1962, *1,* 141–166.

Shultz, T. & Zigler, E. Emotional concomitants of visual mastery in infants: The effects of stimulus movement on smiling and vocalizing. *Journal of Experimental Child Psychology,* 1970, *10,* 390–402.

Selman, R. L. *The growth of interpersonal understanding: Developmental and clinical analyses.* New York: Academic Press, 1980.

Sroufe, L. A. The developmental significance of the construct of wariness. *Child Development*, 1977, *48*, 731–746.

Sroufe, L. A. Socioemotional development. In J. Osofsky (Ed.), *Handbook of infant development*. New York: Wiley, 1979. (a)

Sroufe, L. A. The coherence of individual development: Early care, attachment, and subsequent developmental issues. *American Psychologist*, 1979, *34*, 834–841 (b)

Sroufe, L. A., & Waters, E. The ontogenesis of smiling and laughter: A perspective on the organization of development in infancy. *Psychological Review*, 1976, *83*, 173–189.

Sroufe, L. A., Waters, E., & Matas, L. Contextual determinants of infant affective response. In M. Lewis & L. Rosenblum (Eds.), *The origins of fear*. New York: Wiley, 1974.

Sroufe, L. A., & Wunsch, J. P. The development of laughter in the first year of life. *Child Development*, 1972, *43*, 1326–1344.

Stern, D. *The first relationship*. Cambridge, Massachusetts: Harvard Univ. Press, 1977.

Tomkins, S. *Affect, imagery, consciousness* (Vol. 1). New York: Springer, 1962.

Tomkins, S. *Affect, imagery, consciousness* (Vol. 2). New York: Springer, 1963.

Watson, J. S. Smiling, cooing and "the game." *Merrill Palmer Quarterly*, 1972, *18*, 323–339.

Werner, H. *Comparative psychology of mental development*. New York: International Universities Press, 1948.

White, R. Motivation reconsidered: The concept of competence. *Psychological Review*, 1959, *66*, 297–333.

Wolff, P. H. Observations on the early development of smiling. In B. M. Foss (Ed.), *Determinants of infant behavior* (Vol. 2). London: Methuen, 1963.

Zajonc, R. Feeling and thinking: Preferences need no inferences. *American Psychologist*, 1980, *35*, 151–175.

Chapter 6

# EMOTIONAL SEQUENCES
# AND CONSEQUENCES

*HARRY F. HARLOW*
*CLARA E. MEARS*

## ABSTRACT

*The maturation of the emotions of love, fear, and anger among socially reared primates, both human and nonhuman, customarily follows the same sequence. Three of the love systems—maternal love, infant love for the mother, and peer love—have every chance to become firmly established before the strong emotions of fear appear, and these, in turn, precede aggression with intent to harm. Social rearing requires exposure and experience with a biological mother or an adequate surrogate as well as agemate love accompanied by appropriate play. All of these contexts offer innumerable opportunities for the alleviation of both fear and aggression. The interlocking backgrounds of undesirable fears and violent aggression create a situation that allows the amelioration of these fears to aid in prevention of aggression. Should these early loves be prevented through the many avenues of deprivation or denial that are no respecters of economic levels, fear and aggression frequently fill the vacuum. Once established, the rehabilitation of the individual becomes very difficult; prevention of these extreme states is far more economical than is its treatment.*

EMOTION
Theory, Research, and Experience
Volume 2

## THE EMOTIONAL TRIUMVIRATE: FEAR, ANGER, AND LOVE

There are three emotions—fear, anger, and love—that have held the emotional attention of both psychologists and physiologists intermittently over the past century. At the Wisconsin laboratory, throughout the years, while pursuing research on completely different behavioral areas such as learning, motivation, love, and psychopathology, we began to perceive relationships among emotional factors that were not intrinsically related to the subject being studied. A folded diaper, placed in the cage of a rhesus monkey solving matching-from-sample learning problems, facilitated learning, and a similar piece of gauze, years later, led to the creation of the terry cloth surrogate mother.

In another instance, while using the facilities of the Vilas Park Zoo to start our learning research, even before we had acquired a laboratory of our own, we ran into problems while trying to test Terrible Tommy, the baboon. Tommy would begin the test with admirable cooperation, which lasted until he was required to make a difficult decision. With frustration, rage would strike. Tommy shook the bars of his cage and hurled away any test object within reach. He pulled the testing table against the bars of the cage, attempting to shred it into bits. Fortunately, three tables later, beautiful Betty, a new student tester, appeared. Betty liked Tommy. She groomed his hands and gently talked sweet nothings. Tommy obviously fell in love with Betty, and she began to test him. When Tommy came to a challenging selection, he would start to react, then would look at Betty, pause and stare hard at the test tray, then make his choice. Tommy began to enjoy solving the puzzles.

Instances of the interaction between fear, anger, and love have accumulated throughout the years, in pairs or as a trio. They have created their own importance by intruding, uncourted, into our research. The core of concern of this chapter is the effect of these various interrelationships on the development of the emotions during the early years of the human and subhuman primate.

## HISTORICAL PERSPECTIVES

### WILLIAM JAMES

The breadth of vision of William James (1893) is such that, had experimental methods been more thoroughly developed during his lifetime, psychology might have made some giant strides. James anticipated many facts that have since been corroborated by scientific research.

Among James' factual musings was that infant fears progressed from the fear of sudden loud noises, which appeared as early as 3 months, to the fear of the sight of new objects. He observed the increase of fear on the part of his own child at the age of 10 months and identified the child's fear of strange men and strange animals.

Interrelationships of fear and anger were part of the picture of the emotions as portrayed by James. The same bodily changes precipitated both, and each at times involved aggression. As James said, "We both fear, and wish to kill anything that may kill us [p. 407]." Fear, anger, and love, in the form of lust, form part of a group that James called the *coarser emotions;* they are the most exciting of all emotions and have very strong reverberations.

## JOHN B. WATSON

The smell of fear has been so dramatized in mystery and horror stories that we shall not imply that fear, by any other name, would smell the same. We may ask, however, if fear, by the same name, is always the same emotion. In his description of the three basic emotions (1919, p. 219), Watson states that his list of the emotions is identical to that of James, except for James' inclusion in descriptions of the coarser emotions, the emotion of grief, as well as fear, rage, and love. The latter three may be the same in name, almost the same in number, but far from the same in breadth and depth of behavioral content. James, without qualms, uses the terms *emotions* and *instincts* interchangeably, whereas Watson was on the brink of replacing *instincts* with limited *behaviors,* consistent with his adoption of a more objective psychological theory.

In order to delineate the beliefs of John B. Watson, one must be prepared to name the year to which one is referring. In 1919, he was on the verge of tossing his instincts to the somewhat perverse winds of the Dry Tortugas Islands on which he had pursued them, with the noddy and sooty tern. When he had returned from the Dry Tortugas, Watson (1914) wrote an outstanding book in which he described instincts as complicated, concatenated behaviors unfolding serially to appropriate stimulation. By 1919, however, he had cast aside instincts and found himself with a theory of conditioned responses without any unconditioned, unlearned responses to which to attach them.

Watson's three emotions were described in nonintrospective terms, and the range of emotion covered might well be described, as Dorothy Parker once said, as running the gamut of emotions from A to B. These reflexes demanded presence at birth, freedom from antecedent learning, and freedom, also, from the taint of any maturational complexities that might later appear.

Fear was elicited by simple, specific stimuli or situations capable of objective measurement. Basically, fear was engendered by loud sounds, especially sudden sounds, and by loss of support. Anger was produced by stimuli just as specific and by situations even more narrow or limited. Limitation and restraint of the infant's movements were responsible for subsequent behaviors characterized by Watson as rage. His favorite example was that of holding the child's nose.

It may be possible to extrapolate from a sudden, loud noise, the more than 200 abnormal fears listed in behavioral dictionaries. It may also be possible to make the transition from holding the nose of an infant, or even an adult, to aggravated aggression, but it requires an incalculable amount of imagination.

When Watson faced love as a theoretical topic, he radically reduced the emotion, not only to sex but to specifically located sex. His reflex love behavior consisted of the stimulation of the erogenous zones. Whether or not this definition met his criterion of observable behavior is a debatable question.


## COMPLEX, UNLEARNED RESPONSES

### DEFINITION OF EMOTIONS

By our definition, love, fear, and anger, in that order, are experienced as emotions. They are not themselves behaviors, but each may be the generator of a whole set or sets of behaviors that can be defined and delineated by observation.

There is very little question that the potential for these behaviors is inherited. Any social organism will express these responses throughout its existence, through maturation later, if not at birth. However, the form, frequency, and intensity of these behaviors will be shaped by environmental factors. Harlow used to think in terms of the evil emotions of fear and anger as opposed to the good emotion of love, but considering that all of these can lay claim to having had survival value over the evolutionary eras, none can properly be considered to be entirely evil.

Before we consider the case closed on the subject of emotions as being either innate or learned, we must now present the possibility of a third source of origin. That which is innate may be presumed to have an origin that is also prenatal, but that which is prenatal may not necessarily be innate. There has been extensive research in the past few years on the effect of fetuses of sex hormones injected into pregnant females. The experiments of greatest significance to our present concern were performed on rhesus monkeys by Goy and Phoenix (1971), who discovered that the genetically female babies proved to be masculinized in certain characteristics as a result of the male sex-hormone injections.

Harlow's (1965) experiments statistically separated the sexes in playroom behaviors. The young, male monkeys displayed more social threats than did the young female monkeys. The males also were more frequently initiators of rough-and-tumble play, which they preferred over other play. Goy and Phoenix (1971) compared their testosterone-injected female infants with normal male and female infants in regard to the same behaviors and found that they ranked at a level intermediate to that of the two normal groups. These effects were displayed after the prenatal injections were given between 46 and 90 days of pregnancy. There was some evidence that these prenatal injections may masculinize the nervous system (Phoenix, 1974), but probably only in the case of characteristics more common to the male originally (Phoenix, Goy, & Resko, 1968).

Just as the effects of hormonal injections have fairly recently been confirmed, other factors may also be discovered. To date, we can say that evolution and certain specific prenatal influences provide the basic material on which fear, anger, and love are built. Interpersonal, combined with impersonal environmental experiences, determine the variations of expressions of these emotions.

Not all of the potentials implied by the evolutionary process are present at birth, since that assumption would negate the importance of maturational factors for development. Emotions can be defined not only in terms of the variables on which they depend but also in terms of the behaviors through which they are expressed. An indisputable characteristic of the emotions of the human being and of the nonhuman primate, from birth onward, is that these behaviors are of such complexity that emotional analysis throughout the century has produced many more theories than there are emotions themselves.

There is a category within which our three emotions may be placed, to keep company with other responses such as play, both individual and social. This category of complex, unlearned responses involves the same variables underlying the behaviors themselves.

## CRITERIA FOR
## COMPLEX, UNLEARNED RESPONSES

There are three criteria to be met to determine the inclusion of responses in this category:

1. In orderly progression, the unlearned response follows developmental maturation stages. A study of these stages reveals that learning is inevitable after the very start of these behaviors. The start may be early or late, but the completion of maturation is often quite late.
2. The response is based on multiple variables. Because primate behavior is not simple, it cannot be explained by a single variable, but is based on an interaction of more than one innate or prenatal factor. There may be many learned ways of expressing the response, no matter how many or few the variables.
3. The unlearned response is very persistent, even through the entire duration of life itself.

Research on human subjects exposed during gestation to androgen-based pro-
gestin (Reinisch, 1980) confirms the fact that the resultant responses meet this
third criterion. Not only did the human subjects become masculinized on the
measures on which sex differences might be expected during childhood, but
these differences also persisted over many life stages. A unique aspect of a
reported portion of this research is that the original injections of norlutin were
administered to the pregnant mothers for a multiplicity of medical needs.

## DEVELOPMENTAL, MATURATIONAL SEQUENCE OF THE THREE EMOTIONS

### LOVE'S HEADSTART

In the relationships among the three emotions, the fact of primary importance
for primates, be they man or, as James has said, ''brutes,'' is that love has a
headstart over both fear and anger.

### Maternal–Infant Love Variables

Of the three emotions under our present scrutiny, love has strayed the farthest
and spread its influence over the broadest new area in the years elapsed since the
times of William James and John B. Watson.

James listed love as the latest of the three to develop, with fear the first. Love
was scientifically neglected over the years, and when it was even discussed, it
was usually limited to heterosexual, man–woman relationships. Infant, mother,
and peer love, the three loves that bear the brunt of developmental significance,
as such, were practically ignored. Without them it would be difficult to discuss
maturation or sequencing of the emotions.

Although they may not be aware of the fact, there are mothers who do not feel
immediate love for their newborn babies. It may be necessary for them to
exercise the mechanisms underlying some of the variables for maternal love in
order to recognize the maternal love experience.

Contact comfort has proven to be the most important of variables in cementing
the two-way maternal–infant bond, at least in rhesus monkeys (Harlow, 1958). It
is most effective through contact of the two soft bodies when mother nurses the
baby. This may be the reason why both Freudians and behaviorists decided that
the libations of the breast were the essential source of the love of the infant for
the mother. Fortunately, contact comfort may be achieved by many methods and
at many times by soft, close cuddling and cradling.

The newborn rhesus monkey has a great advantage over the human neonate in maturational development. The rate of physiological growth of the rhesus monkey is four times faster than that of the human infant, although it ceases relatively sooner. The upward climbing reflex of the rhesus is ready at birth to take the tiny baby in the right direction for finding mother's breast. The human mother has a much greater responsibility in providing the opportunity for both contact comfort and the flow of milk, whether the milk is breast milk or formula.

The same principle holds for the receipt of love benefits from the pleasure of rocking motion. The neonate monkey can already cling to the mother's body and swing gently along, underneath, while she moves around. The human mother must resort to rocking baby in her arms, in a cradle, or rocking chair to equal this contribution to the inception of love. Had Watson had the chance to observe rhesus monkeys as well as the noddy and sooty tern, he might have found a measurable and observable basis for keeping the baby's cradle instead of banning it. In the course of providing contact comfort, rocking motion, and the flow of milk in the proper fashion, whether breast or bottle, the caretaker should find that another important variable—warmth—follows naturally.

Since 1960, research has contributed so much knowledge concerning infant–mother communication from birth onward that we feel that two-way maternal–infant communication should be added to the list of variables on which the first two love systems depend. This factor also plays a vital role in interactions between love and both fear and anger. Reciprocal communication and the human baby begin life together, if given the chance. Eye contacts between the mother and baby are shared within the first hour after the birth (Brazelton, School, & Robey, 1966; Robson, 1967). Many observers consider this eye contact exchange as one of the main factors in creating caretaker responsiveness on the part of the mother. The lack of this communication with a blind infant may, on the other hand, produce a feeling of rejection and almost anger in the mother (Fraiberg, 1974). The blind infant and the mother find their smile language confused as well. Whereas the smile occurs at the same time, the fourth week, at the sight of the mother by the normal baby and at the sound of the mother's voice by the blind baby, the smile does not occur regularly with the blind baby, because it lacks the reinforcement of seeing the mother smile back.

The research reported by Fraiberg (1974) follows closely the timing guidelines described by Wolff (1973) on the development of the smile. The first clear indication of a social smile appears in the third week, and the fourth week produces more visual attention to faces. Originally, a high-pitched voice elicited the smile most frequently. The nearest the rhesus monkey comes to smiling is the facial grimace called "the silly grin," an expression for which no learning by imitation has been found. This grimace is used in the training of the infant in desirable habits of obedience, one of which is to return to mother at the appropriate times.

## Peer Love

When human mothers refused to allow an infant to learn how to be independent, the saying was that mother would not untie the infant from her apron strings. The need for infant independence still exists, even if the apron may have lost its priority. When the human and the monkey mother feel that the young have the maturity and have learned proper caution, they gradually increase the freedom to explore the world away from mother's restraining arms.

As early as the second month of a rhesus monkey infant's life, its mother may appear to be rejecting the baby and urging it to leave, but typically the infant is curious about its environment, and is ready to go, as long as mother will be right there when it rushes back to find her. As soon as the infant begins to meet other little monkey agemates on its sorties away from mother, new love bonds—those of friendships with peers—begin to be cemented.

The human baby, long before the crawling stage, shows a strong interest in other children, even babies in other baby buggies or strollers. Peer preferences appear long before most adults would suspect. For example, a study by Lee (1973) describes the proven preferences of a group of five babies in a Cornell University day-care nursery by 9 months of age, well prior to the emergence of spoken language.

These agemate friendships or peer loves are among the longest-lasting loves in our society, often outlasting marital love or even marital loves. In the nonhuman primate, peer loves are also strong (Erwin, 1979). Experiments demonstrated that social bonds between female pairs of rhesus macaques, housed in pairs during the second year of life, outlasted 2 years of separation. Upon reunion, no female aggressed against her previous cagemate, although she did show aggressive behavior toward unfamiliar females. The reunited pairs, in contrast, displayed affectionate embracing, grooming, and a maintenance of proximity toward each other.

## THE EMOTION OF FEAR

The emergence of fear into the developing lives of human and nonhuman primates is neither a suddenly occurring event nor a totally predictable and invariable sequence of gradual developmental changes. Some fears depend more than others on physiological maturation of specific motor skills, such as those necessary for the manipulation of objects by the fingers and hands or for the skills required in crawling and walking. The fear of the visual cliff, for instance, follows the perceptual awareness of the cliff, itself (Stone, Smith, & Murphy, 1973).

We now know that many fear behaviors, from the scanty Watsonian reflexes

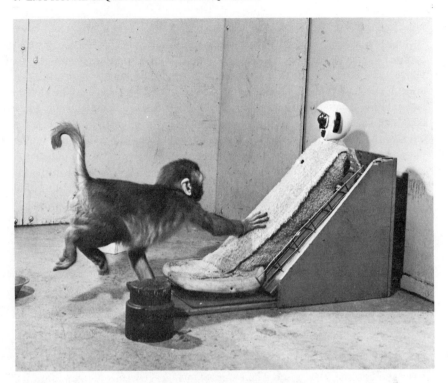

FIGURE 6.1. A safe base to which to return.

to the much more complex fear of strangers and strange places, are primordially unlearned. We also know, from Darwin (1872), that many facial and gestural patterns involved in fear stimulation or responses are primordially unlearned. Additionally, many factors contribute to the continuum of learning effects, and individual differences in the specific learning histories of subjects themselves increase the complexity to a point that would challenge the canniest computer. Yet we can now trace, in primate behavior, many changes in the development of many specific behaviors characteristic of fear. Soon after birth, the baby rhesus startles and jerks to no apparent stimulus in the environment. This reaction has been termed *geckering*. (Suomi & Harlow, 1976) and is accompanied by sharp, simian vocalizations.

Rhesus monkey mothers keep their babies close by their side or in their arms during the first month of life. When an infant first begins to stray, almost any object encountered sends the little adventurer scurrying back to mother's arms for security, or to a suitable surrogate substitute. Harlow and Zimmerman (1959) found that for the first few weeks, novel stimuli such as a plastic butterfly and a stuffed monkey doll would send infant monkeys back to a cloth surrogate for more security but, after rubbing in courage from the cuddly terry cloth body, back to the novel stimuli they went, and soon were on a course of fairly steady approach. The stuffed monkey doll probably shared some of the affectional variables of the cloth-covered surrogate mother. In the same experiment, even after 3 weeks of daily exposure, a mechanical teddy bear caused considerable amounts of avoidance behavior. From the sixth week on, the little monkeys could not quite make up their minds, but avoidance reactions won and peaked at 80 days. Avoidance of a mechanical dog and withdrawal to the surrogate mother both appeared and peaked sooner.

Soon after birth, the human infant's reflex behavior to loud sounds or loss of support produces crying, holding of the breath, and clutching at the air. With increasing age, the early reflex-eliciting stimuli lose their sting, and the responses also begin to change. Loud noises practically lose their effectiveness as fear stimuli by the age of 20 months. By that time the young child is producing most of the noise by itself. Loss of support becomes a game when daddies toss their babies up in the air and catch them, often to the tune of gurgles and giggles.

Two separate teams of experimenters (Ball & Tronick, 1973; Bower, Broughton, & Moore, 1970) studied the appearance of early avoidance reactions in human infants. The latter research group reported the responses of 6–20-day-old infants to an object coming from above their heads on a seeming collision course. In this experiment the babies were seated in a supporting chair. A typical neonate would move his head back and away, bring his arms forward toward the face, and become very upset. The older infants, 2–11 weeks of age, confirmed the responses of the first group and added another response. These babies were being held in adult arms, and in each case the person holding could feel a stiffening of the baby's body suggestive of an early symptom of the freezing response.

In tracing the development of social fears, which we all experience sooner or later in varying degree, we find experiments of great diversity substantiating a limited range in the timing of the maturation of fear. There are some monkey fears that are much more evident to the observer than are avoidance of a mechanical dog and consequent withdrawal to a monkey or surrogate mother. The most extreme monkey fears are much more apt to occur when there is no mother, live or surrogate, to whom to withdraw.

Griffin and Harlow (1966) found that when rhesus monkeys were raised from birth to the age of 3 months in total social isolation, there was no question but that they emerged afraid. The customary reaction of 3-month-old monkey in fear is to screech or cry, to repetitively rock on its haunches, to walk on its hind legs while clasping its own body, or to curl up in a ball. Upon exposure to any part of the world outside its cage, the 3-month isolates would go into a state of panic. The maturation of fear was just upon them but, fortunately, though the effects were dramatic, they were not irreversible. Fear had not yet had a chance to produce any lasting behavioral scars in these infants. From all indications from extensive experimentation, the monkey maturation time for unlearned social fears is between 70 and 90 days.

Social fears, above all, clearly reflect their maturation date. One of the most innovative of the fear experiments at the Wisconsin Primate Laboratory was that of Sackett (1966). The subjects were eight rhesus infants raised without any social experience before or during the experiment. From the age of 14 days to 9 months, their only visual stimulation was a series of picture slides projected onto one wall of each monkey's separate cage. There were two slides centering around fear behavior—a monkey threatening and one displaying a fear grimace. The other slides were of everyday monkey relationships plus one blank and a picture of Sackett's living room, for neutral controls. Fear behavior was consistently very low or absent for every slide except threat and the fear grimace. Highest levels of fear behavior were displayed from 2½ to 3 months, after a good start from 2 to 2½ months. These reactions were universal, including fear grimaces, but they were only elicited by the threat picture. Sackett convincingly corroborated the time of maturation of the fear as well as the innateness of the fear grimace that had had no opportunity to be learned in these isolate-reared infants.

Mother monkeys living in large social groups show fearful respect toward the offspring of dominant females and exercise the fear grimace toward them. An interesting index for dominance has been identified by Buirski, Kellerman, Plutchik, Weininger, and Buirski (1973). In the sample population of seven baboons, the most dominant animal proved to be the one with the highest mean score for being groomed by others. He was also the most aggressive, the second most destructive, and the most rejecting. Needless to say, he spent the least amount of time grooming others.

Scarr and Salapatek (1973) traced the onset and development of fears in human infants, using as fear stimuli a mechanical dog, various noises, a jack-in-the-box, masks, and the visual cliff. The subjects were 91 babies from 2 to 23 months of age. The criteria for fear responses were crying or fretting and fleeing—not just withdrawing—to mother. There are, surely, even more intense responses to this emotion but, probably because of the ages and species of the subjects, the mother was a muted but present part of each fear situation except the visual cliff.

Scarr and Salapatek (1973) found that the percentage of the infants showing the fear reactions to all stimuli generally increased up to the eleventh month, although the fear responses to the visual cliff reached much higher levels than did the reactions to the other stimuli. In this investigation, with age variance removed, greater fear of the visual cliff, the jack-in-the-box, and noise were evidenced if the duration of creeping had been relatively brief before the testing. If the subjects had a very short history of walking, fear increased for the cliff, the jack, the mechanical dog, and masks. The complexity of the human being continues to be constantly with us.

## Fear of the Strange

We have but scratched the surface of research results on the subject of fear, but have saved for the last an area in which interest has been most steadily maintained. This is the fear of the strange—strange objects, strange places, strangers, and strangeness itself. The fear of the unfamiliar has become one of the most familiar fears for human and nonhuman primates alike, as well as many other species.

For example, ethologists have found fear of the strange in chicks, ducks, and geese (Hinde, 1974). They have also determined that the tendency to follow the mother or other chosen object—*imprinting*—declines when a competing tendency to flee in any other direction begins to appear. Only as the bird becomes familiar with its environment do strange new objects, especially strange moving objects, elicit fear.

A good point of departure for a consideration of strangeness is Hebb's (1946, 1949) theory, which has been described as an incongruity or discrepancy theory. His discourses centered on violent expressions of emotions, both fear and aggression. He observed that when chimpanzees were shown a head severed from the body, they were convulsed with fear and yet, almost at the same time, were consumed by rage and aggression. These reactions, according to Hebb, resulted from a disruption of a set schema that had already been established. The discrepancy, mild though the term seems, sparked the violent reaction.

Hebb's theory introduces an important interrelationship—the fact that anger to the point of aggression is but the other side of the coin of fear. Van Lawick-Goodall (1968) has added a parallel observation concerning a chimpanzee who sees a former friend whose body has become paralyzed. The fear that is first provoked turns into active aggression.

In a longitudinal study with human infants, Wolff (1973) found the fear of discrepancies present in 5½-month-old infants who did not show the slightest evidence of any fear of strangers. Incongruous and discrepant configurations may well form a natural bridge to the subject of the fear of strangers. Monkey fears of strange objects or events include any intense or unusual stimulation of many kinds, such as unusually bright or strangely shaped spotlights (Dodsworth, cited in Suomi & Harlow, 1976), and various unusual combinations of sounds and lights. Practically without exception, the studies support the 70–90-day period as the time when important specific fears mature.

Fear studies of infants have concentrated more on the studies of strangers than on strange objects, but the research of Schaffer and Parry (1973) is an exception.

They researched the reactions of 6- and 12-month-old babies to strangely shaped objects unlike any toy or useful gadget. The two investigators demonstrated not only maturation of fear of strange objects but also the fear, shown by 12-month-old babies, of the act of manipulating the strange object. Most 6-month-old babies manipulated what 12-month-olds feared to touch.

It is impossible, after reading the extensive research on the fear of strangeness, to think of the fear of strange places without thinking of the amelioration of that fear by the mother or peers. The picture is much more meaningful when presenting both sides simultaneously. A strange, empty room and an empty, strange "open field" may hold both fear and even terror for children and monkeys, respectively.

Hinde (1974), in his separation studies, found parallel results in a similar but not identical situation. When rhesus infants are removed from both their mother and their familiar environment and are housed in a strange place, the separation protest of fear and distress is long and lasting. When, instead, the mother is separated, leaving the infant with agemates and other older monkeys, the infant protests, but its protest is cursory and not very fearful. Play and peers assuage the infant's grief under these conditions.

There is a tendency to interpret the onset of stranger anxiety as if it were acquired more suddenly than other fears. However, many mothers have noticed a gradual lessening of positive responses toward individuals other than the primary attachment figures. Not suddenly, but little by little and even one by one, monkey and human infants alike respond differentially to the less-familiar individuals encountered.

Brooks and Lewis (1975; Lewis & Brooks, 1978) have carried the analysis of stranger interactions into a field that we approach, in part, during later discussion of the amelioration of fears. We cannot, in this chapter, discuss experiencing emotions, since we are involved with a discussion of developing emotions of both human and nonhuman primates. Self-awareness of the monkeys and higher apes is more difficult to determine. The mirror technique, effectively employed by Brooks and Lewis in spotting self-awareness from the response to mirror-viewing of rouge on the nose, would not be very effective with either the rhesus or the mandrill. The mandrill would not even wonder how the rouge came to be on his nose and, if the rhesus could see it on the nose in the mirror, he would run around to find the monkey on the other side.

There have been innumerable controversies over identifying the actual determinants of the fear of strangers. Many of these conflicts have arisen from an attempt to create overall theories to include and account for exceptions as well as for the rule. We believe that many of these seeming contradictions disappear upon acceptance of the fact that early experience can affect the time of onset of the fear, the intensity of the fear, and the duration of the fear of strangers. These will be discussed under the topic of amelioration of fears.

The discrepancy theory cannot account, in one lump sum, for all the unlearned and the complex learned aspects of the fear of strangers. It is, rather, a description of an important set of fears, all by themselves, with their own exceptions. The fear of strangers may not necessarily appear suddenly and full-blown, but if the stranger appears very suddenly and unexpectedly, fear is more likely. On the average, most investigators (Scarr & Salapatek, 1973; Schaffer, 1966) have found human onset of fear of strangers to center around the ninth month of life, although the range is clearly much broader. Schaffer (1966) found that the number of positive responses to relatively unfamiliar people declined prior to the expression of fear of strangers itself, which had a mean of close to 9 months. In addition, Schaffer found some instances of fear of familiar people that might have been sparked by specific, unpleasant encounters.

The picture of human fears, like most human behaviors, is complicated by a tangle of environmental factors. The time range for the onset of real human fears may be broader than with nonhuman primates. The important fact, however, is that there is still no doubt that the early love systems have every chance to be firmly established before the bona fide social fears appear.


## THE EMOTION OF ANGER, RAGE, OR AGGRESSION

In making the transition to the development of anger and the real antagonist, aggression, we are again reminded of the juxtaposition of fear and rage. James (1893) took thorough note of the similarity of the basic bodily changes in both fear and anger. Wolff (1973) describing the early developmental history of crying, identifies a "mad" cry as well as a cry of distress upon contact with noxious substances or situations. As children increase in age, they cry in anger and they cry when afraid.

To fear is to avoid or to flee. To aggress is to approach, to attack. In an interview with Evans (1975), Lorenz beautifully presented the paradox in his example of a goose described as the "aggressive coward." This is a goose with a low threshold for both escape and aggressive behaviors. It attacks in dastardly fashion, from behind, and then it runs away.

For many decades, and even in the 1960s, there was intense theoretical insistence that aggression or aggressiveness was exclusively a learned behavior. While describing the love systems and the various stages in sexual development in monkeys, Harlow (1961, 1962) reviewed the sex differences evident in play patterns. These patterns are of interest for enlightenment on the acquisition of not only sexual but also social roles of the individual and the formation of social groups.

The young male rhesus monkeys adopted facial threat gestures significantly sooner and to a greater degree than did young female monkeys. The young males also showed greater aggressiveness in initiating rough-and-tumble play. They chose this play form much more frequently as it became progressively more aggressive. These facts have been corroborated by many researchers, but there have remained a few staunch adherents of aggression's learned foundation.

We believe that doubt of the accuracy of this assumption became widespread when the results of prenatal testosterone injections in various species began to accumulate. Clearly, aggressiveness in an individual could be measurably affected prenatally. As mentioned earlier in the chapter, testosterone injections of the pregnant mother at the proper stage of pregnancy could increase the aggressiveness of the female infants, whoso play patterns, themselves, became more masculine.

Like her human counterpart, the female rhesus monkey is more precocious, both physiologically and behaviorally, than is the male, except when it comes to aggression. These facts have a special significance when the monkeys concerned have been raised with surrogate mothers. The terry cloth surrogate mother cannot selectively train the young to display gender-appropriate behavioral patterns or social roles.

Aggression is, to date, one of the few behavioral characteristics to appear earlier in the male than in the female, and with greater frequency (the others are rough-and-tumble play, and mounting and thrusting behavior). More complex aggressive behavior, such as self-aggression, enters the picture even later than do threat gestures, but with the same male–female sequence and relative frequency. Externally directed monkey aggression reaches its first peak in the male at 2 years but, depending on the behavioral forms, continues to rise until the fourth to seventh years. The female may have her own subtle methods but, to the observer, it is not until the fifth or sixth year that aggression makes any striking appearance (see Figure 6.2).

The earlier appearance of aggressive behavior in the male, as well as the greater amount of aggression displayed by the male, both human and monkey, is consistent with the long-time social role of the male as a protector. The man has protected the social group from outside predators. The father rhesus monkey has protected the younger and smaller animals from abuse by the larger and older ones. He has even chastised the mother if he believed she was harming an infant. The adult male would seldom harm an infant even if the baby were pestering papa at the same time. Occasionally, an adult male may succumb to some tiny baby monkey that has been separated from its mother, adopt it and display some striking signs of affection. If breast feeding were the primary base for infant affection, the infant adopted by the male would be in an unfortunate position.

Fear and anger or fear and aggression may appear to be very uncomfortable bedfellows, but they are sure to be found together frequently. Nowhere, experimentally, has this been more evident than with the rhesus infants after 6 or more

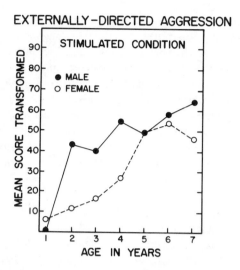

**FIGURE 6.2.** Sex differences in development of aggression in rhesus monkeys.

months of asocial rearing. On the basis of the ethological theory that fear of strangeness follows a certain amount of familiarity with one's surroundings, the rhesus monkeys fresh from isolation faced a world of near-total strangeness but had become very familiar with their very limited isolation environment. When placed with other rhesus monkeys, the 6-month isolates prostrated themselves in fear, and the other monkeys aggressed against the strange creatures. To refer again to the statement of William James (1893), the isolates wished to kill those they feared would kill them. So, they aggressed in return. They violently assaulted male monkeys much larger than they were, yet they also attacked infants smaller than they, a behavior almost never encountered in socially raised rhesus monkeys. For their own protection, the isolates had to be speedily removed from the group by laboratory personnel.

A comparable human situation, unfortunately not as far-fetched as the comparison may at first seem, has existed in many overcrowded orphanages over the years. The babies, because of insufficient and inadequate caretakers, were often kept in their cribs far past the ages of either creeping or walking. The cribs themselves were often placed in separate cubicles from which the infants could neither see nor hear the other babies (Provence & Lipton, 1962). The little ones were not held, even for their bottle feedings, and, when more solid food was added, the bottles were still propped up against pillows in the cribs, but the holes in the nipples were enlarged. There was no time for smiling or for cooing, and bathing was dispatched with no nonsense, on a table top. It was a strange sight to see so many children playing so little. These waifs had been raised in a partial isolation that suffocated the sources of play before they could become organized. When visiting adults interested in adopting one of the orphans arrived, the children often hurled themselves against the visitors. They apparently did not know the meaning of social behavior as it is commonly acquired.

Angers, both the common household variety and the aggressive forms, are structured throughout the evolutionary process to preserve the individual or the group without concern for any other individual or clan.

In turning our attention to the alleviation of fear and primarily, of aggression, we find a number of facial and postural gestures in use by human and nonhuman primates, gestures of special effectiveness in temporary alleviation or redirection of the aggressive intent. The most common of these measures in the human being is the smile, a universal gesture (Eibl-Eibesfeldt, 1980). Blurton-Jones (1972) discovered that among nursery-school children, the smile was used more often by children low in dominance when initiating interaction with more dominant peers than in the reverse situation, when the dominant wished to engage the more submissive. Since it is an accepted scientific fact that girl babies smile sooner and smile more often than boys, the smile may be responsible for the later and lighter onset of aggression in women.

However, the same general statistics on the appearance and the strength of aggression between the sexes apply to the nonhuman primates to whom the same type of smile does not come as naturally. The "silly grin" is not quite a fair comparison, but grooming might fill the same need, that is, reduction of aggression by the female rhesus. Like the smile, grooming starts earlier with the female, develops more rapidly, and is useful to the submissive in placating the more dominant male.

Many species of nonhuman primates display a different facial gesture that also may serve to alleviate the onset of violent or vicious behavior. This is a generally relaxed face that features a very relaxed, open mouth. This face might be effective for human use as well, but it is found especially in mock fighting, rough-and-tumble play of monkeys and chimpanzees. It indicates submission, nonhostility, and subsequent friendliness (Hinde, 1974). It may even be used by some dominant animals toward subordinates, possibly to suggest a pleasant change of heart.

Years ago we learned not to look a monkey directly in the eye since that behavior, for the nonhuman primate, is synonymous with threat, and threat begets threat; a threat such as a dangerous stranger might present. This is what the mother monkey teaches her young. In the fear experiments of Novak (1974), the mother-reared juveniles used the threat face to test the intentions of monsters with fearsome flashing lights and loud noises. The surrogate- and peer-raised rhesus had not mastered that art of encounter. In the laboratory, we maintained friendly, cooperative behavior by looking from the side or at the side of the monkey's face. The monkey remained alert and observant of any change.

Many behavioral traits that have developed and continued because of their survival value have also served to ameliorate excessive expressions of fear and aggressive anger. Countless animals add postural gestures to their behavioral repertoires in avoidance of aggression and expression of fear. Squirrel monkeys (Rosenblum, 1968) control behavior through postural gestures of dominance, beginning as juveniles, and submissive gestures of avoidance and defense. One of the most common fear responses from nonhuman and human primates is the posture of complete prostration, or freezing in fear. This may be one version of fleeing that also may fool only the subject, like our reaction to the ostrich that buries its head in the sand, but there is no doubt that it has also saved many lives, primarily because the aggressor believes that the victim is already dead.

## Violence and Isolation

We have produced the sequential and maturational statistics showing, without a doubt, that, in the plan of primate development over millennia, love has had every chance for a headstart over both fear and hate. Love offers the most thorough prevention of destruction through fear and violence. Nature abhors a vacuum, and if love fills it, there is not much place left for negative emotions. If an infant is brought into the world to find no loving mother or father or other adequate surrogate and meets neglect, either physical or psychological or both, aggression is in possession of an open invitation.

In this day and age, at any economic level and in many countries, television will probably be the earliest companion who talks freely to the lonely, neglected child. Not only is the viewing of violence on television or in the motion pictures reflected in the behavior of the viewer (Berkowitz, 1968, 1969; Eron, 1963; Eron, Huesmann, Lefkowitz, & Walder, 1972), but, again, the sentiments of William James are experimentally confirmed. Agonistic behavior of an individual is not cathartic, a reducer of aggression, but an accelerator. Each subsequent expression is more violent than the one prior.

Violence may be initiated in human young by imitation of antagonistic, physically fighting, or abusive parents, or by television viewing to ease the boredom of neglect. From nursery-school age, the child may graduate to the school of street gangs, where the appeal of agemates is just as strong, but the social roles taught are quite different from those of social play. Again we find the close association of fear and aggression. Rival street gangs fear each other and, often at the same time, may fear the police. Both the fear and the agonistic aggression become cemented without the amelioration of prior love bonds. This, then, is the background with which many ineffective attempts at rehabilitation have tried to cope.

As many of our readers will be well aware, the discovery of the behavioral deficits and miseries created by partial or total asocial rearing was a side effect of a very different enterprise at the Wisconsin Primate Laboratory. We had reached a stage of desperation from the loss and illness of monkeys from tuberculosis imported along with the rhesus from India. The health of the laboratory personnel and their families was also threatened. Experiments in progress were cut off at different intervals. The only solution was to start our own breeding colony. In order to prevent any and every possibility of infection, we raised our would-be breeders alone, in single wire cages. The cages were wholly hygienic, the food excellent. We raised very healthy animals and we not only eliminated tuberculosis, we also thoroughly eliminated the ability to breed.

One year after another we devised experiments testing different methods of rehabilitation to undo the damage of asocial rearing and create animals whole in personality as well as in physical health. We first placed them with peers, hoping that the power of peer play would work wonders, but the isolates did not know how to play. We tried surrogate mothers—unheated, heated, and rocking. Acceptance of contact was achieved, but nothing more.

We had no notable success until we were able to take fear out of the picture. This we achieved with the aid of junior therapists (Harlow & Suomi, 1971; Suomi & Harlow, 1972). The 3-month-old therapists were just one-half the age of the isolates, young enough to still seek gentle contact with other monkeys. The therapists were so gentle that they did not present any threat to the fearful 6-month isolate. At 3 months of age, the little rhesus monkeys were just learning to play, and they led the isolates along with them, little by little. It took approximately 5 months for virtually complete reversal of the behavioral deficits to occur, a year of one-to-one therapy to develop play and social interaction along with social roles and rules. And eventually, maturation produced realistic sex.

## THE AMELIORATION OF
## FEAR AND AGGRESSION

The fact that fear and aggression often go hand-in-hand, or fist-in-fist, sometimes makes it difficult to separate facts concerning amelioration into facts concerning just fear or just aggression. We do know that certain variables are effective in alleviating the harmful effects of both, and these, of course, are concerned with the early and strong formation of love bonds.

## INFLUENCE OF MOTHER, OTHER CARETAKERS,
## AND COMPANIONS

The maternal development of the sense of security through the love variables, beginning with contact comfort, establishes the firmest foundation for security and trust. The implications of these terms can be visually pictured if you consider mothers' contributions to the exploratory behavior of infants. We refer to human mothers, monkey mothers, and surrogate mothers who become secure bases from which to leave and see the world without being upset and beset by unnecessary minor fears of unfamiliar objects (Ainsworth, 1967; Harlow, 1958; Rheingold & Eckerman, 1969). These bases remain firm and secure as long as the explorer is certain that they will be there when s/he returns for reassurance. For persistent trust, these same pillars of comfort and solace should be there when needed to prevent a variety of fears that might grow into major fears. Encircling arms can help distract the infant from startling, thunderous sounds.

Since the 1960s, mothers have voluntarily been taking part, with their babies, in developmental research. We believe that many mothers are excited by the discovery of how much a baby can understand and learn, how early a baby communicates in a multitude of ways. The years between the first solid food and the first serious school experiences have become fertile years for fond parents and older siblings to teach the infants. Of course, many families have done this all along, including the monkey families.

The rhesus mother, with the infant within her encircling arms, teaches the baby rhesus the secret of threat faces in identifying unsafe and unsound strangers (Figure 6.3). The mother chimp assists the young ones in early climbing, to ensure safe footing and safe handling. Some knowledge that used to be thought innate is now found to be within the scope of nonhuman parental teaching. For example, live bull snakes and their make-believe counterparts brought fear responses from feral-born rhesus monkeys (Joslin, Fletcher, & Emlen, 1964). These investigators, however, decided that this trait must be learned since it did not exist among laboratory-reared rhesus monkeys and the capacity for such teaching was well within range of the monkey mother.

The human family uses this same relative period to teach dangers to be overcome. Preferably, the caretakers present positive ploys to replace disruptive fears and prevent destructive fires, to avoid accidents on the streets or on skates and swings, or to escape the dangers from some strangers.

The fear of strangers is one of the more complex of the unlearned responses. The unfamiliar covers broad ground, and the familiar friend may become a stranger when a mask is donned. The incongruity or discrepancy theory initiated by Hebb (1946) became a starting point for explaining the fear of strangers in a variety of theories that are as diverse, but not as numerous, as the theories of emotion itself during the past century. As we have mentioned earlier in the chapter, the fear of strangers is at its most intense and has its greatest frequency from approximately the ages of 9 to 12 months, but it ranges in a shifting fashion from the seventh to the fourteenth months. Surely, not all factors involved are yet known, but probably the breadth and variety of social experience prior to the onset will prove to be one of the most, if not the most, important determinants.

FIGURE 6.3. Positive behavior to replace helpless fear.

The amount and duration of both creeping and walking are known to affect other fears, but it would be quite plausible to find social influences in the background of fear of strangers.

Animal experimenters have made their own contributions to this social research. Rosenblum and Kaufman (1968) introduced the scientific community to the affable families of the bonnet macaques, in which the bonnet infants enjoy more multiple mothering at any one time than do the children of the kibbutzim of Israel. The bonnet monkey mothers are very permissive about sharing their infants with other adult females almost from the moment of birth. Kaufman and Rosenblum (1969) have compared the bonnets with pigtail macaque monkeys, who more clearly resemble the rhesus in their protective and more possessive maternal manner.

When separated from their mothers, the pigtail infants showed the customary separation stages found by Spitz (1945) and Bowlby (1964) in mother–infant separation (Kaufman & Rosenblum, 1967), including agitated protest followed by abject despair or depression. Play and other social contacts practically evaporated on the heavy air. There was one pigtail who showed no depression or despair, and this was the offspring of a dominant pigtail female. Dominant monkey mothers are a type apart. They attract bevies of other adult females around them, a fortunate situation to precede infant–mother separation because it provides some familiar surrogate mothers who allow the mother to leave without causing severe separation ripples of fear and anxiety.

The next research of Rosenblum and Kaufman (1968) studied bonnet mother and infant separation. When mother left, the bonnet babies each attached themselves so quickly to a living surrogate, already familiar, that fear lost its function. The infants almost forgot to stop playing, and did not forego the pleasure long. Several of the babies did not immediately desert the surrogate mother when the real mother returned.

We must not forget the power of peer love in ameliorating separation fears and anxiety. Research has determined that the time for recovery from separation fears is significantly reduced if the separated infant is housed with a familiar peer.

The intensity of the relationship between a mother and her offspring has been thought by several investigators to influence the infant's fear of strangers, but this observation is not consistent enough to be significant in comparison with the breadth and variety of social encounters prior to the age of onset of the fear of strangers (Schaffer, 1966). The more gradual the initiation to social encounters in our successive therapeutic experiments, the more successful and the sooner the fears were alleviated. Schaffer and other investigators have observed that quiet, immobile strangers may stand looking at the child without causing a panic, but let the stranger advance upon the infant and start to make physical contact and the fear is apt to be reflected, full-fledged, in the youngster's reactions.

We feel that there is an element of similarity between the situation just described and Rheingold's (1969) strange room, which was not strange as long as the infant took the initiative upon entrance. The infant is still in the midst of the acquisition of self-awareness at the time of the onset of fear, but as long as the child feels in control, all is well. An advancing stranger brings the unknown into the picture and out of the knowledge of the baby.

Novak's successful therapy of the 12-month isolate included an additional step in the therapy procedure (Novak & Harlow, 1975). She allowed the isolates to decide for themselves whether or not they wished to watch the therapists at play. Throughout the centuries, our contradictory companions—fear and aggression—have both been triggered by the introduction of strangers. In the nonhuman primates the fear of strangers, as a rule, has lasted much longer than with the human being, even through entire lifetimes.

## THE POWER OF PLAY

We cannot conclude the topic of amelioration of fears and aggression without once more mentioning the powers of play. It is no wonder that play is here to stay. It has so much survival value that we would not dare be without play. The earliest form of play, *peragration* (Mears, 1978), conveys to the developing child a knowledge of the capacities of the body as a whole in relation to the natural elements of water, air, snow, and earth. Peragration prepares the individual for entry, without fear, into the world of social play by removing self-consciousness in such simple movements as walking, running, and jumping.

One aspect of the survival value of play that we observed from the accidental asocial rearing of our breeding colony, is that without peer play in the developmental years, the growing offspring do not learn to accept, not only the presence of and social interaction with agemates, but also the physical bodily contact that is a natural component of children's play and sports. At the time of ordinary maturity, sex did not appear. It did not exist. Without sex behavior, survival of a species is impossible.

Play is the proving ground for sexual roles and also for social roles and rules. With social pressure, aggression becomes unrecognizably altered into roles of dominance, compliance, and cooperation. When parents play rough-and-tumble with their children, they play less vehemently than do the agemates in order to convey the information that play is not supposed to hurt. Pleasure may replace injury, and laughter replace wrangling.

There is no doubt but that the training of the mother or other adequate surrogate, especially in the enforcement of discipline, albeit with love, is a companion force with play in determining the development of positive social roles. This is true even for the nonhuman primates among whom the social roles have been credited with the maintenance of the cohesiveness of the troop. In the development of the human child, training in compliance with commands becomes intertwined with the mother's sensitivity, cooperation, and frequency of both commands and physical intervention (Stayton, Hogan, & Ainsworth, 1973). Here again, the freedom of exploration also adds its potency to the development.

## SOCIETAL IMPLICATIONS

Many religions have promoted individual and world peace, and statesmen have also made admirable attempts, but, in the past, the family has been the most successful dispenser of preventive remedies for the amelioration of fear and aggression. Just as we are experiencing our most vicious onslaught of violence in the form of crime and international aggression in a period of pseudopeace, the family presents its least unified composite of a century. The increased incidence of two working parents or one working divorced or widowed head of a household has fostered a mushrooming growth of day-care centers with unpredictable varieties of surrogate caretakers.

We do not have the answers to such global problems, but we do have a small suggestion as to how one desirable factor of family life might be introduced into the day-care centers and make a contribution to the care of the young clientele. At the same time, there might be created a nucleus of trained future babysitters and future mothers and fathers representative of most economic and ethnic groups. This project may not be expensive enough to interest paid lobbyists, but a comprehensive group of concerned citizens should be able to form one of the most effective lobbies against fear and aggression one could desire.

The schematic sketch for such an undertaking in day-care centers, a beginning solution, would be an educationally trained force of day-care siblings—boys in the 10–11-year-old age group and girls in the 9–10-year-old range—to act as concerned big sisters and brothers, selected as an honor in the schools. These older siblings of the day-care centers should be trained by thoroughly prepared developmental child psychologists and should receive school credits for the hours spent in training and at the day-care centers. The students should, preferably, be consistently sent to the same day-care centers since the number of caretakers might be too numerous and would already be too varied without adding to the problem. Younger caretakers should add a spark of interest through the enthusiasm of their age group. In order to introduce the strangers, even fairly young strangers, gradually, the trained crew should first appear as observers who would let the day-care children initiate the first communication or social contacts. A minimum requirement for the day-care centers should be planned areas for indoor and outdoor play areas. The big sisters and brothers could participate in and guide social play and games.

One authority (Izard, 1978) has suggested that training babies in positive skills to replace the frustrations of early anger can be worthwhile as early as 4–6 months of age. And that is just about the age that babies are beginning to join the day-care center population.

## REFERENCES

Ainsworth, M. D. S. *Infancy in Uganda*. Baltimore, Maryland: Johns Hopkins Univ. Press, 1967.
Ball, W., & Tronick, E. Infant responses to impending collision: Optical and real. In L. J. Stone, H. T. Smith, & L. B. Murphy (Eds.), *The competent infant*. New York: Basic Books, 1973.

Berkowitz, L. Impulse, aggression, and the gun. *Psychology Today,* 1968, *2,* 18–23.

Berkowitz, L. (Ed.) *Roots of aggression.* New York: Atherton, 1969.

Blurton-Jones, N. G. Categories of child–child interaction. In N. G. Blurton-Jones (Ed.), *Ethological studies of child behaviour.* London and New York: Cambridge Univ. Press, 1972.

Bower, T. G. R., Broughton, J. M., & Moore, M. R. Infant responses to approaching objects: An indicator of response to distal variables. *Perception and Psychophysics,* 1970, *9,* 193–196.

Bowlby, J. *Attachment and loss.* Vol. 1. *Attachment.* New York: Basic Books, 1969.

Brazelton, T. B., School, M. L., & Robey, J. S. Visual responses in the newborn. *Pediatrics,* 1966, *37,* 284–290.

Brooks, J., & Lewis, M. *Mirror-image stimulation and self-recognition in infancy.* Paper presented at a meeting of the Society for Research in Child Development, Denver, Colorado, April 1975.

Buirski, P., Kellerman, H., Plutchik, R., Weininger, R., & Buirski, N. A field study of emotions, dominance, and social behavior in a group of baboons (*Papio anubis*). *Primates,* 1973, *14,* 67–78.

Darwin, C. *Expression of the emotions in man and animals.* London: Murray, 1872.

Eibl-Eibesfeldt, I. Strategies of social interaction. In R. Plutchik & H. Kellerman (Eds.), *Emotion: Theory, research, and experience* (Vol. 1): *Theories of emotion.* New York: Academic Press, 1980.

Eron, L. D. The relationship of T.V. viewing habits and aggressive behavior in children. *Journal of Abnormal and Social Psychology,* 1963, *67,* 193–196.

Eron, L. D., Huesmann, R. L., Lefkowitz, M. M., & Walder, L. O. Does T.V. violence cause aggression? *American Psychologist,* 1972, *27,* 253–263.

Erwin, J. Aggression in captive macaques: Interaction of social and spatial factors. In J. Erwin, T. L. Maple, & G. Mitchell (Eds.), *Captivity and behavior.* New York: Van Nostrand Rheinhold, 1979.

Evans, R. I. *Konrad Lorenz: The man and his ideas.* New York: Harcourt, 1975.

Fraiberg, S. Blind infants and their mothers: An examination of the sign system. In M. Lewis & L. A. Rosenblum (Eds.), *The effect of the infant on its caregiver.* New York: Wiley, 1974.

Goy, R., & Phoenix, C. The effects of testosterone administered before birth on the development of behavior in genetic female rhesus monkeys. In C. Sawyer & R. Gorski (Eds.), *Steroid hormones and brain function.* Berkeley: Univ. of California Press, 1971.

Griffin, G. A., & Harlow, H. F. Effects of three months of total social deprivation on social adjustment and learning in the rhesus monkey. *Child Development.* 1966, *37,* 533–547.

Harlow, H. F. The nature of love. *American Psychologist,* 1958, *13,* 673–685.

Harlow, H. F. The development of affectional patterns in infant monkeys. In B. M. Foss (Ed.), *Determinants of infant behaviour* (Vol. 1). London: Methuen, 1961.

Harlow, H. F. The heterosexual affectional system in monkeys. *American Psychologist,* 1962, *17,* 1–9.

Harlow, H. F. Sexual behavior in the rhesus monkey. In F. A. Beach (Ed.), *Sex and behavior.* New York: Wiley, 1965.

Harlow, H. F., & Suomi, S. J. The nature of love—Simplified. *American Psychologist,* 1970, *25,* 161–168.

Harlow, H. F., & Suomi, S. J. Social recovery by isolation-reared monkeys. *Proceedings of the National Academy of Sciences,* 1971, *68,* 1534–1538.

Harlow, H. F., & Zimmermann, R. R. Affectional responses in the infant monkey. *Science,* 1959, *130,* 121–132.

Hebb, D. O. On the nature of fear. *Psychological Review,* 1946, *53,* 259–276.

Hebb, D. O. *The organization of behavior.* New York: Wiley, 1949.

Hinde, R. A. *Biological bases of human social behaviour.* New York: McGraw-Hill, 1974.

Izard, C. E. On the ontogenesis of emotions and emotion–cognition relationships in infancy. In M. Lewis & L. A. Rosenblum (Eds.), *The development of affect*. New York: Plenum, 1978.

James, W. *Psychology*. New York: Holt, 1893.

Joslin, J., Fletcher, H., & Emlen, J. A comparison of the responses to snakes of lab- and wild-reared monkeys. *Animal Behaviour*, 1964, *12*, 348–352.

Kaufman, I. C., & Rosenblum, L. A. The reaction of separation in infant monkeys. Anaclitic depression and conservation–withdrawal. *Psychosomatic Medicine*, 1967, *29*, 648–675.

Kaufman, I. C., & Rosenblum, L. A. The waning of the mother-infant bond in two species of macaque. In B. M. Foss (Ed.), *Determinants of infant behaviour*. Vol. 4. London: Methuen, 1969.

Lee, L. C. *Social encounters of infants: The beginnings of popularity*. Paper presented at a meeting of the International Society for the Study of Behavioral Development, Ann Arbor, Michigan, 1973.

Lewis, M., & Brooks, J. Self-knowledge and emotional development. In M. Lewis & L. A. Rosenblum (Eds.), *The development of affect*. New York: Plenum, 1978.

Mears, C. E. Play and development of cosmic confidence. *Developmental Psychology*, 1978, *14*, 371–378.

Novak, M. A., & Harlow, H. F. Social recovery of monkeys isolated for the first year of life. I. Rehabilitation and therapy. *Developmental Psychology*, 1975, *11*, 453–465.

Phoenix, C. Prenatal testosterone in the nonhuman primate and the consequences for behavior. In R. C. Friedman, R. M. Richart, R. N. Van der Wiele (Eds.), *Sex differences in behavior*. New York: Wiley, 1974.

Phoenix, C., Goy, R., & Resko, J. Psychosexual differentiation. In M. Diamond (Ed.), *Reproduction and sexual behavior*. Bloomington: Indiana Univ. Press, 1968.

Provence, S., & Lipton, R. C. *Infants in institutions*. New York: International Universities Press, 1962.

Reinisch, J. M. *Long-term influence of norlutin on human behavioral development: Preliminary results*. Paper presented at a meeting of the International Society for Sexual Research, Tucson, Arizona, December 1980.

Rheingold, H. L. The effect of a strange environment on the behavior of infants. In B. M. Foss (Ed.), *Determinants of infant behaviour* (Vol. 4). London: Methuen, 1969.

Rheingold, H. L., & Eckerman, C. O. The infant's free entry into a strange environment. *Journal of Experimental Child Psychology*, 1969, *8*, 271–283.

Robson, K. The role of eye-to-eye contact in maternal–infant Attachment. *Psychology, Psychiatry, and Allied Disciplines*, 1967, *8*, 13–25.

Rosenblum, L. A. *The squirrel monkey*. New York: Academic Press, 1968.

Rosenblum, L. A., & Kaufman, I. C. Variations in infant development and response to maternal loss in monkeys. *American Journal of Orthopsychiatry*, 1968, *38*, 418–426.

Sackett, G. P. Monkeys reared in visual isolation with pictures as visual input: Evidence for an innate releasing mechanism. *Science*, 1966, *154*, 1468–1472.

Scarr, S., & Salapatek, P. Patterns of fear development during infancy. In L. J. Stone, H. T. Smith, & L. B. Murphy (Eds.), *The competent infant*. New York: Basic Books, 1973.

Schaffer, H. R. The onset of fear of strangers and the incongruity hypothesis. *Child Psychology and Psychiatry*, 1966, *7*, 95–106.

Schaffer, H. R., & Parry, M. H. Perceptual–motor behavior in infancy as a function of age and stimulus familiarity. In L. J. Stone, H. T. Smith, & L. B. Murphy (Eds.), *The competent infant*. New York: Basic Books, 1973.

Spitz, R. A. Hospitalism: An inquiry into the genesis of psychiatric conditions in early childhood. *Psychoanalytic Study of the Child*, 1945, *1*, 53–74.

Stayton, D. J., Hogan, R., & Ainsworth, M. D. S. Infant obedience and maternal behavior: The origins of socialization reconsidered. In L. J. Stone, H. T. Smith, & L. B. Murphy (Eds.), *The competent infant*. New York: Basic Books, 1973.

Stone, L. J., Smith, H. T., & Murphy, L. B. Editors' introduction. In L. J. Stone, H. T. Smith, & L. B. Murphy (Eds.), *The competent infant*. New York: Basic Books, 1973.

Suomi, S. J., & Harlow, H. F. Social rehabilitation of isolate-reared monkeys. *Developmental Psychology,* 1972, *6,* 487–496.

Suomi, S. J., & Harlow, H. F. The facts and functions of fear. In M. Zuckerman & C. D. Spielberger (Eds.), *Emotions and anxiety*. New York: Basic Books, 1976.

Van Lawick-Goodall, J. Behavior of free-living chimpanzees of the Gombe Stream area. *Animal Behavior Monographs,* 1968, *3*.

Watson, J. B. *An introduction of comparative psychology*. New York: Holt, 1914.

Watson, J. B. *Psychology*. Philadelpha, Pennsylvania: Lippincott, 1919.

Wolff, P. H. Observations on the early development of smiling. In L. J. Stone, H. T. Smith, & L. B. Murphy (Eds.), *The competent infant*. New York: Basic Books, 1973.

Chapter 7

# ON THE RELATIONSHIP BETWEEN
# ATTACHMENT AND SEPARATION PROCESSES
# IN INFANCY

*MYRON A. HOFER*

## ABSTRACT

*Maternal separation responses and attachment behavior are generally consid-*
*ered to be different aspects of a single psychophysiological system. However,*
*recent evidence from animal studies argue against a unitary emotional system*
*underlying attachment and separation responses. Hidden within the interactions*
*between infant and mother, we and others have found a number of processes by*
*which the mother serves as an external regulator of the infants' behavior, its*
*autonomic physiology, and even the neurochemistry of its maturing brain. Many*
*of the more slowly developing separation responses may thus be due to with-*
*drawal of the previous regulation supplied by the mother rather than being part*
*of the acute emotional response to disruption of attachment.*

*This formulation of separation phenomena turns attention to an analysis of*
*processes within the preexisting thermal, nutrient, and sensorimotor interaction*
*between parent and infant. It is possible that some of these processes and their*
*effects on the infant's developing systems may support early stages in the forma-*
*tion of attachment and of other emotional systems as well.*

One of the settings in which emotions first appear in early development is in
response to maternal separation and in the attachment that infants show toward

EMOTION
Theory, Research, and Experience
Volume 2

their mothers. Research on maternal separation responses and research on attachment behavior have developed together, historically, and the two sets of phenomena are generally considered to be different aspects of a single psychophysiological system. The degree of interdependence of our explanations for the two kinds of behavior is quickly realized when we ask ourselves why an infant is distressed when separated from its mother and answer in terms of the strength of the attachment 'bond' the infant had formed to the mother. For if we then ask how we can tell that such an attachment exists, the answer is given in terms of the observation that the infant always tries to stay close to its mother and becomes distressed when separated from her. Vulnerability to circular reasoning such as this is a constant hazard for those attempting to use 'bond' theories to generate new and clear understanding of early social relationships.

What is it about maternal separation that gives it such impact on the developing infant? Most stressful events involve an increase in some form of outside stimulation, whereas in this experience there are *reduced* levels of stimulation. Yet the infant, be it a rat (Hofer & Shair, 1978), cat (Seitz, 1959), dog (Scott, 1962), monkey (Seay, Hansen, & Harlow, 1962), or human (Bowlby, 1969), acts as if it were acutely distressed when isolated from its mother and siblings. The stressful impact is explained by current theory, which infers, both from the distress of separation and from the many behaviors organized so as to keep the infant in close physical proximity to the mother, that an attachment has been formed, a ''bond'' (at the psychological level) between the infant, its mother, and its siblings. John Bowlby (1969, 1973) has presented this theory in elegant form in his books.

Separation breaks this inferred bond and disrupts the attachment system by preventing attainment of its goals. Attachment behavior (searching and vocalization) escalates, and distress ensues. The distressed behavior closely resembles the response of the infant to physically painful stimuli, presumably because the importance of maintaining proximity with the mother at an early age is at a level of biological importance similar to the importance of avoiding physical harm. This distress is thought to be accompanied by an integrated psychophysiological response similar to emotional responses occurring in adults. An early phase of agitation has been found to give way to a later phase of apathy and social withdrawal in some species of monkeys under some conditions (Kaufman & Rosenblum, 1969; Kaufman & Stynes, 1978) and is the usual but not uniform response for human infants (Bowlby, 1973). This concept is summarized in Table 7.1.

In fact, evidence in animals is mounting against the existence of a single emotional system underlying attachment and separation responses. The results of experimental work in our own laboratory and othes have shown that hidden within the interactions between infant and mother are a number of processes by which the mother serves as an external regulator of the infant's behavior, its

TABLE 7.1
Summary of Attachment Theory and Its Application to Infant Separation Responses

| Attachment | Separation |
|---|---|
| 1. Goal-directed behavior to attain proximity (e.g., vocalization, following, clinging) | 1. Intensification of attachment behavior (e.g., vocalization, locomotion, rocking) |
| 2. Bond (at psychological level) associated with affects characteristic of security and comfort | 2. Disruption of bond associated with affects characteristic of distress, followed by depression |
| | 3. Results in an integrated psychophysiological response pattern |

physiological state, and even the neurochemistry of its maturing brain. These processes were unexpected and were revealed only by experiments involving maternal separation in which questions were asked about exactly how the experience might be producing some of the more slowly developing responses of the infant. Once these processes were discovered, it became possible to see that several of the responses to separation resulted from *withdrawal* of the previous regulation supplied by the mother and thus represented gradual shifts to new sources of regulation, either within the infant or in its new environment. This concept is summarized in Table 7.2.

The two concepts need not be mutually exclusive since the motivational system that we call *attachment* serves to maintain the proximity between mother and infant that allows the several regulatory processes to act. It is, however, possible that the attachment system itself is built up out of a number of interactional processes similar to the regulatory processes described in Table 7.2. This possibility is described later.

The emotions that we attribute to infants during various phases of attachment and separation are inferred from the patterns of behavioral and physiological changes exhibited by the infants. This chapter is aimed at understanding the processes through which these changes are brought about by the action of stimuli hidden within the fabric of the parent–infant relationship.

TABLE 7.2
Summary of Regulator Hypothesis and Its Application to the More Slowly Developing Infant Separation Responses

| Regulation | Separation |
|---|---|
| Multiple sources of stimulation control or direct physiology and behavior of infant over multiple (relatively independent) pathways | Withdrawal of regulatory control leads to altered levels, patterns, and rhythms in individual systems |

## THE PARENT–INFANT RELATIONSHIP
## AS A REGULATOR

In order to illustrate the idea of the parent–infant relationship as a regulator of function in the infant and to show the implications of this idea for an understanding of the infants' responses to separation, I will give some examples from my own and others' research. I will begin with heart rate changes, a physiological sign that is often used as an indicator of infant emotions within the mother–infant affectional system.

### HEART RATE

The heart rates of infant rats (and humans) follow a developmental course characterized by a small rise in the first days (or months) followed by a plateau of high heart rates during mid-infancy, which gives way to a slow decline during preadolescence. The high range of heart rates during infancy are the result of an initial high sympathetic tone, and the subsequent decline is the result of the gradual establishment of predominant parasympathetic (vagal) restraint (Hofer, 1974). These developmental stages and transitions had been assumed to be the result of maturation of central neural homeostatic systems, and the set point at any age had been assumed to be an intrinsic neural function, probably genetically programmed and heavily buffered from environmental influences. In our studies, we found that the age-characteristic level of heart rate in the rat was the result of the infant's nutritional relationship with its mother and could be delicately tuned, over periods of a few hours, by variations in the amount of milk the mother provides.

The demonstration of this relationship depended on separating the mother and the 2-week-old infant rat, finding that there was a 30% decrease in cardiac rate and that this, in turn, was the result of a marked reduction in sympathetic cardiac tone (Hofer & Weiner, 1971). When this reduction in rate persisted unchanged despite maintenance of normal body temperature and return of the infants to nonlactating "maternal" females, our attention turned to a nutritional mechanism. At first this might appear to be a nonspecific debilitative effect of the weight loss sustained by these infants, except that their hearts were capable of beating at normal rates if the animals were simply stimulated by tail pinching. Then, we found that the heart-rate decline persisted even if they were fed every 4 hours by gastric intubation so that they gained a small amount of weight over the 24 hours the mother was gone (Hofer, 1970). This showed that the low heart rates were not the result of starvation. But the mother provides milk even more frequently (every 1–2 hours) at this age. A series of systematic studies with graded amounts of feedings by stomach tube demonstrated that cardiac rate was delicately tuned to the amount of milk given within the normal range of weight gain for infant rats (Hofer, 1973c). If enough milk was given by tube to produce as much weight gain as in a group of mothered infants, then heart rates of separated infants remained at the level of the mothered infants.

Variations ordinarily occur in the amount of weight gained each day by mothered infants. If the mother is disturbed or the litter size is increased, the usual weight gain does not occur or is reversed. Other factors, such as reduction of litter size, seem to promote weight gain. Heart rates follow these fluctuations in the weight gain of mothered infants and illustrate the cumulative action of repeated nursing bouts resulting in long-term regulation of the infants' cardiac rate by the amount of milk supplied over time by the mother.

A series of physiological studies (Hofer & Weiner, 1975) showed that this effect of nutrient on heart rate was most likely mediated by spinal sympathetic pathways and the β-adrenergic receptors on the efferent side. Since lactose and amino acids were effective only if administered intragastrically and not if administered intravenously, the receptors of the afferent mechanism appeared to be located in the gut wall. Simple gastric distension, various gastrointestinal hormones, and the afferent vagus have been ruled out, but afferent mesenteric sympathetic nerves (Sharma & Nasset, 1962) remain a possible pathway by which the brain is informed of the amount of nutrient in the gut.

Why is a vital internal function such as regulation of heart rate at the mercy of such an unreliable control system as the relationship with the mother? The very word *autonomic* is used to denote the autonomous nature of the neural system that regulates certain vital internal organ systems (e.g., sympathetic and parasympathetic cardiac control). Instead, we see heart rate in a very nonautonomous role, dependent on extrinsic regulation by another animal. The adaptive value of this regulatory phenomenon in early life may hinge on the cardiovascular tasks involved in the absorption and circulatory transport of the relatively enormous amounts of milk consumed by infant rats. At 2 weeks of age, young rats gain between 12% and 15% of body weight per day. In order to produce these weight gains by milk infusion, 10 ml of milk must be given per day to a 25–30-gm animal. This means that infant rats process 30–40% of their own body weight in milk each day. A "wide-open" cardiovascular system would appear to be appropriate for this task, allowing maximal rates of transport of nutrient from the gut and delivery to all the rapidly growing peripheral tissues. With a wide-open system, resistance to pumping is low and the heart must have a relatively high output with rapid pumping rates in order to maintain blood pressure at levels necessary for tissue processes. With reduced nutrient levels, blood vessels would constrict and cardiac rates decrease. This is our working hypothesis, supported by evidence that blood pressure is maintained at normal levels during 24-hour separations and that a drug that blocks blood vessel constriction returns the low heart rates of separated pups to normal levels, (Shear, Brunelli, Shair, & Hofer, 1981).

This unexpected regulatory phenomenon of the early social relationship in the rat was revealed by the use of mother–infant separation followed by analytic studies based on a concept of the relationship as a regulator, rather than on the concept of attachment and social bond formation. To have inferred that the low heart rates of recently separated infants were a reflection of an emotional state precipitated by disruption of an attachment bond (such as "conservation– withdrawal" [Engel & Schmale, 1972]) would have been wrong and could have obscured other processes from view. Thus, the slowly developing changes in cardiac and respiratory rates following separation of the young from their mothers are "release phenomena" that occur as a result of withdrawal of a physiological regulatory process hidden within the fabric of the previous mother–infant relationship.

## STEREOTYPED ROCKING

The next example is a behavioral one and involves one of the prototypical maternal deprivation behaviors, stereotyped body rocking, which occurs in human and monkey infants after several hours or days of separation from their mothers. This behavior, together with self-clasping and nonnutritive sucking, is generally throught to be a patterned emotional response indicating the emotional anguish experienced as a result of loss of the attachment object.

Several species of nonhuman primate infants show this behavior abnormality, most often as a consequence of early maternal deprivation, whether reared with artificial surrogate mothers or not. Those artifical surrogates were not mobile. Mason and Berkson (1974) gave rhesus monkey infants a standard terry cloth surrogate suspended on a wire so that it could swing when jumped on by the infant. Furthermore, they gave the surrogate independent mobility by having it moved, on the end of its wire, in a circle within the cage, at irregular intervals during most of the day. The infants spent the same amount of time clinging to this mobile surrogate as to the standard stationary one, but the mobility of the surrogate completely prevented all self-rocking in these infants. Two other self-directed behaviors, self-clasping and sucking, were not affected by the mobility of the surrogate, nor was locomotion or distress vocalization. Infants of mobile surrogates spent slightly less total time in contact with the surrogates after the first 3 months, but spent much more time in rough-and-tumble play with their surrogates than infants with stationary surrogates. Even after the surrogates were permanently removed when the infants were 1 year of age, no rocking appeared in the infants previously housed with mobile surrogates. In later tests with novel environment and strange intruder animals, the monkeys raised on mobile surrogates reacted with less timidity, distress vocalization, or extremes of locomotor activity, and with less self-biting and self-rocking.

The implication of these results is that vestibular stimulation of the infant by the mother in the course of their social relationship has effects on the development of certain behavior patterns. This form of stimulation, as delivered in the normal mother–infant interaction, may function to channel the development of motor behavior into patterns other than self-rocking. In the absence of vestibular stimulation and the regulatory effects it has on developing motor behavior, the self-rocking emerges as early as 1 month postnatally and becomes characteristic and habitual in the juvenile and young adult.

In this example, one aspect of the mother–infant interaction, the vestibular stimulation ordinarily supplied, regulates one aspect of behavioral development, so that it is the withdrawal of this particular process, hidden within their previous relationship, that is responsible for the appearance of this singular action pattern within the set of behaviors constituting the separation response.


## DEPRIVATION DWARFISM

A series of studies by Schanberg and associates (Butler, Suskind & Schanberg, 1978; Kuhn, Butler, and Schanberg and Kuhn & Schanberg 1979) has contributed to our knowledge of the neurochemistry and endocrinology of maternal separation. The studies concern the enzyme ornithine decarboxylase (ODC), which is thought to regulate the rate-limiting step in polyamine synthesis and which is elevated in most rapidly growing tissues. They found that this enzyme, in the brain and heart of infant rats 10 days of age, fell rapidly after the mother rat was removed from her litter. They went through the procedures we had used with cardiac effects of separation and found ODC not to be regulated by nutritional level or ambient temperature but to be regulated by some aspect of the pup's active behavioral interaction with its mother. An anesthetized mother would not do, but one with mammary ducts ligated was as good as a normal mother at maintaining brain and heart ODC levels. In fact, a nonlactating mother promptly reversed the fall in brain ODC much as the intragastric milk restored cardiac rate in our studies. This effect of interaction with the mother took place equally well after bilateral adrenalectomy, indicating that the brain enzyme changes were not induced by a corticosterone response to separation.

Further studies on the endocrinology of maternal separation demonstrated that growth hormone was reduced nearly 50% by a 2-hour maternal absence, whereas TSH, prolactin, and corticosterone were not significantly affected. All these hormones are known to induce ODC, but these studies show that growth hormone is the most likely actually to mediate the brain enzyme changes.

Further studies showed how close the temporal patterns of growth hormone and ODC responses were during maternal separation and reunion. Blood levels of growth hormone have a 15–30-min half-life, and the level of this hormone appeared to be very closely tied to the stimulation received by the infant during its behavioral interaction with its mother. Furthermore, observations by the Duke University group shows that stimulation of the back of the infant with a stiff brush, but not tail pinch or anogenital stimulation, can maintain growth hormone levels in maternally deprived pups. These studies should soon tell us precisely which aspects of the mother–infant interaction are crucial for regulation of growth hormone levels in the pup.

That a decrease in growth hormone may indeed be the mediator of maternal separation effects on brain ODC was supported by the finding that cyprohep-tadine, a serotonin antagonist that decreases serum growth hormone levels in normally mothered infant rats, also lowers brain ODC, despite the continued presence of the mother.

Work reported by Kuhn and Schanberg (1979) shows that after the mother has been absent for 2 hours the low brain ODC levels become unresponsive to growth hormone injection although they remain responsive to other inducers of this enzyme, such as cyclic AMP or insulin.

Similar hormonal abnormalities have been reported in human "deprivation dwarfism [Powell, Brasel, & Blizzard, 1967]," a condition of developmental retardation in infants from chaotic homes where parent–infant interaction is severely disturbed. These children grow and mature only if provided with an attentive caretaker. Such studies in animals may provide an animal analog of this distressing human condition.

## OTHER REGULATORY PROCESSES

These three examples, given in some detail, show how different aspects of the mother–infant relationship serve to maintain levels of function within the in-fants' autonomic, endocrine, and neurochemical systems, as well as to influence the development of relatively discrete aspects of behavior. We have, in addition, found evidence for the regulation of sleep–wake patterns by the rhythmicity of nutrient delivery (Hofer & Shair, 1982) and the regulation of brain cate-cholamines by the thermal input provided by the mother's body (Stone, Bonnet, & Hofer, 1976).

Is there evidence that such processes may also take place in humans? Of course it is much more difficult to design human studies that give unequivocal answers, but the work of Condon and Sander (1974) suggests that the rhythms of human speech entrain the rhythms of neonatal limb movements. And the work of Fraiberg (1974) on blind infants shows how the infants' experience of the expressive facial movements of the mother are necessary for the development of the child's facial expressiveness beyond the fourth to sixth week after birth.

It seems likely that these are just a beginning and that many more regulatory systems will be discovered, hidden within the mammalian infants' early social relationships. Many of the consequences of maternal separation may be the result of withdrawal of these powerful influences on the behavior and physiology of the infant. Since each operates in relative independence of other regulatory systems and each is activated by its own stimulus configuration, qualitative variations in the prior relationship and in the setting of separation are likely to result in marked differences in the pattern of changes shown by individual infants.

## TWO FORMS OF SEPARATION HYPERACTIVITY IN THE SAME-AGE INFANT

If the withdrawal of regulatory processes accounts for some of the infants' responses to maternal separation, what room is left for the impact of the rupture of the attachment bond as an explanatory concept for the phenomena of maternal separation? Obviously, age and species differences will be important. Older children who spend relatively little time with their parents and whose behavioral, cognitive, and physiological development is relatively advanced, are unlikely to respond primarily in terms of the withdrawal of regulatory systems similar to those just described. The same seems true for the acute distress of sudden social isolation. So far, the psychological processes of attachment are a better conceptual framework for dealing with such events. Yet it may be possible to apply regulator and withdrawal concepts, even to the immediate distress reaction of a separated child, as will be discussed in a later section.

We were concerned with these questions and determined to find out if the 2-week-old rat, which showed so well the independent regulatory systems just described, would also show one of the cardinal phenomena of attachment: acute isolation distress upon separation from its social companions, as is seen in puppies, monkeys, and children. If this were true, then at least we would know that regulatory and attachment processes were not mutually exclusive and that the rat would be a reasonable species in which to try to work out some of the principles of the relationship between the two.

## ACUTE SOCIAL ISOLATION IN THE INFANT RAT

Psychological attachment is usually inferred from the strong tendency of the infant to maintain proximity to familiar social companions and from the infant's immediate responses to separation, which generally consist of an intensification of attachment behaviors accompanied by emotional behaviors indicative of distress. Clinging and huddling are the most proximal attachment behaviors, whereas following, intermittent vocalization, and locomotor search are the more distal forms. The behavior most consistently reported as an index of emotional distess after separation, across mammalian species, is vocalization, with aimless locomotion, self-grooming, rocking, or apathetic withdrawal less consistently found. Characteristically, the vocalization of separation distress is rapidly alleviated by reunion with the object of attachment, the social companion. In the rat infant, vocalizations are in the ultrasonic range (35–45 kHz) but can be observed and recorded with a Holgate bat detector (Sales & Pye, 1974).

First, we wanted to know whether 2-week-old rats responded to the periodic maternal absences that normally occur in this species, and whether the mother returns to her young because of an increase in their vocalization after a lengthy absence. We found that vocalizations increased more than four-fold immediately after the mother left the nest, but that these levels dropped to basal rates within 4 min and did not increase again until *after* the mother returned, when they showed the same pattern of a sharp rise and decrement (Hofer & Shair, 1978). Pups observed in a group in the home cage for as long as 24 hours after maternal separation showed no increase in ultrasonic vocalization. Next, we asked whether sudden separation of the infant from all social companions would elicit increased vocalization even if the infant remained undisturbed in the home cage nest area. We found that even sleeping pups usually sensed their isolation within a minute or two and began an outcry with much higher rates than observed in the previous litter situation. Pups maintained vocalization steadily throughout a 30-min observation period, at an average level of 12 pulses/min, in response to no other disturbance than the absence of their littermates and mother. In addition to vocalizing, isolated pups spent more than one-half the time either locomoting or self-grooming. Rates of ultrasound were highest during locomotion.

These experiments demonstrated that young rats responded to separation from familiar social companions with high levels of vocalization, locomotion, and self-grooming, even in their own home cage. Would their response to isolation in an unfamiliar place be even greater, as has been found in monkeys and humans? And if so, would interaction with mother or littermates be sufficient to reduce vocalization significantly? We found that a single pup placed in an unfamiliar test area vocalized at twice the home cage isolation rate (25 pulses/min) during 80–100% of the 7-min observation period and often moved ceaselessly about the enclosure, whereas when allowed access to an anesthetized mother, or when groups of four pups were placed in the same situation, they became virtually silent within 2 min, as they huddled together with their companions.

Our results showed that an unfamiliar environment intensified the response to isolation. These findings led us to an extensive enquiry into the properties of the social companion critical to the alleviation of the high-intensity vocalization produced by separation in an unfamiliar area (Hofer & Shair, 1980). An active behavioral interaction was not found to be necessary, for a single anesthetized pup was as effective as an awake one. The mother, anesthetized, was more effective than a single littermate, whereas a plastic object in the shape and size of a littermate and warmed to body temperature did not influence vocalization rate at all. A series of surrogates were then designed, each with a different sensory modality or combination of modalities. From these experiments we learned that the odor of home cage shavings, warmth, and a familiar contour were not in themselves sufficient to reduce vocalizations, but they added to the effectiveness of a furry texture. Synthetic fur, even when laid on the cage floor, reduced vocalizations partially, but consistently. The possibility that infant rats possess a skin odor, not present in home cage shavings, that acts as a cue to reduction of distress vocalizations was tested in two additional experiments and found to be unlikely.

These experiments have extended our understanding of the control of ultrasonic vocalization in relatively old rat pups, 2-weeks of age. Most of the previous work on this subject was done on pups in their first week of life, when vocalizations are predominantly under the control of ambient temperature (Allin & Banks, 1971; Okon, 1971) and during their second week, when olfactory and tactual nest cues come to replace thermal properties (Oswalt & Meier, 1975).

The duration of body contact elicited by the different surrogates bore a clear relation to the amount by which the surrogates reduced the ultrasonic vocalization of the pup in the test box with them. The more body contact elicited by a surrogate, the more those pups reduced their vocalization. This relation between the elicitation of body contact and of reduced vocalization across experiments was not nearly as clear within each experiment, when the correlation across individuals was examined. Some pups appeared to make only occasional contact, by nosing the surrogate, but they emitted little or no ultrasound throughout. This kind of observation in primates has led to inferring the existence of a memory trace of the social companion, which can be maintained by repeated brief periods of contact, providing a "safe base" for exploration of a novel environment.

Taken together, these experiments provide evidence for behavioral responses to separation in the young rat that closely resemble those of kittens, puppies, monkeys, and human infants, behavioral characteristics that have been used as the basis for inferring "isolation distress," "comfort," and the concept of "attachment" in those species. Obviously, we are not dealing here with the highly specific attachments and internal cognitive representations apparent in older human infants and children. The young rat apparently employs a strategy of adding cues in different sense modalities in the alleviation of separation distress and apparently has come to regard littermates as more or less complete surrogates for the mother, in so far as separation distress is concerned. However, this strategy allows a fairly high degree of specificity and is not too different from that employed by young primates and human infants before the development of highly differentiated schemata.

## SLOWLY DEVELOPING
## BEHAVIORAL HYPERACTIVITY

We have found that, in addition to the acute separation response, the infant rat also undergoes a set of more slowly developing changes in behavioral responsiveness that can be attributed to the continued absence of the mother in particular. Every day, infant rats experience about 17 short periods of maternal absence. These range in average length from 5 to 10 min for the newborn to 2 hours or more for 3-week-olds. At the age we are considering (2 weeks), these absences are 45 min–1 hour, and her visits with them last 15–20 min, when all nursing takes place (Grota & Ader, 1969). Thus, a regular cycle of interaction and withdrawal is provided by the mother. This pattern, characteristic of the rat, is actually more like the schedule of human mother–infant interaction in most civilized countries than is the nonhuman primate and primitive human pattern of holding the infant in nearly continuous physical contact throughout the day and night.

If the mother is removed from the cage by the experimenter during one of her periodic absences, the litter is exposed to a withdrawal of this periodic behavioral interaction. After a period of time has elapsed, the pups can then be tested for their behavioral response to being placed in an unfamiliar test box.

After 18 hours of maternal absence, heart rates, predictably, were markedly down. This was true whether the infants were left in their home cage without additional heat (resulting in a 3° C fall in body temperature over this time period) or whether their temperatures were maintained at 35° C by a regulated heating pad under the cage floor. But whether they were warmed or left at room temperature made a dramatic difference in their behavior when they were placed alone in an unfamiliar test box for observation at the end of the experiment. The cool pups showed fewer characteristic behavioral responses than their normally mothered littermates, whereas the warm pups were very hyperactive on the same measures of locomotion, rearing, and self-grooming (Hofer, 1973a).

This picture is quite different from the usual integrated psychophysiological response to stressful stimulation. Here an animal with a very low resting heart rate was found to be markedly hyperactive behaviorally, but the same low heart rate did not predict the same thing at all about the behavioral response of the cool infants. The role of the mother as a source of thermal input and its importance for behavior regulation is illustrated here. We can have either "agitation" or "apathy" as a response to maternal deprivation, depending on whether the separated infant has had the regulating effect of the mother's body heat withdrawn or whether this aspect of the relationship has been provided artifically.

The infant's behavioral state can be shown to be affected by separation even while it is resting in a group in the home cage nest with its littermates. Electrophysiologic studies of sleep and wakefulness (Hofer, 1976) revealed that the separated infant became markedly insomniac after 24 hours separation, with the major sleep loss coming out of rapid eye movement (REM) sleep time. Separated infants took longer to fall asleep, and their sleep was fragmented, with frequent awakenings and shortened duration of slow wave sleep periods as well as REM periods. The effect of separation at room temperature was to exaggerate these changes, in contrast to the room temperature effects on waking behavior just described.

A further understanding of the behavioral changes following separation has been provided by neurochemical studies by Stone et al. (1976). Tissue growth, brain DNA and RNA, as well as brain catecholamines were measured in 12–15-day-old pups after 3 days of maternal deprivation either at nest temperature or at room temperature (20° C). Maturation rates of body tissues were generally temperature-dependent. Catecholamines showed the most striking differences. For the pups separated at room temperature, brain catecholamines fell below the levels of normally reared agemates, whereas the warm, separated pups showed an *increased* rate of accumulation of norepinephrine and dopamine, as measured per brain, compared to normally mothered littermates.

These data suggest that the motor deficit of cool pups resulted from reduced levels of central catecholamines, whereas the hyperactivity of warm, separated pups might have resulted from increased availability of these neurotransmitters at central adrenergic terminals. Indeed, pretreatment with reserpine (which destroys storage vesicles at nerve terminals) at the time of separation prevented the development of behavioral hyperactivity in separated, warm infants at a dose (.5 mg/kg) that has no residual effect on normally mothered pups at the time of behavior testing 24 hours later (Hofer, 1980).

Next we asked how the loss of the mother produces the hyperactivity found if nest temperature is maintained. We had determined that this response takes time to develop. Only after more than 4 hours was there any change. What was it about the increasing length of separation to which the infants were responding? An obvious candidate was the increasing nutritional deficit, since separated pups do not eat well for the first 2 or 3 days. In order to test this idea, separated infants were fed continuously by an indwelling stomach catheter. Regardless of how much milk they received, they behaved no differently than separated pups that were not fed (Hofer, 1973c). On the other hand, if the mother was left with them to provide behavioral interaction, but with her mammary ducts ligated, the hyperactivity was almost entirely prevented (Hofer, 1973b).

Two hypotheses compete for explanation. The hyperactivity could be viewed in the framework of the attachment hypothesis or it could be the result of withdrawal of regulatory processes that had been acting to reduce levels of activity while the social relationship was intact. It is difficult to rule out an attachment separation–distress model, but several predictions of that model failed to be substantiated (Hofer, 1975). First, the hyperactivity was slow to develop (between 4 and 8 hours after separation), which is not at all characteristic of the hyperactivity of separation distress. Second, the maternally separated infants in these experiments were housed in the familiar home cage with seven littermates during separation. Housing them alone and in an unfamiliar environment failed to accentuate the hyperactivity, as predicted by the attachment hypothesis. Thus, this form of behavioral hyperactivity did not meet our criteria for separation distress. As I have described, it is immediately following isolation that infant rats of this age show vocalization and hyperactivity that is alleviated by the presence of a familiar social companion. This earlier response, then, is classical separation distress, and the later changes we have been considering here are not.

What sort of stimulation could serve to reduce or inhibit behavioral arousal levels during the normal mother–infant interaction? Tactile, auditory, olfactory, and vestibular stimulation are the leading candidates, the eyes not yet being open at this age. Since the mother normally licks, noses, scratches, picks up, steps on, rubs, and lies on her infants, tactile stimulation seemed a strong possibility. In order to test this possibility, stimulation was provided for approximately 15 min out of every hour throughout the 8-hour separation period, in accordance with the timing of the visits and absences of the mother at this age. Forty minutes following the last stimulation, pups were observed in the novel test box. Using mild electric current (.05 mA constant amperage, just enough to elicit a response), levels and patterns of behavior were produced in 8-hour separated pups, which were indistinguishable from those seen after normal mothering (Hofer, 1975). A similar, though not so powerful effect was obtained by placing infants in a slowly rotating drum.

What do these results mean? They show that when tactile stimulation, which has the immediate effect of eliciting activity, is repeated, it has the cumulative long-term effect of reducing the pups' level of behavioral reactivity. The results can be said to be consistent with the hypothesis that levels of behavioral arousal of the infant are regulated in part by the levels of tactile stimulation delivered by the mother. A long-term quieting effect from tactile and other forms of stimulation provided to the human infant has been described by Brackbill (1971). Korner and Thoman (1970) have pointed out how effective vestibular stimulation is in calming a crying baby. Cultures differ in how human babies are stimulated, but there appears to be a widespread intuitive understanding of the necessity for regular stimulation in order to avoid fussiness in infants. Such processes may generalize between rats and man.

## IMPLICATIONS

We have found two forms of separation hyperactivity in the 14-day-old rat pup, distinguished by their time of appearance following separation and by the processes underlying them. Although increased vocalization is more prominent in one type than in the other, increased levels of locomotion, rearing, and self-grooming occur in both. If we did not know anything about the processes underlying the two responses, we might easily conclude that the slower developing hyperactivity was simply an extension in time of the acute response and view both in terms of a unitary emotional system of separation distress activated as a result of disruption of an attachment bond. This does not seem to be the case.

Our analysis of the sensory and neurochemical processes underlying these behaviors is pointing the way toward a less global way of thinking about infant separation responses. But is it necessary to conclude that there are two separate forms of responses, the acute response operating by the principles of attachment theory, and the more slowly developing response by the withdrawal of a maternal regulator? Would it be possible to bring the two kinds of phenomena together within a single theoretical approach?

## TOWARD A UNIFIED THEORY

The intuitive belief that early mother–infant separation is stressful and traumatic, the profound abnormalities in behavioral development that have been found to result from prolonged maternal deprivation (Spitz, 1945), and the recent findings that mothers are also adversely affected by separation from their infants (Leifer, Leiderman, Barnett, & Williams, 1972) have directed concepts of separation into the framework of stress psychophysiology. This focus on the response to separation has distracted us from considering what may have been going on during the mother–infant relationship and from realizing that knowledge about this relationship may help explain some of the responses to separation.

At present, the behavioral and physiological responses to mother–infant separation are generally viewed as related to attachment and to the inferred stress of disrupting such a strong social "bond." An emotional distress response is supposed to ensue with behavioral and physiological components, as in classical psychophysiological responses to imposed threat. But I have described physiological and behavioral responses to separation that do not fit this model, and I would now like to examine the concept of attachment and the response to separation from a different point of view.

In altricial mammals such as the rat, the monkey, and the human the growth and formation of attachment appears to take place slowly, throughout a rather prolonged sensitive period. Initially consisting only of primitive biological-approach tendencies (e.g., thermotaxis), the attraction becomes more and more specifically directed. Coincidentally, there develops the reaction to separation, which usually consists of behaviors characteristic of emotional distress, as if the animal were in physical pain or threatened with harm. The intensity of this separation response is often taken as a measure of the strength of attachment. These events have been difficult to explain in terms of learning theory since attachment does not depend on standard reinforcing agents (Bowlby, 1969, 1973; Harlow, 1958; Scott, 1962). Attachment is then viewed as a primary drive, and words are used that convey the sense of an unusual process of stamping in (e.g., *imprinting*), or metaphors are used, such as the *bond,* that convey a sense of the enduring character of some social attachments and the traumatic impact of separation.

But the formation of attachment develops in the young coincidentally with the hidden regulatory processes outlined above. May not the formation of attachment and the expression of separation distress be related to these regulatory processes? The infant cat, for example, is at first attracted to heat and orients along thermal gradients to the nest and to the mother. In the course of development, a gradual transition takes place through a series of intermediate regulatory processes (e.g., olfaction [Rosenblatt, 1971]) to the juvenile stage when attraction is to the unique stimulus configuration of an individual adult, and the regulatory effect is primarily psychological. Coincidentally, biological and behavioral regulation has shifted from the mother–infant dyad to a wide range of environmental events and to newly matured internal homeostatic mechanisms. This transition would appear to be the result of an interaction of rapidly maturing sensorimotor, integrative, and cognitive faculties of the developing young with the changing experiences of the evolving social relationship.

I have reviewed some of the unexpected, persistent, long-range, and cumulative effects of the episodic, repeated stimulation inherent in early social relationships. It seems probable that many other processes will eventually be elucidated. Thus, it may not be too speculative to suggest that one of the enduring effects of early repetitive stimulation is to establish and maintain the goal-directed system of behavior that we call *attachment.* The regulatory nature of attachment has been described by Bowlby (1969, 1973), and a theoretical model for the elicitation of distress behavior upon withdrawal of the attachment object (opponent process theory) has been put forward by Hoffman and Solomon (1974), supported by Hoffman's data on imprinting in ducklings. If we conceive of attachment as a regulatory process, established and governed by repetitive specific stimulation, then the classical separation responses of vocalization, locomotor hyperactivity, and even stereotyped abnormal behavior can be viewed as "withdrawal" or release phenomena, analogous to the withdrawal response of narcotic addicts after separation from their repeated drug injections. By this line of reasoning, the results of separation of an infant (of any species) from its mother (at any developmental age) are in part a function of the tonic or cumulative effects of the stimulation the infant has received from the interaction with its mother. To a variable degree of certainty, we can draw inferences as to the prior regulatory processes from the responses shown. But only by analytic experiments with specific stimulus configuration and rhythms can we positively identify them.

It appears that withdrawal responses can occur with different latencies. Those classically ascribed to attachment in older infants occur immediately upon separation or even upon signs that separation is imminent (Bowlby, 1969, 1973). Those we have found in younger infants, develop slowly in the hours after separation, as if the regulatory effects of the stimulation took time to dissipate. Clearly, different neural mechanisms may underlie withdrawal effects in different systems, just as the regulatory effects of stimulation vary among the different systems and the different sources of stimulation.

It is not yet clear which aspects of the stimulation provided by the mother are critical to the formation of attachment, but the following partial formulation is offered. In birds that show imprinting, moving objects or flashing lights appears to be sufficient to establish following. In slowly developing mammals, elicitation of approach, clinging, and following may depend on a series of stimuli in a developmental progression depending on the maturation of sensory capacities. These stimuli become gradually combined into a highly specific complex or gestalt. Stimulation from these sources appears to be reinforcing at appropriate ages, eliciting approach and maintaining proximity. This stimulation also has the long-term cumulative effect of reducing emotional distress and the behavior associated with it. Removal of the mother withdraws the regulatory effect of the repetitive stimulation on the emotional state of the young, and the classical separation distress ensues.

The advantage of this formulation is not only that it allows separation experiments to be used to learn more about the effects of parent–infant interaction but also that it permits us to seek to understand some of the more slowly-developing effects of maternal separation (Reite, Kaufman, Pauley, & Stynes, 1974; Spitz, 1945) as the result of loss of specific regulatory actions previously provided by the mother, rather than some form of prolonged, complex emotional response. It allows us to separate out each developmental effect of separation in relation to its specific mechanisms rather than viewing the phenomenon globally as an "emotional stress response," words that do not lead to further understanding. For example, a rat pup separated for 18 hours has a low heart rate and is hyperreactive behaviorally in unfamiliar surroundings. This is not an integrated psychophysiological stress response like the threat of electric shock. Rather, I have shown how the experience of maternal separation in this instance becomes translated into physiological and behavioral changes by separate and different mechanisms. By altering specific aspects of the experience, we can produce an animal that is hyperreactive and has normal heart rates or one that is normally active with low heart rates.

This approach to the formation of attachment and the genesis of separation responses can be taken a step further and applied to early stages in the development of other emotions. The speculation would be that the organized systems for the experience and expression of different emotions in adults may have been built up out of component parts, or *subunits,* during early infancy, by the patterning of the parent–infant interaction. What I mean by *subunits* are the brief, fragmentary behaviors of the late fetal and newborn period, the frowns and smiles that follow each other in rapid succession, the opening and closing of hands, the waving and reaching of arms—and, of course, the various physiological changes that occur concomitantly. Early rudimentary body rocking may also be considered as one of these subunits. The experiment on the freely swinging terry cloth surrogate shows how this mobility on the part of the parent surrogate supplied an interaction that specifically modified the bodily expression of emotion in the later lives of these infants, in comparison to their agemates reared without this interaction. It was not so much a global effect on an emotional state or drive system but rather one by which a specific component of emotional expression, rocking, was regulated by a specific component of the interaction with the surrogate, mobility. Initially, the quantity of vestibular stimulation may be the key factor. Later the rhythms of this stimulation may facilitate rhythmic characteristics of emotional expression such as sobbing or stroking. Later, at a more cognitive level, the contingency and responsive aspect of the mobility may be a key element in the integration of the child's emotions with those of other people. Initially the effect of the mobility interaction is discrete and limited; later it becomes more widespread and integrated into patterns of behavior.

Infants presumably are born with a predisposition to organize certain patterns of behavior and certain inner experiences together so as to form the coherent patterns we call emotional states. But the evidence tells us that this predisposition will not be expressed in a recognizable form in adulthood without certain crucial infantile and childhood experiences. The enormously deficient emotional expressions of feral children were argued to be examples of defects in predisposition (e.g., brain damage at birth) until Spitz's, (1945) and Harlow's (1958) studies demonstrated that the parent–infant interaction was curcial for the organization of a full range of emotional expression.

How may the parent–infant interaction work to facilitate the development of emotions? Obviously, we are far from being able to answer this question with any degree of certainty. But on the basis of the experimental results described in this chapter and other evidence described elsewhere (Hofer, 1981), we can outline the following train of thought. The human infant begins to show fragments or subunits of facial expressive patterns as early as the last trimester of pregnancy, and, in the newborn period, smiling, for example, occurs first as a part of one of the sleep states (REM sleep) and later at 1½–2 months as a nonspecific response to a broad range of stimulation. Smiling and fussiness also occur in 2–3-month-old infants when nobody is present, during the process of learning on instrumental task, for example. How the parent responds to these early subunits of affective expression is probably critical for determining the characteristics of the adult pattern of expression of such emotions as joy, fear, or anger. The normal development of rudimentary affective expressions in blind infants up to 2 months of age and of prespeech through early babbling in deaf infants suggests the strength of predisposition behind these subunits. The subsequent decline and disappearance of facial expressiveness and of speech, respectively, in these two types of sensory handicap, attests to the crucial importance of feedback in the development of facial and vocal expression of emotion. But in addition to contingent feedback, levels and rhythms of general stimulation may also be important, judging from the swinging surrogate data.

Thus, parents appear to facilitate, differentiate, and shape the organization of subunits of emotional behavior during infancy through various aspects of their interaction with their offspring. Individual adult variations in the form of emotional states, and in their threshold, timing, intensity, and dynamics are likely to have been heavily influenced by childhood interactions with parents. And judging from the evidence described in this chapter, individual subunits may be regulated, initially at least, by individual processes within the parent–infant relationship.

This regulation of subunits of emotional behavior by part processes of the parent–infant interaction is likely to occur predominantly during early development. Gradually, as the infant begins to organize the subunits into patterns that usually occur together, the parents will begin to respond differentially to certain patterns and identify them as individual emotional states. But already, distinctive individual differences will have occurred as a result of each infant's particular predispositions and each parent's particular pattern of interaction with the early subunits. The differences will be expressed as an additional degree of variability in the form of emotional expression from one child to the next.

Clearly, what we need to know a great deal more about is how the subunits are themselves facilitated in development and how they are gathered together and integrated by the events of the parent–infant interaction. This "particulate" view of early emotional development raises questions rather than answering them, but it should at least open our eyes to the possibility of discovering unexpected new principles through analytic studies.

The formulation put forward in this chapter shifts the emphasis in studies on parental separation toward the preexisting parent–infant relationship. The concept of the regulatory effects of repeated stimulation is congruent with what is currently known about neurobiological mechanisms and allows an experimental approach to the processes underlying separation phenomena, social bonds, and the long-range developmental effects of early social relationships.

## REFERENCES

Allin, J. T., & Banks, E. M. Effects of temperature on ultrasound production by infant albino rats. *Developmental Psychobiology*, 1971, *4*, 149–156.

Bowlby, J. *Attachment and loss* (Vol. 1). *Attachment*. New York: Basic Books, 1969.

Bowlby, J. *Attachment and loss* (Vol. 2). *Separation*. New York: Basic Books, 1973.

Brackbill, Y. Effects of continuous stimulation on arousal levels in infants. *Child Development*, 1971, *41*, 17–26.

Butler, S. R., Suskind, M. R., & Schanberg, S. M. Maternal behavior as a regulator of polyamine biosynthesis in brain and heart of the developing rat pup. *Science*, 1978, *199*, 445–447.

Condon, W. S., & Sander, L. W. Neonate movement is synchronized with adult speech: Interactional participation and language acquisition. *Science*, 1974, *183*, 99–101.

Engel, G. L., & Schmale, A. H. *Conservation–withdrawal: A primary regulatory process for organismic homeostasis*. In Ciba Foundation Symposium No. 8, Physiology, Emotion and Psychosomatic Illness. New York: Elsevier, 1972.

Fraiberg, S. Blind infants and their mothers: An examination of the system. In M. Lewis & L. A. Rosenblum (Eds.), *The effect of the infant on its care giver*. In Origins of Behavior Series. New York: Wiley, 1974.

Grota, L. J., & Ader, R. Continuous recording of maternal behavior in *Rattus Norvegicus*. *Animal Behavior*, 1969, *17*, 722–729.

Harlow, H. F. The nature of love. *American Psychologist*, 1958, *12*, 673–685.

Hofer, M. A. Physiological responses of infant rats to separation from their mothers. *Science*, 1970, *168*, 871–873.

Hofer, M. A. The effects of brief maternal separations on behavior and heart rate of two week old rat pups. *Physiology and Behavior*, 1973, *10*, 423–427. (a)

Hofer, M. A. Maternal separation affects infant rats' behavior. *Journal of Behavioral Biology*, 1973, *9*, 629–633. (b)

Hofer, M. A. The role of nutrition in the physiological and behavioral effects of early maternal separation on infant rats. *Psychosomatic Medicine*, 1973, *35*, 350–359. (c)

Hofer, M. A. The role of early experience in the development of autonomic regulation. In L. DiCara (Ed.), *The limbic and autonomic nervous system: Advances in research*. New York: Plenum, 1974.

Hofer, M. A. Studies on how early maternal separation produces behavioral change in young rats. *Psychosomatic Medicine*, 1975, *37*, 245–264.

Hofer, M. A. The organization of sleep and wakefulness after maternal separation in young rats. *Developmental Psychobiology*, 1976, *9*, 189–206.

Hofer, M. A. Effects of reserpine and amphetamine on the development of hyperactivity in maternally deprived rat pups. *Psychosomatic Medicine*, 1980, *42*, 513–520.

Hofer, M. A. *The roots of human behavior: An introduction to the psychobiology of early development*. San Francisco, California: Freeman, 1981.

Hofer, M. A., & Shair, H. Ultrasonic vocalization during social interaction and isolation in 2 week old rats. *Developmental Psychobiology*, 1978, *11*, 495–504.

Hofer, M. A., & Shair, H. Sensory processes in control of isolation-induced ultrasonic vocalization by 2-week old rats. *Journal of Comparative and Physiological Psychology*, 1980, *94*, 271–279.

Hofer, M. A., & Shair, H. Control of sleep–wake states in the infant rat by features of the mother–infant relationship. *Developmental Psychobiology.* 1982, *15*, 229–244.

Hofer, M. A., & Weiner, H. The development and mechanisms of cardiorespiratory responses to maternal deprivation in rat pups. *Psychosomatic Medicine,* 1971, *33*, 353–363.

Hofer, M. A., & Weiner, H. Physiological mechanisms for cardiac control by nutritional intake after early maternal separation in the young rat. *Psychosomatic Medicine,* 1975, *37*, 8–24.

Hoffman, H. S., & Solomon, R. L. An opponent-process theory of motivation. III. Some affective dynamics in imprinting. *Learning and Motivation,* 1974, *5*, 149–164.

Kaufman, I. C., & Rosenblum, L. A. Effects of separation from mother on the emotional behavior of infant monkeys. *Annals of the New York Academy of Sciences,* 1969, *159*, 681–695.

Kaufman, I. C., & Stynes, A. J. Depression can be induced in a Bonnet macaque infant. *Psychosomatic Medicine,* 1978, *40*, 71–75.

Korner, A. F., & Thoman, E. B. Visual alertness in neonates as evoked by maternal care. *Journal of Experimental and Child Psychology,* 1970, *10*, 67–68.

Kuhn, C. M., Butler, S. R., & Schanberg, S. M. Selective depression of serum growth hormone during maternal deprivation in rat pups. *Science,* 1978, *201*, 1034–1036.

Kuhn, C. M., & Schanberg, S. M. Loss of growth hormone sensitivity in brain and liver during maternal deprivation in rats. *Society for Neurosciences (Abstract),* 1979, *5*, 168.

Leifer, A., Leiderman, P. H., Barnett, C., & Williams, J. Effects of mother–infant separation on maternal attachment behavior. *Child Development,* 1972, *43*, 1203–1218.

Mason, W. A., & Berkson, G. Effects of maternal mobility on the development of rocking and other behaviors in rhesus monkeys: A study with artificial mothers. *Developmental Psychobiology,* 1974, *8*, 197–211.

Okon, E. E. The temperature relations of vocalization in infant golden hamsters and Wistar rats. *Journal of Zoology (London),* 1971, *104*, 227–237.

Oswalt, G. L., & Meier, G. W. Olfactory, thermal and tactual influences on infantile ultrasonic vocalization in rats. *Developmental Psychobiology,* 1975, *8*, 129–135.

Powell, G. F., Brasel, J. A., & Blizzard, R. M. Emotional deprivation and growth retardation stimulating idiopathic hypopituitarism. *New England Journal of Medicine,* 1967, *276*, 1271–1283.

Reite, M., Kaufman, I. C., Pauley, J. D., & Stynes, A. J. Depression in infant monkeys: Physiological correlates. *Psychosomatic Medicine,* 1974, *36*, 363–367.

Rosenblatt, J. S. Suckling and home orientation in the kitten: A comparative developmental study. In E. Tobach, L. Aronson, & E. Shaw (Eds.), *The biopsychology of development.* New York: Academic Press, 1971.

Sales, G., & Pye, D. *Ultrasonic communication by animals.* New York: Wiley, 1974.

Scott, J. P. Critical periods in behavioral development. *Science,* 1962, *138*, 949–958.

Seay, B., Hansen, E. W., & Harlow, H. F. Mother–infant separation in monkeys. *Child Psychology and Psychiatry,* 1962, *3*, 123–132.

Seitz, P. F. D. Infantile experience and adult behavior in animal subjects. II: Age of separation from the mother and adult behavior in the cat. *Psychosomatic Medicine,* 1959, *21*, 353–378.

Sharma, K. N., & Nasset, E. S. Electrical activity in mesenteric nerves after perfusion of gut lumen. *American Journal of Physiology,* 1962, *202*, 725–730.

Shear, K. M., Brunelli, S. A., Shair, H. N., & Hofer, M. A. The effects of 24-hr. maternal separation on blood pressure and vasoconstrictor tone in 2-week-old rat pups. *Psychosomatic Medicine,* 1981, *43*, 93.

Spitz, R. A. Hospitalism: An enquiry into psychiatric conditions in early childhood. *Psychoanalytic Study of Child,* 1945, *1*, 53–80.

Stone, E., Bonnet, K., & Hofer, M. A. Survival and development of maternally deprived rats: Role of body temperature. *Psychosomatic Medicine,* 1976, *38*, 242–249.

Chapter 8

# EMOTIONS IN EARLY DEVELOPMENT: A PSYCHOEVOLUTIONARY APPROACH

*ROBERT PLUTCHIK*

## ABSTRACT

*Some implications of a psychoevolutionary theory of emotions for an under-standing of infant development are presented. The concepts of schemata, sentic states, and epigenetic rules are elaborated as central ideas for a theory of affects. An attempt is then made to apply the basic ideas of the theory to infancy. These ideas are that emotions must be considered within an evolutionary context; that emotions are complex chains of events; that emotions are hypothetical constructs that can be known only approximately, and only by inferences from many sources of data; that emotions have certain structural relations to one another; and that emotions have certain derivatives. Ethological and other evidence is reviewed and the gaps in knowledge and unanswered questions are identified.*

It is intriguing to consider the appearance and development of emotions in young organisms, for a number of reasons. First, the language behaviors we typically use as evidence of emotions are not available. Second, the expressive behaviors of emotions that are so striking in mature animals are more limited in young ones. Third, what appears as stable emotional behavior in adults is seen as highly variable and changing behavior in infants. These facts raise several impor-

EMOTION
Theory, Research, and Experience
Volume 2

tant questions for a theory of emotion as applied to young organisms: What evidence do we use as indicators of emotion? How many emotions are there? What is their changing character during the course of development? These questions and various related issues will be examined from the point of view of the psychoevolutionary theory of emotion developed by Plutchik (1962, 1970, 1980).

## CENTRAL CONCEPTS OF A PSYCHOEVOLUTIONARY THEORY OF EMOTIONS

### EMOTIONS AND EVOLUTION

There are five important ideas that are fundamental to a psychoevolutionary approach to emotions. The first is that emotions must be considered in an evolutionary context. Darwin (1872/1965) was among the first to point out the basic continuity of emotional expressions from lower animals to humans. For example, he pointed out that the baring of the fangs of the wolf is related to the sneer of the human adult. Also, many species of animals, including humans, show an apparent increase in body size during rage, due to the erection of body hair or feathers, changes in posture, or expansion of air pouches. According to Darwin, emotions in all animals increase the chances of individual survival because they are appropriate reactions to emergency events in the environment. In addition, he noted, emotions act as signals of intentions or future actions.

Scott (1958) has pointed out that there are only a few general classes of adaptive behavior found in most species and phylogenetic levels. He describes them in the following terms: ingestive behavior, shelter-seeking behavior, care-soliciting behavior, agonistic (fight or flight) behavior, sexual behavior, caregiving behavior, eliminative behavior, allelomimetic (imitative) behavior, and investigative behavior. Wilson (1975) has also commented on the similarity of behavioral adaptations found in higher and lower animals. He notes, for example, that both termites and monkeys form cooperative groups that occupy territories, and that group members communicate hunger, alarm, hostility, caste status or rank and reproductive status among themselves by means of something on the order of 10 to 100 nonsyntactical signals.

These observations of similar classes of adaptive behavior identifiable at various phylogenetic levels suggests that organisms have developed innate (genetically programmed) responses to deal with certain common survival-related problems. The psychoevolutionary theory assumes that certain classes of adaptive response are the prototype patterns of emotions in lower animals and humans. The theory assumes that the environment of all organisms creates certain common problems, for example, identifying prey and predator, food and mate, caregiver and care-solicitor. Emotions are attempts of the organism to achieve control over these kinds of events that relate to survival. Emotions are the ultra-conservative evolutionary behavioral adaptations, based on genetic codings, that have been successful (like amino acids, DNA, and genes) in increasing the chances of survival of organisms. Therefore, they have been maintained, in functionally equivalent form, through all phylogenetic levels.

## EMOTIONS AS COMPLEX CHAINS

A second key idea of the psychoevolutionary theory is that an emotion is more than a verbal reaction or a facial expression. Emotions are conceptualized as conplex chains of events that are triggered most often by environmental stimuli. The stimulus event has to be recognized, or evaluated, as an important survival-related emergency. Such a cognitive evaluation may be automatic, as when a puppy emits distress signals in the absence of its mother, or it may be based on learning. The cognition will then be followed by a subjective feeling state (such as fear or sadness) that we infer on the basis of various classes of evidence. Either simultaneously with the subjective feeling or following it, there will be a pattern of physiological changes that occur in the body. These physiological changes have the character of anticipatory reactions associated with various types of exertions. Stanley-Jones (1966) has suggested that these physiological changes are fundamentally related to temperature adjustments necessary to survival by cold-blooded animals. These adjustments, he suggests, have evolved as the basis of emotional reactions in warm-blooded mammals.

The feeling state and physiological reaction will be followed, with a certain probability, by an impulse to action. These impulses include the urge to attack, to explore, to reject, or to mate, among others. Such impulses to action will then interact with each other on the assumption that more than one impulse to action can exist simultaneously. Depending on the relative strengths of these various impulses, a final, vectorial resultant will occur in the form of action or overt display behavior. Examples of the interactions of various emotional impulses are given by Morris (1954) for birds, Hinde (1966) for cats, and Eibl-Eibesfeldt (1971) for dogs. Eibl-Eibesfeldt (1971) shows how different facial expressions in the dog result from an interaction of different intensities of fighting and flight impulses.

This complex chain of events defining an emotion is represented schematically in Figure 8.1. Figure 8.1 shows not only the various links of the chain but also points out another important idea. Emotional behavior is not random, meaning-less, overflow behavior, but is directly related to the stimulus event that triggered the complex chain of events in the first place. The overt behavior is designed to

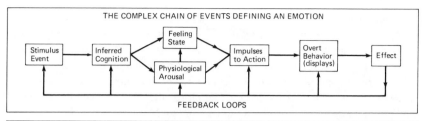

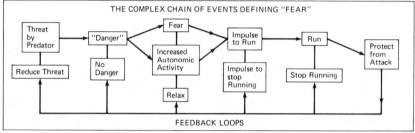

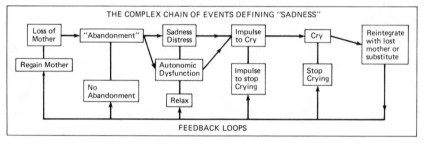

**FIGURE 8.1.** Illustrations of the complex chain of events defining an emotion.

have an effect on the environment in such a way as to affect the initial triggering stimulus. For example, the overt behavior of running decreases the likelihood that the threat of attack will be effective. Distress signals by a puppy or the crying of an infant will increase the probability that the mother or a mother substitute will arrive on the scene. There is, therefore, a feedback loop in which the overt behavior changes the stimulus event and thereby also changes the inferred cognition, the feeling state, the arousal, and the impulses to action. The overall effect of this complex feedback system we call an *emotion* is to reduce the threat, the stress, or the emergency and to recreate a kind of behavioral homeostatic balance.

## EMOTIONS ARE KNOWN THROUGH INFERENCES

The psychoanalysts have made us aware of the fact that subjective reports of emotion cannot always be an accurate description of the emotion. Not only are some emotions totally repressed and thus unavailable to introspection, but others are frequently modified or distorted as a result of partial repressions or as the result of the operation of ego defense mechanisms. Studies of the language of emotions, such as those by Davitz (1969), have shown that people define emotions in terms of physical symptoms ("tired," "sleepy"), self-attitudes ("feel vulnerable"), impulses to action ("want to withdraw"), and physiological changes ("no appetite"). Any one class of descriptions is only a partial image of the total state called an emotion.

Other evidence against the view that an emotion is nothing but a subjective feeling state revealed by verbal reports, is as follows: (a) verbal reports of emotion may sometimes be deliberate attempts to deceive; (b) an observer may erroneously assume that no emotion exists because none has been reported; (c) reports of emotion depend on an individual's particular conditioning history as well as his or her facility with words; (d) emotions are usually mixed, so verbal reports are unable to unequivocally specify them; (e) emotions are generally believed to occur in the mentally ill, the mentally retarded, young children, infants, and lower animals. Such beliefs must be based on other types of information than verbal reports of subjective states.

An emotion may be conceptualized as a hypothetical construct or inference based on various classes of evidence. This evidence may include verbal reports about inner feelings, but will include other types of data as well. The work of Hebb (1972) and Van Hooff (1973), for example, suggests that the kind of evidence we use to infer emotions in nonverbal organisms includes (a) knowledge of stimulus conditions; (b) knowledge of the organism's behavior over an extended period of time; (c) ability of the inference to predict the organism's behavior in the near future; (d) knowledge of what the species-typical behavior is; (e) knowledge of how the organism's peers or conspecifics react to it; (f) knowledge of what choices an individual makes in a comparative free choice situation; and (g) knowledge of the effect of an organism's behavior on others. Illustrations of these various sources of inferences about emotions may be found in Plutchik (1980).

## THE STRUCTURE OF EMOTIONS

It is evident that emotions vary in intensity, as reflected by the distinctions we make between fear and panic or annoyance and rage. They also vary in degree of similarity to one another. We recognize, for example, that shame and guilt are more similar than are joy and disgust. Finally, emotions have the character of polarity. We recognize that joy is the opposite of sadness and that acceptance is the opposite of rejection.

These characteristics of intensity, similarity, and polarity may be represented geometrically by means of a three-dimensional structure shaped like a cone, somewhat like the three-dimensional color solid. The vertical dimension represents intensity, the circle defines degree of similarity, and polarity may be represented by the opposite emotions on the circle.

There is one other important element needed to complete the structural model of emotions. This is the concept that some emotions are fundamental, or primary, and others are derived, or secondary, in the same sense that some colors are primary and others are mixed.

On the basis of factor-analytic evidence, similarity scaling studies, and certain evolutionary considerations, the psychoevolutionary theory of emotions assumes that there are eight basic emotions that can occur at various intensity levels; all other emotions are derived through various combinations of these eight. The eight basic emotions may be given different names depending in part on the vagaries of language and in part on whether we are considering the subjective language of emotions, the behavioral language, or the functional language. From the subjective language viewpoint, the basic emotions consist of the following (arranged as pairs of opposites): joy versus sadness, anger versus fear, acceptance versus disgust, and surprise versus anticipation.

If we add these ideas to the structural model, the three-dimensional emotion cone looks somewhat like half an orange with eight slices, each slice representing a basic emotion dimension. Studies indicate that emotions may be mixed to produce a variety of dyads (Plutchik, 1980). Conversely, it is possible to demonstrate that judges will show considerable consistency in judging the emotion components of words representing the complex language of emotions.

## THE DERIVATIVES OF EMOTION

Another key idea of the theory is that the eight primary emotions have a variety of derivatives. These derivatives represent alternative or derivative languages that reflect some aspect of the transformation of the basic emotions. For example, the theory has shown that the language of interpersonal personality traits is, in fact, the language of mixed emotions. Personality traits such as sociable, hostile, gloomy, or adventurous reflect the persistent appearance of certain mixed emotions. Hostility, for example, is judged to·be composed of anger and disgust, whereas sociability is rated as being composed of joy plus acceptance. It is of some interest to note that personality traits may also be organized by means of a circular (or circumplex) order, reflecting the existence of the dimensions of similarity and polarity in this domain (Conte & Plutchik, 1981).

Another derivative language is the language of diagnostic labels. Terms such as *hysteric, paranoid, schizoid,* and *obsessive–compulsive* have been shown to be related to one another by means of a circular order (Plutchik & Platman,

1977). These terms also represent extreme manifestations of certain personality traits. Thus the trait of gloominess in extreme form is recognized as depression; the trait of contempt in extreme form is diagnosed as paranoid; methodical planning, in extreme form, is described by the diagnostic label obsessive-compulsive.

Still another derivative language is the ego defense language. We have tried to show that ego defenses are actually ways to handle emotions (Plutchik, Kellerman, & Conte, 1979). Displacement, for example, is a way to deal with feelings of anger that cannot be expressed in a direct way. Similarly, repression is a way to deal with feelings of anxiety that are threatening, and projection handles feelings of disgust against oneself by unconsciously attributing them to other people. Other derivative languages are also in existence and have been described by Kellerman (1979, 1980).

In summary, I have indicated that there are at least five key concepts that characterize my psychoevolutionary theory of emotions. The first is that emotions must be considered in the context of evolution. The second is that an emotion is a complex chain of events designed to have an effect on important or survival-related stimulus events in a kind of behavioral-homeostatic way. The third is that emotions can only be known through inferences based on a variety of types of evidence. The fourth is that emotions have certain systematic relations to one another than can be described in terms of a three-dimensional structural model. Fifth is the important idea that the basic emotions may go through all sorts of transformations to produce certain derivative domains of discourse. The point of the remaining sections of this chapter is to apply these ideas to both human and animal infants. The major focus, however, will be on humans.

## INFANT ETHOGRAMS

It is obvious that inferences about emotion in infants must be based on evidence other than verbal report. Most discussions of this issue rely on an infant's facial expressions or vocal output such as crying, and relatively little attention has been paid to other responses or behavior. However, from an evolutionary point of view, it is likely that too much attention has been paid to the face. In most lower animals, there are relatively few facial expressions to communicate information, but many other display behaviors reflect emotional states. For example, in lower animals the displays, which involve various parts of the body, are used in special ways in the following contexts: greeting, recognition, courtship, mating, dominance, submission, warning, alarm, defense, challenge, distress, defeat, victory, feeding, and food-begging. These kinds of displays are thought of by the ethologists as *social releasers,* that is, they function to communicate important information from one animal to another. In most cases these display reactions appear without prior learning or experience and are apparently genetically programmed. Some of these displays are found in young organisms as well as mature ones.

From an ethological point of view, it would be expected that some of these display behaviors should be found in humans, at least in rudimentary form. For example, the cry of the newborn human infant is remarkably like the cry of the newborn chimpanzee and newborn gorilla (Lieberman, 1975), and the grasp reflex is found in human newborns just as it is found in monkeys. It should, therefore, be useful if we are to understand the nature of emotions in infants, to consider the many different expressive behaviors of which infants are capable. This involves the consideration of what ethologists call *ethograms*.

Table 8.1 presents an ethogram of facial–vocal behavior seen in 8–12-month-old human infants. Also indicated are the positive and negative hedonic tones inferred to be associated with each of the behaviors (Young & Decarie, 1977). Some of the terms are simple descriptions and involve little inference, for example, *tongue out, tremble,* or *square-mouth face.* Others, such as *sad face, sober frown,* and *semismile* involve moderate degrees of inference. Some, such as *coy*

TABLE 8.1

An Ethogram of Facial and Vocal Behaviors in 8–12-Month-Old Infants[a]

| Positive | Negative | Ambiguous |
|---|---|---|
| Close-mouth smile | Tremble | Yawn |
| Coy smile | Tight-lip face | Wide-eyed stare |
| O-mouth smile | Square-mouth face | Tongue out |
| Shy smile | Kidney-mouth face | Blink |
| Semi-smile | Clenched-teeth face | Brow-raise stare |
| Slight open-mouth smile | Pout | Lip roll |
| Positive face | Sad face | Sigh |
| Brighten | Negative face | Sober frown |
| Play face | Grimace | Sober stare |
| Babble | Fear face | Perplexed face |
| Coo | Disgust face | Shy face |
| Laugh | Harsh wail | Detached face |
| Squeal | Soft wail | Frozen face |
| Positive vocalization | Wail | Attentive face |
| | | Ambivalent face |
| | | Ambivalent smile |
| | | Undifferentiated face |
| | | Normal face |
| | | Ambivalent vocalization |
| | | Undifferentiated vocalization |

[a] Adapted from Young and Decarie (1977).

*smile, ambivalent face,* and *negative face,* appear to require a considerable amount of inference. However, considerable reliability of judgment has been obtained for most of the categories, including those that clearly refer to emotional states.

Marler and Tenaza (1977) have reviewed the vocal characteristics of the apes. Table 8.2 is based on their research and compares vocalizations in infants and adults in chimpanzees and gorillas. Comparison across species is not easy because the descriptive terminology of vocal sounds is not consistent, but comparisons between adults and infants have been made. Generally speaking, infants do not pant, hoot, grunt, roar, growl, or wraaa. They do laugh or chuckle, cry, whine, and whimper.

Marler and Tenaza (1977) also describe the circumstances under which these various sounds are emitted. They point out, for instance, that laughter occurs when an animal is playing, especially when it is being tickled. Infants scream when fleeing from attack, when lost, and while attacking a dominant animal. Whimpers occur when a chimpanzee is begging, when a strange sound or object appears, and when infants are separated from parents. These various sounds

TABLE 8.2

Frequency of Use of Vocalizations in Infant and Adult Male Chimpanzees and Gorillas[a]

|  | Chimpanzees | | Gorillas | |
|---|---|---|---|---|
|  | *Adult* | *Child* | *Adult* | *Child* |
| Pant–hoot | 7 | 2 | 83 | 0 |
| Pant–grunt | 7 | 7 | 89 | 0 |
| Laughter (chuckle) | 7 | 68 | 0 | 100 |
| Squeak | 12 | 8 |  |  |
| Scream | 11 | 8 | 56 | 4 |
| Whimper | 7 | 37 |  |  |
| Bark | 3 | 5 |  |  |
| War Bark | 18 | 7 |  |  |
| Rough grunt | 8 | 10 |  |  |
| Pant | 4 | 4 | 23 | 0 |
| Grunt | 12 | 0 |  |  |
| Cough | 3 | 3 |  |  |
| Wraaa | 6 | 0 | 92 | 0 |
| Lip smack | 47 | 0 |  |  |
| Cries |  |  | 0 | 100 |
| Roar |  |  | 94 | 0 |
| Growl |  |  | 87 | 0 |
| Whine |  |  | 11 | 44 |

[a] Figures represent the percentage of renditions of each type of vocalization. (Adapted from Marler & Tenaza, 1977).

therefore clearly have affective connotations. The fact that they vary in frequency in infants and adults implies that a structured developmental sequence of changes occurs.

Infants are capable of a great variety of facial expressions. Ekman and Friesen (1976) have developed a facial action code that defines 24 rather specific facial expressions. Oster and Ekman (1978) claim that virtually all of the facial action code movements can be seen in both premature and full-term newborns. Extensive video recordings have been made of infants facial expressions during the first few months of life. Attempts have been made to establish the meaning of different facial expressions on the basis of two types of criteria: (a) evidence of patterning based on the simultaneous occurrence of independent muscle actions; and (b) the timing of particular facial movements. Oster and Ekman (1978) report, for example, that the earliest smiles are produced by the action of a single muscle, but smiles become increasingly complex, in terms of muscle action unit involvements, as they become more related to social interactions. Another illustration of the possible usefulness of the system is the alternative explanation it provides for the origins of human smiling. Van Hooff (1972) has suggested that smiling is a derivative of the nonhuman primate defensive grimace related to fear and distress. Oster and Ekman (1978) claim that this interpretation is based on the assumption that the actions of *risorius* muscles, which draw the lip corners back laterally but not upward, are the basis of the smile. Instead, they relate the "smile" only to the action of *zygomaticus major,* which draws the corners of the mouth up. They also point out that rapid onset and gradual fading seems to be more characteristic of affect expressions than they are of random, reflex expressions.

Another description of a large variety of infant behaviors has been reported by Pawlby (1977). He recorded the frequency with which infants imitated their mother's activities when mother–infant pairs were observed. Table 8.3 lists 49 imitated activities that have been grouped under five general headings, namely:

1. Acts involving face–head movements
2. Acts involving hand–body movements
3. Acts involving speech sounds
4. Acts involving nonspeech sounds
5. Acts involving manipulation of objects

Speech sounds were most frequently imitated (42% of the time), whereas facial expressions were least frequently imitated (5% of the time). The major point emphasized in Table 8.3 is the large number of discrete behaviors that the human infant is capable of imitating. Many of these behaviors could be part of the emotional chain of events described earlier.

Another set of behaviors not often considered in the study of emotion is the

TABLE 8.3
Imitated Activities (with the Frequency with which Each Occurred in the Course of the Study)[a]

| 1. Acts involving face–head movements | 2. Acts involving hand–body movements | 3. Acts involving speech sounds |
|---|---|---|
| Opens mouth wide (40) | Waves (4) | Vowel-like sounds (480) |
| Smiles (20) | Arm movements (8) | Early consonantal |
| Pokes tongue (3) | Scratches (2) | sounds (65) |
| Purses lips (5) | Covers face in peek-a-boo manner (2) | Late consonantal sounds |
| Frowns (2) | Tickles (1) | (140) |
| Puts head on one side (6) | Bangs (295) | |
| Shakes head (7) | Claps (22) | |
| Nods (5) | Hand game (35) | |
| | Finger movements (7) | |
| | Hits own hand (3) | |
| | Moves backwards (3) | |

| 4. Acts involving non-speech sounds | 5. Acts involving manipulation of objects | |
|---|---|---|
| Whimpers (34) | Sucks object (4) | |
| Laughs (112) | Gives object (7) | |
| Blows raspberries (23) | Pushes or rolls object (50) | |
| Coughs (23) | Shakes object (16) | |
| Sighs (21) | Presses object parts (42) | |
| Yawns (11) | Bangs two objects together (15) | |
| Smacks lips (4) | Takes object out of another (18) | |
| Panting sound (36) | Puts object into another (6) | |
| Sneezes (4) | Builds (1) | |
| Hiccoughs (4) | Spins object (44) | |
| Clicking sound with | Stops object spinning (1) | |
| Tongue (3) | Bounces object (4) | |
| Snuffling sound (2) | Puts object to mouth appropriately (3) | |
| | Turns pages of book (7) | |
| | Uncovers object to find it (1) | |

[a] Adapted from Pawlby (1977).

position of the infant's hands. Papousek and Papousek (1977) have identified five different hand positions that reflect different behavioral states of infants. If we assume that states of alertness and states of distress express emotions then these hand positions are at least as revealing as facial expressions. Papousek and Papousek (1977) also point out that with regard to vocal behavior, infants show crying from birth, vowel-like sounds in relaxed waking states at about 4 weeks of age, and repeated syllabic sounds beginning at about 5–6 months of age.

Brazelton (1976) has also described the range of behaviors of which newborns are capable. His Neonatal Assessment Scale lists 26 behavioral and 20 reflex activities of the human neonate in interaction with an adult. These include the following:

1. Turning head in direction of human voice
2. Responding to a female vocal pitch over a male voice
3. Humanoid sounds preferred to pure tones
4. Using the eyes to follow a picture
5. Responding to milk smells rather than sugar water

In a similar vein, Barnett (1973) has pointed out that newborn infants have a surprising ability to process sensory information. Infants show the pupillary reflex; visual pursuit behavior; sustained fixation; color sensitivity; tracking objects with coordinated movements of the head and eyes; visual accomodation; the ability to discriminate visual patterns; differential attention and preferences for some patterns over others; sensitivity to pitch, intensity, and duration of sounds; head and eye movements to locate a source of sound; and a preference for human speech over other types of sound.

Various types of rhythmic and stereotyped movements also are evident in infants and have been related to mood states. Thelen (1979) has observed thousands of instances of rhythmical stereotyped movements of the legs, arms, and torso of 20 normal infants in their first year of life. These movement stereotypes were observed in many settings including interactions with the mother, in feeding situations, and in nonalert states.

Thelen (1979) points out that the onset of particular stereotyped movements is highly correlated with motor development and that the rhythms are probably indications of incomplete cortical control of maturing neuromuscular pathways. The rhythmical movements are probably transition behaviors between uncoordinated movements and mature, goal-corrected behavior. Thelen (1981) also suggests that the quality of the rhythmic movements call attention to the infant's mood, just as voice inflection or hand movements in an adult emphasize the mood of the individual. Thelen (1981) also points out that the frequency of these stereotyped movements appear to increase under high states of arousal. At later points of development, infants may use earlier patterns of rhythmic movement, as is seen in temper tantrums. It is worth noting that ethologists have reported many examples of stereotyped behavior that tend to be associated with situations of high conflict (Andrew, 1974). Such behaviors can also be made to increase in frequency by raising animals in restricted environments or by administering certain drugs (Valenstein, 1976).

Many other authors have mentioned the behavioral characteristics of infants. For example, infants show automatic walking movements, eyes-closed smiling, and spontaneous erections (Freedman, 1974). They also show size, shape, and movement constancy, slant perception, and object permanence (Bower, 1974). They are able to imitate mouth and tongue movements, vocalizations and hand movements, and often synchronize hand or arm movements with vocalizations or facial grimaces (Trevarthen, 1977). Trevarthen (1977) also claims that when a mother shows a lack of response or an inappropriate response, 8-week-old infants show expressions of confusion, distress, or withdrawal. Spitz (1957) has pointed out that infants show rooting behavior (a head-turning response to touching of the cheek called an *oral orientation reflex*), as well as head nodding. Kinsey, Pomeroy, and Martin (1948) have described evidence of orgasm in infants. Andrew (1972) has drawn our attention to patterns of behavior that are found in the young of lower animals (as well as in the mature animal). He mentions respiratory reflexes that cause dilation of the nostrils and contribute in some degree to facial expressions. He describes thermoregulatory responses such as sweating, panting, and flushing, which act to cool the body, and the total body response of freezing or immobility. He also mentions secretions (odors) and excretions (defecation), which play an important role in social displays.

In general, Andrew (1972) suggests that there are three types of reflexes that play some role in animal communication as well as in the expression of emotions in young as well as mature animals. These three types of reflexes are respiratory, thermoregulatory, and postural. The latter categories includes such behaviors as clinging, huddling, back arching, crouching, slinking, and shivering. He also suggests that most of these reflexes play a fundamental role in either warming or cooling the body.

This section, dealing with the concept of an infant ethogram, has revealed the presence of well over 100 different behaviors or expressions or patterns of movement which have been observed and catalogued in human infants in the first year of life. Most have not been studied extensively and only a few of them have been· considered as measures of emotion. However, it is certainly possible that many of the behaviors described may be incorporated into our descriptions of the patterns we call emotions.

## SCHEMATA

The presence of so many discrete as well as coordinated behaviors in the newborn has bearing on an important issue, that is, the extent to which these behaviors may be considered to express basic neurological programs, sometimes called *schemata*. A second related question is whether emotions in infants reflect the existence of such schemata.

The concept of a schema refers to a configuration within the brain that acts as a pattern against which the input to nerve cells is compared. Such a configuration may be learned or unlearned. The schemata have several functions: (*a*) they may screen out certain types of inputs in favor of others; (*b*) they may allow one type of stimulus to be perceived more vividly than another, and thus favor one kind of decision over another; (*c*) they can fill in details that are missing from actual sensory input and create a pattern or gestalt that is not entirely present in reality;

and (d) they can program the sequence of developmental changes that occur as an organism matures (Wilson, 1978).

However, the concept of schemata has been described in other terms as well. Piaget and Inhelder (1969) describe schemata as central theoretical structures that relate the perception of stimuli to action. They assume that these schemata are constructed from combinations of innate reflexes such as looking, sucking, and grasping. The particular schemata that an infant possesses determines how it reacts to the environment. Piaget and Inhelder (1969) do not explore the issue of the extent to which schemata are innate, although the consistency in the timing of language acquisition despite the diversity of social environments strongly suggests that at least some schemata are genetically based.

The notion of schemata has been described in still another way by Arbib and Kahn (1969). They point out that children show developmental sequences that procede relatively independently of the environment. To account for this and other observations, they assume that the brain contains a model of the world. However, just as a computer contains a hierarchy of languages ranging from the basic "inherent" machine language, through assembly and high-level (learned) languages, so, too, does the brain contain a hierarchy of elements, some of which are innate and some of which are acquired. Such things as receptor structures, short-term memory characteristics, and effector patterns have strong built-in properties. Decision making and goal-setting characteristics tend largely to be programmed by experience.

Such a system is not a passive one. It actively seeks information to update its internal model of the environment (the schemata) as well as to obtain current information for decision making. The schemata can so adjust the input system (e.g., by focusing the eyes) as to limit the sensory input. There is thus a constant interaction between the system and the environment.

Still another alternative view that bears on the issue of schemata was proposed by Clynes (1980) in his writing on emotional communication; the study of such communications he calls *sentics*. Clynes points out that there are discrete characteristic expressive patterns in the different arts that can express the same emotional states. For example, certain lines in a drawing may express anger or sadness, whereas certain sequences of tones may express the same emotions. Bodily movements in dance may also express these emotions.

In general, such expressive patterns have a beginning and an end. The character of each expressive act is also determined before it begins (i.e., is preprogrammed in the brain), just as the arm movements involved in the throwing of a ball at a target are preprogrammed before the throw occurs. In Clynes's view, each emotion has a preprogrammed motor pattern of this sort associated with it. He calls this an *essentic form;* it can be described through the use of evoked potential techniques. According to Clynes, "the same genetic change that produces the form of expression also produces its corresponding experiential quality

[Clynes, 1980, p. 275]." In addition, sentic states are assumed to have certain properties: For example, only one state can be expressed at a time, a sentic state may be expressed by any of a number of different output modalities, and the recognized form of a sentic state tends to produce a sentic state in the perceiver. Clynes (1980) has reported some empirical evidence that support these ideas.

A theory of schemata has also been presented by Lumsden and Wilson (1981) in their theory of the coevolutionary process. They argue that the genes prescribe a set of biological processes that they call *epigenetic rules* that direct the "assembly of the mind." These epigenetic rules act as "filters" that may be either "loose" or "tight" and that determine what kinds of information are allowed into the system and how that information is to be processed. The epigenetic rules determine the constraints that genes place on development, and they affect the probability of using one cultural activity as compared to another. For example, genetic controls are known to affect the ability to detect certain odors and are believed to underlie sex differences in the perception of and reaction to musklike fragrances. Similarly, epigenetic rules determine incest avoidance.

Lumsden and Wilson (1981) believe that the epigenetic rules determine the schemata in the brain that in turn influence the choices and actions made by organisms. The application of epigenetic rules to emotions may be seen in the consistent developmental sequences in the appearance of certain facial expressions, in the fear of strangers and in the fear of falling found to occur in all infants at comparable ages, and in the consistent average differences found between men and women in certain emotional expressions such as aggressiveness.

It appears that the concept of schemata, or epigenetic rules, is an important theoretical notion that is found in the writings of scientists representing a diversity of views. The common elements seem to be that genetic processes determine certain aspects of the intake of information, the processing and organization of information, and the expression of behavior. There appear to be both strong and weak constraints on the functioning of organisms in these various areas. In brief, infants at birth perceive only selected aspects of their environment and begin organizing the information so obtained into conceptual categories, some of which are determined by genetically programmed schemata. Emotions in infants may be conceptualized as an expression of these schemata or epigenetic rules.

An important point that must be emphasized is that the schemata affect not only the patterns of messages sent by the organism (e.g., emotional responses) but also influence the reception of messages from others. Green and Marler (1979) make this same point when they note that "in communication, senders and receivers benefit most from closely matched procedures [p. 107]," and that "common genetic control of signal production and reception is indicated [p. 110]." Just as there is an innate basis for song production and recognition for birds, there appears to be an innate basis for both the perception and production of human speech. The frequency of cooing is the same in deaf and normal infants until at least 6 months of age. Birds deafened in early life show the same pattern of vocal development as normal birds. Many animals appear to have auditory detectors "tuned" to signals that are of special significance to them. For example, studies of single brain cells in the squirrel monkey demonstrated that some cells responded only to one or a few types of sounds representing the vocal repertoire of this species (Lieberman, 1975). Prespeech infants respond to some of the same distinctions between phonemes that adults do, and the ability to acquire language syntax and grammar appears to be based on a biological propensity. As Freedman (1974) puts it, "No baby is taught to laugh or to cry, nor do adults need previous experience with babies to read these signals expertly and immediately [p. 42]." Freedman (1974) also points out that the cry of the infant, typically associated with separation, is a nearly universal mammalian event. In dogs, when a separated pup cries, the mother becomes excited and looks for it. This reflects the existence of two complementary evolved, unlearned, emotional mechanisms that contribute to the survival of the species.

Another illustration of this kind of schematic control of interaction has been given by Papousek and Papousek (1977). They have observed that mothers unconsciously keep their heads centered in the infant's visual field, with their eyes on the same plane as their baby's. They tend to keep an optimal distance of 20–25 cm during the first few weeks, as if respecting the infants limited capacities for focusing. After achieving eye-to-eye contact, the mother shows "greeting behavior," that is, she briefly lifts her head, raises her eyebrows, and opens her mouth (with or without a sound).

Finally, we may briefly consider the evidence for the existence of innate schemata as the basis for two affective states: smiling and play. Social smiling appears in blind infants at about the same time as it appears in sighted infants. Identical twins show a greater concordance of smiling patterns than do fraternal twins, thus suggesting hereditary control. Infant smiling apparently cannot be conditioned, thus further supporting its unlearned nature. Strong visual stimuli facilitate smiling more readily than weak ones, implying that ethological-type releasing stimuli may be at work. And smiling may be more readily observed in response to a high-pitched voice than a low-pitched one, further suggesting the existence of a tuned innate detector. Other indirect evidence for innateness of smiling is its universal presence in all cultures, its appearance in congenitally blind and deaf children, and its role in increasing "bonding" or attachment behavior (Freedman, 1974).

With regard to play, most authorities agree that it is intrinsically motivated (Vandenberg, 1978) and that it tends to follow a predictable course. In monkeys, Harlow and Harlow (1966) have identified three stages of play that occur under a wide variety of conditions: rough-and-tumble play, pursuit-and-retreat play, and aggressive play. These in turn are related in a mutually reciprocal way to maternal patterns of development that they call: (*a*) attachment and protection; (*b*) ambivalence and disattachment; and (c) separation and rejection. In most species, play behavior is often preceded by a sign (such as a chimpanzee "play face") as a meta communication. The play of male animals is generally more aggressive than that of females, and mothers who were injected with male hormones when pregnant produced female infants who were more aggressive in play than were female infants whose mothers were not treated. Both the motivation to play and the types of behavior engaged in by young organisms are determined largely by innate schemata.

The various examples that have been given of the concept of schemata suggests that the organized behavior of infants reflects the existence of such underlying neural mechanisms. In addition, since emotional expressions in infants are patterned, species-specific, communication signals, they too must reflect the existence of schemata. The next sections will explore this idea in more detail.

## RELATION OF PSYCHOEVOLUTIONARY THEORY TO EMOTIONS IN YOUNG ORGANISMS

At the beginning of this chapter, a brief overview was presented of a psychoevolutionary theory of emotion. Five elements were identified as the major components of the theory. These are that emotions should be considered in the context of evolution; that emotions are complex chains of events; that emotions are known through inferences; that emotions have a systematic, structural relation to one another; and that many domains of discourse are derivatives of emotions. The following sections will examine evidence that relates each of these five areas to emotions as seen, expressed, and evaluated primarily in human infants, but also in young organisms of other species.

## EMOTIONS, EVOLUTION, AND INFANCY

From an evolutionary point of view, the newborn organism is most vulnerable to the vicissitudes of the environment, including predation. This reality is the basic reason behind the various signals, displays, communication patterns, and behaviors that are found in immature organisms and that are present at or shortly after birth. These various behaviors have effects that increase the chances of survival in the newborn. And since the problems of survival exist from the moment of birth, certain mechanisms must exist both in the child and in the mother or caretaker to help ensure survival. If young organisms had to wait until the infant learned how to attract its mother's attention and support, and if the mother had to learn how to provide it, the chances of species survival would be small. Communication patterns have to work the first time they are used. From this viewpoint, emotions may be thought of, in part, as communication signals emitted by the infant that have various adaptive consequences for survival.

From an ethological point of view, the study of behavior requires the examination of two questions: From what did this piece of behavior evolve? What is the adaptive significance of this behavior (Beer, 1970)? The answer to the first question is usually given in terms of homologies (i.e., the identification of common evolutionary origins). An example of a homology may be seen in the common structural plan underlying the wing of the bird, the forelimb of the monkey, and the arm of the human. A possible example of a behavioral homology is the dilation of the nostrils in anger, which may be related to a respiratory reflex that functions to cool the body at a time of exertion (Andrew, 1974).

A number of writers have commented on the function of affect in young organisms. Watson in 1929 wrote that

> Man at birth and at varying periods thereafter is supplied with a series of protective attack and defense mechanisms, which while not nearly so perfect as in animals, nevertheless form a substantial repertoire of acts. They need supplementation by habit before being of direct utility to the individual in his struggle for food, against enemies, etc. These are the protective and defense reactions—the unlearned part activities at first predominate [p. 98].

By *affect,* Watson clearly referred to such behavioral patterns as crying, smiling, erection of the penis, flailing of the arms or legs, etc.

More recently, Sroufe (1974) has written about the function of affect in a different way. He suggests that affects have three functions, namely, the communication of information about internal states, the elicitation of helpful reactions from the mother, and the amplification or exaggeration of behavior. This view implies that an emotion is an internal state that has certain observable indexes. One makes an inference from the observable behavior to the implied state.

Still another way to consider the function of emotions is to consider their origin in primitive reflexes evolved to provide defense against heat and cold. Stanley-Jones (1966) has argued that emotions have been grafted onto autonomic reflexes used to maintain body temperature. In support of this argument, he points out that adrenaline secretion acts to protect the individual from overheating and that hypothalamic mechanisms control temperature regulation just as they control many emotional expressions as well. Color changes in the skin that are typically considered to reflect emotions also regulate heat input and output. This whole thermoregulatory mechanism is available to the infant within a few hours of birth.

From this point of view, Stanley-Jones (1966) argues that emotions are not disruptive, maladaptive states, but rather act to stabilize the internal state of the organism. Emotions are thus autonomic and behavioral patterns that act to maintain thermostasis rather than to disrupt it. A similar viewpoint was presented by

Rapoport (1965), who proposed that emotions are homeostatic devices designed to maintain a steady state in the face of environmental fluctuations. Emotions represent transitory adjustment reactions that function to return the organism into a stable, effective relationship with its immediate environment when that relationship is disrupted.

Andrew (1974) has elaborated on the view presented by Stanley-Jones (1970). He points out that emergency reactions are associated with exertion in general, rather than being restricted to attack or fleeing. Many of these reactions precede behavioral exertion and therefore may become important in communicating an organism's intentions. To that extent, they become part of the complex chain of events called an emotion. Examples of reflex, anticipatory reactions are: vasodilation in skeletal muscles to increase their blood supply, blood pressure increases due to cardiac acceleration, and vasoconstriction in the skin and intestines. "This pattern occurs as a first response to a new stimulus in a previously quiet organism. The function of this pattern is to prepare for a sustained or violent muscle action [Andrew, 1974, p. 195]."

Andrew (1974) suggests that all such reflexes maintain a balance between total inhibition, or immobility, and extreme motor action. These reflexes may be thermoregulatory (for example, sweating, panting, flushing), respiratory (rapid breathing or dilation of nostrils), and postural (crouching, huddling, or arching). Andrew (1974) concludes that the generalized mammalian response to noxious stimulation is characterized by ear withdrawal and flattening, mouth corner withdrawal and lip retraction, and eye closure. Other behaviors that are often found as part of the protective response pattern are tongue protrusion and lateral shaking of head and body. These kinds of protective responses are often seen as part of greeting displays that "are most predictably evoked in primates by sudden mutual perception, particularly if the eyes meet. . . . Vocalizations reflect such states as that the organism is unconfortable, or lost, or wants something, or is likely to flee, or that it has perceived a novel stimulus [Andrew, 1974, p. 190]." These patterns are found in young organisms as well as mature ones.

Ethologists have published many studies that have identified rather specific functions of communication signals or displays. For example, Seyfarth, Cheney, and Marler (1980b) have shown that vervet monkey alarm calls function to designate different classes of external danger related to specific types of predators: "Animals on the ground respond to leopard alarms by running into trees, to eagle alarms by looking up, and to snake alarms by looking down [p. 170]." Context had little relation to the response.

In a series of field trials, recorded alarm calls were played back to monkeys of different ages. It was found that infants were able to distinguish between general classes of predators; for example, between a terrestrial mammal and a flying bird, but that adults could distinguish among predators and other mammals, or eagles and other birds (Seyforth, Cheney, & Marler, 1980a). These observations provide strong support for the thesis that the ability to react appropriately to such calls is a genetically determined characteristic. Although the degree of specificity may be influenced by experience, the initial appearance of such abilities does not appear to depend on learning.

The proposition that emotional calls or vocalization in different species might have some evolutionary continuity has been explored by Morton (1977). He examined the sounds of a large number of birds and mammals in a variety of settings and found that regardless of size, voice, or environment, each animal had a common vocal pattern: An animal that was interpreted as angry makes a low, harsh growl, and a fearful animal makes a high-pitched whine. Animals that were neither angry nor fearful, but active and involved, emit a grunt or barklike sound. Various combinations of these sounds were found; for example, a screech contains components of both anger and fear.

Morton's (1977) theory is that these basic sound patterns are indicators of inner impulses in response to outer stimuli and that they serve to communicate messages that have implications for successful adaptation. Larger animals are generally more capable of making low-pitched, harsher, and louder sounds than smaller animals. The use of such low-pitched growls represents an evolutionary adaptation by which a small animal may imitate a larger animal. This is a pseudo-largeness principle that is analogous to the expansion of body size through feathers, fur, arching, or air pouches in order to provide a threatening appearance. Such displays often prevent actual combat.

Similarly, young animals inherently make higher-pitched sounds than do older ones, generally because their vocal apparatus is not as large as that of an adult. An adult animal that intends to express submission or fear will whine or squeak out high-pitched sounds in mimicry of a younger, more vulnerable creature. According to Morton, "the sounds of largeness have replaced the need to be large, and the sounds of smallness the need to be small [Hopson, 1980, p. 83]."

Extending this type of analysis, Tembrock (cited in Scherer, 1980) suggests that repeated short sounds within the mid-frequency range of the species tend to characterize states of comfort. Dominance calls are identified by lower frequencies, whereas submission sounds have high frequencies and are maintained over a longer period of time.

After investigating vocalizations of the Japanese monkey (*macaca fuscata*), Green (1975) concluded that there were a large number of parallels between human vocalizations and the vocalizations of this monkey:

> Humans also employ roars, cries, shrieks, screams, screeches, and a variety of other sounds. These sounds are not only acoustically homologous with those described here for the Japanese monkey, but they are also used in analogous situations by primates with similar inferred internal states. Roars are used by enraged people, cries by babies abandoned or otherwise distressed, screeches in tantrums of youngsters, and whines as they reach the comfort of a mother's embrace [p. 95].

The sounds made by humans are exceedingly complex partly because a phylogenetically late language coding system has been superimposed upon a very ancient vocal affect system. Therefore, many speech characteristics reflect both linguistic and emotional information. Although there are many studies of infant vocalizations, the complexity of the problem has limited generalizations. For a critique of inadequate methodologies and measurement techniques, see Plutchik (1980) and Scherer (1981).

## Genetics and Behavior

Evidence for the genetic basis of most emotional expressions has continued to accumulate ever since Darwin (1872/1965) first defined some criteria for establishing innateness. He pointed out that there are at least four types of evidence one may use. First, he noted that some emotional expressions appear in similar form in many lower animals. Second, some emotional expressions appear in infants in the same form as in adults. Third, some emotional expressions are shown in identical ways by those born blind as in those who are normally sighted. Fourth, some emotional expressions appear in similar form in widely distinct races and groups of humans. Recent work by Eibl-Eibesfeldt (1971, 1973, 1975) and by Ekman and Friesen (1971), among others, have supported these ideas. In addition, Wilson (1978) has emphasized both the similarities and differences between human societies and societies found among lower animals.

The rôle of genetic determinism is more readily seen when humans are compared with apes and monkeys, who are our closest living evolutionary relatives. There are four major parallels that Wilson (1978) notes: (a) human intimate social groups contain 10–100 members, as is true for most primate groups; (b) males are larger than females, which in turn is related to sex differences in competitiveness, aggression, and timidity; (c) the young are influenced by extensive social training over a long period of time; and (d) social play is the basis for pair-bonding, sex practices, and exploration. Wilson's (1978) point is that these social patterns that include emotions are strongly influenced by the primate genotype. "The grimace of fear, the smile, and even laughter have parallels in the facial expressions of chimpanzees [Wilson, 1978, p. 25]."

However, Wilson (1978) also points out that genes do not directly prescribe a particular behavior; they influence thresholds of sensitivity, perceptual inclinations, and motor factors. In some cases, genetic influences almost completely determine a behavioral trait such as avoidance of visual cliffs or smiling in the young infant. In other cases such as phobias, genetic factors act simply as predisposing factors. Of considerable importance in this view is the idea that humans approach certain kinds of choices and not others in the first place because of innate, genetically determined influences. Examples of such innate predispositions are the preferential tuning of the newborn to the sound of the human voice; the preference for human faces rather than random patterns; and the need to avoid snakes, spiders, and rats rather than inanimate but potentially more dangerous objects such as knives, guns, or electrical outlets.

Lumsden and Wilson (1981) try to make a case for the idea that there are certain classes of behavior that are incorporated into all human societies under the influence of epigenetic rules. These include deep grammar (consistent, rapid sentence formation), incest avoidance, consumption of sugar, fear of strangers, smiling, holding an infant on the left side of the body, fear of snakes, laughing, crying, mother–infant bonding, and sex differences in temperament, among others. They conclude that "individuals are genetically prepared or contraprepared to learn to respond to particular conditioned stimuli in those behavioral categories of greatest importance to their survival and reproduction, while in other behavioral categories they are typically unprepared or neutral [Lumsden & Wilson, 1981, p. 82]." This same point is made by Kaufman (1974) when he concludes as a result of his study of Bonnet and pigtail monkeys that an infant easily learns the behaviors that characterize its own particular species. Washburn (1978) presents the same idea when he notes that important adaptive behaviors are easier to learn than others because of a genetic basis.

This section has emphasized the idea that emotions in infants must be considered within an evolutionary context. From this point of view, we recognize that emotional expressions in human infants are related to emotional expressions in lower primates and have a genetic (schematic) basis. The functions of emotions in lower animals; that is, communication and survival, are the same functions expressed by human infants when they exhibit a large variety of patterned behaviors.

## EMOTION AS A COMPLEX CHAIN OF EVENTS

The general emotion theory outlined earlier assumes that an emotion is more than a subjective experience; it is defined as a complex chain of events that begins with the perception of a stimulus and ends with an interaction between the organism and the stimulus that precipitated the chain of events. The major components of the chain are cognitive evaluation of the stimulus, feeling state, physiological arousal, impulses to action, and overt behavior.

From the point of view of the phylogeny and ontogeny of emotion, each of these components of the emotion chain has a different evolutionary and developmental history. In the work of Piaget (1952) and Piaget and Inhelder (1969), for example, stages of cognitive development in the infant are related to emotional development. In Stage 2 (1–4 months), the infant shows anticipatory sucking on the basis of visual cues. Such positively toned anticipation has been interpreted by them as an affective reaction. In Stage 3 (4–8 months), signs of fear and wariness appear as the infants' cognitive capacities allow recognition, memory, and rudimentary intentionality. By Stage 4 (8–12 months), the infant has the capacity to evaluate an event and its context to some degree, and signs of fear, anger, surprise, and disappointment become evident. And in Stage 5 (12–18 months), with the development of the cognitive ability to represent the self and external causation, affects such as shame, defiance, and negativism appear. Sroufe (1979) suggests that the development of "object permanence" and "person permanence" as cognitive categories is tied to the appearance of such affective states as fear of strangers, surprise, and laughter. Similarly, both Schaffer (1977) and Ekman (1979) point out that, for anticipation to take place, an expanded memory as well as an increased attention span are necessary. Hunt (1979) adds that the attachment of infants to mothers depends on cognitive development and varies for different species. In certain birds it takes place in a few hours, in ungulates it takes a few days, in dogs, 3–4 weeks, in chimps 5–6 weeks, and in humans, 5–6 months. In connection with a discussion of play from an ethological perspective, Vandenberg (1978) concludes that:

> Phylogenetically, it is interesting to note that next to humans, chimpanzees and dolphins are capable of the most sophisticated linguistic and means–ends activities, and they are also the most socially playful of nonhuman species. This is not to suggest that play per se is responsible for those other activities. Rather, it supports the contention that, phylogenetically, the cognitive requirements for complex play may be similar to those required for means–ends and representational abilities. This suggests that to chart the phylogenetic evolution of play is also to chart the evolution and potentiality of these other abilities [p. 734].

There are two other points worth making about the relation between cognitions and emotions. The first is that certain emotion expressions such as crying, smiling, and cooing appear before there is much cognitive capacity in the infant. Such expressions occur at approximately the same time in blind infants, deaf infants, deaf–blind infants, retarded infants, and in infants in widely different cultures (Freedman, 1974). However, the experience of extensive maternal deprivation does appear to have a marked effect on at least certain emotional expressions, presumably through its impact on cognitive development. For example, total isolation of rhesus monkeys produced a permanent decrease in the animals' ability to form social attachments (Sackett & Ruppenthal, 1973). In another study, rhesus monkeys were found to be able to use the facial expressions of other monkeys as appropriate cues for avoiding an electric shock (Miller, Caul, & Mirsky, 1967). Monkeys who had been raised in total isolation for more than 6 months were markedly inferior in this task than were normal monkeys. The isolate animals were deficient in recognizing the facial expressions of normal monkeys. This finding again emphasizes the point that the *expression* of emotions and the *recognition* of emotions are two different processes and are affected by different variables, one of which may be cognitive development. This supports the idea that an emotion is a complex chain of events, each link of which may be differently influenced by experience as well as the course of ontology. The typical pattern of emotional behavior appears in a certain time sequence in infants only in an average, expectable environment. Under extreme abnormal conditions of rearing, unusual behaviors may appear or "normal" behaviors may fail to appear.

Unfortunately, little data exist on the course of development of certain other aspects of the affect chain of events, particularly, arousal, physiological changes, and preparations for action. In this context, Green and Marler (1979) state that the concept of undifferentiated arousal is inadequate to explain social interaction among animals. They claim that natural selection should favor means by which an emotionally aroused animal could signal to another conspecific something about the nature of the stimulus arousing the emotion. In the interests of survival, it is important to know whether the referent is a predator or a source of food, a sex object or a nurturant one.

## Displays in the Chain of Emotion

Just as the subjective feeling state is only one element in the chain of events that define an emotion, so, too, is the overt behavior one element in this chain. We pay more attention to this component because the subjective element is less accessible to investigation than is the motor one.

The first part of this chapter provided an ethological catalogue of the various behaviors a young infant is capable of showing. Research attention has focused on only a small number of them, such things as cries, smiles, laughter, cooing, and other vocalizations. Only relatively recently has attention been directed to postures; hand, leg, and body movements; stereotyped patterns; and more subtle aspects of facial expressions.

Ekman and Oster (1979) have reviewed the evidence on facial expressions in human infants and have arrived at the following conclusions:

1. The facial musculature is fully formed and functional at birth.
2. Distinctive facial expressions resembling certain adult expressions are present in early infancy. Expressions of crying, smiling, disgust, and startle are observable in the first days of life.
3. Three- to 4-month-old infants show differential facial responses to exaggerated facial responses of caretakers.
4. Imitation of certain facial expressions of caretakers (mouth opening and tongue protrusion) has been shown by 2–3-week-old infants.

5. Preschool children know what the most common facial expressions look like, what they mean, and what kinds of situations typically elicit them.
6. Facial expressions plays a role in social communication.

These generalizations illustrate the important point that facial expressions suggestive of emotions are present at birth and continue to appear long before any language exists. It is evident that an emotion is not a facial expression per se but is somehow inferred to exist on the basis of evidence from facial expressions as well as other sources of information. For example, smiles occur at birth and continue to appear from time to time thereafter. Observations have revealed, however, that the smiles of the first few weeks of life occur without any identifiable stimulus being present. Such smiles tend to occur during states of rapid eye movements (REM states), which are normal concomitants of both sleep and drowsiness in infants. After about 6 weeks, smiles appear in response to the sight of a human face and may also be triggered by rocking the baby or ringing a bell. Thus, conclusions about the emotional significance of a particular facial expression depend on a series of associated events. It is extremely unlikely that there is a one-to-one isomorphic relation between the facial expression of the infant and a unique corresponding subjective experience.

The ethologists have paid the most attention to displays or expressive behavior as signals of emotion, generally without reference to hypothetical subjective states. From their point of view, facial expressions are only one kind of display system that includes such varied communications as mating signals, warning signals, threat signals, food signals, and territory signals, among others. These displays may be vocal, visual, postural, or olfactory (Plutchik, 1980). According to Andrew (1974), in lower vertebrates, expressive emotional behavior tends to be whole body displays. At higher phylogenetic levels, displays are more discrete and, at the same time, the parts of the display are less highly correlated with each other. Also found at higher levels is less all-or-none behavior and more gradation of signals. Such gradation allows greater flexibility in the expression of meanings. Marler (1977a) believes that there is no firm proof that fundamental differences exist between animals and humans in regard to the underlying physiology of signaling.

One final point on emotion as a chain of events. Ekman and Oster (1979) state that facial expressions play a role in social communication. This is true, in general, for all infant emotional expressions. Infants do not simply emit signals that have emotional meaning. The signals are part of an interaction between the infant and its caretaker. For example, pauses during sucking may function to elicit a response from the mother (Kaye, 1977). According to Trevarthen (1977), infants show various movements of their head, trunk, or limbs that are closely synchronized to facial expression changes or vocalizations. Such movements signal a change in the level or direction of communication. "Social interactions are . . . chains of interlocking behavior patterns representing responses, and at the same time acting as stimuli initiating the next step in the interaction [Papousek & Papousek, 1977, p. 73]." The infant– caretaker system uses the response of the infant as a stimulus to the environment in order to change the stimulus that triggered the response in the first place. Such a model implies a rudimentary grammar of the sequence of interactions. One of the tasks of research is to make explicit the nature of the interactions within the infant–caretaker system.

## EMOTIONS AS INFERENCES

The point has been made that an emotion is more than a subjective response, more than a display signal, and more than a physiological state of arousal. The term *emotion* refers to a complex chain of events, most of which can be described only by inference from indirect sources of evidence. From the point of view of ethology, the judgment that a state is emotional is based on a number of recurring themes. These are

> That the states are generalized, affecting many patterns of behavior; that autonomic arousal is often involved; that there is often some connotation of emergency in the tempo, intensity, and demeanor of the signaling animal; that there is often strong "momentum" to the behavior so that once begun it tends to continue for a period of time, resisting rapid change; that is it involuntary, or toward that end of a continuum with voluntary actions; that it is less susceptible to modification by learning or conscious effort, and that it can be placed somewhere on a dimension of pleasantness to unpleasantness [Marler, 1977a, p. 54].

It is important to emphasize that one or more of these characteristics may be absent and the judgment of the presence of an emotion may still be made. Unfortunately, the rules for such inferences have not yet been made explicit, accounting in part, for some of the disagreements between investigators in this field.

An example of the role of inference in judging emotions in infants has already been given in regard to the smile. Certain smiles are not triggered by social events, are not conditionable, and are related to REM states of drowsiness. Other smiles are clearly responses to the caretaker, appear to be anticipatory reactions, and appear at times of high alertness. The latter smiles are inferred to be emotional, the former not.

Similarly, the inference of aggression in the interaction of young animals depends on whether the context is judged to be play or not. This in turn depends on a variety of factors, including the observation of a sign or metacommunication facial expression signal that is apparently interpreted to mean "this is play" (Vandenberg, 1978). Tooker and Miller (1980) also point out that the motor pattern typical of aggression in fish may occur in a nonsocial context. Only when it occurs in a social context is the inference made that it represents aggression.

The inference that vervet monkeys respond differentially to alarm calls was based on a variety of observations (Seyforth *et al.*, 1980). So-called leopard alarms were associated with other monkeys running into trees; eagle alarms were associated with monkeys looking up; and snake alarms with monkeys looking down. These alarms were tape-recorded and played back to the vervets in the absence of actual predators with comparable results. In addition, it was found that age, sex, context, and various acoustic properties had little effect on the animal's reactions. Thus, the convergence of various kinds of evidence led to the conclusion that an emotional signal of a specific kind had been emitted.

The judgment of social attachment is also based on a variety of observations. Freedman (1974) states that social attachment is inferred on the basis of the following kinds of data: (*a*) an apparent desire for physical proximity; (*b*) the appearance of mutual watching; (*c*) mutual smiling; (*d*) mutual cooing; (*e*) mutual laughter and play; and (*f*) signs of protection of the young. It is obvious that even these observational types of judgments are inferences from the specific behaviors engaged in by the mother and infant. The final judgment of attachment is thus a higher-order abstraction based on a series of lower-order inferences.

The judgment of fear in an infant is usually based on observations of gaze aversion and crying when a stranger approaches. But these reactions may also be evoked by a visual cliff and by looming stimuli, among others. Should the inference of fear depend on evidence of crying in all three situations, two out of three, or only one? The problem is equivalent to the psychometric one of constructing a reliable test of a hypothetical construct. How many items does one need to make a reliable and valid judgment of the existence of the hypothetical state of fear in an infant? Unfortunately, little attention has been directed to this problem from a psychometric point of view.

In addition to this item-sampling problem, there also exists the problem that various indexes of emotion are poorly correlated. Facial expressions are only tenuously connected with psychological arousal states or biochemical indexes (Yarrow, 1979). Yet, according to Marler (1977a), "No reaction of an organism to an external stimulus can be understood without taking its current physiological state into account [p. 53]." Inferences about emotions should rely on as many sources of information as possible. Of particular importance is a description of the stimuli that precede the emotional expression, the detailed morphology of the response itself, and the kind of effects the expression appears to have on other organisms in the immediate environment.

An illustration of this approach to defining emotion may be found in the study of kitten vocalizations by Haskins (1979). Kittens were exposed to cold stimuli, restraint, and isolation at various times during their first 6 weeks of life. The results showed that the kittens cried more during restraint than during either cold exposure or isolation. The entrance of the mother into the litter box also increased the frequency of crying, as did shifts in position of the mother during nursing. Crying decreased when kittens congregated in huddles. The crying of the kittens also influenced the mother to come into the litter and to make nursing possible. Sound spectrograph analysis revealed that the peak fundamental frequency of the crying was significantly greater during the cold stress than during either isolation or restraint. These results imply that vocalizations carry information about the stimulus conditions to which kittens are exposed and have an effect on the caretaker that is related to the probability of survival of the young.

Another illustration of a similar approach was reported by Scoville and Gottlieb (1980). They recorded the vocalizations of Peking ducklings from several hours before hatching to 48 hours posthatching. Vocalizations were recorded in a variety of situations, for example, in the presence of other ducklings, during exposure to maternal calls, and during social isolation. Sound spectrograph analysis revealed two acoustically distinct types of sound patterns: (a) *contentment calls,* which have short note durations, fast repetition rates, and low pitch, and are elicited by the presence of peers and/or maternal calls; and (b) distress calls, which have longer note durations, slower repetition rates, and higher pitch, and are emitted during social isolation. The second category of sounds appear to attract attention of the hen to any duckling that has become separated from the brood. Such attraction serves to maintain group cohesion and to increase the chances of survival of the ducklings.

In a similar type of investigation, Scott (1980), recorded distress vocalizations in puppies and tried to identify variables that would either increase or decrease them. Food, novel objects, and tranquilizers had no effect, although an antidepressant (Imipramine) reduced distress vocalizations in certain breeds of dogs. Morphine also reduced these vocalizations as did exposure to a warm (29° C) incubator. The most effective reducer of these vocalizations was social interaction with other puppies or adult dogs. These and other observations led to the conclusion that these vocalizations are, in fact, emotional signals of distress and that they function to increase the probability of social contact with other animals.

There is one further point to be made in regard to the issue of inferring emotions from indirect evidence. One of the important reasons that emotional states are sometimes very difficult to define in a simple, clear-cut way is that emotions are often mixed states and reflect the interaction of opposite tendencies. Hinde (1966) has given many examples from the animal literature of the concept that overt displays often reflect combined impulses of approach and avoidance, attack and flight, or sex and aggression. Van Hooff (1973) has identified five display systems in the chimpanzee that he calls play, aggression, submission, affinity, and excitement systems. He concludes that all facial expressions seen in the chimpanzee are a result of the conflict of two or more of these motivational systems. Harlow and Harlow (1972) point out that mother–infant rhesus monkey separation is produced through a mixture of maternal punishment and infant curiosity. And Sroufe (1979) concludes that infant behavior is a vectorial resultant of opposing forces such as wariness and curiosity, security in the familiar and attraction to the unfamiliar. For all the reasons given, emotions in infants (and adults as well) are complex hypothetical states whose existence and properties can only be determined by a series of inferences and approximations. Ekman and Oster (1979) make a similar point when they write, "Since there is no single, infallible way to determine a person's true emotional state, it is unfortunate that so few investigators have followed the approach of using multiple convergent measures to gain a more reliable indication of the emotion experienced [p. 541]."

## THE STRUCTURE OF EMOTIONS

Although most research on infant emotions focuses on one or another affect such as smiling, fear, or attachment, it is evident that emotions do not exist in isolation from one another. As has already been noted, emotional expressions often result from the interaction of opposing motivations such as approach and avoidance, or dominance and submission. This implies that the concept of emotional polarities is already inherent in our thinking about emotions. What is needed is an explicit statement of the emotional polarities, as well as a description of the relative similarity of emotion and of the implications of these ideas for affect theory. This, in part, is what is meant by the idea of structure.

Relatively few models have tried to include structural elements in a theory of emotion. One of the earliest was that of Plutchik (1958, 1962, 1980), who proposed that there are eight basic emotions, each of which can be described by means of different languages. From a subjective point of view, the basic emotions are anger, fear, joy, sadness, acceptance, disgust, surprise, and anticipation. These terms are only approximations of the basic emotions since each primary emotion dimension can be described by words that reflect different levels of intensity, for example, anger or rage, or fear or panic. There are also behavioral, functional, and trait languages of emotion as well as the subjective one.

Since emotions vary in intensity, similarity, and polarity, these characteristics can be summarized by means of a three-dimensional solid somewhat like the color solid. Mixtures of the basic emotions can be shown to be describable in terms of the words we use to designate personality traits. The basic emotions are assumed to be genetically determined, prototype reactions that have adaptive significance from an evolutionary point of view.

Applying these ideas to infancy suggests that emotional expressions such as smiling or crying should be considered as signals of inner states of disequilibrium that require intervention by the caretaker. Such intervention increases the probability of survival of the infant. Second, since an emotion is a complex chain of reactions, it is highly likely that the different elements of the chain mature, or develop, at different rates, and that life experiences have differential effects on each part of the chain. Thus, for example, diet, stimulus complexity, mothering, and isolation may each have different effects on cognitions, subjective feelings, physiological arousal, impulses to action, and behavior at any given time in the life of an infant. Research should be directed at determining in systematic ways when each component of an emotion appears and what effect various environmental contingencies have on each component.

Another approach to emotions that contains structural elements is the "differential emotions" theory proposed by Izard (1978). He assumes that emotion is one of six relatively independent subsystems of the human personality and that emotions have three major components: a facial expression, a physiological (face–brain) feedback loop, and a communication function. Fundamental emotions are based on innate neural mechanisms and function to ensure a mother–infant attachment critical for survival. Izard assumes that emotion experience is activated by sensory feedback from the face and that environmental events will trigger different emotions, depending on the stage of development of the various subsystems.

One other approach to emotions has included structural elements. The ethologist Marler (1977b) has proposed four dimensions of affective signaling that are assumed to have certain systematic relations to one another: (*a*) arousal– depression; (*b*) locomotor approach–withdrawal; (*c*) object acceptance–rejection; and (*d*) social engagement–disengagement. Marler (1977) assumes that these signaling dimensions have both affective and ethological aspects. For example, he believes that the social engagement–disengagement dimension is related to the subjective states of joy and rage and that the ethological aspects of this dimension refer to touching, courting, or mating versus competing, dominating or killing, respectively. He concludes that both animal and human signaling consists of a mixture of both symbolic and affective components.

This brief overview of structural models suggests that more attention should be given to this aspect of infant development. Research should be directed at the interrelations among the different emotions and emotion expressions that are identifiable in infancy. This would be an important step toward understanding the sequences of development of particular emotions throughout infancy and childhood.

## DERIVATIVES OF EMOTION

A major question asked about emotions concerns their development over time. The psychoanalysts have been particularly interested in tracing personality traits and psychopathological symptoms of adult life to early affective impulses and their viscissitudes. But the interest is more general, and ethologists as well as child psychologists have been concerned with the course of development of emotions and their expressions at different ages.

One of the earliest discussions of this issue was published by Bridges (1932). She observed infants in a Canadian Foundling hospital and concluded that, until 3 weeks of age, they showed only one "emotion" to all stimulating conditions, called "general excitement." After 3 weeks, the infants showed "distress" to painful situations such as hunger and circumcision. By 3 months of age, signs of "bitter distress" or "angry vexation" appeared. Signs of "temper" were seen by the fourth month, and evidence of "revulsion" (i.e., food rejection) were seen by 5 or 6 months. Fear of strangers appeared by the seventh or eighth month, and real temper tantrums occurred by age 14 months. Signs of "jealousy" and "envy" appeared by age 16 months. The "positive" emotions indicated by smiling became evident at about 2 months, and laughter appeared at 4 months. Affectionate attachments to particular people were first noticed at about 1 year of age. These observations are important, but Bridges (1932) never attempted to define the word *emotion*, and it is not evident why she called one pattern of reaction *distress*, another *anger*, and a third *disgust*. Also, no attempt was made to provide a rationale for the particular sequence of emergence of emotions.

A recent attempt to describe the ontogenesis of some human emotions was made by Sroufe (1979). He traces the development of the *pleasure–joy* dimension from the endogeneous smile observed at birth to the *turning toward* reaction seen at 1 month, to signs of pleasure at 3 months (exogenous smile?), to delight (indicated by laughter in response to vigorous stimulation) to *joy* at 7 months, *elation* at 12 months, and *pride* and *love* at 36 months. Similarly, he assumes that the earliest signs of *rage* at birth are seen in the *distress* associated with covering the face, or physical restraint. At 3 months of age, *rage* associated with *disappointment* appears, and *anger* appears at 7 months. *Petulance* appears at 12 months, *defiance* at 18 months, and *guilt* at 36 months.

A major problem with these descriptions of affect development is the use of inherently ambiguous language and the somewhat arbitrary assignment of labels to presumed sequences of emotional growth. For example, it is not clear why pride is considered a derivative of joy, or why guilt is considered a derivative of anger. Is defiance a derivative of anger or of disgust? And to what extent is disgust a primary affect? One might argue that such affects as pride and guilt (and many others) are mixed emotions that reflect two or more of the primary emotions. In fact, pride has been rated as reflecting anger as much as joy, and guilt has been rated as a mixture of joy and fear (Plutchik, 1980). Yarrow (1979) has pointed out that the reactions of infants to strangers may include both smiling and crying, and that dissimilar emotions can be present simultaneously. Research on the ontogenesis of emotions should be devoted to identifying the variables that influence the mixing of primary emotions. In addition, a theory of ontogenesis must derive all affect states and not simply the few such as fear and anger that are usually studied.

In contrast to child psychologists, ethologists have provided a different perspective on the development of emotions and emotional expressions. For example, after studying two carnivores and several primates, including the chimpanzee, Bolwig (1962) presents a number of conclusions about facial expressions. He proposes that the origin of the smile, from a phylogenetic point of view, is the play-bite, whereas the facial expression of anger is related to the preparation for a hard bite. Threat expressions contain components of fear and anger. Love and affection find expression through such actions as lipsmacking, love-biting, sucking, and kissing. The oral caress is believed to originate from infant sucking

In apparent disagreement, Andrew (1974) states that the primate grin is a derivative of the intention movement of attack and reflects conflicting tendencies to attack and flee. He distinguishes between the smile and the grin and suggests that they have different evolutionary origins.

Changes in the frequency of play acts in many species have a predictable schedule, often increasing and then decreasing. Fagan (1980) has identified at least three factors that influence such behavior: (a) the cost of play (i.e., conflict between mother and offspring over food resources); (b) the availability of companions; and (c) genetic constraints related to the effects of natural selection over long periods of time.

A detailed attempt to describe the derivatives of some basic emotions has been made by Eibl-Eibesfeldt (1975) and elaborated by Lumsden and Wilson (1981). The "eyebrow flash" is seen as an accompaniment of attention or surprise in young infants when they are exposed to a strong stimulus. As the infant matures, the raised eyebrow takes on four possible communication meanings. The eyebrow may be lifted in friendly surprise, angry surprise, curiosity, or as a question. In many different societies, the eyebrow flash is a sign of greeting, flirting, thanking, emphasizing, or approving. In other societies, the eyebrow flash is an expression of indignation, arrogance, or disapproval. Lumsden and Wilson (1981) conclude that "much of nonverbal communication is built upon the ritualization of elementary behavior patterns [p. 78]." However, still unknown and unspecified at the present time are the eipigenetic rules that presumably determine this ritualization process.

Another major attempt to describe the derivatives of the basic emotions has been made by Plutchik (1980). In the psychoevolutionary theory of emotion, personality traits are considered to be mixtures of two or more basic emotions that are expressed with some frequency. Thus, the trait of *gloominess* is conceptualized as a mixture of sadness and expectation, and the trait of *optimism* is considered to result from a mixture of joy and expectation. When certain personality traits are expressed to an extreme degree, we use a diagnostic language to describe the individual. Thus, extreme gloominess is diagnosed as depression, extreme sociability is diagnosed as mania, and extreme rejection (distrust) is diagnosed as paranoia.

Carrying these ideas one step further, we recognize that ego defenses such as repression, displacement, and projection function to deal with particular emotions. Repression attempts to deal with high levels of unacceptable anxiety, displacement deals with anger that cannot be directly expressed, and projection attempts to handle feelings of disgust about oneself. Other ego defenses handle other basic emotions. Finally, certain coping styles such as minimizing the importance of a stress, substituting one behavior for a less acceptable one, and blaming others can also be conceptualized as derivatives of the basic emotions (Wilder & Plutchik, 1982). However, relatively little is known about the variables that determine why the derivatives of emotion take one form rather than another in particular individuals.

It is evident that a theory of development has a number of tasks to perform. It needs to use or obtain basic information about the many forms of expressive behavior observable in young organisms, particularly human infants. It needs a conceptualization of emotion as a hypothetical construct deeper and more fundamental than the particular expressive behaviors that can be observed. The theory should help identify those behaviors that clearly reflect emotional processes as distinct from those that do not. The theory should also provide some insight into the developmental course of emotional expressions, recognizing that the appearance of a particular behavior (e.g., wariness of strangers) at 8 months does not indicate that fear began at that point any more than the absence of fear of strangers at 12 months indicates that fear is no longer an emotion in the repertoire of an individual. A general theory of development should also have something to say about the classes of variables that influence the appearance and development of emotional behaviors. And finally, the theory should attempt to be explicit about the many derivatives of emotion that are part of the adult organism's repertoire of behaviors and feelings. Although no current theory deals with all these issues, their explicit formulation may provide a salutary step toward a new synthesis.

## REFERENCES

Andrew, R. J. The information potentially available in mammalian displays. In R. A. Hinde (Ed.), *Nonverbal communication*. London and New York: Cambridge Univ. Press, 1972.

Andrew, R. J. Arousal and the causation of behavior. *Behavior*, 1974, *51*, 135–165.

Arbib, M. A., & Kahn, R. M. A developmental model of information processing in the child. *Perspectives in Biology and Medicine*, 1969, *12*, 397–416.

Barnett, S. A. Animals to man: The epigenetics of behavior. In S. A. Barnett (Ed.), *Ethology and behavior*. London: Heinemann, 1973.

Beer, C. C. Comparative ethology and the evolution of behavior. In N. F. White (Ed.), *Ethology and psychiatry*. Toronto: Univ. of Toronto Press, 1970.

Bolwig, N. Facial expression in primates with remarks on a parallel development in certain carnivores. *Behavior*, 1962, *22*, 167–192.

Bower, T. G. R. *Development in infancy*. San Francisco, California: Freeman, 1974.

Brazelton, T. B. Early parent–infant reciprocity. In V. C. Vaughan, III & T. B. Brazelton (Eds.), *The family: Can it be saved?* New York: Year Book Medical, 1976.

Bridges, K. M. B. Emotional development in early infancy. *Child Development*, 1932, *3*, 324–342.

Clynes, M. The communication of emotion: Theory of sentics. In R. Plutchik & H. Kellerman (Eds.), *Theories of emotion*. New York: Academic Press, 1980.

Conte, H. R., & Plutchik, R. A circumplex model for interpersonal personality traits. *Journal of Personality and Social Psychology*, 1981, *40*, 701–711.

Darwin, C. *The expression of the emotions in man and animals*. Chicago, Illinois: Univ. of Chicago Press, 1965. (Originally published, 1872).

Davitz, J. R. *The language of emotions*. New York: McGraw-Hill, 1969.

Eibl-Eibesfeldt, I. *Love and hate*. New York: Holt, 1971.

Eibl-Eibesfeldt, I. The expressive behavior of the deaf-and-blind-born. In M. von Cranach & I. Vine (Eds.), *Social communication and movement*. New York: Academic Press, 1973.

Eibl-Eibesfeldt, I. *Ethology: The biology of behavior* (2nd ed.). New York: Holt, 1975.

Ekman, P. About brows: Emotional and conversational signals. In M. von Cranach, K. Foppa, W. Lepenies, & D. Ploog (Eds.), *Human ethology*. London and New York: Cambridge Univ. Press, 1979.

Ekman, P., & Friesen, W. V. Constants across cultures in the face and emotion. *Journal of Personality and Social Psychology*, 1971, *17*, 124–129.

Ekman, P., & Friesen, W. V. Measuring facial movement. *Environmental Psychology and Nonverbal Behavior*, 1976, *1*, 56–75.

Ekman, P., & Oster, H. Facial expressions of emotion. *Annual Review of Psychology*, 1979, *30*, 527–554.

Fagen, R. M. Ontogeny of animal play behavior: Bimodal age schedule. *Animal Behavior*, 1980, *28*, 1290.

Freedman, D. G. *Human infancy: An ethological perspective*. Hillsdale, New Jersey: Erlbaum, 1974.

Green, S. Communication by a graded vocal system in Japanese monkeys. In L. A. Rosenblum (ed.), *Primate behavior*, vol. 4. New York: Academic Press, 1975.

Green, S., & Marler, P. The analysis of animal communication. In P. Marler & J. G. Vandenbergh (Eds.), *Handbook of behavioral neurobiology* (Vol. 3): *Social behavior and communication*. New York: Plenum, 1979.

Harlow, H. F., & Harlow, M. K. Learning to love. *American Scientist*, 1966, *54*, 244–272.

Harlow, H. F., & Harlow, M. K. The language of love. In T. Alloway, L. Krames, & P. Pliner (Eds.), *Communication and affect: A comparative approach*. New York: Academic Press, 1972.

Haskins, R. A causal analysis of kitten vocalizations: An observational and experimental study, *Animal Behavior*, 1979, *27*, 726–736.

Hebb, D. O. *Textbook of psychology*. Philadelphia, Pennsylvania: Saunders, 1972.

Hinde, R. A. *Animal behavior: A synthesis of ethology and comparative psychology*. New York: McGraw-Hill, 1966.

Hopson, J. Growl, bark, whine and hiss. *Science '80*, 1980, *1*, 81–84.

Hunt, J. McV. Psychological development: Early experience. *Annual Review of Psychology*, 1979, *30*, 103–143.

Izard, C. E. Emotions as motivations: An evolutionary–developmental perspective. In R. A. Dienstbier (Ed.), *Nebraska Symposium on Motivation* (Vol. 26). Lincoln Univ. of Nebraska Press, 1978.

Kaufman, I. C. Mother/infant relations in monkeys and humans: A reply to Professor Hinde. In N. F. White (Ed.), *Ethology and psychiatry*. Toronto: Univ. of Toronto Press, 1974.

Kaye, K. Toward the origin of dialogue. In H. R. Schaffer (Ed.), *Studies in mother–infant interaction*. New York: Academic Press, 1977.

Kellerman, H. *Group psychotherapy and personality: Intersecting structures*. New York: Grune & Stratton, 1979.

Kellerman, H. A structural model of emotion and personality: Psychoanalytic and sociobiological implications. In R. Plutchik & H. Kellerman (Eds.), *Theories of emotion*. New York: Academic Press, 1980.

Kinsey, A. C., Pomeroy, W. B., & Martin, C. E. *Sexual behavior in the human male*. Philadelphia, Pennsylvania, Saunders, 1948.

Lieberman, P. *On the origins of language*. New York: Macmillan, 1975.

Lumsden, C. J., & Wilson, E. O. *Genes, mind, and culture: The coevolutionary process*. Cambridge, Massachusetts: Harvard Univ. Press, 1981.

Marler, P. The evolution of communication. In T. A. Sebeok (Ed.), *How animals communicate*. Bloomington: Indiana Univ. Press, 1977. (a)

Marler, P. Primate vocalization: Affective or symbolic? In G. A. Bourne (Ed.), *Progress in ape research*. New York: Academic Press, 1977. (b)

Marler, P., & Tenaza, R. Signaling behavior of apes with special reference to vocalization. In T. A. Sebeok (Ed.), *How animals communicate*. Bloomington: Indiana Univ. Press, 1977.

Miller, R. E., Caul, W. F., & Mirsky, I. R. Communication of affects between feral and socially isolated monkeys. *Journal of Personality and Social Psychology*, 1967, *7*, 231–239.

Morris, D. J. The reproductive behavior of the zebra finch (*Peophila guttata*) with special reference to pseudofemale behavior and displacement activities. *Behavior*, 1954, *6*, 271–322.

Morton, E. S. On the occurrence and signifance of motivation: Structural rules in some bird and mammal sounds. *American Naturalist*, 1977, *111*, 855–869.

Oster, H., & Ekman, P. Facial behavior in child development. In W. A. Collins (Ed.), *Minnesota Symposia on Child Psychology* (Vol. 11). Hillsdale, New Jersey: Erlbaum, 1978.

Papousek, H., & Papousek, M. Mothering and the cognitive head-start: Psychobiological considerations. In H. R. Schaffer (Ed.), *Studies in mother–infant interaction*. New York: Academic Press, 1977.

Pawlby, S. J. Imitative interaction. In H. R. Schaffer (Ed.), *Studies in mother–infant interaction*. New York: Academic Press, 1977.

Piaget, J. *The origins of intelligence in children*. London: Rutledge & Kegan Paul, 1952.

Piaget, J., & Inhelder, B. *The psychology of the child*. London: Rutledge & Kegan Paul, 1969.

Plutchik, R. Outlines of a new theory of emotions. *Transactions of the New York Academy of Sciences*, 1958, *20*, 394–403.

Plutchik, R. *The emotions: Facts, theories and a new model*. New York: Random House, 1962.

Plutchik, R. Emotions, evolution and adaptation. In M. Arnold (Ed.), *Feelings and emotions: The Loyola Symposium*. New York: Academic Press, 1970.

Plutchik, R. *Emotion: A psychoevolutionary synthesis*. New York: Harper & Row, 1980.

Plutchik, R., Kellerman, H., & Conte, H. R. A structural theory of ego defenses. In C. E. Izard (Ed.), *Emotions, personality and psychopathology*. New York: Plenum, 1979.

Plutchik, R., & Platman, S. R. Personality connotations of psychiatric diagnoses. *Journal of Nervous and Mental Disease*, 1977, *165*, 418–422.

Rapoport, A. The impact of cybernetics on the philosophy of biology. In N. Wiener & J. P. Schode (Eds.), *Progress in biocybernetics* (Vol. 2). New York: Elsevier, 1965.

Sackett, G. P., & Ruppenthal, G. O. Development of monkeys after varied experiences during infancy. In S. A. Barnett (Ed.), *Ethology and development*. Philadelphia, Pennsylvania: Lippincott, 1973.

Schaffer, H. R. Early interactive development. In H. R. Schaffer (Ed.), *Studies in mother–infant interaction*. New York: Academic Press, 1977.

Scherer, K. R. Speech and emotional states. In J. Darby (Ed.), *The evaluation of speech in psychiatry and medicine*. New York: Grune & Stratton, 1980.

Scherer, K. R. The assessment of vocal expression in infants and children. In C. E. Izard (Ed.), *Measuring emotions in infants and children*. London and New York: Cambridge Univ. Press. (1982)

Scott, J. P. *Animal behavior*. Chicago, Illinois: Univ. of Chicago Press, 1958.

Scott, J. P. The function of emotions in behavioral systems: A systems theory analysis. In R. Plutchik & H. Kellerman (Eds.), *Theories of emotion*. New York: Academic Press, 1980.

Scoville, R., & Gottlieb, G. Development of vocal behavior in Peking ducklings. *Animal Behavior, 1980, 28,* 1095–1109.

Seyfarth, R. M., Cheney, D. L., & Marler, P. Monkey responses to three different alarm calls: Evidence of predator classification and semantic communication. *Science, 1980, 210,* 801–803. (a)

Seyfarth, R. M., Cheney, D. L., & Marler, P. Vervet monkey alarm calls: Semantic communication in a free-ranging primate. *Animal Behavior, 1980, 28,* 1070–1094. (b)

Spitz, R. A. *No and yes: On the genesis of human communication*. New York: International Universities Press, 1957.

Sroufe, L. A. Socioemotional development. In J. D. Osofsky (Ed.), *Handbook of infant development*. New York: Wiley, 1979.

Stanley-Jones, D. The thermostatic theory of emotion: A study in kybernetics. *Progress of Biocybernetics 1966, 3,* 1–20.

Stanley-Jones, D. The biological origin of love and hate. In M. Arnold (Ed.), *Feelings and emotions*. New York: Academic Press, 1970.

Thelen, E. Rhythmical stereotypes in normal human infants. *Animal Behavior, 1979, 27,* 699–715.

Thelen, E. Kicking, rocking, and waving: Contextual analysis of rhythmical stereotypes in normal human infants. *Animal Behavior, 1981, 29,* 3–11.

Tooker, C. P., & Miller, R. J. The ontogeny of agonistic behavior in the blue gourami trichogaster trichopterus (Pisces, Anabantoidei) *Animal Behavior, 1980, 28,* 973–988.

Trevarthen, C. Descriptive analysis of infant communicative behavior. In H. R. Schaffer (Ed.), *Studies in mother–infant interaction*. New York: Academic Press, 1977.

Valenstein, E. S. Stereotyped behavior and stress. In G. Servan (Ed.), *Psychopathology of human adaptation*. New York: Plenum, 1976.

Vandenberg, B. Play and development from an ethological perspective. *American Psychologist, 1978, 33,* 724–738.

Van Hooff, J. A. R. A. M. A comparative approach to the phylogeny of laughter and smiling. In R. A. Hinde (Ed.), *Non-verbal communication*. London and New York: Cambridge Univ. Press, 1972.

Van Hooff, J. A. R. A. M. A structural analysis of the social behavior of a semicaptive group of chimpanzees. In M. von Cranach & I. Vine (Eds.), *Social communication and movement*. New York: Academic Press, 1973.

Washburn, S. L. Human behavior and the behavior of other animals. *American Psychologist, 1978, 33,* 405–418.

Watson, J. B. *Psychology from the standpoint of a behaviorist* (3rd ed.). Philadelphia, Pennslyvania: Lippincott, 1929.

Wilder, J., & Plutchik, R. Preparing the professional: Building prevention of burnout into professional training. In W. Payne (Ed.), *Job stress and burnout*. Beverly Hills, Calif.: Sage, 1982.

Wilson, E. O. *Sociobiology: The New synthesis*. Cambridge, Massachusetts: Harvard Univ. Press, 1975.

Wilson, E. O. *On human nature*. Cambridge, Massachusetts: Harvard Univ. Press, 1978.

Yarrow, L. J. Emotional development. *American Psychologist*, 1979, *34*, 951–957.

Young, G., & Decarie, T. G. An ethology-based catalogue of facial/vocal behavior in infancy. *Animal Behavior*, 1977, *25*, 95–107.

Chapter 9

# EMOTIONAL DEVELOPMENT AND EMOTIONAL EDUCATION

*ROSS BUCK*

## ABSTRACT

*This chapter outlines a readout model of emotion that assumes that emotion involves an ongoing progress report of the state of primary motivational/ emotional systems located in subcortical and paleocortical systems in the brain. The independent evolution of three kinds of readout systems is considered: readout via autonomic or endocrine systems (Emotion I), spontaneous ritualized displays (Emotion II), and direct subjective experience (Emotion III). The ways in which these different emotional responses are experienced by the child in self and others, and the implications of differences in the accessibility of different responses to the social learning of emotion, are considered. The chapter then considers the course of emotional development and education, first using animal and infant studies to illustrate how communication mechanisms, social experience, and primary motivational/emotional systems have evolved to develop hand-in-hand. This involves discussion of what emotions are innate in humans and the developmental sequence of their appearance. It then considers the differences in emotion in humans and in animals. Specifically, the relationships between cognitive and emotional development are discussed, as well as the*

EMOTION
Theory, Research, and Experience
Volume 2

*concept of emotional education, which involves the acquisition of knowledge of emotion via experience and instruction. Emotional education involves making different aspects of emotion accessible via the education of attention, and the acquisition of knowledge about the meaning of emotional behaviors. It is suggested that the quality of this emotional education may have important personal and social implications.*

It is a truism that creatures learn from experience, and it is widely accepted that the concept of emotion refers in large part to events and processes that are internal to the organism and thus normally unavailable to direct observation. In these statements lies the difficulty and fascination of the study of emotional development. The scientist must study emotion indirectly, through its complex and often contradictory effects on overt behavior, self-reported feelings, and physiological responses. The growing child is in an analogous situation. Just as the scientist cannot directly observe emotion in all of its aspects, the child is confronted by a welter of subjective feelings, expressive behaviors and reports of feelings in others, feedback from his or her own behavior, etc. The development of emotion in the child depends on the ways in which these various phenomena associated with emotion are experienced by the child during the course of development. In other words, the child learns from experience. But in the case of the learning of emotion, we must recognize the complexity of this experience, and any complete analysis of emotional development must consider how the child experiences the various aspects of emotion.

This experience involves all of the ways in which we become acquainted with emotional states, both in ourselves and in others. There are many cues that may potentially be associated with emotional states, including observation of instrumental behaviors (hugging, hitting, running) in ourselves and others; observation of expressive behaviors (facial expressions, tone of voice, posture) in ourselves and others, observation of subjective feelings in ourselves and reports of such feelings in others, and observation in ourselves of a variety of cues from proprioceptive, cutaneous, and interoceptive feedback. No one can attend to all of these cues all of the time; we must learn not only what these cues mean, but also which cues to attend to.

This chapter considers emotional development in infancy and early childhood from the point of view of how the developing individual becomes acquainted with emotion. It considers a number of basic issues, including (*a*) how *emotion* should be defined; (*b*) whether the human infant is born with emotions; (*c*) whether there are developmental sequences in the appearance of emotion; (*d*) whether there are differences in emotions in children versus in animals; and (*e*) why older children seem to show more emotion than younger children. I shall begin by suggesting a general model of emotion.

## THE PRIMARY
## MOTIVATIONAL/EMOTIONAL SYSTEMS

### DEFINING EMOTION

The point of view of this chapter is based on several propositions that, since Sylvan Tomkins' pioneering work (1962, 1963), have been widely accepted: (a) that emotion is ultimately based on activity in neurochemical systems in the central nervous system (CNS); (b) that these systems are the product of evolution and as such reflect survival requirements within each species; and (c) that activity in these systems can be modified by learning. These major elements appear in a number of recent theories of emotion, including Ekman and Friesen's (1969b) neurocultural theory and Izard's (1971, 1977) evolutionary developmental view. These theories, however, regard emotion as consisting of a few primary affects or fundamental emotions such as happiness, sadness, fear, anger, surprise, and disgust; they distinguish between these emotions and motivational states or drives such as hunger, thirst, and sex. Unlike them, I propose that what is termed *motivation* (i.e., the process by which behavior is activated and directed, [Young, 1961]) and what is termed *emotion* (i.e., involving expressive behaviors and subjective experiences) are both aspects of the same underlying processes, which I shall term *primary motivational/emotional systems* (Buck, 1976a, in press).

I shall begin with the assumption that neurochemical systems in the CNS constitute the basis structural elements underlying primary motives and emotions. A schematic drawing of the major motivational or emotional systems in humans, showing their approximate locations in the brain, is presented in Figure 9.1. I shall not discuss these systems in detail, except to note that the general structural location of the systems within the CNS has functional implications (cf. Buck, 1976a, in press).

### EVOLUTIONARY ORIGINS

#### Adaptation and Homeostasis

I shall further assume that the primary motivational/emotional systems evolved to serve the basic functions of bodily adaptation and the maintenance of homeostasis. Originally, these functions could be served largely within the organism, and it was not necessary to take into consideration other organisms or the nature of the environment. In simple organisms, essential nutrients are provided almost as automatically as oxygen is provided to us. If the supply is cut

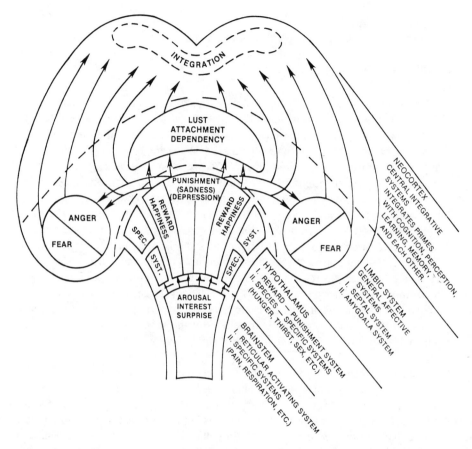

**FIGURE 9.1.** General location of the major motivational/emotional systems in the human brain.

off, the organism must die or perhaps revert to a state where nutrients are not necessary, as when simple creatures may dry up when a pond evaporates, only to resume their lives when water is restored.

As species evolved and became more complex, there was a corresponding increase in the complexity of the systems involved in adaptation and homeostasis. The autonomic and endocrine systems evolved to serve such functions as respiration, digestion, temperature regulation, etc., as well as basic emergency "fight or flight" responses to threat, stress, and injury. The specific motivational/emotional systems that evolved with a given species tended to be ones that were tuned to the particular requirements of that species. Because of similarities in species' requirements within the Earth's ecosystems and because of the relationship among species during the course of evolution, some motivational/emotional systems are relatively universal. Examples include the needs for food, water, and oxygen in animals. Other motivational/emotional systems are more specific to the particular species, such as the tendencies to gnaw, burrow, and hoard in small rodents.

The match between the motivational/emotional systems and species requirements is not, however, perfect. Physiological responses appropriate for fighting and fleeing continue to occur in humans even in situations where such overt responses are inappropriate socially (for example, when asking the boss for a raise). Such responses may be harmful to the internal economy of the body and ultimately contribute to the etiology of a wide variety of stress-related diseases (Anderson, 1981; Benson, 1975; Selye, 1976).

## Social Coordination

Perhaps the most basic motivational/emotional system that went beyond a solitary, virtually automatic homeostatic process involved sexual reproduction. Successful sexual reproduction ordinarily requires a coordination of behavior with another organism and cannot therefore be an entirely internal affair. Communication mechanisms must exist and must involve signals that are sent by one organism and received by another. These signals identify potential mates, attract them to each other, and encourage the process of courtship and mating. In some respects, sex may be the most complex of the motivational/emotional systems in humans: Neural mechanisms that deal directly with sex are found in the CNS from the lower spinal cord to cortical structures in the brain.

In highly social species, it became important for individuals to signal certain motivational/emotional states to each other beyond purely sexual signals (Darwin, 1872). This led to the evolution of, for example, the complex chemical communication system of ants, gestures of dominance and submission in many species, and a wide variety of facial expressions and calls in primates (cf. Andrew, 1963).

The process by which such *displays* evolve has been termed *ritualization* (Blest, 1961; Tinbergen, 1952). The source or precursor of a display is often an aspect of responses that serve basic adaptive or homeostatic functions and that, for one reason or another, is available or "accessible" to others via sensory cues. For example, Eibl-Eibesfeldt (1972) has noted that a widening of the eyes increases visual acuity in primates and that it therefore commonly occurs in situations where the responder confronts some unusual or unexpected circumstance. This widening is naturally accompanied by a raising of the skin above the eyes. Eibl-Eibesfeldt argues that this raising of the skin is both (*a*) potentially informative about a state of surprise or interest in the responder, and (*b*) accessible to others via visual cues, and that it has evolved into a display for these reasons. He feels that the eyebrow has evolved in part to emphasize this display, making it more visible against the field of the face. He also notes that, in humans, the "eyebrow flash" has acquired different meanings in different cultures, making the important point that social learning must play a part in determining the communicative role in the display.


## SUBJECTIVE EXPERIENCE AND EMOTION

Thus far we have considered two relatively "automatic" sorts of emotional functioning: adaption and homeostasis via the autonomic and endocrine systems, and external expression via spontaneous displays. Neither of these kinds of emotional response necessarily involves much in the way of cognitive mediation or involvement, and they do not require consideration of intention and planning. Both kinds of processes can be seen at work in the very simplest of creatures. At the same time, it is possible that both these kinds of emotional responses can be the source of a kind of subjective experience of emotion. As the James–Lange theory suggests, our perception of feedback from our visceral and skeletal muscle responses to emotion may contribute to our subjective experience of emotion.


### Visceral Feedback

There is convincing evidence for the importance of visceral feedback in emotional experience (Buck, 1980). One of the most persuasive studies is that done by Hohmann (1966), who demonstrated deficits in reported emotional experience among veterans with spinal cord injuries. The higher the lesion in the cord, and thus the greater the loss of visceral sensation, the greater the reported loss of emotional experience. Another observation is provided by Delgado (1969), who noted that a patient who underwent a unilateral sympathectomy reported that he could no longer be thrilled by music on the sympathectomized side of his body, although the response on the other side was unchanged. Finally, animal studies have shown that bilateral sympathectomy retards the acquisition of emotional responses although it does not affect the retention of previously learned emotional behavior (Wynne & Solomon, 1955).


### Proprioceptive and Cutaneous Feedback

Although it seems clear that visceral feedback contributes to emotional experience, it is doubtful that it is either necessary or sufficient for *all* kinds of emotion experience (cf. Buck, 1976a, pp. 42–49). In Cannon's (1932) critique of the

James–Lange theory, he noted that visceral responses are too slow and too undifferentiated to account for the speed and variety of human emotional experience. However, Cannon did not take skeletal muscle responses into account, even though James specifically stated that such responses could contribute to emotional experience. Proprioceptive and cutaneous feedback from such responses, and particularly facial expressions, are clearly sufficiently differentiated and respond sufficiently quickly; a number of theories of emotion have put forward the *facial feedback hypothesis* that facial expressions provide feedback to the responder that is necessary or sufficient to alter emotion experience. As Ekman, Friesen, and Ellsworth (1972) put it: "The face might . . . fill the information gap left by a solely visceral theory of emotion, distinguishing one emotion from another, changing rapidly and providing feedback about what is occurring to the person [p. 173]."

The facial feedback hypothesis has not gained the empirical support enjoyed by the proponents of visceral feedback and, in fact, it has been the subject of considerable controversy (Buck, 1980; Ellsworth & Tourageau, 1981; Hager and Ekman, 1981; Izard, 1981; Tomkins, 1981; Tourangeau & Ellsworth, 1979), in which for the first time the hypothesis and its implications have been explored specifically and in detail. In summary, it appears that no one now holds the strong version of the facial feedback hypothesis, which states that facial expression *is* emotional experience, and like visceral feedback it seems clear that feedback from facial expressions or other skeletal muscle activity is neither necessary nor sufficient for subjective emotional experience, although it might still contribute to some kinds of emotional experience.

## Cognitive–Physiological Interactions

Thus although there is evidence that both visceral and facial or bodily feedback may contribute to some kinds of emotional experience, it appears that neither is necessary or sufficient for all kinds of emotional experience. Another possibility, suggested in 1927 by Bertrand Russell, is that cognitions arising from the responder's understanding of the emotional situation account for the quality and speed of the emotion experience (Russell, 1961). This notion is basic to Schachter's (1964) self-attribution theory of emotion, which holds that emotional experience results from an interaction between cognition and physiological factors. Schachter originally emphasized the interaction between visceral feedback and cognition, although more recent authors have emphasized facial feedback as well (Laird, 1974).

This "interactionist" viewpoint is powerful and is able to integrate much of the research on the James–Lange of theory of emotion (cf. Buck, 1976a, pp. 46–49). However, it cannot easily deal with certain observations that have been made on humans with brain disorders and/or implanted brain electrodes. Apparently irresistible and uncontrollable feeling states have been reported from brain stimulation to certain portions of the limbic system; these bear little relationship to the external situation. For example, Mark and Ervin (1970) report the case of a young woman who was stimulated in the region of the amygdala via telemetery while she was quietly playing a guitar, who suddenly and violently smashed the guitar against the wall. Similarly, Heath (1964) has found that stimulation of the septal area in humans is often associated with subjective reports of unexpected pleasure in depressed patients who cannot explain its origin.

### Direct Emotional Experience

These and other observations indicate that apparently complete and well-integrated emotional states involving appropriate expressive behavior, instrumental behavior, and self-reported experience, can be created via brain stimulation and via diseases that affect certain brain centers (cf. Buck, 1976a, pp. 77–108, 182–190). The strongest of these effects seem to involve the limbic system. Significantly, it has been reported that stimulation of the hypothalamus in humans often does *not* elicit strong subjective reactions, even though substantial autonomic changes occur (Sem-Jacobson, 1968; White, 1940). In general, more positive states such as pleasure and sexuality seem to occur with septal stimulation, whereas fearful and aggressive responses are associated with the amygdala, a result consistent with MacLean's (1968, 1970, 1978) general conceptualization of limbic system functioning. This suggests that emotional experience must to some extent be a direct function of neurochemical activity in relevant brain regions.

It could be argued that such a direct "readout" of emotion into conscious experience may have evolved in a way analogous to the evolution of emotional displays in social species. Specifically, it may be useful for a creature with significant cognitive capacities to have a direct knowledge of the state of certain of its own neurochemical systems associated with primary motivational/emotional states, just as it is useful for a social animal to have knowledge of certain of the motivational/emotional states of its fellows. Note that this reasoning does not apply to *all* motivational/emotional states. Nature is frugal and provides displays only of motivational/emotional states that must be displayed, that is, ones that are useful for survival. Thus, although both hunger and thirst are apparent subjectively in humans, there are no specific facial or gestural displays associated with hunger or thirst in most animals because there is no evolutionary requirement for such a display as there is for anger, fear, interest, etc. (An exception is that in many birds, "gaping" associated with hunger in nestlings is an important display [Koenig, 1951]). Similarly, the lack of air leads to very strong subjective subjective reactions in humans, but a lack of oxygen does not. A lack of oxygen, or anoxia, was never a significant threat in the evolution of the human species, so that although there are bodily responses to oxygen deprivation, these are not experienced in consciousness as threatening, and, in fact, gradual anoxia may lead to euphoria. Similarly, dangerous levels of nuclear radiation are not directly experienced as painful or threatening. Thus, I am suggesting that a direct subjective experience of the state of certain motivational/ emotional systems evolved in ways analogous to the evolution of the external display of certain motivational/emotional systems.

## EMOTION AS READOUT

### Types of Emotion

In essence, I am suggesting that emotion involves a kind of running progress report or "readout" of neurochemical mechanisms within the CNS. The most basic kind of readout, which I shall call *Emotion I*, involves homeostasis and adaptation and takes place via the autonomic and endocrine systems. In the case of anoxia, only these kinds of responses occur. The second kind of readout, *Emotion II*, is the external display of the state of the neurochemical system via ritualized displays: chemical odors, bodily postures, facial expressions, color changes, etc. These displays occur only in social species and only with motivational/emotional states whose display is useful to social coordination and thus to survival. The third kind of readout, *Emotion III*, involves the direct experience of the state of certain neurochemical systems in consciousness. It occurs in species with significant cognitive capacities and functions to allow the cognitive system fast and easy access to the current state of relevant neurochemical systems, that is, ones in which cognitive processes may be instrumental in the process of satiation. Thus, it should be useful for a creature with important cognitive capacities to be aware of its need for food, drink, and air, as well as the state of its own tendencies toward fight, flight, and courtship. Such awareness could constitute a *feedforward* mechanism that allows a creature to anticipate homeostatic deficits before they actually occur (cf. Mogenson & Phillips, 1976).

### Types of Emotional Responses

Different kinds of emotional behavior are differentially relevant to Emotions I, II, and III, as just defined. Autonomic and endocrine measures are clearly most relevant to Emotion I and should reflect most closely the state of adaptation and homeostasis. Expressive behaviors such as facial expressions, gestures, and postural shifts are most relevant to Emotion II, although they may also be influenced by display rules that reflect learning and cognitive functioning. Instrumental or goal-directed behavior is most relevant to Emotion III, as are voluntary self-reports of subjective experience.

## A General Model of Emotion

Figure 9.2 illustrates a general model of emotion that includes these four kinds of emotion responses and their hypothesized relationships with Emotion I, II, and III processes. The model assumes that internal or external affective stimuli impinge on the neurochemical motivation/emotional systems directly, without cognitive mediation (cf. Kunst-Wilson & Zajonc, 1980; Wilson, 1979). The response of these systems depends on their current state of arousal and also on their arousability or their capacity to become aroused (Whalen, 1966). Arousability is dependent on a large number of factors, including short-term influences (drugs, blood chemistry), long-term influences (heredity, early experience, disease), and interactions with other neurochemical systems.

Variations in arousal and arousability function in part to increase or decrease the range of affective stimuli that will trigger a response. Moyer (1971) suggests that high arousability in neurochemical circuits associated with aggression is associated with subjective feelings of anger and a high readiness to respond aggressively, even to inappropriate stimuli. For example, von Holst and von Saint Paul (1962) showed that electrical stimulation in such systems in roosters causes them to attack a stuffed polecat that they had previously ignored. Cases of violence associated with temporal lobe disease may be due to hyperactivity to

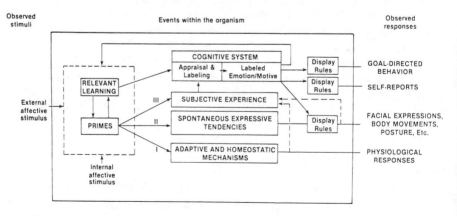

**Figure 9.2.** Four kinds of emotional responses and their hypothesized relationships with Emotion I, II, and III processes. (See text for explanation.)

mild stimuli caused, in turn, by abnormal electrochemical activity in aggressive circuits (Mark & Ervin, 1970).

The response to affective stimuli is also in part a function of the individual's relevant learning experiences. The latter may involve classically conditioned associations as well as direct or vicarious social learning experiences about the affective stimuli. For example, a person may have a slight fear of heights caused by a negative experience in high places. Because of this, the person may experience a fear of high places at times when neurochemical systems are arousable (i.e., with fatigue, or in the premenstrual week). Together, the responsiveness of the neurochemical systems and the individual's relevant learning experiences determine the impact of the affective stimulus for that particular person in that particular situation.

This impact is felt at both cognitive and emotional levels. On the emotional level, adaptive and homeostatic processes are activated (Emotion I), spontaneous expressive tendencies occur (Emotion II), and subjective experiences occur, both directly from the activation of the motivational/emotional systems (Emotion III) and indirectly via visceral and proprioceptive or cutaneous feedback (dashed lines in Figure 9.2). On the cognitive level, work by Schachter (1964, 1968, 1970), Lazarus (1966), and others suggests that the individual labels or appraises the affective stimuli on the basis of past experience, the present situation, and the present subjective emotional experience. Once the stimulus is appraised or labeled, the individual has a basis for making appropriate goal-directed instrumental coping responses and self-reports describing the subjective response to the stimulus. These overt responses will be affected by *display rules* in that the individual will only make responses that are appropriate in that situation and may not respond according to his or her true feelings. Such display rules may also interfere with spontaneous expressive behaviors (Ekman & Friesen, 1975). The labeled motivational/emotional state may at the same time itself become an internal affective stimulus, beginning another cycle of response.

## SOCIAL LEARNING AND EMOTIONAL DEVELOPMENT

I have suggested that there are four general types of emotional responding: instrumental behavior, self-reports, expressive behavior, and physiological responses. It is often argued that, since these various measures presumably reflect the same emotional process, they should vary together. However, they often do not. Not only are there wide individual differences in the tendency to respond on a given measure, but the magnitude of response on one measure is not necessarily related to the response on another and, in fact, these responses are sometimes negatively related to each other. For example, there is evidence that overt emotional expression is often negatively related to autonomic responding in that some persons may show an "externalizing" pattern of high overt and low autonomic responding, whereas others show the opposite, "internalizing" pattern of response (Buck, 1979). Field & Walden (1982) have identified this phenomenon in infants.

The simplest and perhaps most common way to eliminate the dilemmas posed by the complex relationships between various measures of emotion is to choose and analyze only a single measure. However, there is no adequate rationale for deciding what kind of measure is appropriate in a given situation. Furthermore, as the externalizing–internalizing phenomenon suggests, these different measures represent different aspects of a complex multidimensional process and they cannot be expected to vary together because they are affected by different underlying variables. In this section I suggest that the different types of emotional response tend to be associated with different sorts of social learning experiences due to the fact that they tend to be accessible to the responder and to others to different degrees.

## THE ACCESSIBILITY DIMENSION

We have seen that the candidacy of a motivational/emotional response for the evolutionary process of ritualization is partly a function of the *accessibility* of that response, that is, the degree to which it is available to others via sensory cues. Just as the accessibility of a response is important in the process of ritualization, it must also be important in the process of social learning. Here it is not only the accessibility of the response to others that is important but also the accessibility of a response to the responder.

We shall define *accessibility* as the degree to which a response is normally perceivable and apparent to the responder and to others around the responder via sensory cues. Any sensory cues may be involved: A response may be apparent to others via visual, tactile, auditory, or olfactory cues; it may be apparent to the responder from these cues and via proprioceptive, cutaneous, or interoceptive cues as well. Observational learning studies suggest that the visual channel is undoubtedly highly important relative to other channels in human social learning, although other channels should not be ignored.

Social learning theory, in emphasizing the role of imitation and social reinforcement in the development of response patterns (Bandura, 1977; Bandura & Walters, 1963), implies that responses with different degrees of accessibility must be associated with different patterns of social learning. Highly accessible responses that are easily available to the responder and to others can undergo thorough training via imitation and social reinforcement. Responses that are not accessible to the responder or to others must not be susceptible to this kind of direct social learning. Social influences must affect them indirectly, outside the awareness of everyone involved. Responses that are accessible to the responder but not to others, and responses accessible to others but not to the responder, must be subject to still different kinds of social learning and influence. Let us now consider the types of responses to emotion from this point of view.

## Instrumental Behavior

Goal-directed instrumental behavior is normally the most accessible type of response to emotion. It can be seen both by the responder in other persons and by others in the responder, so that it may undergo thorough training through imitation and social reinforcement: A child can see and learn directly from the overt emotional behaviors of his or her parents and other models, and others can "shape" the overt behaviors of the child through social reinforcement. In addition, since goal-directed instrumental behavior involves a contingency between the responder's behavior and reinforcement, the reinforcement (reward or escape or avoidance of punishment) occurs only if a correct instrumental response occurs: It is generally thought to be voluntary (Miller, 1969). Therefore, it presumably must be at least potentially accessible to the responder in his or her own behavior.

Thus, a child is at least potentially conscious of his or her own instrumental emotional behavior and can learn to make many discriminations both from personal and from vicarious experience about how one is supposed to respond in different sorts of emotional situations. For example, in our culture a young girl will find relatively few female models who respond to anger-inducing situations with overt aggression, and they will be more likely to be punished for expressing overt aggression than will a young boy (learning, for example, that "young ladies don't hit").

## Subjective Experience

This kind of fine discrimination learning cannot apply to the subjective feelings associated with emotions. A child has no direct access to the subjective emotional experiences of others, and others have no direct access to those of the child. Learning about subjective events must take place indirectly, via the reports and descriptions of subjective experiences that the child gains from others, and the reports that he or she gives to others.

Several theorists, including Skinner (1953) and Schachter (1964), have discussed the process by which such learning is achieved. Through the process of associating one's private experiences with interpretations provided by the community, the child develops a set of labels by which to identify and categorize his or her subjective experience. Thus, a child might learn to correctly identify and label the subjective experience associated with activation of neurochemical systems of anger by repeated direct and vicarious experience with situations that arouse such feelings and label them appropriately. When a child is overtly expressing felt anger, a parent might say, "I see that you are angry," or the child may see others overtly angry and/or in a situation that would commonly evoke anger and hear them describe their feelings as *anger*. It should be noted that this process depends on overt emotion responding: If there is no overt response, such learning cannot occur. Also, the labeling process may be erroneous. A child could conceivably learn to mislabel the subjective experience associated with anger as *fear* or *guilt*.

### Expressive Behavior

Whereas instrumental behavior is visible to both the responder and to others, and subjective experience is visible to the responder but not to others, expressive behavior tends to be more visible to others than it is to the responder. People are often unaware of how they appear to others and are often surprised when viewing themselves on film. Frequently they report learning more about themselves when they view their own behavior from the perspective of others (Storms, 1973).

A number of studies have suggested that people are more aware of some of their own expressive behaviors than they are of others. Ekman and Friesen (1969a) suggest that people are most aware of the actions of the face, less aware of the hands, and least aware of the legs and feet, and they present evidence that "nonverbal leakage" occurs with the latter behaviors. Thus, the behaviors that in our terms are less accessible to the responder tend to be more "leaky"—they are more spontaneously expressive of the actual emotional state.

Although the responder is generally less aware of his or her expressive behavior, it is accessible to others and thus is subject to shaping via social reinforcement. Similarly, the expressive behavior of others is accessible to the child and is thus available for modeling and imitation. Thus, a young boy in our culture is likely to find few male models for the open expression of many emotions and is likely to experience punishment when openly expressing them: As girls learn that they must not hit, boys learn that they must not cry.

### Relationships among Measures

It is likely that measures of expressive behavior will be positively correlated with measures of instrumental behavior and accurately labeled self-reports since social pressures that encourage or discourage one of these kinds of responses would tend to have similar effects on the others. If instrumental behavior is discouraged in a given kind of emotion situation, it is likely that expressive behavior will be discouraged in that situation as well, and it is less likely that the subjective experience will be correctly labeled or openly admitted in self-reports if it is labeled. For example, if women are discouraged from expressing aggressive behavior, it is likely that they will also be discouraged from looking angry and from admitting to angry feelings.

**Physiological Responding**

Physiological responses must be associated with a quite different kind of social learning process. Most physiological events normally take place outside conscious awareness, so a child would not ordinarily learn to identify or label them. For example, there are relatively few interoceptive afferent neurons carrying feedback from the viscera, so it is difficult, if not impossible, to determine the position of food in one's digestive tract. In contrast, knowing the position of one's arm from proprioceptive or cutaneous feedback is relatively easy (cf. Markov, 1950). Also, most physiological events are inaccessible to others, although a careful observer might detect changes in coloration or sweating that are associated with such events.

Since normally physiological events are relatively inaccessible, they are not greatly affected by the social pressures that influence other emotional responses. However, they can be modified by learning experiences. Both Russian studies of interoceptive conditioning and studies of biofeedback indicate that subtle physiological events are readily alterable (cf. Orne, 1979; Razran, 1961). Other investigators have demonstrated that such conditioning can be vicarious as well as direct (Berger, 1962). These findings suggest that conditioning involving physiological responses must be a complex but constantly occurring process and that a given person's physiological response in a given situation may be determined in great part by his or her conditioning history in similar kinds of situations (cf. Buck, 1976a, pp. 112–124). For example, one might expect that the more stimuli that have been conditioned to cause autonomic arousal in the past, the higher that arousal will be. If a child has intensely arousing experiences in situations involving anger, it is likely that he or she will show strong arousal in situations involving anger as an adult. This explanation has been used to account for the finding that the spontaneous expression of emotion is often negatively correlated with autonomic responses: Situations that result in the inhibition of overt responding may tend to be stressful and associated with arousal (cf. Buck, 1979, 1980; Buck, Miller, & Caul, 1974).

## TABLE 9.1
### Social Learning Process Underlying Different Kinds of Emotional Responses

| Type of response | Normal Accessibility | Social Learning Process | Relevant Feature of the Arousing Situation |
|---|---|---|---|
| Instrumental behaviors | Accessible to responder and others | Imitation and social reinforcement | Responder's past experience of what behavior is appropriate and expected by others in the situation |
| Physiological responses | Not easily accessible | Conditioning of physiological responses | The actual motivational/emotional state (Emotion I) plus the stimuli in the situation previously conditioned to alter physiological responses for the responder |
| Spontaneous expressive behaviors | Accessible to others more than responder | Imitation and social reinforcement are relatively less important the more "leaky" the expressive behavior | To the extent that the expressive behavior is spontaneous, it reflects the actual motivational/emotional state (Emotion II). Less "leaky" behaviors are similar to instrumental behaviors |
| Subjective experience | Accessible to responders only | Association of labels and interpretation with subjective experience | The actual motivational/emotional state (Emotion III). *Reports* of subjective experience are similar to instrumental behaviors except that they uniquely reflect the labeling process |

## Summary

To summarize, I am suggesting that emotional responses that differ in accessibility tend to be associated with different kinds of social learning. This analysis is summarized in Table 9.1. It implies that different kinds of emotional responses should be related to different features of an emotion-arousing situation. Instrumental responses, since they are highly salient to the responder and have been subjected to much discrimination learning via imitation and social reinforcement, should be closely related to the responder's expectations about what behavior is appropriate and expected by the community. This should also be true of expressive behavior to some extent, but since it tends to be less accessible to the responder, expressive behavior is likely to be more closely related to the actual emotional state, particularly if the responder does not realize that his or her expressions are being observed or if "leaky" behaviors are chosen for analysis. Subjective experience should be related to the actual emotional state, but *reports* of that experience should reflect the labels and interpretations that the responder has associated with that state, and also expectations about what experiences are appropriate and socially acceptable. The responder's physiological responding should reflect, among other things, the intensity of the prior conditioning of arousal in similar situations for that particular person.

## ACCESSIBILITY AND THE EDUCATION OF ATTENTION

I have argued thus far that the accessibility of a response is largely a function of the nature of the response, and indeed, it seems that some responses, such as voluntary overt behaviors, are normally more accessible than others, such as physiological reactions. However, it should be noted that response accessibility is not an invariant property of these response systems. It is clearly possible for an individual to learn to attend to, and thus access, responses that to others remain unaccessed, a process that might be termed an *education of attention*.

For example, it may be that certain Eastern traditions encourage a greater attention to internal cues than do most Western cultures. In a 1933 study of muscle relaxation, M. A. Wenger noted that the level of relaxation achieved by a student from India trained in Yoga exercises was far superior to the performance of American students. In subsequent studies in India, Wenger and his colleagues found that students of Yoga could demonstrate impressive control of autonomic functions, including changes in heart action, blood pressure, and skin temperature (Wenger & Bagchi, 1961; Wenger, Bagchi, & Anand, 1961). Possibly such control is dependent on learning to attend to bodily functions that are ignored by most Westerners. One of the goals of biofeedback training is to teach control of normally automatic bodily functions by making them artificially accessible via the feedback. Studies have demonstrated that such control can often be achieved in the presence of the feedback, although evidence of long-term changes in the absence of feedback is as yet inconclusive.

Regarding expressive behavior, I noted earlier that some kinds of behaviors are more accessible to the responder—and thus less "leaky"—than others. It is also clear that individuals learn a variety of expression management techniques to intensify or mask their displays of emotion in conformance with the display rules appropriate to that situation (Ekman & Friesen, 1975).

There are undoubtedly both individual and situational differences in the tendency to attend to emotional expression in others. Some persons may learn to attend to nonverbal cues more than others, and for that reason may be generally more empathic with the feelings of others. However, there is increasing evidence that such empathy varies considerably with the situation and the type of nonverbal behavior in question. A number of researchers have recently begun to systematically examine developmental changes in how nonverbal behavior is decoded (cf. Blanck & Rosenthal, 1982; DePaulo & Rosenthal, in press). These studies have shown that we learn to attend to expressive cues in some situations more than in others. For example, it is probable that a therapist learns to use quite different patterns of attention to expressive cues when with a patient than when with a friend (Buck & Lerman, 1979). In fact, if a therapist "reads" friends like patients, he or she may end up with few friends. Also, we learn to attend to some expressive cues and ignore others. In this regard, Rosenthal and DePaulo (1979) have suggested that although females are superior to males in decoding accessible expressive cues, they may not learn (or *learn not*) to attend to "leakier" cues that reveal emotion states that others would rather hide.

It might be noted that conventional tests of nonverbal decoding ability, such as Rosenthal's Profile of Nonverbal Sensitivity (PONS, Rosenthal, Hall, DiMatteo, Rogers, & Archer, 1979) and my Communication of Affect Receiving Ability Test (CARAT, Buck, 1976b) generally instruct the subject to attend to nonverbal cues, thus missing possible individual differences in the spontaneous tendency to attend to such cues. One way of assessing the attentional focus of the individual is via behavior segmentation techniques in which subjects are instructed to watch a film and indicate by pressing a button when "meaningful events" occur (Dickman, 1963; Newtson, 1976). The definition of what is meaningful is left to the subject, thus allowing an analysis of the subject's pattern of attention to the film. Reuben Baron, myself, and our students have applied these techniques to the study of emotion expression (Buck, Baron, & Barrette, 1982; Buck, Baron, Goodman, & Shapiro, 1980). For example, Goodman (1980) used a videotape of a person showing both instrumental actions (sitting down, picking up a magazine, lighting a cigarette, etc.) and emotion expressions (frowns, smiles, shaking of the head, shrugging the shoulders, etc.). Subjects were instructed in one condition (Action Focus) to press the button when the person on the videotape showed meaningful actions; in another Emotion Focus condition, subjects were told to focus on emotions. The patterns of button-pressing in these two conditions were quite different, with subjects in the Action Focus condition pressing to instrumental actions and those in the Emotion Focus condition pressing to emotional expressions. In a third, No Focus, condition, the subjects were not specifically instructed to focus on either actions or emotions, and examples of both were given in the instructions, leaving them free to respond to either. Interestingly, the pattern of button-pressing in this condition was quite similar to that of the Action Focus condition and dissimilar to that of the Emotion Focus condition, suggesting that under the circumstances of this study these subjects tended to attend to instrumental actions and (at least consciously) to ignore emotional expressions.

## THE COURSE OF EMOTIONAL DEVELOPMENT AND EDUCATION

In the first section of this chapter, I considered the evolution of emotion and outlined a general model that posited four kinds of emotional response. In the second section, I outlined how these responses differ in accessibility and must therefore be influenced by different kinds of social learning experience. In the present section, I suggest the broad outlines of the course of normal emotional development, first using animal studies to demonstrate the contribution played by the maturation of the neurochemical systems that underlie emotion and the importance of the provision of appropriate opportunities for social learning and experience. The course of cognitive development in humans is then considered, which, though usually considered independently of emotional development, must play a major role in the child's growing understanding of his or her feelings and those of others. In considering the latter, we move into the realm of *emotional education,* which involves the acquisition of knowledge of emotion via experience and instruction.

## THE ANIMAL MODEL OF EMOTIONAL DEVELOPMENT

Perhaps the most important single research program in the study of emotional development has been that of Harlow, whose studies with rhesus monkeys convinced many of the compelling nature of the analogies between human and animal emotional development. Indeed, from his studies there has emerged what might be termed an "animal model" of emotional development. A central in-

TABLE 9.2
Summary of the Affectional Systems[a]

| Affectional System | Necessary Conditions | Functions |
| --- | --- | --- |
| Maternal affectional system | Contact comfort | Establishes basic sense of trust |
| Peer affectional system | Basic sense of trust<br>Relative independence from mother | Social experience, with associated learning of emotional communication[b] |
| Heterosexual affectional system | Social experience<br>Accurate emotional communication | Basis of social life and group organization |

[a] Adapted from Harlow, 1971.
[b] Accurate emotional communication involves the abilities to send and receive courting, threat, submission, etc., gestures associated with sex, anger, fear, etc.

sight of this model is that communication mechanisms and patterns of social experience evolve hand-in-hand with motivational or emotional systems that are relevant to social relations.

The initial evidence of the importance of social experience came when it was demonstrated that providing a scrap of cloth for contact comfort increased significantly the survival rate of infants isolated in wire cages. Later, it was found that early isolation, even with the provision of adequate contact comfort via cloth-covered surrogate mothers, led to severe social maladjustment in adulthood (Harlow, 1971). Subsequent studies showed that experience with other monkeys is essential for normal socioemotional development in rhesus monkeys. Observation of the normal course of social development in rhesus monkey groups suggested the reason: There is a pattern in the series of social relationships normally experienced by the infant rhesus monkey that seems to function to introduce the infant to the kinds of social relationships necessary for adults. Harlow termed this pattern of adult relationships the *heterosexual affectional system* (see Table 9.2).

## The Maternal Affectional System

The maternal affectional system forms the essential base for later socioemotional development. Harlow suggests that the infant monkey has the capacity at birth to feel (and signal to others) affectionate emotions and perhaps also curiosity and pain, but that fearful and aggressive behaviors are absent. Since the young infant shows curiosity about everything and fear of nothing, the protective presence of the parent is essential for survival. Deets and Harlow (1971) suggest that the neurochemical systems underlying fear and aggression are not fully mature at birth, so that the infant monkey comes into a world populated by other monkeys who literally cannot elicit fearful and angry emotions. Instead, they can elicit only affection, and thus the helpless infant comes to know, trust, and love his or her irascible conspecifics.

Deets and Harlow (1971) suggested that the neurochemical mechanisms underlying fear do not become fully mature until 6 months of age, and that those underlying aggression require 1 year to become fully mature. Thus, the full appearance of fear and aggression does not take place until affectional social ties have had much time to become established. Apparently, the system has evolved so that the maturation of motivational/emotional systems is synchronized with the normal social experience of the infant: The maternal affectional system provides a basic sense of trust in other monkeys that is essential to later social behavior.

The maternal affectional system does not, however, represent a period in which the infant experiences unconditional positive regard. There is evidence, in fact, that excessive maternal attention may be socially damaging if it restricts contact with agemates. The *stage of contact,* which involves relatively unrestricted contact with the mother, only lasts for the first few months. This is the time when the infant is at its most vulnerable, with few locomotor skills. As its skills improve, the *stage of rejection* occurs, in which the mother begins to punish unrestricted contact, increasing the punishments in frequency and intensity as the infant grows. This is consistent with the infant's high level of curiosity, and it encourages the infant to become more independent, resulting in the *stage of relative separation* from the mother, which begins at about 5–6 months of age. Since similar-age peers are normally present in the environment, the separation from the mother tends to naturally encourage increased interaction with peers, leading to the peer affectional system.

**The Peer Affectional System**

Harlow (1971) suggests that during the frequent sessions of rough-and-tumble play, the young monkey acquires the social skills necessary for adult functioning. One of these skills involves the practical use of the system of emotion communication that has evolved within the species. Although these systems are based on sending and receiving mechanisms that must be innate to some extent (cf. Sackett, 1966; Winter, Handley, Ploog, & Schott, 1973), there is evidence that in rhesus monkeys they require social experience to function effectively (Miller, Caul, & Mirsky, 1967). Such experience is naturally provided to the young monkey during the affectional systems. In the peer affectional system, elements of adult social behavior appear during play, including immature sexual posturing, threat gesturing, submissive behavior, greeting, etc. The youngster learns how to use the communication system during these bouts, which leads naturally to the development of monkey social behavior that is considered normal.

## The Heterosexual Affectional System

The heterosexual affectional system encompasses normal monkey social behavior, including a dominance order that is maintained largely by signals of threat and submission, a process of courting and sexual behavior, proper maternal behavior, and a variety of behaviors signaling greeting, grooming, warning, etc. It is apparent that animals isolated in infancy cannot function effectively in this system, both because the presence of other monkeys may be emotionally overwhelming due to a failure to experience others under the proper emotion conditions and because the normal monkey communication system cannot be used effectively due to a lack of social experience.

## THE ANIMAL–HUMAN ANALOGY

### Scope of the Analogy: The Analysis of Infancy

In general, the relationships between the developing child and its caregivers and peers provide social experiences that appear to serve many functions analogous to those served by the affectional systems in rhesus monkeys: creating an emotional basis for later social behavior and teaching the use of the human emotional communication system (cf. Buck, 1981b; Sroufe, 1979). In this view, human development may be regarded as involving stages analogous to those outlined by Harlow: An initial state in which the infant's relationships with caregivers provides a basis for later social development, a period of experience in relationships with peers, and a period encompassing normal adult social behavior. One of the more interesting implications of this view is that it suggests that these stages are based on deeply rooted biological systems that include the involvement of largely unrecognized and unverbalized motivational and emotional processes. Because of the complexities introduced by langauge learning, which I shall consider later, these processes are difficult to demonstrate in older children. However, we do have evidence of their importance in infancy.

As noted earlier, a central tenet of the animal model of emotional development is that communication mechanisms, patterns of social experience, and motivational/emotional mechanisms have evolved so that their development is normally coordinated. We saw that in monkeys, mechanisms underlying fear and anger apparently do not mature until certain social experiences have normally taken place. Izard and his colleagues have found evidence that the course of the maturation of emotion systems in humans is broadly similar to that suggested by Deets and Harlow (1971) in monkeys in that younger infants do not show facial expressions of anger or fear when receiving a painful injection (Izard, 1979; Izard, Huebner, Risser, McGinnes, & Dougherty, 1980).

Also, the animal model implies that the infant must be involved in communication with caregivers virtually from birth. This implication is contrary to a view of communication as an inherently voluntary, cognitive activity (e.g., Bruner, 1975), but is quite consistent with demonstrations of affective communication in infants. For example, Thoman (1981) has argued that the infant is a communicating organism from birth: "communication of the newborn with the mother, or caretaker, is biologically determined, is based on interactive capabilities of the infant organism that have derived from the evolutionary processes, and is a critical form of early adaptation that assures the infant's survival [pp. 3–4]." Studies indeed suggest the importance of the mutual influence of infant and caregiver on one another: The caregiver's behavior is often a function of the infant's behavior (e.g., Lewis & Rosenbloom, 1974; Thoman, 1975, 1981).

Another implication from the animal model is that if this coordination of communication, social experience, and motivational/emotional maturation is significantly disrupted, it should have serious consequences that should not be expected from a strictly cognitive point of view. There are indications that such disruptions can indeed have powerful effects on infant–caregiver relationships. For example, studies suggest that certain kinds of responsiveness in the infant are needed to elicit appropriate responses from the caregiver and that, in the absence of such reponsiveness, caregiving may be deficient even to the extent of abuse. Thus, Fraiberg, (1974) has noted that observers are less responsive to blind infants—that, for example, they do not tend to talk to blind infants as they do to sighted infants—apparently because of a lack of differentiated facial signs in the blind infant. Also, several studies have suggested that certain characteristics of premature infants—particularly an aversive quality to their cry—may trigger aggressive abuse (Frodi, 1981; Frodi & Lamb, 1978; Zeskind & Lester, 1978).

Thus, there is evidence that communication systems, motivational/emotional mechanisms, and social experiences combine in the interactions between infant and caregiver to help to lay the emotional and communicative groundwork for later social behavior. Similarly, the interactions with peers in older children and adolescents clearly function in part to teach communication patterns associated among other things with courtship, sex, dominance, submission, and other social behaviors remarkably similar to those observed in monkeys.

**Limits of the Analogy**

Although it is clear that the human–animal analogy is useful in understanding many aspects of human motivational/emotional development and expression, it is also clear that some aspects of human behavior are quantitatively and qualitatively different from animal behavior. It may be that the boundary between the domain where the human–animal analogy is useful and that where it is not involves the development of linguistic competence. Only in humans does behavior come so completely under the influence of principles of logic and reasoning that are mediated primarily by language.

Studies of cerebral lateralization have suggested that the affective systems involved in the animal model of emotion development may, in humans, be particularly associated with the right cerebral hemisphere, whereas the cognitive bases of language are associated with the left cerebral hemisphere. For example, Tucker (1981) has contrasted the wholistic and imagal cognition of the right hemisphere with the sequential and linear cognition of the left and suggested that the left hemisphere comes to exert a verbally mediated control over the emotionality of the right (cf. Buck & Duffy, 1980; Shearer & Tucker, 1981; Tucker & Newman, 1981). Extending Tucker's reasoning, I have suggested that the right hemisphere involves the processing of the primary motivational/emotional states based on subcortical and paleocortical systems, whereas the left hemisphere involves the processing of cognitive motivation. The latter includes the motivation involved in the learning of language, in the efforts to secure accurate and consistent knowledge about the world and oneself, and in the intrinsic rewards provided by behaviors and experiences that enrich the developing cognitive system (Buck, 1976a, 1981b, in press).

Thus, our attention is directed from animal studies to approaches to human development that take such processes into account: Specifically, these include theories of cognitive development, which have not heretofore been widely used in the analysis of emotional development and expression.

## COGNITIVE DEVELOPMENT AND EMOTION

**Piaget's Theory**

According to Piaget, the cognitive system constructs its own structure in the course of adaptation to the external world. Through the process of *assimilation,* elements of the external world (reality data) are integrated into the existing cognitive structure. Once assimilated, they may then modify and enrich the existing structure to fit the new data, a process termed *accommodation* (Piaget, 1971; Piaget & Inhelder, 1969). In essence, this is a spontaneous restructuring of the individual's experience in such a way that the experience adds new elements to the structure, thus altering it.

The individual must be able to assimilate a new experience to some extent before accommodation is possible. Piaget states that a situation that is partially but not completely assimilated is intrinsically motivating because it demands accommodation—it constitutes a challenge. Piaget terms experience with such a situation to be a food or *aliment* for the cognitive structure. Elkind (1971) similarly believes that the first stage of any cognitive growth cycle is characterized by stimulus-seeking behavior; that novel (but not too novel) situations serve as an aliment of food for further growth; and that the individual is intrinsically attracted to such situations. The motivational state involved in the attraction to such situations is similar to White's (1959) *effectance motivation* and it is a central construct in analyses of exploratory behavior, stimulus-seeking, personal causation, and achievement motivation (cf. Buck, 1976a, pp. 278–290).

Piaget proposed that cognitive development proceeds in a series of stages, each of which involves a qualitatively distinct style of mental functioning (cf. Baldwin, 1967; Piaget & Inhelder, 1969). Stage 1 is the *sensorimotor period* (from birth to 18 months), in which the child gains the basic sensory and motor skills for exploring the environment and acquires the object concept. Stage 2 is the *preoperational period* (from 18 months to 6–8 years), which is ushered in by positive evidence of the *semiotic function*—the ability to internally store symbolic representations of the external world. In this period, the child generally acquires the ability to use logical operations in guiding his or her behavior: The internal cognitive representations of reality become organized according to such logical principles as the conservation of volume and number. This process requires *decentering:* The child must experience a "Copernican revolution" in his or her own thinking to understand that the world appears different to other persons and from other points of view. Stage 3 is the *concrete operational period* (from 6–8 years to 12–14 years), in which the child has the ability to reason, but only about concrete logical operations centered on real objects. The ability to use abstract or formal propositions that are removed from the actual observation of real objects (i.e., to consider alternatives and nonpresent possibilities) must await Stage 4, or *formal operational period* (from 12–14 years to adulthood).

## Applications of the Theory

Piaget's theory was designed to explain the process of cognitive development, but it has been used to study other phenomena where cognitive development plays a major role. One example is in the analysis of moral development (Kohlberg, 1963; Piaget, 1932/1948), where the theory was employed to study the development of moral judgment (i.e., the reasoning about right versus wrong, good versus bad, the interpretation of rules, etc). Another example is Selman's analysis of role-taking ability as the ability to view the world and oneself from the perspective of another person (Selman, 1973; Selman & Byrne, 1973).

It can be argued that Piaget's theory could also be applied to the study of emotional development. It is widely accepted that cognitive factors influence emotion, but the implication that cognitive development should influence emotional development has not been clearly spelled out. Such an analysis would involve the child's simultaneous adaptation to the external world of events and the internal world of subjective experience. Such an analysis should prove quite fruitful, and indeed it seems essential to the eventual understanding of the uniquely human aspects of emotional development and expression.

## Emotional Aliments

One potential application of Piaget's theory to emotion involves the concept of aliments. If there are situations that intrinsically motivate attempts at cognitive understanding and mastery, there may also be situations that intrinsically call forth attempts at emotional understanding and mastery. The child who experiences novel feelings associated with activity in a neurochemical system (i.e., when first feeling anger toward a parent, or at puberty when sexual systems become more active) is in a situation analogous, in many respects, to that of a child who experiences a novel external event. Indeed, the situation of the former child may be even more compelling, for unlike an external event the child cannot run away from or avoid his or her own feelings.

If the experience is beyond the child's capacity to assimilate, the child would presumably soon forget it, but the experience might well leave a lasting impression of some kind in a process perhaps analogous to psychoanalytic concepts such as repression or fixation. One could reasonably suggest a variety of ways in which "unconscious" influences could persist and affect later behavior (i.e., via interoceptive conditioning [cf. Buck, 1976a, pp. 115–122; Razran, 1961]). There is, unfortunately, very little empirical data on which to base any discussion or even speculation in this area.

If the experience is within the capacity of the child to assimilate, Piaget's theory predicts that the situation would be intrinsically attractive to the individual, even if the emotions involved might not necessarily be pleasant ones. One study that may be interpreted as supporting this prediction was reported by Boyanowsky, Newtson, and Walster (1972). Following the tragic stabbing murder of a woman student at a large university, the investigators called randomly selected women from the victim's dormitory and a comparable "control" dormitory. The women were given a telephone interview unrelated to the murder, for which they were given a choice of tickets for two movies playing downtown at the time: *The Fox,* a story of a lesbian relationship, and *In Cold Blood,* based on the brutal murder of a family. One week following the murder, students from the victim's dormitory showed a significant preference for *In Cold Blood.* The authors interpret the preference for the violent film as involving an attempt to reduce fear and anxiety via desensitization (i.e. subjecting oneself to a mild form of the feared stimulus while relaxing). However, it is also possible to interpret the preference as indicating an attempt to cognitively accommodate feelings evoked by the murder.

Such a process might account for the human fascination with depictions of emotion of many kinds, both pleasant and unpleasant, and in many forms, from novels and stories to mass media programming. I have suggested that important aspects of emotion often remain inaccessible to the outside observer. It may be that one important determinant of the assimilability either of a depiction of emotion or of an actual emotional situation may be the degree to which the emotion is made accessible in all of its aspects. The situation that teaches us something about our feelings and helps us to understand our emotions more completely may constitute an emotional aliment regardless of the quality of the emotion. The parent who openly admits his or her anger and the reasons for it may find a ready audience even in the child or adolescent who is the target of the anger.

## Stages of Emotional Development

The child's readiness to comprehend such lessons will naturally depend on the child's level of cognitive development. The egocentric, preoperational child should have difficulty understanding that others have different feelings; the concrete, operational child should be able to comprehend the emotional response of a specific other in a given situation but might have difficulty generalizing this to classes of persons or classes of situations. Such a child should also have difficulty conceiving of feelings that he or she has not actually experienced (witness the expansive boredom of many children with love scenes in movies). Many such predictions can be made on the basis of Piaget's theory and what is known about the process of cognitive development, and the investigation of such questions will undoubtedly contribute to the understanding not only of emotional development but of cognitive development as well and of how the two relate to one another. It may also lead to new insights into emotional education and into how emotional development in children can be fostered in ways that are beneficial both to the child and to society.

Another implication involving emotional development involves one of the questions that I posed originally but have not yet addressed concerning why older children seem to show more emotion than do younger children. After the age of 2 or so, all the neurochemical systems underlying the primary motives/emotions are presumably mature, so that the child should show evidence of all of these emotions, given the right circumstances. However, apparent emotional expressiveness may still increase with age. It may well be that this is due to the increasing control of emotional expression by verbally mediated display rules. It has been noted that if only "real" emotions appeared on our faces, we would be expressionless most of the time, because the occurrence of strong emotion is relatively rare. However, the child learns to use emotional expression symbolically, as a tool in linguistic communication. As a result, facial expressions, gestures, and postures that normally are expressive of emotion occur in the stream of linguistic communication. Birdwhistell (1970) and his colleagues have analyzed in detail how bodily and facial movements come under the control of language. I have suggested elsewhere that many of the bodily and facial movements expressive of emotion are organized as systems in the brain, possibly in the midbrain, and that they can be expressed in two ways—spontaneously via the activation of the subcortical or paleocortical systems, and also voluntarily (Buck, 1982, in press). The increasing expressiveness in the older child may reflect his or her increasing facility at the symbolic expression of emotion in the service of linguistic communication.

## Emotional Education

We have seen that a society, culture, or family group can make different aspects of emotion states more or less accessible via the education of attention, and that the child may learn a variety of lessons about the meaning of emotional behaviors. The quality of this emotional education must have important personal and social implications. Consider, for example, the social impact of the mass media and its role in the development of children. Most research on this question has focused on media depictions of sex and violence. It may be that the depictions of many other kinds of emotion are equally important. One indication of the potential importance of the depiction of emotion within a society is provided by D. C. McClelland's (1961) work on achievement motivation in different societies. McClelland reasoned that cultural values encouraging or discouraging the need for achievement should be reflected in literature and in children's stories, which would play a part in the socialization of these values. He found that the levels of achievement imagery in children's stories published in a variety of societies in 1925 were positively correlated with the economic development of those societies as measured by per capita electrical production between 1929 and 1950. Similarly, periods of growth and decline of achievement imagery in Spanish literature (1350–1700 A.D.) and British literature (155–1800 A.D.) preceeded periods of growth and decline of economic activity.

If this kind of analysis may be applied to other motivational/emotional systems, the implications are considerable. It suggests that the flavor and ambience of a culture may reflect to a great degree the emotional education of its young. It is also a testament to the ultimate freedom of human beings from the animal model of emotion. Although the processes that we see in animals undoubtedly lay the groundwork and foundation for the emotional life of human beings, the family and culture provide the architectual style and detail that make the emotional life unique and truly human.

## SUMMARY AND CONCLUSIONS

In this chapter I have addressed the following basic questions: (a) how *emotion* should be defined; (b) whether the human infant is born with emotions; (c) whether there is a developmental sequence to the appearance of emotions; (d) whether there are differences in emotions in children and in animals; and (e) why older children seem to show more emotion than younger children. I outlined a readout model of emotion, that assumes that the individual is born with a number of primary motivational-emotional systems based on subcortical and paleocortical neural mechanisms. Not all of these are active at birth, but some become active as the individual matures. The implications of this model to the analysis of early development were explored, considering how the growing individual becomes acquainted with emotion in self and others, how this process of social learning may come to modify emotional responding, and how emotional expression may influence the development of social relationships.

The foregoing issues may be investigated with animals as well as humans, and I suggested that there are important analogies in animal and human social or emotional development. However, at some point, this animal–human analogy breaks down, largely because emotional responding in humans becomes powerfully influenced by verbally mediated controls associated with language and with cognitive development. From that point, emotional development in humans becomes largely a story of the relationship between the primary motivational/ emotional systems based on subcortical and poleocortical mechanisms on one hand, and verbally mediated processes associated with cognitive motives on the other. The former may be particularly associated with right-hemisphere processes, and the latter with left-hemisphere processes.

Regarding the implications of this view of emotional development, I suggest that the relationship between emotional development and cognitive development has been almost completely ignored, both by researchers and by educators, that a consideration of cognitive development gives the researcher a new view of the process of emotional development, and that a consideration of emotional education may provide new insights into what society does, and should be doing, to influence the emotional health of its members.

# REFERENCES

Andrew, R. J. The origin and evolution of the calls and facial expressions of the primates. *Behavior,* 1963, *20,* 1–109.

Baldwin, A. L. *Theories of child development.* New York: Wiley, 1967.

Bandura, A. *Social learning theory.* Englewood Cliffs, New Jersey: Prentice-Hall, 1977.

Bandura, A., & Walters, R. H. *Social learning and personality development.* New York: Holt, 1963.

Benson, H. *The relaxation response.* New York: William Morrow, 1975.

Berger, S. Conditioning through vicarious instigation. *Psychological Review,* 1962, *69,* 450–466.

Birdwhistell, R. L. *Kinesics and context.* Philadelphia: Univ. of Pennsylvania Press, 1970.

Blanck, P. D., & Rosenthal, R. Developing strategies for decoding "leaky" messages: On learning how and when to decode discrepant and consistent social communications. In R. Feldman (Ed.), *The development of nonverbal behavior in children.* New York: Springer-Verlag, 1982.

Blest, A. D. The concept of ritualization. In W. H. Thorpe & O. L. Zangwill (Eds.), *Current problems in animal behavior.* London and New York: Cambridge Univ. Press, 1961.

Boyanowsky, E. O., Newtson, D., & Walster, E. Effects of murder on movie preference. *Proceedings of the 80th Annual Convention of the American Psychological Association,* 1972, *2,* 235–236.

Bruner, J. S. From communication to language: A psychological perspective. *Cognition,* 1975, *3,* 255–287.

Buck, R. *Human motivation and emotion.* New York: Wiley, Inc., 1976. (a)

Buck, R. A test of nonverbal receiving ability: Preliminary studies. *Human Communication Research,* 1976, *2,* 162–171. (b)

Buck, R. Individual differences in nonverbal sending accuracy and electrodermal responding: The externalizing–internalizing dimension. In R. Rosenthal (Ed.), *Skill in nonverbal communication: Individual differences.* Cambridge, Massachusetts: Oelgeschlager, 1979.

Buck, R. Nonverbal behavior and the theory of emotion: The facial feedback hypothesis. *Journal of Personality and Social Psychology,* 1980, *38,* 811–824.

Buck, R. *The development of emotional and conversational nonverbal behaviors.* Paper presented at the convention of the Society for Research in Child Development. Boston, 1981. (a)

Buck, R. The evolution and development of emotion expression and communication. In S. Brehm, S. Kassin, & F. Gibbons (Eds.), *Developmental social psychology.* London and New York: Oxford Univ. Press, 1981. (b)

Buck, R. A theory of spontaneous and symbolic expression-implications for facial lateralization. Paper presented at the convention of the International Neuropsychological Society, Pittsburgh, Pennsylvania, February, 1982.

Buck, R. *Emotion and nonverbal behavior: The communication of affect.* New York: Guilford. (In press)

Buck, R., Baron, R., & Barrette, D. The temporal organization of spontaneous nonverbal expression: A segmentation analysis. *Journal of Personality and Social Psychology,* 1982, *42,* 506–517.

Buck, R., Baron, R., Goodman, N., & Shapiro, N. The unitization of spontaneous nonverbal behavior in the study of emotion communication. *Journal of Personality and Social Psychology,* 1980, *39,* 522–529.

Buck, R., & Duffy, R. Nonverbal communication of affect in brain-damaged patients. *Cortex,* 1980, *16,* 351–362.

Buck, R., & Lerman, J. General vs. specific nonverbal sensitivity and clinical training. *Human Communication,* 1979, 269–274.

Buck, R. W., Miller, R. E., & Caul, W. F. Sex, personality and physiological variables in the communication of emotion via facial expression. *Journal of Personality and Social Psychology*, 1974, *30*, 587–596.

Cannon, W. B. *The wisdom of the body*. New York: Norton, 1932.

Darwin, C. *Expressions of the emotions in man and animals*. London: John Murray, 1872.

Deets, A., & Harlow, H. F. *Early experience and the maturation of agonistic behavior*. Paper presented at the convention of the American Association for the Advancement of Science, New York, December, 1971.

Delgado, J. M. R. *Physical control of the mind*. New York: Harper & Row, 1969.

DePaulo, B. M., & Rosenthal, R. Measuring the development of nonverbal sensitivity. In P. B. Read & C. Izard (Eds.), *Measuring emotions in infants and children*. London and New York: Cambridge Univ. Press. (In press)

Dickman, H. R. The perception of behavior units. In R. G. Barker (Ed.), *The stream of behavior*. New York: Appleton-Century-Crofts, 1963.

Eibl-Eibesfeldt, I. Similarities and differences between cultures in expressive movements. In R. A. Hinde (Ed.), *Nonverbal communication*. London and New York: Cambridge Univ. Press, 1972.

Ekman, P., & Friesen, W. V. Nonverbal leakage and clues to deception. *Psychiatry*, 1969, *32*, 88–105. (a)

Ekman, P., & Friesen, W. V. The repertoire of nonverbal behavior: Categories, origins, usage and coding. *Semiotica*, 1969, *1*, 49–98. (b)

Ekman, P., & Friesen, W. V. *Unmasking the face*. Englewood Cliffs, New Jersey: Prentice-Hall, 1975.

Ekman, P., Friesen, W. V., & Ellsworth, P. *Emotion in the human face*. New York: Permagon, 1972.

Elkind, D. Cognitive growth cycles in mental development. In J. K. Cole (Ed.), *Nebraska Symposium on Motivation* (Vol. 19). Lincoln: Univ. of Nebraska Press, 1971.

Ellsworth, P. C., & Tourangeau, R. On our failure to disconfirm what nobody ever said. *Journal of Personality and Social Psychology*, 1981, *40*, 363–369.

Field, T. M., & Walden, T. A. Perception and production of facial expressions in infancy and early childhood. In H. Reese & L. Lipsett (Eds.), *Advances in child development and behavior* (Vol. 16). New York: Academic Press, 1982.

Fraiberg, S. Blind infants and their mothers: An examination of the sign system. In M. Lewis & L. A. Rosenbloom (Ed.), *The effect of the infant on its caregiver*. New York: Wiley, 1974.

Frodi, A. M. Contribution of infant characteristics to child abuse. *American Journal of Mental Deficiency*, 1981, *85*, 341–349.

Frodi, A. M., & Lamb, M. E. Fathers' and mothers' responses to the faces and cries of normal and premature infants. *Developmental Psychology*, 1978, *14*, 490–498.

Goodman, N. R. *Determinants of the perceptual organization of ongoing action and emotion behavior*. Unpublished doctoral dissertation, University of Connecticut, 1980.

Hager, J. C., & Ekman, P. Methodological problems in Tourangean and Ellworth's study of facial expression and experience of emotion. *Journal of Personality and Social Psychology*, 1981, *40*, 353–362.

Harlow, H. F. *Learning to love*. San Francisco, California: Albion, 1971.

Heath, R. G. Pleasure responses of human subjects to direct stimulation of the brain: Physiologic and psychodynamic considerations. In R. G. Heath (Ed.), *The role of pleasure in behavior*. New York: Hoeber, 1964.

Hohmann, G. Some effects of spinal cord lesions on experiential emotional feelings. *Psychophysiology*, 1966, *3*, 143–156.

Izard, C. E. *The face of emotion*. New York: Appleton-Century-Crofts, 1971.

Izard, C. E. *Human emotions*. New York: Plenum, 1977.

Izard, C. E. Differential emotions theory and the facial feedback hypothesis of emotion activation. *Journal of Personality and Social Psychology,* 1981, *40,* 350–354.

Izard, C. E., Huebner, R. R., Risser, D., McGinnes, G. C., & Dougherty, L. M. The young infant's ability to produce discrete emotion expressions. *Developmental Psychology,* 1980, *16,* 132–140.

Izard, C. E. *Emotion as motivation: An evolutionary–developmental perspective.* Colloquium presented at the University of Connecticut, April, 1979.

Koenig, O. Das aktionssystem der Bartmeise (*Panurus biarmicus L.*). *Österreichische Zoologische Zeitschrift,* 1951, *3,* 247–325.

Kohlberg, L. Moral development and identification. In H. W. Stevenson (Ed.), *Child psychology.* Chicago, Illinois: Univ. of Chicago Press, 1963.

Kunst-Wilson, W. R., & Zajonc, R. B. Affective discrimination of stimuli that cannot be recognized. *Science,* 1980, *207,* 557–558.

Laird, J. D. Self-attribution of emotion: The effects of expressive behavior on the quality of emotional experience. *Journal of Personality and Social Psychology,* 1974, *29,* 475–486.

Lazarus, R. S. *Psychological stress and the coping process.* New York: McGraw-Hill, 1966.

Lewis, M., & Rosenblum, L. A. *The effect of the infant on its caregiver.* New York: Wiley, 1974.

McClelland, D. C. *The achieving society.* Princeton, New Jersey: Van Nostrand, 1961.

MacLean, P. D. Contrasting functions of limbic and neocortical systems of the brain and their relevance to psychophysiological aspects of medicine. In E. Gellhorn (Ed.), *Biological foundations of emotion.* Glenview, Illinois: Scott, Foresman, 1968.

MacLean, P. D. The limbic brain in relation to the psychoses. In P. H. Black (Ed.), *Physiological correlates of emotion.* New York: Academic Press, 1970.

MacLean, P. D. Effects of lesions of globus pallidus on species-typical display behavior of squirrel monkeys. *Brain Research,* 1978, *149,* 175–196.

Mark, V. H., & Ervin, F. R. *Violence and the brain.* New York: Harper & Row, 1970.

Markov, P. O. A study of interoception in human subjects. *Uchenye Zapiski Leningradskogo Universiteta, Seriya Biologicheskikh,* 1950, *22,* 345–368.

Miller, N. E. The learning of visceral and glandular responses. *Science,* 1969, *163,* 434–445.

Miller, R. E., Caul, W. F., & Mirsky, I. A. Communication of affects between feral and socially isolated monkeys. *Journal of Personality and Social Psychology,* 1967, *7,* 231–239.

Mogenson, G. J., & Phillips, A. G. Motivation: A psychological construct in search of a physiological substrate. In J. M. Sprague & A. N. Epstein (Eds.), *Progress in psychobiology and physiological psychology.* New York: Academic Press, 1976.

Moyer, K. E. *The physiology of hostility.* Chicago, Illinois: Markham, 1971.

Newtson, D. Foundations of attribution: The perception of ongoing behavior. In J. H. Harvey, W. J. Ickes, & R. F. Kidd (Eds.), *New directions in attribution research* (Vol. 1). New York: Wiley, 1976.

Orne, M. T. The efficacy of biofeedback therapy. *Annual Review of Medicine,* 1979, *30,* 489–503.

Piaget, J. *The moral judgment of the child.* Glencoe, Illinois: Free Press, 1948. (Originally published, 1932)

Piaget, J. Piaget's theory. In P. Mussen (Ed.), *Handbook of child development* (Vol. 1). New York: Wiley, 1971.

Piaget, J., & Inhelder, B. *The psychology of the child.* New York: Basic Books, 1969.

Razran, G. The observable unconscious and the inferable conscious in current Soviet psychophysiology. *Psychological Review,* 1961, *68,* 81–147.

Rosenthal, R., & DePaulo, B. Sex differences in accommodation in nonverbal communication. In R. Rosenthal (Ed.), *Skill in nonverbal communication.* Cambridge, Massachusetts: Oelgeschlager, 1979.

Rosenthal, R., Hall, J. A., DiMatteo, M. R., Rogers, P. L., Archer, D. *Sensitivity to nonverbal communication: The PONS test.* Baltimore, Maryland: Johns Hopkins Univ. Press, 1979.

Russell, B. *An outline of philosophy*. Cleveland-World, 1961. (Originally published 1927)

Sackett, G. P. Monkeys reared in isolation with pictures as visual input: Evidence for an innate releasing mechanism. *Science*, 1966, *154*, 1468–1473.

Schachter, S. The interaction of cognitive and physiological determinants of emotional state. In L. Berkowitz (Ed.), *Advances in experimental social psychology* (Vol. 1). New York: Academic Press, 1964.

Schachter, S. Obesity and eating. *Science*, 1968, *161*, 751–756.

Schachter, S. Some extraordinary facts about obese humans and rats. *American Psychologist*, 1970, *26*, 129–144.

Selman, R. *A structural analysis of the ability to take another's social perspective—stages in the development of role taking ability*. Paper presented at the Society for Research in Child Development, Philadelphia, Pennsylvania, April, 1973.

Selman, R., & Byrne, D. *Manual for scoring stages of role-taking in moral and non-moral social dilemmas*. Unpublished manuscript, Harvard University, 1973.

Selye, H. *The stress of life*. New York: McGraw-Hill, 1976.

Sem-Jacobson, C. W. Depth-electroencephalographic stimulation of the human brain and behavior. Springfield, Illinois: Thomas, 1968.

Shearer, S. L., & Tucker, D. M. Differential cognitive contributions of the cerebral hemispheres in the modulation of emotional arousal. *Cognitive Theory and Research*, 1981, *5*, 85–93.

Skinner, B. F. *Science and human behavior*. New York: Macmillan, 1953.

Sroufe, A. The coherence of individual development. *American Psychologist*, 1979, *34*, 834–849.

Storms, M. D. Videotape and the attribution process: Reversing actors' and observers' points of view. *Journal of Personality and Social Psychology*, 1973, *27*, 165–175.

Thoman, E. *How a rejecting baby affects mother–infant synchrony*. Parent–Infant Interaction, Ciba Foundation Symposium 33. New York: Associated Scientific Publishers, 1975.

Thoman, E. Affective communication as the prelude and context for language learning. In R. L. Schiefelbusch & D. Bricker (Eds.), *Early language: Acquisition and intervention*. Baltimore, Maryland: University Park Press, 1981.

Tinbergen, N. "Derived" activities: Their causation, biological significance, origin and emancipation during evolution. *Quarterly Review of Biology*, 1952, *27*, 1–32.

Tomkins, S. *Affect, imagery, and consciousness: The positive affects* (Vol. 1). New York: Springer, 1962.

Tomkins, S. *Affect, imagery and consciousness: The negative affects* (Vol. 2). New York: Springer, 1963.

Tomkins, S. The role of facial response in the experience of emotion: A reply to Tourangean and Ellswoth. *Journal of Personality and Social Psychology*, 1981, *40*, 355–357.

Tourangeau, R., & Ellsworth, P. C. The role of facial response in the experience of emotion. *Journal of Personality and Social Psychology*, 1979, *37*, 1519–1531.

Tucker, D. M. Lateral brain function, emotion, and conceptualization. *Psychological Bulletin*, 1981, *89*, 19–46.

Tucker, D. M., & Newman, J. P. Lateral brain function and the cognitive inhibition of emotional arousal. *Cognitive Theory and Research*. (in press)

von Holst, E. & von Saint Paul, U. Electrically controlled behavior. *Scientific American*, 1962 (March), *20*, 50–59.

Wenger, M. A., & Bagchi, B. K. Studies of autonomic functions in practitioners of Yoga in India. *Beh. Sci.* 1961, *6*, 312–323.

Wenger, M. A., Bagchi, B. K., & Anand, B. K. Experiments in India on "voluntary" control of the heart and pulse. *Circulation*, 1961, *24*, 1319–1325.

Whalen, R. E. *Sexual motivation. Psych. Rev.*, 1966, *72*, 151–163.

White, J. C. Autonomic discharge from stimulation of the hypothalamus in man. *Research Publications of the Association for Research in Nervous and Mental Disease*, 1940, *20*, 854–863.

White, R. W. Motivation reconsidered: The concept of competence. *Psychological Review,* 1959, *65,* 297–233.

Wilson, W. R. Feeling more than we can know: Exposure effects without learning. *Journal of Personality and Social Psychology,* 1979, *37,* 811–821.

Winter, P., Handley, P., Ploog, D., & Schott, D. Ontogeny of squirrel monkey cells under normal conditions and under acoustic isolation. *Behavior,* 1973, *47,* 230–239.

Wynne, L. C., & Solomon, R. L. Traumatic avoidance learning: Acquisition and extinction in dogs deprived of normal peripheral autonomic function. *Genetic Psychology Monographs,* 1955, *52,* 241–284.

Young, P. T. *Motivation and emotion.* New York: Wiley, 1961.

Zajonc, R. B. Feeling and thinking: Preferences need no inferences. *American Psychologist,* 1980, *35,* 151–175.

Zeskind, P. S., & Lester, B. M. Acoustic features and auditory perceptions of the cries of newborns with prenatal and perinatal complications. *Child Development,* 1978, *49,* 580–589.

Chapter 10

# ON THE EMERGENCE, FUNCTIONS, AND REGULATION OF SOME EMOTION EXPRESSIONS IN INFANCY

*SANDRA BUECHLER*
*CARROLL E. IZARD*

## ABSTRACT

*Divergent theoretical positions on the emergence, functions, and regulation of emotion expressions in infancy are delineated in this chapter. The emotion of anger is used to illustrate the implications of three theoretical perspectives on the onset and significance of a discrete emotion in the life experience of the infant.*

*The study of the capacity to regulate the expression of an emotion is complicated by terminological differences and procedural variations. These problems are illustrated by considering the empirical evidence supporting each of these viewpoints on age-related changes in the infant's fear response to a stranger. Comparing these results yields contradictory findings regarding the age at which the infant no longer shows the fear response. The differential emotions theory holds that each new emotion expression that emerges in infancy is a major determinant of changes in the infant's experience. Each emotion is seen as having a separate, discernible expression and a unique impact on perceptual, cognitive, and social growth.*

Theoretical perspectives on the emergence and function of emotions in infancy affect how the onset of each new emotion expression is viewed. Investigators and theoreticians holding psychoanalytic viewpoints, those subscribing to the differ-

EMOTION
Theory, Research, and Experience
Volume 2

entiation hypothesis, and those adhering to the discrete systems approach conceptualize the appearance and role of emotion expressions differently. Similarities and differences among the divergent positions on the onset and functions of emotion expressions will be illustrated by a discussion of the onset and functions of the expression of anger.

## THE EMERGENCE AND FUNCTIONS OF THE EXPRESSION OF ANGER

Investigators with different positions on the nature of human emotions use different terminologies to describe the onset of anger in infancy. These differences in terminology often make it difficult to generalize across experimental studies or theoretical discussions. If, for example, one is attempting to assess whether the irritability described by temperament theorists is the same phenomenon or on the same dimension as the rage described by Sroufe (1976) and irritability and rage are measured in different stimulus situations with different criteria for judging their presence, the nature of their relationship to each other cannot be assessed. Furthermore, even if irritability and rage could be considered to account for the same behavioral phenomena, the link between these infant phenomena and later manifestations of anger would have to be established in order to maintain that irritability represents the onset of the expression of anger. Despite these problems in interpretation, it is possible to isolate some issues in the treatment of the emergence of anger by investigators holding psychoanalytic, differentiation, discrete systems, and other theoretical positions.

### PSYCHOANALYTIC PERSPECTIVES

Psychoanalytically oriented theoreticians and experimental investigators have differed in their concepts of the onset and significance of the infant's expression of anger. Several theoreticians, who use the term *aggression* or *aggressive drive* to describe the source of infant anger, see it as present from birth. Storr (1968) summarizes the psychoanalytic view that the infant is "potentially aggressive from the time that it is born [p. 38]." Storr sees this view as reasonable:

> Since it makes no sense to assume that aggression, sexuality, or any other drive suddenly appears from nowhere without any precursors, it is perfectly reasonable to suppose that even the newborn have aggressive impulses in spite of the fact that we cannot enter their phantasy world direct [p. 41].

Thus, this perspective is based on assumptions about the fantasies of the infant, which are presumed to contain aggressive themes from birth. Klein describes the impact of these early aggressive fantasies, suggesting that "a hungry, raging infant, screaming and kicking, phantasies that he is actually attacking the breast, tearing and destroying it, and experiences his own screams which tear and hurt him as the torn breast attacking him in his own inside [Segal, 1964, p. 2]."

The earliest manifestations of aggression in the infant, according to this view, are known through reconstructions of early fantasies. Aside from difficulties in testing these assumptions empirically, this position is complicated by the different ways analytically oriented theoreticians use the terms *anger* and *aggression*. Whereas some see the "raging" infant as expressing destructive aggression, others attempt to differentiate destructive anger and rage from aggression, which may have a clearly constructive function. Thompson (1964), for example, wrote:

> Aggression is not necessarily destructive at all. It springs from an innate tendency to grow and master life, which seems to be characteristic of all living matter. Only when this life force is obstructed in its development do ingredients of anger, rage, or hate become connected with it [p. 179].

Similarly, some analytically oriented theoreticians consider motility and other behavioral manifestations of the infant's assertion of separateness as expressions of "positive aggression." Aggression drives the infant to escape from the restrictions of dependency and is so essential to healthy growth that it can be "almost considered synonymous with activity [Winnicott, 1958, p. 204]."

Stephan (1941) presents another analytical interpretation of the differences between rage and aggression in the experience of the infant. In her view, aggression can either serve a useful function for the infant or, if inhibited by fear, it can be experienced as a threatening rage that excites anxiety. When used constructively, aggression aims at getting needed supplies from the outside world or at destroying sources of pain through attack. If aggressive attempts are unsuccessful, a fear reaction can develop. Since fear inhibits the expression of aggression, these two emotions block each other, and both become exacerbated. This vicious cycle of fear and rage results in acute anxiety, to which the infant responds with defenses such as repression, psychic withdrawal, projection, or introjection. Thus constructive aggression becomes destructive rage through the addition of fear:

> When the child suffers frustration or indeed privation or pain, whatever its origin, it may find itself in danger from within because of the unmanageableness of its own impulses, which cannot find satisfactory discharge and so threaten to get out of control and overwhelm the ego [Stephan, 1941, p. 189].

The analytic viewpoints just discussed have in common their reliance on fantasy reconstruction and theoretical deduction in their descriptions of the onset of aggression. Other analytically oriented theoreticians have applied their concepts in a more experimental framework. In a series of longitudinal studies, Emde, Gaensbauer, and Harmon (1976) and Emde (1978) have tested the usefulness of concepts derived from psychoanalytic theory to the study of emotion development in infancy. Emde (1978) reported a growing appreciation in more recent analytic literature of the view that emotions have adaptive functions and are continuous elements of experience rather than disruptive events (cf. Izard, 1971, 1978). Emde's data lend support to Spitz's (1965) conception that major organizational shifts occur regularly in development and are signaled by the emergence of new affective behavior. Emde (1978) concurs with the view that anger becomes a prominent feature of infant behavior in the latter half of the first year of life. This estimated time of the emergence of anger coincides with the period proposed as the second major developmental shift, a time during which fearfulness also has its onset. Citing findings of changes in heart rate organization (Campos, Emde, Gaensbauer, & Henderson, 1975) and cognitive advances in the development of means–end relationships (Piaget, 1936–1952), Emde considers the period of 7–9 months a time of rapid change in the organization of the infant's experience. This conception of periods of rapid reorganization marked by the emergence of new emotions contrasts with the differentiation hypothesis of the onset of emotions (discussed later). One implication of Emde's view is that in the 7–9-month-old infant, emotion expressions can lead to behavior (the infant can show a fearful expression and then avoid). Although Emde does not elaborate on his view of anger in this context, his concept of the second organizational shift implies that the anger expression, as it emerges, can lead to defensive or aggressive behavior. The expression of anger provides a signal to the infant as to how to behave, as well as providing a communicative social signal to the caregiver. Emde's view of the psychological and social motivating functions of emotion expressions give them a central role in his concept of infant development.

## THE DIFFERENTIATION HYPOTHESIS

The differentiation theory of the development of human emotions suggests that, by a process of differentiation, the various emotions derive from a single state of emotional arousal. In contrast to the analytic perspectives, the differentiation hypothesis suggests that the emotion of anger does not exist in the first weeks of life but gradually develops from its early precursors.

The first proponent of the differentiation view was Bridges (1932), who supported the theory with a study of the expressions of emotions in infants from a few hours after birth to 2 years of age. Although Bridges' work has been criticized for its weaknesses in methodology (Izard, 1977), few empirical studies have provided data to challenge her results. Her theory suggests that generalized excitement is the only emotion present at birth, but that distress emerges early in the first months, and the first signs of anger evolve from distress between the third and sixth months of life. Clear indications of the presence of anger are evident by the age of 12 months.

Bridges based her theory of the ontogenesis of anger on the following behavioral observations of infants at 3 months of age:

> The slight change in vowel sound of the cry, the long holding of breath combined with more than usually vigorous leg thrusts and arm movements, seemed to suggest that the emotion of anger is beginning to evolve from general distress at about this age. Although for the most part the distress shown at discomfort differs almost imperceptibly from distress in response to disappointment, occasionally the latter includes, to a marked degree, those behavior elements peculiar to the emotion of anger. The situations which evoke these demonstrations of temper in the tiny infant are a stop or check in the progressive satisfaction of a physical need. In the above instance the child's appetite was aroused but not satisfied [Bridges, 1932, p. 329].

Several aspects of these observations invite comparison with the data of other investigators:

1. Wolff (1969) described the "frustration cry" as differing from the response to pain in the former's lack of prolonged breath-holding after the initial cries. In contrast, what differentiates the anger cry from distress in Bridges' (1932) observations is the presence of breath-holding.
2. Bridges (1932) assumes that the criteria for judging the presence of anger in infants can consist of "behavioral elements" that resemble temper tantrums in older subjects. These elements are, however, only vaguely described. It seems from these observations that the infant was judged angry if it gave an impression of expressing any element of a temper tantrum.
3. The first elicitor of anger is frustration of a need for satisfaction when the need has already had some satisfaction. This contradicts Marquis's (1943) finding that frustration responses decreased as satisfaction increased. The frustration of a partially satisfied need can be seen as similar to Mandler's (1975) concept of the interruption of behavior, but he holds that such an event leads to anxiety when no alternative behavior is available.

Throughout Bridges (1932) observations, the behavioral criteria for judging the presence of new emotions are chosen because they reminded the observer of that emotion (e.g., the flat *a-a-a* sound of the frustrated 3-month-old is categorized as an anger response to frustration because it is "reminiscent of an older child's 'paddy' or temper cry [p. 329]." Besides being open to other interpretations and unsystematic, occasionally these observations use different criteria for judging the presence of anger at differing ages (e.g., the 12-month-old infant is considered angry when it screams, flushes, and trembles, but flushing and trembling are not mentioned as criteria for judging the presence of anger at several other ages). This suggests a logical contradiction: The young infant is considered angry when its behavior resembles that of the older child, yet the behaviors expressing anger are thought to differ by age.

Sroufe (1976) has amended and amplified the differentiation hypothesis in attempting to explain how each emotion emerges from its precursors. In his view of the onset of anger, early distress gives rise to rage, then anger, angry mood, and defiance. Sroufe sees rage as emerging at about the age of 3 months, and anger at 7 months. Sroufe describes how anger develops from rage and is stimulated by a variety of elicitors.

The emotion of anger is seen as elicited by a "disappointment—the failure of a motor expectation or the interruption of specific ongoing activities [Sroufe, 1976, p. 43]." In contrast, in the earlier rage response "the negative reaction comes from blocking the flow of behavior, analogous to the wary reaction described above, though in this case the stoppage of behavior is physical [Sroufe, 1976, p. 43]." How Sroufe distinguishes between "blocking the flow of behavior," which is presumed to elicit rage, and "interruption of specific ongoing activities," which is described as eliciting anger, is not clarified. In any case, he agrees with Bridges (1932) in indicating that interruption of a behavioral sequence produces anger rather than anxiety, as suggested by Mandler (1975).

In contrast to some of the psychoanalytic writers, the proponents of the differentiation hypothesis based their theory of the onset of anger on specific behavioral observations, but they have not established several important elements of their view:

1. It is difficult to judge, from their descriptions, how anger differs from its precursors (rage and distress) in its behavioral manifestations and elicitors. The differences cited are often vague or contradict the findings of other investigators.
2. The process of differentiation has not yet been described. Although Sroufe implies (1976, p. 43–44) that cognitive factors (e.g., intentionality, awareness of causation) are important in the change from rage to anger responses, the cognitive–affective interactions that dictate anger responses to anger elicitors are unknown. Writing of the emergence of anger from rage, Sroufe (1976) states that "the outline above is speculative and the ontogenesis of this system awaits systematic study (p. 44."
3. The relationship between the infant emotion expressions of rage and anger and the adult emotions is unclear. The presence of infant rage and anger has generally been assessed using behavioral criteria such as latency to cry, intensity of crying, kicking, and other behaviors that do not generally characterize adult anger expressions. Facial expression changes, which do

occur in both infants and adults, would represent an objective criterion for ongoing emotion assessment, but their systematic use in studies of emotion development has been limited. For the differentiation hypothesis, this means that the only link between the descriptions of early rage and the description of its later anger variant is the observers' impression of some inherent similarities between the "protest shouts" of the 3-month-old, the foot stomping, kicking, slapping, and pushing of the 1-year-old, and the angry facial expression of the adult.

## DISCRETE EMOTIONS THEORY ON THE EMERGENCE OF ANGER

The discrete emotions theory of the ontogenesis of emotions (Izard, 1977) suggests that each emotion develops as a discrete system. In contrast to the differentiation theorists, Izard proposes that anger does not evolve in a continuous process from "precursor" emotions but emerges at a distinct point in development. According to the discrete systems view, there are separate, innate neural programs for the expression of each of the fundamental emotions. Whereas the expressions of interest, the neonatal smile, startle, distress, and disgust are present at birth, for the other emotions a period of maturation is required before they can be expressed and experienced [Izard, 1978].

In the case of anger, Izard suggests that, like the other emotions, it emerges when it becomes adaptive in the life of the infant (Izard, 1971, 1978). The onset of anger is suggested to be between the fourth and sixth months of life. Since anger serves to motivate actions that remove restraints, or circumvent barriers, and fosters the infant's concept of self as causal agent, its emergence would only be adaptive after the infant is able to locomote, push or kick, swat, etc. If anger emerged prior to these developments, it could only result in mounting frustration experiences and negative exchanges with the social and object world.

In a cross-sectional study of the facial expressions of 5-, 7-, and 9-month-olds, Parisi and Izard (1977) videotaped responses to 20 brief stimulus situations. Trained judges were able to reliably identify anger expressions (as well as expressions of other discrete emotions) at all three age levels, suggesting that the infant is able to communicate anger by the fifth month of life. This places the onset of anger expressions as several months earlier than the age hypothesized by Sroufe (although Sroufe suggested that precursors of anger emerge in the first months of life).

Unlike psychoanalytic or differentiation theorists, proponents of discrete emotions attempt to gain support for their viewpoint from empirical studies of the emergence of the facial expressions of the emotions. By using sets of patterns of specific facial movements as criteria for the presence of a particular emotion expression, it is possible to design comparable studies for different age groups, since facial expressions (unlike temper tantrums and other emotion-related behaviors) occur throughout the life span.

Discrete emotions theory emphasizes the adaptive role of emotion expressions and their active, organizing functions. It differs from some of the psychoanalytic views that focus on the disruptive effect of anger, but has more in common with some analytically oriented viewpoints, such as Emde's (1978), that posit organizing functions for infant emotions. Unlike the differentiation hypothesis, discrete emotions theory views anger as emerging as a new expression at 4–6 months rather than as an elaboration of earlier rage responses. Anger directly contributes to the infant's self-development by motivating active efforts to cope with frustrating barriers. As a result, the infant adds to its experiences of the object and social world and gains a sense of self as causal agent (Izard, 1978). Interactions motivated by anger provide opportunities for the infant to experience itself as a capable individual.

This concept of anger is not inconsistent with some views of the dynamics of the process of individuation. As conceptualized by Mahler, Pine, and Bergman (1975), separation–individuation begins in a tentative, exploratory fashion at about 6 months of age. They maintain that the infant at this age is emerging from symbiosis and is beginning to differentiate from the mother. Unlike its previous, more passive, behavior, the infant in this phase has "a certain look of alertness, persistence and goal directedness [Mahler, *et al.;* 1975, p. 54]." The discrete systems view of anger as emerging at 4–6 months and motivating active coping with barriers can be seen as directing the infant's efforts to fend for itself against frustrations instead of relying solely on the caregiver by signaling its distress. However, anger-motivated behavior may yield repeated experiences of inadequacy and weakness. The commerce with the social and object world that is motivated by anger may be seen as furthering the process of learning to cope with the positive and negative aspects of being a separate individual.

## THE REGULATION OF THE EXPRESSION OF EMOTIONS IN INFANCY

The capacity to regulate the expression of an emotion is difficult to examine experimentally. When an infant of 12 months does not show fear, for example, in a situation that elicited fear at 9 months, is this evidence of the advent of the ability to delimit fear expression? Or does the stimulus have a different meaning for the older infant? Or do aspects of the context (such as the presence of mother) make the situation less threatening for the older infant?

The discussion of emotion regulation is also complicated by the differences in terminology across theories. Whereas some refer to *controlling* or *regulating* emotion expression, others discuss *mastering* and *coping styles*. Terminology differences reflect, to some extent, the author's bias on the question of the relationship between subjective emotion experiences and observable emotion expressions. For those who assume a close correspondence between experience and expression, the absence of a fear response connotes that the infant construes the stimulus as nonthreatening. For those who separate the issues of emotion experience and expression, the absence of expressed fear reflects a new coping capacity to deal with that which still threatens.

A further complication, in our view, is the tendency for some theoreticians to treat emotion regulation as a unitary process, rather than separately addressing the capacity for delimiting the expression of the various discrete emotions such as distress, anger, fear, and shame. Whether the infant gains, at some recognizable point in development, the overall ability to regulate the expression of all the emotions is an area for future study. At the present time, it would seem more appropriate to assume that, just as the onset of expression of the various emotions occurs at different points in development, so the age at which the infant is able to regulate expression may differ for each of the discrete emotions.

The following discussion presents a brief review of several perspectives on the regulation of the expressions of emotions in infancy. Where possible, alternative interpretations of the means by which the infant first regulates the expression of an emotion are contrasted.

## EMPIRICAL STUDIES OF
## THE REGULATION OF
## THE EXPRESSION OF FEAR IN
## RESPONSE TO STRANGERS

Rather than study the course of infants' fear expressions in a variety of situations, most researchers have limited their investigation to the onset of fear as a response to a particular situation. Interaction with a stranger is the incentive event that has received the most concentrated attention as a potential elicitor of fear. However, some investigators have focused on the infant's changing responses to separation, the visual cliff, and unusual visual stimuli.

The experimental literature on age-related changes in the infant's response to a stranger is subject to three contrasting interpretations:

1. The fear response to the stranger has its onset in most infants by the age of 8–9 months, and thereafter the infant begins the process of regulating any observable fear response to strangers.

2. The fear response to the stranger has more than one period of peak expression during the first 2 years of life, and the infant does not begin active regulation of stranger fear expression until the end of the second year.
3. Fear responses to strangers are relatively uncommon events in infancy. Their appearance in experimentally controlled situations is due to a complex of factors and is present only in some infants.

Before examining the evidence that supports each view it is important to note that procedural variations across these studies complicate interpretation of their findings regarding age-related changes in the stranger response. Factors that have varied across stranger response studies have included the sex, height, manner, speed of approach, and facial behavior of the stranger, the type and duration of infant–stranger contact, the presence or absence of competing emotion elicitors in the context, physical constraints on the movement of the infant, the presence and proximity of the mother, and the criteria for judging the presence or absence of a fear response. Clearly, the stranger has not been studied as a standard stimulus. More importantly, since it is likely that some of these variables are differentially salient to infants of varying ages, some of the experimental procedures that have been used were more likely to elicit fear at the younger ages tested, whereas other procedures were probably unlikely to elicit fear at any age. Hence, discrepancies in their findings regarding the age at which the infant expresses and limits expression of stranger fear may be the result of these procedural variations.

• The first view, that stranger fear has its onset and peak expression by about 8–9 months and is subject to increasing control thereafter, is supported by the investigations of Tennes and Lampl (1964), Gaensbauer, Emde, and Campos (1976), Schaffer (1966), and Bronson, 1972. Tennes and Lampl, studying infants from their third through their twenty-third month, found that two-thirds of their subjects reached the peak of their stranger fear response between 5 and 10 months of age. Gaensbauer *et al.* (1976) and Schaffer (1966) found the age of onset of stranger fear to occur most often in the eighth month, whereas over 75% of Bronson's subjects showed fear responses to strangers by 6½ months of age. Although the termination of fear expression was not the main focus of these three investigations, Tennes and Lampl did study their subjects' waning expression of fear of strangers and found that one-third of their subjects had terminated the expression of a fear response by the end of the tenth month. Taken together, these data support the view that the peak expression of stranger fear occurs in the first year of life.

Scarr and Salapatek (1970) present evidence supporting the second view, that there are two peak periods of expression of stranger fear in the first 2 years of life. Looking at infants from 2 to 23 months of age, they found that over 60% of the 9–11-month-old infants and 80% of the 18–24-month-old infants showed fear of strangers. This contradicts the notion that the capacity to regulate fear expression is a developmental milestone that should be present by the middle of the second year, an interpretation that is compatible with much of the previously reviewed findings. However, several factors warrant caution in interpreting the data regarding the responses of the 18–24-month-old subjects in Scarr and Salapatek's sample. Their scoring procedures categorized children as either not showing any fear or as sober, cautions, quitting ongoing activity, fretting, crying, or fleeing to mother. It might be argued that by using such broad criteria, the investigators may have included in the "fearful" group some infants who were expressing shyness in response to the stranger. Shyness is thought to increase at this age (Lewis & Brooks, 1978), and without analysis of the infants' facial expressions it is possible that behaviors such as fleeing to mother, quitting an ongoing activity, or sobering could have accompanied shy expressions. Thus, the determination of whether Scarr and Salapatek's data support the hypothesis that there are two periods of stranger fear or the assumption that there is an early period of stranger fear followed by a later period of shyness in response to strangers awaits more extensive longitudinal analysis of the range of the infant's emotion responses to strangers and more systematic analysis of objective criteria for specific emotion expressions.

The third view, that the fear response to the stranger is either an uncommon event, resulting from individual difference factors, or an experimental artifact, is supported by the data of Rheingold and Eckerman (1974). The 24 subjects in this cross-sectional study were 8, 10, and 12 months of age. The investigators report no signs of stranger distress or fear in their subjects. Although Rheingold and Eckerman interpret their results as a challenge to the existence of the stranger response, it is also possible that their subjects were already able to control expression of the response in this particular experimental condition. The presence of a wide range of interest elicitors (posters, mobiles, brightly colored pull toys), the slow approach of the strangers, the freedom afforded the subjects to crawl away from the stranger, and the stringent criteria for judging the presence of fear (only fussing and crying were rated as evidence of fear, but no measures of type of visual regard, facial expression, or attempts at withdrawal were taken) may have mitigated against obtaining fear responses. Thus, if (as will be discussed later) one were to argue that emotions such as interest and interest-motivated exploratory behavior are factors in the infant's regulation of fear expression, the Rheingold and Eckerman (1974) data are subject to the interpretation that their procedures elicited interest (in the toys) and encouraged regulation of what otherwise might have emerged as fear responses. The issue of whether the Rheingold and Eckerman subjects expressed some stranger fear modulated by interest is made more difficult to resolve since the facial expressions of the infants were not analyzed.

A further complication in relating the findings of this study to the issue of fear regulation is its cross-sectional design. Had the subjects been tested longitudinally some might have shown an early onset and course of decreasing expressions of stranger fear. In emphasizing the importance of longitudinal approaches to the study of stranger fear, Gaensbauer *et al.* (1976) noted that

> The extent to which cross-sectional data can be misleading is demonstrated when we look at our own data cross-sectionally. An increasing number of infants showed distress with increasing age, yet at any given age, one third to one half of the infants tested did not show distress. When considered longitudinally, however, all infants at some point between 6 and 12 months showed distress which tended to recur in subsequent months [p. 104].

In addition to highlighting the need for longitudinal investigation of the course of expression of stranger fear, this comment suggests the possibility that within the 6–12-month age range individual differences determine onset of stranger fear expression; once stranger fear has been expressed, it tends to recur during this period. Since the monthly testings did not proceed beyond the infants' twelfth month, these data do not attest to whether the subjects would have shown another peak of stranger fear in the second year, preceeded and followed by less fearful responses. Since, like the Gaensbauer *et al.* (1976) study, most other investigations of stranger fear have focused on the onset of the response rather than its regulation, the course of the response in the second year and the variables that affect its eventual control require further exploration.

To summarize, experimental approaches to the infant's regulation of the expression of stranger fear have yielded contradictory findings regarding the age at which the infant no longer shows the response. Some of the discrepancies may be the result of procedural differences across investigations and of the use of cross-sectional designs. Apart from these difficulties, none of the studies reviewed offers evidence as to whether or how older infants regulate fear expressions; they indicate merely that older infants show less fear, at least in some experimental situations. In order to clarify the course of the infant's emotion responses to the stranger, or any other fear elicitor, it would be necessary to study, longitudinally, all of the infant's emotion expressions to that stimulus from the time of onset of fear through the age at which fear is replaced (or, perhaps, blended) with another emotion response.

## CLINICAL CONCEPTS OF EMOTION REGULATION

For clinicians, the capacity to regulate emotion expression is a crucial aspect of personality development. Often, their focus has been on the regulation of anger, fear, shame, and guilt, with less emphasis on emotions such as interest, joy, surprise, disgust, and comtempt. The clinical focus is frequently centered on individual differences in emotion regulation, with inadequate regulation seen as pathology. In contrast with differential emotions theory, which centers on the adaptive motivating properties of each emotion, the clinician has frequently been concerned with the disruptive effect of emotions on cognition and behavior, and so has seen emotion regulation as a process necessary for adequate social and intellectual growth.

One point of view that has been espoused with some frequency by clinical investigators is that emotion control is a process that results from socialization or social pressure on the infant. This approach considers individual differences in emotion control to be partially a result of differing degrees of effectiveness of socialization. In contrast to the major emphasis differential emotions theory places on the tendency for one emotion (e.g., interest) to alter conscious experience and effectively regulate the expression of another emotion (e.g., fear), the clinical approach sees the impetus for emotion regulation as deriving, at least at first, from outside the infant. Such a schema has obvious clinical implications since modifying the social and interpersonal context are seen as effective means of altering the infant's ability to control emotion expression.

Writing in 1931, Goodenough suggested that emotion expressions are expressed in their purest form in early infancy. As the infant becomes subject to social pressures and to learning experiences, it modifies its natural responses. Reflecting on the controversy regarding whether infant emotion expressions can be reliably described, Goodenough (1931) answers in the affirmative stating that infancy is the time to capture pure emotion expressions: "The optimum period for the study of emotional expression is to be found in early childhood before the original patterns of response have become too extensively overlaid by the habits resulting from social experience [p. 100]."

More recently, Escalona and Heider (1959), Murphy (1962) and Murphy and Moriarty (1976) have described an extensive research project with a clinical emphasis on individual differences in controlling emotion expressions. Drawing on extensive longitudinal observations, these investigators have studied the long-term effects of different coping styles. Individual differences in coping with emotion are seen as the product of innate equipment and environmental influences: "It does not take a great leap of the imagination to suggest that some children are like a closely woven textile that does not stretch or shrink much, while others are more elastic and react to the pushes and pulls, the storms and heat waves of life [Murphy & Moriarty, 1976, p. 168]."

Using the language of temperament theory, Thomas, Chess, and Birch (1968), Thomas and Chess (1977), and their associates also refer to the interplay of individual difference factors and environmental forces as determining the degree of the infant's emotion expression control. Different profiles of scores on primarily hereditary factors such as activity level, mood, adaptability, and withdrawal define the Easy, Difficult, and Slow-to-warm-up child. The interaction between these variables and maternal responses ("goodness of fit" between their temperaments) is significant in determining the individual infant's ability to modulate emotion responses.

While drawing on the analytically oriented writings of Spitz, Emde, in both his experimental and theoretical work (Emde, 1978; Emde *et al.*, 1976), emphasizes more clearly than his predecessors the adaptive role of emotions. Emde sees current psychoanalytic thinking as compatible with the concept of affects as constructive forces in development, playing a role in the conflict-free ego sphere as well as the conflict sphere. Expression control results not merely from outside social pressures but from the organizing, regulating force of emotions themselves. In 1978, Emde suggested that "There is now new need for delineating when it is that emotions are organizing and when they are disorganizing, not only for anxiety but also for a variety of discrete emotions, such as anger, fear, sadness, and joy [p. 22]." By extending the view of emotions as adaptive, Emde suggested that excesses of control of any of the discrete emotions may be another form of disorganization. The blunting of any emotion has as serious clinical implications as its excessive expression. Whereas the extreme control of emotions such as anger has long been considered maladaptive, Emde extended this concept to the exploration of the "psychological signal value" of each of the emotions. His view of affects as the medium for infant–caregiver interactions and, later, as internal psychological signals, deemphasizes the need for their control and focuses on their healthy expression:

> Furthermore, from the developmental considerations reviewed in this paper, it can be concluded that affects do not have to be "tamed." They do not become signals as a consequence of socialization. They are signals to begin with. In this, we must realize that "socialization" must be considered other than from a drive-reduction point of view; affects are active participants in developing social transactions rather than passive chaotic structures needing to be shaped [Emde, 1978, p. 32].

Emde's adaptive view of the role of emotions has much in common with the differential emotions perspective, discussed more fully in a subsequent section of this chapter.

## COGNITIVE APPROACHES:
## THE REGULATION OF SURPRISE

When emotions are seen as responses to cognitions, emotion regulation can be viewed as a process of modifying the content of the cognitions. Consciousness, in this view, is cognitively regulated, and emotion responses are results, rather than causes, of changes in awareness.

From the extensive literature on cognitive development, the present discussion will draw only two examples of its implications for emotion regulation. Charlesworth (1969) views surprise as the result of misexpectation and suggests that this emotion is a response to a cognitive event. According to this view, adequate memory facility for recognizing expected versus unexpected occurrences is necessary for the onset of surprise. Reasoning in this way, Charlesworth places the emergence of surprise at about 7 months. However, facial expression of surprise has been identified in 4-month old infants (Izard, Huebner, Risser, McGuinnes, & Dougherty, 1980).

Although Charlesworth has focused more on the onset of the surprise expression than on its control, it would follow from his theory that an expansion of the infant's realm of expectations would limit surprise expressions. Extensive acquaintance, for example, with a variety of masks of faces, should delimit expressions of surprise at the presentation of subsequent masks if the infant has become aware of an increased expectable array of facial features.

In his concept of "uncertainty," Kagan (1972) also emphasizes the role of cognitive expectations. *Uncertainty*, for Kagan, is an alerted affect state that gives rise to achievement, affiliation, and other derivatives. Although this approach preserves the primacy of cognitions in directing awareness, responses are seen as resulting from a cognition–emotion interaction. Although not explicitly expressed by Kagan, this view might be extended to suggest that control of emotion expressions such as surprise is achieved through increased schema for the familiar and possible.

## DIFFERENTIAL EMOTIONS THEORY: THE MOTIVATIONAL AND REGULATORY FUNCTIONS OF EMOTION EXPERIENCE

The differential emotions theory of the role of emotions (Izard, 1971, 1972, 1980) focuses on the unique motivational properties of each of the fundamental emotions of interest, joy, surprise, distress, anger, disgust, contempt, fear, shame–shyness, and guilt. Emotions are seen as the primary motivational system for human beings, with each discrete emotion having characteristic neural, expressive, and experiential components. Each emotion is seen as emerging as it becomes adaptive in the life of the infant and as having a role in the structuring of conscious experience, cognition, and action. Extensive discussions of the role of emotions in infant development may be found in two papers extending differential emotions theory to infant development (Izard, 1977, 1978). The present discussion will be limited to the implications of this theoretical perspective for understanding the regulation of emotion expressions.

In a general sense, as has been mentioned in the discussion of Emde's view, differential emotions theory suggests that the emphasis on emotion control should be tempered by the recognition that emotions are not a disruptive, maladaptive force to be tamed, but rather an organizing, mobilizing experience. It is most probable that certain emotions, such as shame (which enhances self-awareness), play an active role in emotion expression regulation. Thus, the emotion system itself motivates and, in interaction with other systems, provides the structure for emotion control.

Although much experimental work is needed to clarify the role of the emotions in regulating emotion expression, differential emotion theory suggests that interest, joy, shame, and guilt have central roles in this process. The theory postulates (Emde, 1978, p. 17) that, beginning around the age of 5 months, the emotion of interest–excitement plays a significant role in motivating sustained contacts with objects and persons. Caregivers have probably always used interest-elicitors informally to delimit rage and fear expressions in their infants. By expanding the infant's conscious awareness of its surround, interest alters the environment as it is sensed, perceived, and cognized. When combined with joy, interest motivates attachments to persons, objects, and the self. Awareness of self, of self-in-relation to others, and, eventually, of the effect of expressing or controlling emotion displays is based on the initial intrapersonal and interpersonal experiences motivated by interest and joy. Being cognizant of a variety of interest-eliciting stimuli widens the narrowed attentional focus or phenomenal field of the enraged or fearful infant. Interest, with joy, provides the motivation to regulate negative emotion expressions for the furtherance of positive relations to others and to the self. By allowing for the expansion of consciousness of response possibilities, interest also provides an important medium for emotion regulation.

Shame is another important motivational source for emotion expression regulation. Shame, which involves heightened self-awareness and the feeling of exposure (Izard, 1977), may motivate attempts to attain seemly, acceptable modulation of the expressions of emotions. In focusing consciousness on how the self appears, shame provides both the motivation and an element of the medium for control of emotion expression. Shame and its resultant self-awareness and self-reflection allow for intense experiencing of the relationship between what one "shows" to the world and how one is treated.

Guilt is central to establishing a sense of responsibility for one's actions, particularly actions that may hinder self or others. The effects of this emotion become readily observable in the second year of life. Guilt may be important in the development of empathy and prosocial behavior (Hoffman, 1978). It is capable of regulating emotion expressions or emotion-related actions that are conceived as violating connections or as unjust.

In addition to the important regulatory roles of the foregoing emotions, any of the other emotions can serve such a function. Surprise can interrupt severe distress. Anger can attenuate unbearable fear. In turn, anticipatory fear can regulate or inhibit the impulsive actions that tend to occur in anger or rage. The age at which each of the emotions assumes particular regulatory functions is an important area for future research.

In contrast to the approaches that view the emotions as responses to be controlled by cognitions or social forces, the differential emotions perspective focuses attention on their unique organizing, adaptive, regulatory roles. Emotions provide the motivation for self-control, awareness of the variety of the surround, consciousness of self-expression and its effect on others, and the structure for positive involvements that delimit negative emotion experiences.


## DEVELOPMENTAL, CLINICAL AND RESEARCH IMPLICATIONS OF DIFFERENTIAL EMOTIONS THEORY

Differential emotions theory suggests numerous developmental, clinical, and research applications for future study. In this discussion, several implications of the central tenets of the theory will be suggested, followed by brief mention of implications related to specific discrete emotions.

If each emotion has an adaptive function in development, an important task for research investigation is the charting of the normal course of the age of onset, peak expression, and initial regulation of each of the fundamental emotions. Only after such a schedule of normal emotion development is available can we begin investigation of the effects of irregularities or abnormalities in this pattern. If, for example, research findings suggest that normal infants generally begin to regulate their expression of fear during the second year of life, when we encounter a 3-year-old infant without this capacity we will have a basis from which to explore the causes and consequences of this individual difference.

Consideration of each emotion as having a separate, discernible expression suggests that the criteria for judging the presence of each emotion should differ. Current research on the infant's expression of stranger and separation responses, for example, often uses crying as evidence of fear, when it might be the case that the crying infant is expressing distress or anger. To date, facial expressions are the only reliable, measurable indicators that distinguish among the fundamental emotions. When our interest is in a particular emotion response (e.g., fear) rather than a global negative response, we should use the facial expression as the criterion for judging the presence of that emotion.

The socialization of each of the emotion expressions is a vast area for future clinical and research investigation. Among the questions to be explored are whether there are long-term effects of various methods of socialization of each emotion expression, whether parents typically respond to particular emotion expressions differently depending on the infant's age, sex, and other individual difference variables, and whether there are reliable differences in emotion socialization patterns among parents differing in sex, social class, and personality attributes. It would be important to explore, for example, the variables that affect parents' responses to their infants' expressions of anger. What are the infant and parent individual difference variables that affect their pattern of interaction when the infant is angry? What are the long-term consequences (if any) of a consistently negative or punitive parental response to infant anger expressions? Similarly, it would be of interest to study the variables affecting the socialization of each of the other fundamental emotions and the consequences for the infant of differing socialization patterns.

Differential emotions theory invites a reconsideration of several of the traditional diagnostic categories of psychopathology in childhood. For example, do autistic children differ from normal children in the range of their facial expressions with adults, or in the intensity of these expressions? Do they express the full range of anger, fear, and the other fundamental emotions with peers but not with parents? What are the effects of unusual infant emotion expression patterns on parents' emotion response? Emde, Katz, and Thorpe (1978) have found that the smile of the Down's syndrome infant is dampened in intensity and late in appearance. The positive, joyful, infant–caregiver interactions that are fostered by the infant's smile may be affected by this irregularity. Other infant and child abnormalities may be associated with unusual patterns of emotion expression that may affect the infant–caregiver bond and have consequences for perceptual, cognitive, personality, and social growth.

Differential emotions theory implies that we should look for major changes in perceptual, cognitive, and social behavior after the emergence of an emotion expression or, more specifically, after its emergence in response to a particular incentive event. This suggests a somewhat different emphasis from that of Emde *et al.* (1976), for example, who see new emotion expressions as signals that a major biobehavioral reorganization has occurred. Differential emotions theory holds that the new expression is more than a signal of a major biobehavioral shift; it is a major determinant of the change. Once the ontogeny of expression of each of the fundamental emotions is known, the next step will be a reexamination of perceptual, cognitive, and social growth in terms of their interrelationships with affective experience. As an example, the study of infant emotion expression ontogeny has implications for future examinations of Piaget's sequence of stages of cognitive growth. What cognitive learning experiences, for example, are newly available to the infant when it expresses anger? How do these experiences further cognitive attainments such as the understanding of self-as-causal agent, of space, time, and physical barriers. Does fear, once it emerges, heighten the infant's experience of the independent action of causal agents? Separated from the caregiver, does the fearful infant newly cognize the meaning of ''person permanence'' upon the caregiver's return? More generally, differential emotions theory implies that rather than search exclusively for cognitive prerequisites for emotion expressions (as has been attempted in the study of the relationship between object permanence and the stranger response), it is more fruitful to look for the cognitive attainments that follow the emergence of emotion expressions in response to particular incentive events.

The child's growing awareness and appreciation of the role of each of the fundamental emotions is another area for study. At what point in development do we become aware, for example, of the fact that we blush when embarrassed? At this point, do children become better decoders of emotion expression in others and in themselves? Are children (from infancy onward) better able to decode the parents' expressions than those of other adults? Are there significant individual differences in emotion expression decoding ability and are there social consequences of these differences?

The concept that emotions themselves furnish the motive and the medium for negative emotion regulation has important clinical and research implications. How do some children learn to use one emotion (e.g., interest) to regulate or inhibit another (e.g., fear)? Can others be taught to widen their conscious awareness of the possible positive emotion elicitors in their environs when fear threatens? Following Emde's (1978) concept of all emotions as having psychological signal functions, it might be possible to find therapeutic applications of the conscious use of these signals.

Finally, the theory has implications that are specifically related to the role of particular emotions in development. For example, whereas the search for longitudinal continuities in intellectual measurement has proven difficult, a study by Birns and Golden (1972) suggests a role that emotion expression analysis can play in this area. These investigators found that an index of pleasure or enjoyment in the tasks on the Cattell Infant Intelligence Scale at 18 months was significantly correlated with Binet I.Q. at 3 years. This suggests the possibility that the blend of interest and joy or sustained interest alternating with moments of joy is particularly important as a motivator for learning.

Each of the fundamental emotions provides an area for future clinical and experimental investigations. An emotion's normal course of expression in various contexts, its role in perceptual, cognitive, personality, and social growth, the variables that affect the process of its socialization, and the therapeutic implications of its use as a resource for coping require further research.

## REFERENCES

Birns, B., & Golden, M. Prediction of intellectual performance at three years from infant test and personality measures. *Merrill-Palmer Quarterly*, 1972, *18*, 53–58.
Bridges, K. M. B. Emotional development in early infancy. *Child Development*, 1932, *3*, 324–341.

Bronson, G. Infant's reactions to unfamiliar persons and novel objects. *Monographs of the Society for Research in Child Development*, 1972, *37*(3).

Campos, J. J., Emde, R. N., Gaensbauer, T., & Henderson, C. Cardiac and behavioral interrelationships in the reactions of infants to strangers. *Developmental Psychology*, 1975, *11*(5), 589–601.

Charlesworth, W. R. The role of surprise in cognitive development. In D. Elkind & J. Flavell (Eds.), *Studies in cognitive development*. London and New York: Oxford Univ. Press, 1969.

Emde, R. N. *Towards a psychoanalytic theory of affect* (Parts I and II.) Unpublished manuscript, 1978.

Emde, R. N., Gaensbauer, T., & Harmon, R. J. *Emotional expression in infancy: A biobehavioral study*. New York: International Universities Press, 1976.

Emde, R. N., Katz, E. L. & Thorpe, J. K. Emotional expression in infancy: II. Early deviations in Down's syndrome. In M. Lewis & L. A. Rosenblum (eds.), *The development of affect*. New York, Plenum Press, 1978.

Escalona, S. K., & Heider, G. M. *Prediction and outcome: A study in child development*. New York: Basic Books, 1959.

Gaensbauer, T., Emder, R. N., & Campos, J. J. "Stranger" distress: Confirmation of a developmental shift in a longitudinal sample. *Perceptual and Motor Skills*, 1976, *43*, 99–106.

Goodenough, F. L. The expression of the emotions in infancy. *Child Development*, 1931, *2*, 96–101.

Hoffman, M. L. The arousal and development of empathy. In M. Lewis & L. Rosenblum (Eds.), *The development of affect*. New York: Plenum, 1978.

Izard, C. E. *The face of emotion*. New York: Appleton-Century-Croft, 1971.

Izard, C. E. *Patterns of emotions: A new analysis of anxiety and depression*. New York: Academic Press, 1972.

Izard, C. E. *Human emotions*. New York: Plenum, 1977.

Izard, C. E. On the development of emotions and emotion–cognition relationships in infancy. In M. Lewis & L. Rosenblum (Eds.), *The development of affect*. New York: Plenum, 1978.

Izard, C. E. The emergence of emotions and the development of consciousness in infancy. In J. M. Davidson & R. J. Davidson, (Eds.), *The psychobiology of consciousness*. New York: Plenum, 1980.

Izard, C. E., Huebner, R., Risser, D., McGuinnes, G., & Dougherty, L. The young infant's ability to produce discrete emotion expression. *Developmental Psychology*, 1980, *16*(2), 132–140.

Kagan, J. Motives and development. *Journal of Personality and Social Psychology*, 1972, *22*, 51–66.

Lewis, M., & Brooks, J. Self knowledge and emotional development. In M. Lewis & L. Rosenblum (Eds.), *The development of affect*. New York: Plenum, 1978.

Mahler, M. S., Pine, F., & Bergman, A. *The psychological birth of the human infant*. New York: Basic Books, 1975.

Mandler, G. *Mind and emotion*. New York: Wiley, 1975.

Marquis, D. A study of frustration in newborn infants. *Journal of Experimental Psychology*, 1943, *32*, 123–138.

Murphy, L. *The widening world of childhood*. New York: Basic Books, 1962.

Murphy, L., & Moriarty, A. *Vulnerability, coping, and growth*. New Haven, Connecticut: Yale Univ. Press, 1976.

Parisi, S., & Izard, C. E. *Five-, seven-, and nine-month-old infants' facial responses to twenty stimulus situations*. Unpublished manuscript, 1977.

Piaget, J. *The origins of intelligence in children*, (2nd ed.). New York: International Universities Press, 1952. (Originally published, 1936)

Rheingold, H., & Eckerman, C. O. Fear of the stranger: A critical examination. In H. W. Reese (Ed.), *Advances in child development and behavior*. New York: Academic Press, 1974.

Scarr, S., & Salapatek, P. Patterns of fear development during infancy. *Merrill-Palmer Quarterly,* 1970, *16,* 53–90.

Schaffer, H. R. The onset of fear of strangers and the incongruity hypothesis. *Journal of Child Psychology and Psychiatry,* 1966, *7,* 95–106.

Segal, H. *Introduction to the work of Melanie Klein*. London: Heinemann, 1964.

Spitz, R. A. *The first year of life*. New York: International Universities Press, 1965.

Sroufe, L. A. *Emotional expression in infancy*. Unpublished manuscript, 1976.

Stephan, K. Aggression in early childhood. *British Journal of Medical Psychology,* 1941, *18,* 178–191.

Storr, A. *Human aggression*. New York: Atheneum, 1968.

Tennes, K., & Lampl, E. Stranger and separation anxiety in infancy. *Journal of Nervous and Mental Disorders,* 1964, *139,* 247–254.

Thomas, A., & Chess, S. *Temperament and development*. New York: Bruner/Mazel, 1977.

Thomas, A., Chess, S., & Birch, H. G. *Temperament and behavior disorders in children*. New York: New York Univ. Press, 1968.

Thompson, C. *Interpersonal psychoanalysis*. New York: Basic Books, 1964.

Winnicott, D. W. Aggression in relation to emotional development. In *Collected papers of D. W. Winnicott*. London: Tavistock, 1958.

Wolff, P. H. The natural history of crying and other vocalizations in early infancy. In B. M. Foss (Ed.), *Determinants of infant behavior* (Vol. 4). London: Methuen, 1969.

Chapter 11

# AN EPIGENETIC THEORY OF EMOTIONS IN EARLY DEVELOPMENT

HENRY KELLERMAN

## ABSTRACT

The nature of emotion is considered as an epigenetic phenomenon containing a structure with a deep substrate. This epigenetic formulation proposes a system of dispositional elements that exists at birth and is contained within the program of emotion. A network of the relationships of this emotion program is presented along with a discussion of the interaction between the epigenetic framework and object relations experience. The dispositional network of elements within emotion that is considered includes traits, defenses, intrapsychic components, and diagnostic and cognitive properties. It is proposed that the elements of this network appear in discrete form during various stages of infancy. The theoretical analysis of the structure of this network of dispositions is considered in a psychosexual developmental context and within a psychoanalytic framework. A first approximation linking basic emotions with corresponding cognitive orientations is also presented.

## EMOTIONS AS UNLEARNED—
## AN EPIGENETIC VIEW

Several researchers have proposed that affects, or emotional patterns, exist at birth. These authors provide precursor models for the epigenetic view of affect

EMOTION
Theory, Research, and Experience
Volume 2

structure. For example, Bowlby (1969), in his landmark work on attachment and loss, states that all newborns show unlearned patterns. This point is not new, of course, and was first referred to in the psychoanalytic literature by Freud (1905/1961, 1908/1959, 1931/1961) in the analysis of libidinal types and character. In addition, Rapaport and Gill (1959) accept epigenetic formulations and recognize the importance of innate phenomena that comprise the basis of other psychological systems. Kernberg (1976) also considers affect dispositions, in essence, to comprise the subject's primary motivational system. Watson (1929) postulated basic protective and attack mechanisms that are unlearned and, in addition, identified so-called unlearned affect patterns of fear, rage, and love. Emde, Gaensbauer, and Harmon (1976) have suggested the adaptive role of emotions and have proposed that affects are primary signals. Izard (1978) also shares this position.

## CRITICAL PERIODS

Many of the formulations proposing the appearance of emotion in discrete form as well as those that identify the appearance of patterns of emotion create a rationale for a *critical period* theory. Emde *et al.* (1976) for example, propose that the emotion of anger appears in the second half of the first year of life. It may also be proposed that the natural appearance of certain emotions during critical periods, that is, periods when these emotions normally emerge, can either be facilitated or complicated by interpersonal conditions existing at those times. These emotions can emerge in a normal form or they may appear in a distorted form. It is proposed here that interpersonal conditions can determine this difference.

Other illustrations of specific emotions occuring in discrete form during normative developmental periods include Bell and Ainsworth's (1972) identification of stranger distress at 5 months and of the appearance of a fear system at 7–9 months, Emde *et al.* (1976) have identified smiling responses in the first few weeks of life, and Tennes and Lampl (1964) identified separation distress at 4 or 5 months. Izard (1978) has also identified the five emotions of distress, pleasure, startle, interest, and disgust in the neonate. These emotions exist at this initial stage presumably as part of the subject's preparedness and repertoire for relating. It is proposed that such a repertoire contains the emotional ingredients for the development of a social program.

When caregiver behavior is responsive during critical initial stages, then these initial emotion patterns in the neonate remain relatively uncontaminated. The epigenetic program in the subject then is embedded in an object-related social context. This social context can determine the relatively normal expression of emotional responses in the subject. Thus, in the epigenetic formulation, both

Freudian instinct theory and object-relations development theory are based on the proposition that critical periods are defined more saliently when epigenetic elements of the subject are considered along with corresponding social responses of the environment. Finally, Plutchik (1980a) encapsulates the epigenetic issues of normative appearance of emotion, the appearance of emotion in discrete form, and the importance of critical periods in a discussion of the data on stranger distress and laughter. Plutchik states that the data on stranger distress suggests the presence of a genetic variable and that this phenomenon will appear during critical times of maturation.

## THE SUBSTRATE OF EMOTION

An epigenetic view of emotion was also formulated by McDougall (1921) in an early classic text in social psychology. McDougall, who was interested in the theoretical formulation of biologically determined instincts, indicated that emotion refers to dispositions that are etched in the substrate of instinctive behavior. Scott (1958) and Plutchik (1980a) also relate basic emotions to prototype categories of behavior within an evolutionary framework. Although it is not entirely congruent with the system proposed by McDougall, in all cases, a biologically given program involving the emotions is nevertheless proposed. In a similar vein, Kaywin (1960) proposed an epigenetic approach to a psychoanalytic theory of instincts and affects and hypothesized that the mental system is in part derived from biological organization. Accordingly, the mental system has potentials that, to whatever extent they can be realized, depend on the interaction between individual potentials and environmental conditions. This epigenetic view is also discussed by Needles (1964) in a theoretical study of the role of biological factors on the experience of pleasure and unpleasure.

The relation between epigenetic and developmental considerations is suggested by Kellerman (1980), who states that "genetically coded dispositions may be understood as epigenetic or biologically given phenomena, whereas development viewed in a psychoanalytic context is considered to be adaptational [p. 350]." Furthermore, Kellerman indicates that the vicissitudes of psychosexual development become superimposed on existing basic emotion and personality structure, in part, joining biological and interpersonal phenomena and ultimately revealing an epigenetic framework. Kellerman also presents an analysis of the relationship between emotions and personality and cites a series of studies to suggest that the structure of emotion is at the core of the personality.

The interaction between psychosexual developmental experience and existing dispositions of the personality can facilitate the expression of certain aspects of the epigenetic emotion program such as the appearance of discrete emotions that then are called forth during appropriate normative and critical periods. In this respect, it also may be proposed that what becomes differentiated over time and as a function of development is not simply the appearance of specific emotion; rather, it may be the intensity dimension of emotions that is affected most by environmental experience. For example, it is not that fear and sorrow are differentiated; rather, fear and its higher-intensity state of terror or lower intensity state of apprehension become differentiated. Similarly, it is not that anger and disgust are differentiated; rather, anger and its higher-intensity state of rage or lower intensity state of annoyance become distinguished. Differentiation, then, may refer to the discrimination of shades of any single, basic emotion. The emotion system as an epigenetic formulation is viewed as a system of a few basic emotions that become expressed in discrete form during normative or critical periods. Interpersonal experiences, then, generate differentiation *within* each of these basic emotions.

## THE DEEP STRUCTURE OF EMOTION

In the substrate of emotion, the code for personality is etched in dispositional tendencies. These dispositions may include key elements of personality formation such as diagnostic tendencies, defenses, and even intrapsychic properties such as id or superego inclinations (Kellerman, 1979, 1980). In this proposal, it is implied that the predispositional personality program becomes salient during suitable developmental periods. These are the critical periods; they provide a bridge between the epigenetic appearance of emotion and the adaptational requirements of psychosexual developmental experiences. These psychosexual developmental experiences exist within the context of object relations contact. This means that aspects of the emotion structure become reinforced and more highly differentiated during normative periods of development. These aspects of the emotion structure are elements of diagnostic disposition, intrapsychic nature, and defensive orientation. One important implication of this theory is that object relations development, as it is related to psychosexual adaptation, is linked to the intrapsychic apparatus engraved in the substrate of emotion structure. Thus, it is proposed that an implicit correspondence occurs between the epigenetic system and environmental conditions. This correspondence between the epigenetic emotion system and interpersonal events can also be examined through a theoretical analysis of the relation of emotion and language.

## EMOTION AND LANGUAGE

In a sense, infant babbling can be viewed as a pre-language of emotion; that is, babbling is a vocal medium for the expression of feelings. It is proposed that babbling is an early example of the relation between emotion and cognition. For example, one implication of this proposition would be that concept formation exists at first as affective tonal representation. This idea is an oblique reference to the proposition that cognition is derived from uncrystalized affect; that is, thought is the consolidation in language of a feeling, mood, or cluster of emotions.

Lacan (1968) states that phonemes, the smallest distinguishable unit of sounds, are the elementary particles of language. In a qualification to the Lacanian position, it has been proposed that indeed the elementary particles of language are phonemes—but, phonemes with valency (Kellerman, 1977, 1979). Phonemes are not merely random sounds. Along with the component of intonation (or valency) they reflect some meaning—the meaning of the affect. The intonation or inflection of the phoneme is an early indication that the individual is a communicating organism equipped with an epigenetic program, part of which is ultimately expressed in language. This program awaits its developmental salience and is quite dependent on the interaction of maturation and object-relations experience.

Infant babbling, for example, generally contains intonational nuances. Intonation or inflection is the emotion of the phoneme. Since the expression of emotion can deliver connotative meaning, then pre-language babbling prior to the full experience of object relations development (when the infant can deliver messages or signals through facial expressions, posture, and the inflection of the babble) may be the root of the intersection between the epigenetic emotion program and the rational aspect of the interpersonal contact.

The question becomes one of locating the point at which the child is "born into language" (Lacan, 1968). This is an interesting question because it addresses the issue of the role of emotion during both pre-language periods and language acquisition periods. Lacan states that the moment at which desire enters human experience is also the moment at which the child is born into language. Yet this proposition of Lacan's seems somewhat circumscribed within the epigenetic emotion context described here. First, the difference between pre-language babbling periods and actual language acquisition is a developmental matter depending in part on object experiences; second, there is probably no specific time when object experiences become palpable. These experiences are present and essential at birth. An alternate proposition concerning the point at which the child is "born into language" would be to postulate that the moment in which emotion takes an object is the true moment in which the child is born into language. Thus, if the tacit assumption is accepted that emotion becomes associated with objects at birth—albeit at first, as an amorphous association—then it seems that emotion is first associated with pre-language or what is here proposed as babbling periods. Accordingly, pre-language is fundamentally tied to the structure of emotion, and by implication language is tied to the structure of emotion. The issue is not when is the child born into language. Rather, it is simply that because the emotion program exists at birth, the axiom is suggested that the child *is* born into language.

Poor object experiences will necessarily interfere with critical period requirements in the appearance of emotion, and hence language development under such conditions is likely to be adversly affected. In fact, there is clinical literature to demonstrate the correlation between impairment of language and emotional disturbance and interpersonal maladjustment (Chess, 1966; Kanner, 1949). Because of the proposed correlation that ties language to emotion, it follows that since the individual is born with the capacity to potentially experience and express a full range of basic emotions, then the capacity for language, in the pre-language babbling period, also exists at birth.

Since all emotion is presumably connected to objects, then the structure of emotion may also contain rudimentary interpersonal inclinations. This implication suggests that the infant is born with interpersonal proclivities etched in the fiber of emotion structure and hypothetically ultimately expressed through emotion–personality dispositions and moods.

The epigenetic program of emotion structure therefore provides a bridge (through intonational pre-language) to interpersonal object experience. As referred to earlier, the emotion–object relationship may be a bridge to cognition; that is, knowing is inherent in feeling. Such a relation reflects the connection of the intrapersonal with the interpersonal. Kagan (1979) states that interactions between child and adult are embedded in a given context of understanding based upon past interactions. Such past experiences may even exist implicitly in virtual state as part of the epigenetic emotion program; that is, the program awaits critical periods and depends on maturation for its eventual expression. The operation of emotion in developing or accumulating its repertoire of objects roughly parallels what Lacan calls the developmental movement of "other to 'I'." It is a developmental movement reflecting the emergence of ego and corresponds to the interaction between the critical periods of emotional expression and the development of objects.


## EMOTION AND
## OBJECT RELATIONS DEVELOPMENT

The expression of emotion and its relationship to the development of a repertoire of objects is also referred to by Yarrow (1979), who states that most emotions have social concomitants. They are directly or indirectly associated with people. A corollary proposition would be that a greater differentiation of emotion in an individual corresponds to an increase in a repertoire of healthy objects. In essence, the one consistent underlying object in the individual's overall repertoire of objects is the primary object–caregiver. The consistent and normal care given by the primary object (as the foundation of all other object relations) may produce a clear opportunity for the infant to develop the healthy expression of emotions in their discrete form as well as the differentiation of emotion in terms of the varied intensities of each emotion. The implicit equation between objects and emotions seems to be that stability in the development and differentiation of others (objects) corresponds to a more stable expression of the entire spectrum of emotions.

The epigenetic view held here is basically Freudian. An analysis of this view is provided by Klein and Tribich (1981), who review and contrast the Freudian view with the object relations position regarding issues of internalization, primary objects, and primacy of innate states versus environmental conditions. According to Freud (1915/1957) "the object of an instinct is the thing in regard to which or through which the instinct is able to achieve its aim. It is what is most variable about an instinct and is not originally connected with it, but becomes assigned to it only in consequence of being peculiarly fitted to make satisfaction possible [p. 122]." Klein and Tribich further reveal the biological allusions of object relation theorists and how these views are fundamentally different from the Freudian one. These authors point out that the presence of the human object is unconditionally necessary within the object relations literature. "In Bowlby's (1969) terms the object relation is analyzed through *attachment;* in Balint's (1952) view the nature of the object is seen in terms of *primary love;* in Fairbairn's (1952) view the intrinsic object relation is based on *object-seeking;* in Winnicott's (1965) orientation, object relatedness is *ego-relatedness;* in Guntrip's (1961) view it is understood as *personal relations;* and in Suttie's (1935) approach the object relation is discussed in terms of *love* [p. 30]."

Thus, Klein and Tribich (1981) state, "For Freud the person was driven to release something from within. Non-Freduian object-relations theorists have as their motivational concept the requirement of a human object. For them the person has no need to release, rather only to attach himself to another person [p. 30]." The fact that emotions take objects is now revealed as a proposition bridging the Freudian position (the individual needs to release emotion) and encapsulating an epigenetic biological–interpersonal interaction; that is, the individual then seeks to get emotions attached. The epigenetic theory seems to better integrate Freudian instinct theory with object relations considerations because within the epigenetic framework the object is not solely necessary in the expression of motivation, drive, or affect of the subject. The presence of objects simply increases the possibility that the epigenetic program will be expressed to its fullest. According to Klein and Tribich, this is an important point because it shows that within the epigenetic framework the drive concept is retained. Emotion will be released or expressed whether or not a human subject is present. Emotional expression, however, will develop normally when the object is present and responds appropriately to the subject.

The variables involved in defining specifically the nature of the primary human object will be considered in the following section as a prelude to the discussion of patterns of attachement.

## OBJECT RELATION VARIABLES

The behavioral properties involved in the attachment process—those of object development—include elements such as object constancy, degree of object lability, or consistency in object behavior. The object may be evaluated along these dimensions. The infant develops particular response patterns based on certain biological imperatives (here referred to as *epigenetic dispositions*) that can be facilitated in their expression by relatively unencumbered object relations development. Similarly, because of problematic object development due to inconsistency of caregiver response, inconstancy of caregiver presence, or unpredictability of caregiver attitude, emotional expression in the infant can become distorted and misshapen.

In this view the infant develops by identifying basic personality patterns, moods, or attitudes of the caregiver. Thus, the attachment relationship may be largely based on the identification of personality style of the caregiver. Emotion, as Sroufe (1979) indicates, resonates with the object and thus contains an implicit sense of the object relationship. Because the infant is able to identify and understand the object through the constancy, consistency, and relative degree of lability of the object, the infant's emotional response can encapsulate or offer a validating reciprocal meaning to the interaction with the object—to seal the exchange, as it were. In this sense, the infant is identifying the personality, mood, and attitude of the object. The infant's emotional response can be an organizer or encapsulation of the interaction within the object relation and can help facilitate whatever reorganization is needed in subject–object relations. What this means is that a discrete basic emotion and difference in intensity of that emotion both gain meaning from the object interaction as well as help to shape the behavior of the object.

The kinds of attachments described in the psychological research of "subjects" and "objects" reveal that only a few basic patterns are reported. In the following section, the few patterns of attachment appearing in the literature and characterizing most object relations are reviewed. The development of these patterns of attachment both depend on the interface of subject–object emotionality and affect this emotionality.

## PATTERNS OF ATTACHMENT

Ainsworth, Blehar, Waters, and Wall (1978) have identified three patterns of attachment at 6 weeks of life. One pattern is reflected in relatively secure behavior that seems to imply a sense of independence and contentment. Another pattern seems clearly to reflect a sense of avoidance of the caregiver (a negative pattern of attachment), whereas a third pattern seems to be described by a cluster of responses including poverty of exploration, dissatisfaction, and squirming behavior. A similar three-part possibility in identifying emotional style in early development appears in a study of the childhood origins of psychopathology (Schwarz, 1979). In this study, the subject's emotional pattern is theorized to result from the caregiver's overall attitude toward the child. Here again, three basic styles of emotionality may emerge. First, a cooperative contentment pattern can appear. Second, a fearful avoidance pattern can be seen, and third, antagonstic or agitated behavior may appear. This particular system relies heavily on object relations theory and interpersonal considerations to clarify and understand the pattern of emotionality in the infant. Schwarz conceives of a tree of personality. As one develops higher in the tree, one becomes more committed to either of the three basic patterns; that is, to be out on a limb in the sense of developing any one of these basic patterns. The pattern of cooperativeness that is based on a typically appropriate response from the caretaker assures the position of the center of the tree. If the caretaker consistently frustrates the child, then the subject's emotional repertoire becomes organized around a basic pattern of anger—the agitated pattern. When the caretaker mismanages the child's separation experience and his or her response to novel situations, then the subject's emotional pattern becomes organized around the response of fearfulness—the fearful avoidance pattern. It is only when the caregiver is positively responsive to the child that the subject's emotional pattern reflects contentment.

A further theoretical point of view in this system of patterns of attachment concerns a basic belief in the child's ability to transform one pattern for another, largely based on consistent changes in the caretaker's overall relatedness. A focus on the interpenetration or reciprocal interaction between the nature of infant and caretaker typical responses is also cited in Stern, Caldwell, Hersher, Lipton, and Richmond, (1969), in which mother–infant dyads are studied.

Stern et al. attribute the shaping of emotional responses in the infant and child to their specific interactions with the caregiver and imply that the influence of envronmental conditions determines differentiation and the nature of emotional expression. These studies identify only a few basic patterns of emotional style, or trait style, and such styles are labeled with similar and even overlapping definitions. Basic styles of emotionality include a contentment style, an assertiveness or aggressiveness style (or even perhaps a pathological variation such as an agitated style), and a style of emotional response that is characterized as avoidant or fearful. It is interesting to note that these basic styles or patterns of emotional response are even reported in certain animal groups. For example, Kellerman (1966), in a study of the emotional behavior of dolphins, identified two basic styles of emotion. These were labeled *pleasure* and *fear*. In a study comparing baboon with human groups (Kellerman, Buirski, & Plutchik, 1974), a basic homeostatic group mechanism was identified, composed of three primary emotion response patterns that, when in effect, seemed to balance the group. These patterns were labeled *assertion, caution,* and *aggreeableness*.

Thus, in a variety of settings of infant–caregiver interactions, studies of attachment patterns, animal studies, and even in the study of group effects on individuals, commonalities emerge with respect to the appearance of what perhaps can be considered basic infrastructural emotion patterns that can be called forth or reinforced by environmental conditions. Because of the seeming universality of these patterns, the proposition is advanced regarding the relationship between object experience and emotional expression. This proposition does not, in fact, minimize the role of object relations on the shaping of emotional expression; rather it places this role in an epigenetic framework. This proposition holds that the appearance of emotions in early development must inexorably be viewed in terms of its social context, but certain imperatives with respect to an already existing dispositional program (including the preparedness for discrete emotions to appear) must also be considered.

One issue emerging from these studies is to understand how the three emotion patterns of contentment, anger, and fear relate to the expression of all other basic emotions. It is proposed here that these three patterns are essentially behavioral patterns and reflect clusters of emotion that, in aggregate, chatacterize each pattern. For example, the pattern of contentment consists of the emotions of acceptance, pleasure, joy, tranquility, and perhaps even hopeful expectation. The pattern of fear consists of emotions of avoidance, apprehension, rejection, and perhaps elements such as alarm reactions. The third pattern of anger consists of emotions such as rage, agitation, irritibility, aggressiveness, disgust, and perhaps elements such as sorrow or deprivation.

There are vicissitudes of such an epigenetic program that are not well understood and that are affected by maturational considerations. For example, Ames (1963), in a paper on a developmental approach to the child's emotions, indicates that there are periods when the emotional demeanor of the individual is considerably well integrated, and that these periods or ages of the individual appear to alternate with those in which emotional demeanor is poorly organized. This could suggest that at birth patterns of emotion may be poorly organized and perhaps may become better organized in response to object development. That the infant cannot express the full range of emotion at birth does not in any way eliminate the possibility of the existence of an epigenetic emotion program. Such a program may simply await necessary object experiences in order to become organized. It awaits object development, not emotion development; that is, that all emotions take objects, and without objects there can be no healthy or normal emotion organization. What the object does however, is to facilitate the aim of the subject's emotion. For example, in a reasonably healthy object experience, the infant's expression of distress or pleasure achieves an appropriate response from the caregiver, thereby reinforcing the social context in which the emotion is being expressed. In essence the object experience then lends meaning and logic to such emotional expression.

The richness of this proposed epigenetic program with respect to its implications for personality and adaptation will be discussed in the following section on psychoanalytic and epigenetic interactions. It is a theoretical examination of the deeper structure of emotion.

## THE DEEPER STRUCTURE OF EMOTION

In the previous sections of this chapter it has been proposed that an epigenetic program of emotion exists and that this program contains a deep structure. This structure is one in which certain dispositions of personality are etched in the emotion substrate. When normal or adaptive object development occurs, then the expression of this program is facilitated. Implied in this conception is the consideration that even when the entire emotion program is somehow imperfect, healthy object experiences can perhaps minimize more problematic dispositional parts of the program. For example, an epigenetic dispositional inclination toward withdrawal or depression can be minimized by healthy object experiences and, subsequently, other, less prominant, etchings of that particular emotion program, such as needs for contact, may be emphasized and maximized. Hence the epigenetic emotion program seems to be inextricably tied to conditions of the environment or to the development of object relations. This reciprocal phenomenon between the emotion program and the experience of particular object development is also conceived as one that contributes to the differentiation of emotion intensity; that is, object experience aids in the ultimate sharpening of differences along a specific emotion dimension rather than among basic emotions. Object development therefore (as discussed earlier) helps an individual to be able to easily distinguish between apprehension and fear, but is less likely, for example, to contribute to the distinction between fear and disgust. Those basic emotions of fear and disgust appear in discrete form during normative developmental periods and, in part, as a function of maturation.

In this section, a further examination of the deep structure of emotion is undertaken, with special emphasis on the presentation of a theoretical framework proposing intrapsychic and psychosexual properties inherent in the epigenetic emotion structure. This formulation is also examined in Kellerman (1979, 1980).

## INTRAPSYCHIC ENCODINGS
## WITHIN EMOTION STRUCTURE

Kellerman (1979, 1980) has suggested that the ego is an intrapsychic form solely dependent on object development for its fundamental nature, whereas id and superego exist as part of the epigenetic emotion program. Kellerman has proposed that id and superego inclinations are etched in the substrate of emotion and are responsible for the psychological quality of basic emotions. As these basic emotions with inherent id or superego inclinations begin to become expressed within the framework of object relations experiences, this infusion of intrapsychic forces with environmental experience generates the new mediating, form of ego—an accultured form. Hence *ego* becomes defined as the acculturation of intrapsychic forces. The ego represents a bridge between the intrapersonal and interpersonal. Even in infants and nonhuman primates, in the absence of any significant ego development, a wide range of emotions are expressed. Thus, the expression of emotion does not require the presence of ego. Rather, the nature of ego is determined in large measure by the nature of emotional development.

Accordingly, an emotion may be either an id emotion or a superego one. Since it is proposed that id and superego predispositional forces are encoded within emotion structure, then it is also assumed that each emotion contains mood imperatives derived either from an id or superego influence (the psychological quality of emotion). For example, if the emotion of disgust were to be identified as a superego emotion, then the overall quality of this emotion can be characterized as one with a superego mood—that is, the mood implies a superego sense that something is wrong or bad or harmful or dangerous.

Social traits that permit greater access to pleasure experiences may reflect id derivative formations, whereas negative temperament characteristics such as depression may reflect superego derivatives. The id emotions are emotions such as joy, anger, and acceptance, whereas superego emotions are emotions such as sorrow, disgust, and fear. Expression of the basic id emotions correlates with the possibility of experiencing pleasure. This is also true in the expression of anger. Expression of the basic superego emotions correlates with the possibility of experiencing pain. It is proposed that in the beginning—that is, at birth—id emotions are represented by a focus on the pursuit of pleasure and the relief from pain or discomfort. Superego emotions are correspondingly represented chiefly by crying. Although many researchers identify the appearance of infant anger or temper at 3–5 months, it may be reasonable to speculate that initial crying at birth represents both superego and id expressions insofar as the crying reflects superego elements of distress in the absence of gratification and, simultaneously, can be the vehicle for id release of anger and dissatisfaction. The relation between basic emotion states and their particular intrapsychic id or superego designation is examined by Kellerman (1979, 1980) with respect to defense organization as well as through an analysis of a theory of the structure of nightmares.

The issue of an existing id–superego aspect of emotion that is rooted in biology is an epigenetic one. The issue of differentiation of ego is one based on developmental vicissitudes and object relation experiences. The idea of an intrapsychic apparatus existing at birth was also postulated by Melanie Klein (1955). The present proposal linking intrapsychic id–superego structure to emotion is a new theoretical idea and perhaps may reveal further insights regarding the connections of various emotion–personality domains. Many other researchers have also suggested that both structural and intrapsychic—as well as psychosexual formulations—need modification in light of newer-theoretical and clinical understanding (Blum, 1953; Brenner, 1975; Klein, 1948).

How psychosexual imperatives based on object development experiences may be linked with intrapsychic engraved underpinnings of emotion is suggested by the proposition that intrapsychic forces of id and superego are not just forces with valence that need expression but in an environmental object relations context are also revealed as forces with aims. In the following section the relation of psychosexual development to the epigenetic emotion program will be proposed. It is a discussion of the interpenetration of epigenetic emotion properties with psychoanalytic adaptational considerations.

## PSYCHOSEXUAL RESOLUTION, DEFENSES, AND INTRAPSYCHIC AIMS

The extent to which object relations are successfully developed is, in part, dependent on the nature of psychosexual conflict and its ultimate balance. In turn, psychosexual conflict becomes balanced on the basis of the extent to which the intrapsychic aim—that is, the aim of id or superego—of each basic emotion is achieved during particular psychosexual time periods.

The ego as the only intrapsychic state to develop adaptationally is an example of how intrapersonal and interpersonal mechanisms become linked within a single person–environment system. It is proposed that the ego emerges through the accumulation of both achieved and frustrated id–superego aims during psychosexual periods. Since defense mechanisms are also involved in the extent to which id and superego aims become gratified, then ego formations should contain information regarding the operation of particular defense mechanisms. In this respect, defenses are here distinguished specifically as those that are etched in the structure of emotion on the one hand, and those that may be considered part of ego on the other. In the epigenetic system presented here, a modification is proposed with respect to the conventional acceptance of typical defenses such as denial, reaction formation, and projection as ego defenses. These defenses are now considered to be emotion defenses (Kellerman, 1979, 1980). The ego defenses are best described as identification mechanisms—those that depend on acculturation experiences and object relations development. These include internalization, identification, splitting, introjection, and perhaps isolation (Kellerman, 1980). Since it is proposed that certain defenses are part of the epigenetic emotion system and since id–superego forces are also assumed to be part of this system, it is further proposed that id–superego forces within basic emotion are also associated with defense propensities.

A possible major function of emotion defense may be to regulate the id and superego properties of respective basic emotions. Rado (1956) also suggests that emotions and defenses are intimately linked. The system of basic emotions, their intrapsychic id–superego properties and defensive purpose, are given in Table 11.1. The theoretical connections portrayed in Table 11.1 represent parts of a personality theory developed by Kellerman (1979, 1980) that is based on the psychoevolutionary theory of emotion formulated by Plutchik (1962, 1980a,b).

What is conventionally considered differentiation of emotion is in the present theory considered differentiation of personality. This means that in the gradually evolving organization of personality, the individual becomes identified in behavior in terms of sequences of traits that are considered typical for that person. These are trait clusters that reflect a proliferation of traits or a differentiation of traits. Yet, according to the theory outlined by Plutchik and Kellerman (1974) the composition of these traits are all based on a system of a few primary emotions. Correspondingly, the issue of what is discrete and what is differentiated in the personality is here divided between basic emotions consisting, in part,

TABLE 11.1
The Relation of Defensive Purpose to Emotion and Intrapsychic Properties

| Basic emotion | Emotion defense | Intrapsychic element | Defensive purpose |
|---|---|---|---|
| Acceptance | Denial | Id | To block impulse |
| Disgust | Projection | Superego | To release impulse |
| Joy | Reaction formation | Id | To block impulse |
| Sorrow | Compensation | Superego | To release impulse |
| Expectation | Intellectualization | Id | To block impulse |
| Surprise | Regression | Superego | To release impulse |
| Anger | Displacement | Id | To block impulse |
| Fear | Repression | Superego | To release impulse |

of inherent id–superego properties and defense elements on the one hand, and a differentiation process of personality traits associated with the development of the ego and containing identification defenses to manage or regulate the system of traits on the other.

It is proposed here that the differentiation process in personality (that is, differentiation of traits or character structure) occurs through the resolution of conflict during the unfolding of psychosexual stages. This differentiation of trait or character structure essentially refers to ego development within the context of object relations. A similar idea is proposed by Kaywin (1960), who implies that the differentiation process occurs through psychosexual development but that the intrapsychic apparatus—specifically the id and superego—are engraved in the substrate of emotion structure.

Since the id–superego components of the intrapsychic apparatus are proposed to exist at birth, then object relations experiences within the context of psychosexual developmental stages do not create or generate such intrapsychic force. Rather, object relations experiences perhaps act either to minimize or maximize the effects of these id–superego forces. These intrapsychic forces become expressed as a function of working through of object relations problems during salient psychosexual stages. The vicissitudes of psychosexual developmental experiences become superimposed on existing basic emotion—personality structure, in part, lending meaning to the psychosexual developmental experience. For example, it may be expected that id or superego emotions help make logical those events that evoke them during salient developmental periods. This process perhaps further contributes to either the minimizing or maximizing of id and superego intrapsychic expression. In a sense, early and ongoing parental identifications and introjections, the basic nature of object relations, interact with existing id–superego forces and incorporate these forces as part of the system of internalizations.

## DEFENSES AND INTRAPSYCHIC EXPRESSION

In a theory of nightmares (Kellerman, 1979, 1980), basic emotions and their elemental intrapsychic properties were examined. Table 11.1 shows these relationships between basic emotions and defenses, defensive purpose, and intrapsychic property.

Each emotion defense (Table 11.1) has as its main function a releasing or blocking purpose. These defense releasing or blocking mechanisms are designed to manage the nature of corresponding basic emotions. More specifically, defenses are designed to regulate the intrapsychic property of each emotion—that is, the nature of each basic emotion is largely colored by its inherent intrapsychic property: id or superego. The following is an illustration of these connections.

In order to regulate the aim of id imperatives inherent in the emotion of anger, the emotion defense of displacement is utilized to attenuate such impulses. That is, anger is somewhat modulated because of the displacement defense. This permits a more tenable relation to ultimately exist between the epigenetic emotion program and its connection to necessary object development. The proposition that emerges here implies that the defense property of emotion has been etched into the emotion program out of social demands and facilitates the connection between the epigenetic emotion program and object relations experiences. Emotion defenses, therefore, help to create greater resonance between forces of the biological program and corresponding social demands inherent in the object relation experiences. Thus, it is proposed that emotion defenses regulate id–superego urges and ultimately aid the synergistic infant–object relationship.

Freud (1940/1964) developed his motivational theory by proposing that the id contains an aim. The aim is to fuel the underlying instinct. In the present formulation, this instinct is essentially hypothesized to be contained within basic emotion. It is thus further proposed that the emotion substrate contains dispositional diagnostic elements, a defense element, and an intrapsychic nature. The defenses play an integral role in continually frustrating the aim of each basic emotion defined by its intrapsychic element, all in the service of ongoing socialization—that is, to help harmonize social demands with the dispositional nature of the epigenetic emotion program. This process of socialization is composed of the relative extent of working-through that the subject experiences as each psychosexual stage is traversed. In the following section, examples of this socialization process are offered.


## INTRAPSYCHIC AIM
## DURING PSYCHOSEXUAL STAGES

The theoretical position formulated here considers that each of the basic emotions contains dispositional instructions concerning intrapsychic elements, defense, and diagnostic disposition. Kellerman (1979, 1980) offers one possible model in the explication of these connections. In Table 11.2, diagnostic dispositions and their relation to the emotion program are proposed. Based on Table 11.2, many interesting speculations can be made. For example, typical diagnostic states can be related to specific psychosexual stages (Kellerman, 1979). In addition, intrapsychic forces can also be related to these stages. The question can now perhaps be addressed concerning the specific aim of each dispositional category and how this aim is managed in terms of its affect on psychosexual stage experiences? In the following section, the social demands made during each psychosexual stage with respect to the intrapsychic aims of each stage is

TABLE 11.2

Emotion, Diagnostic Disposition, Defense, Intrapsychic Force, and Psychosexual Stage

| Emotion | Diagnostic disposition | Defense | Intrapsychic force | Psychosexual stage |
|---------|------------------------|---------|--------------------|--------------------|
| Joy | Manic | Reaction formation | Id | Oral |
| Sorrow | Depressed | Compensation | Superego | Oral |
| Expectation | Obsessive | Intellectualization | Id | Anal |
| Surprise | Psychopathic | Regression | Superego | Anal |
| Anger | Aggressive | Displacement | Id | Phallic |
| Fear | Passive | Repression | Superego | Phallic |
| Acceptance | Hysteric | Denial | Id | Oedipal |
| Disgust | Paranoid | Projection | Superego | Oedipal |

proposed. Because of the hypothesized relation between emotion and intrapsychic elements, the character of a given epigenetic emotion program may be suggested through this analysis.

## THE ORAL STAGE

During the oral stage, the intrapsychic aim inherent in the emotion of joy is to express impulses characteristic of pleasure needs. The emotion of joy, as it corresponds to the oral stage, is a reference to the fact that the infant strives to experience gratification or to gain possession of the gratifying object. The extent of frustration experienced in the relative achievement of this goal will determine the extent to which superego urges surface—largely in the form of depressive sorrowful feelings. That is, in the absence of gratification and corresponding possession of the primary gratifying object, the infant experiences deprivation and the superego emotion of sorrow or loss. In this sense the feeling that "something is wrong" becomes prevalent. On a practical level, especially in terms of socialization demands, id aims cannot ever be fully met, and along with subsequent relative frustration, the balance between the id and the superego configuration during this oral period is formed. It is a configuration that corresponds to patterns of attachment described earlier in this chapter and perhaps reveals the deeper meaning of any particular attachment pattern. That is, particular attachment patterns are composed of basic id–superego configurations. In terms of diagnostic disposition at this oral stage, Kellerman (1979, 1980) has presented one possible theoretical connection between the basic emotions of joy and sorrow and their respective dispositional elements of manic and depressed.

The ultimate residue of oral stage conflict will thus reflect the result of id–superego aims, the relative impact such aims have on the object, and the extent to which these aims were addressed by the primary object. This residue of conflict or conflict-accomodation of id–superego urges during the oral stage can be conceived perhaps as an emergent ego, a primitive incrustation of ego, or perhaps an initial crystallization of ego. Id and superego as epigenetic elements of the emotion program are therefore hypothesized to be basic components of the emerging ego. This ego begins to form from the interaction of the epigenetic program with object experiences starting at the oral stage.

## THE ANAL STAGE

Inspection of Table 11.2 shows the proposed correlation between the anal stage developmental point and the basic emotions of expectation and surprise. Plutchik (1962, 1980a,b) offers a fuller explanation of the theoretical rationale for the choice of expectation and surprise as basic emotions, and Kellerman (1979, 1980) provides a nomological network that proposes the inherent id nature within the emotion of expectation as well as the superego nature within the emotion of surprise.

Kellerman (1979) has proposed the basic relation between the emotion of expectation and the obsessive diagnosis. During the anal stage, the intrapsychic aim inherent in the emotion of expectation is to express impulses characteristic of an id nature. For example, when obsessive individuals experience nightmares, they invariably awaken with dreams of falling or of losing control in some other way. Obsessive children will report having wet the bed because in the dream they constructed a bathroom scenario that made it then permissible to "let go." In the absence of obsessive id regulating defenses of intellectualization and its variants, a "letting go" occurs; this provides the basis, in part, for the postulate that the true nature of the obsessive is an id nature. During the anal stage, the extent to which this "letting go" aim is frustrated or blocked may determine the extent of superego that surfaces in the form of inhibition and overcontrol.

The overcontrol is a reflection of superego prohibitions becoming manifest in "stopping" experiences of superego feelings of paralysis. The experience of stopping is one that is hypothesized to correspond to the basic emotion of surprise. For example, in the awakening dreams or nightmares (correlated to the anal phase) of psychopathic persons, the superego emotion-regulating defense of regression does not function properly. Instead of a dream in which the subject can remain motoric, that is, in an action orientation (the typical condition of the psychopath), the subject experiences dream contents of being buried alive, drowning, unable to move, or in some other way completely paralyzed or stopped. The stopping event creates a surprise experience and the subject awakens in terror—a superego revelation. Thus, it is proposed that the particular intrapsychic frustrations of the anal period reveal diagnostic obses-sive–psychopathic conflict in the form of an id–superego compromise formation or in a control–dyscontrol compromise. This quantity of id and superego emerges as a response of the demands of socialization during this particular psychosexual developmental point, and the compromise formation reflects a further acculturation of ego development. The ego is now, in part, an object-related one consisting of id–superego compromise formations of the oral and anal stages of psychosexual experiences. Fundamentally, however, it should be noted that in present terms this process of ego development is a representation of object relations experiences deriving from interactions with epigenetic intrapsy-chic elements in the substrate of emotion structure.

## THE PHALLIC STAGE

Inspection of Table 11.2 indicates that the phallic developmental point and the basic emotions of anger and fear are correlated. The intrapsychic aim inherent in the emotion of anger is to express or release impulse. In personality terms, the aim of the aggressive dispositional type is to release the anger directly. This aim is largely managed through the emotion-regulating blocking defense of displace-ment; that is, displacement permits release of anger in more diluted, indirect, and socially acceptable form. Thus, it is hypothesized that due to socialization de-mands, the id aim of the aggressive dispositional type is largely frustrated and calls forth superego feelings of fear as a result of these particular frustrations. The superego urges that emerge are represented in fear of assertion or in disposi-tional passivity, and perhaps in the form of so-called castration anxieties that may be congruent with specific object experiences. In Table 11.2, repression appears as the emotion-regulating releasing defense of fear. The experience of fear is a superego manifestation. The extent of the fear and its superego nature is determined by the amount of displacement utilized to control anger during this period. The ego at this point is further expanded, and its relative strength (and to whatever extent it is resilient) is determined by the configurational balance of id–superego forces inherent in the expression of basic emotions during these first three psychosexual developmental periods.

## THE OEDIPAL STAGE

Also seen in Table 11.2 are the theoretical connections between the basic emotions of acceptance and disgust along with their respective id–superego and emotion defense elements as these are hypothesized to be related to the oedipal developmental stage. The intrapsychic aim of the emotion of acceptance is to express id impulse; that is, to love everything or not to be critical of anything. This id nature of acceptance also facilitates expression of the dispositional hysteric quality in the infrastructure of the emotion program. The aim inherent within hysteric inclinations is to express id needs for incorporation; that is, to take everything in. Because of the emotion defense id-blocking mechanism of denial, the hysterical person can be free of critical thoughts and not need to express negative feelings to external objects. However, because of socialization demands, the denial cannot endure indefinitely, and what emerges is a release of impulse in the opposite form of paranoid projections toward external objects. That is, although the hysteric is not critical, the paranoid is fully critical. This presence of critical thinking that is exemplified in the emotion of disgust or rejection reflects, in essense, a presence of superego. Thus, during the Oedipal period, id–superego conflict presents a still further balance or compromise of expression. It is proposed that the vicissitudes of such a balance developing from the effects of socialization on the emotion program at this stage and at each previous stage represents the first full formative organization of ego in the child's life.

In the final analysis, the successful development of object relations is only in part related to the relatively healthy attachment experiences provided in the external environment. These experiences are also confronted by indigenous forces of the subject that contribute direction, aim, and predisposition to the interaction with environmental object experiences. It is therefore postulated that the ego is a bridge between the intrapersonal (the epigenetic emotion program) and the interpersonal (object experience). In this sense, the ego is also a bridge between emotion and cognition.

In earlier discussions in this chapter, it was proposed that cognitive precursors are also inherent in the epigenetic emotion program. The tentative proposition offered postulated that primitive cognition may exist as uncrystallized intuition within emotion. "You only know (cognition) what you feel (emotion)" would be a first approximation toward understanding this proposition. In the following section, the entre to cognitive connections with the epigenetic emotion program will be proposed. This connection is only presented as one possible approach in the explication of a theory that attempts to discover a structural relationship between emotion and cognition.

## EMOTION AND COGNITION

It would be useful if cognitive categories of analysis could be derived that coincided with the basic categories of the emotion–personality theory. Such a development would necessarily suggest that also engraved in the substrate of emotion are cognitive proclivities, and that to whatever extent the emotion program becomes successfully expressed, these cognitive proclivities in turn also become reinforced. Cognitive correlations to the basic theoretical system presented here may in fact exist. These presumed cognitive categories perhaps simply await discovery and an overall synthesis. A good starting point for such inquiry would be to study the cognitive system in a way that shows intrinsic relations among the domains of cognition, emotion, and personality.


## FREUD AND PIAGET

The proposition that emotion may be the wellspring of cognitive development needs the explication of an intervening explanatory step. Piaget (1972) indicates that the way the ego acts on the external environment is to develop cognitive structures. The question, of course, is how the ego manages to create or facilitate the development of these cognitive configurations. In the theory presented in this chapter, the ego develops out of a series of id–superego compromises occuring through the experience of object relations development within the context of psychosexual considerations. The resulting ego can then be characterized by the degree of its strength, flexibility, plasticity, durability, and solidity. The essence of this process between epigenetic and environmental interactions concerns the fact that emotions seek to be expressed (as an intrinsic nature of the epigenetic program), and that their underlying intrapsychic urges, as previously discussed, seek gratification. If, as Piaget says, it is the ego that acts on the external environment to create cognitive structures, then more fundamentally, according to the epigenetic theory presented here, the emotion program would be ultimately responsible (at least in the rudimentary form) for the presence of such cognitive structure. This should be true if only because the nature of the ego is based on compromise formations of the conflict between id and superego during psychosexual stage progression (especially since such intrapsychic forces are assumed to be embedded in emotion structure). Such cognitive structures that can be conceived as based within the emotion program can become manifest through a series of intervening variables inherent during object relations development. Under this hypothetical set of conditions, cognition becomes a derivative of emotion.

Piaget may be only partially correct in asserting that cognition and emotion reflect parallel lines of development or interdependent processes (Greenspan, 1979). In Freudian terms, affect and cognition become synergistic when, in the infant, in the absence of a drive object and during a high-drive state, thought is derived; that is, in the absence of the object the wish for it creates a hallucination of the image of the object reflecting a wish fulfillment. According to Freud, this wish fulfillment process is then considered to be the precursor of thought. Freudian theory thus predicts that when the object of gratification is missing and instinctual discharges are delayed, the first connection between affects and cognitions arise. The hallucinatory image of the need-satisfying object is an effect of delayed gratification. It is the archetype of thought (Freud, 1915/1957). Thus, according to Freud, emotion can become attached to objects even though these are part objects or object representations derived from within. In this manner, cognition is born from emotion.

Freud posits that the child may view inanimate objects as alive because of projection, whereas Piaget indicates that the child views inanimate objects as alive because of a lack of differentiation between self and other objects (Greenspan, 1979). According to Piaget, it is only toward the end of the sensorimotor period (at about 1½ years) that the infant realizes that objects are imprinted in space and time despite the fact that they are no longer in his perceptual field (Greenspan, 1979). Psychoanalysis claims more ambitious capacities for the infant, placing the expression of mental representation and symbolic behavior at 3–6 months (Arlow, Freud, Lampl-de-Groot, & Beres, 1968). For Piaget, mental image can only be maintained as a function of the acquisition of language, whereas for Freud, maintaining the mental image is more a function of drive and of wish fulfillment. Thus, Freud implies that the connection between affect and thought is more of an epigenetic phenomenon, whereas for Piaget, affect expression through object development experiences and maturational phenomena can only accelerate or retard cognitive development.

Piaget holds that only with the acquisition of language can the child maintain the mental imagery in the absence of the cognitive object. Yet, given the earlier discussion in this chapter of the importance of pre-language intonational expression in the babbling of infants, the whole Piagetian notion of acquisition of language becomes a study only in the denotative element of word representations, whereas the deeper connotative language inherent in the emotion program is essentially ignored.

The point at which Piagetian and Freudian positions on the possible relations between emotions and cognitions intersect is revealed by Piaget's belief in an innate given or functioning capacity that shapes the interaction of the organism with the environment. Piaget labels this view *constructivist structuralism*. Within this theory, the origin of the mental structure is in the subject's actions, and not in the object. Structures are then constructed within the subject as a consequence of interactions between subjects and objects—a theory not unlike the one presented in this chapter, in which the epigenetic emotion program interacts with object experiences to produce a variety of socialization effects. Piaget theorizes that the subject's actions give rise to "affective schemes." In these schemes, affect and cognition are fused.

## PIAGET'S AFFECTIVE SCHEMES

Piagetian affective schemes are essentially behavior sequences that are connected to feelings and can become connected to situations that are similar to an original event. In Freudian terms, such a schema conception would contain three basic ingredients—two that are explicit, and one by implication. The first explicit ingredient relates to the nature of character formations; that is, the scheme or typical behavior itself. These are Piaget's behavior sequences. The second explicit ingredient is that of transference; that is, the transference to other situations—Piaget's similarity to an original event. The third ingredient by implication is the repetition compulsion—that the behavior sequence can occur again and again. Piaget indicates that these schemata determine the relative stability of the emotions; the more solidly formed the schemata, the more stable the emotions. Thus, in Piagetian terms, character structure awaits development of cognitive structure, and affect exists only as part of these action schemata. The affects come into action when schemata are stimulated by an external event (Piaget, 1945). According to Kessen (1971), the Piagetian theory is a cold one. There is no mention of drives, and the development of cognition is only adaptational through the need to function—that is, only as a result of external demands. Piaget also posits the concept of *equilibration*—a mechanical process providing the individual with a compensatory mechanism in managing external disturbances. This equilibration phenomenon in the individual is composed of two parts. The first is an assimilation process in which information is taken in that corresponds to an already established action schema. The second process is that of accomodation—that is, the modification of an assimilatory schema by those elements that have already been assimilated and are part of the schema. Assimilations are possible only to the extent that they may occur in terms of age-appropriate capacities and lead to new accomodations when the system is required to change due to newer external demands (Greenspan, 1979). Thus, although affective or action schemata are discrete, through a differentiation of experiences they are able to become transformed into newer discrete themes. In this sense, Piaget may be considered to be a theorist who posits affect development that occurs as a function of differentiation of external events.

Freudian or even Reichian theorists would argue, of course, that Piagetian action or affect schemata are basically precursor object relations models that account for the formation of character structure. In Piagetian terms, this formation of character depends on external events. In Freudian or in epigenetic approaches, it depends in large measure on the epigenetic emotion program that supplies the component emotions ultimately frozen into position as character traits. These traits are derived from the emotion program but are largely placed into position, so to speak, by object experiences during psychosexual developmental periods. Emotions and traits, according to Freudian structure, are thus expressions of drive and need and therefore may be described as the basis for a hot theory.

To Piaget, object relations and individual action schemata are part of the socialization process and, in this sense, impulses are controlled through values— a highest order of cognition. To Freud, impulses are, of course, controlled through the superego. In terms of the epigenetic program considered in this chapter, impulses reflect id–superego aims within emotion. These aims emerge with respect to object experiences and then the intrapsychic expressions and object experiences reciprocally influence each other. Values then become inextricably bound to ego—the residue of id–superego conflicts as these conflicts become shaped by the vicissitudes of object experiences. In this sense, whatever precognitive qualities may be contained within the deep structure of basic emotions also become represented during id–superego expressions of psychosexual experiences. In terms of the epigenetic program presented here, it is proposed that such cognitive qualities (or uncrystallized thought in the form of mood or intuition) are perhaps also infused in the structure of basic emotions. Thus, as far as the above discussion is concerned, through the use of the theoretical emulsifying agent designated here as the epigenetic formulation, Freudian and Piagetian positions become harmonized with respect to the proposition: *emotion is the wellspring of cognition*. This idea contains both Freudian as well as Piagetian ingredients. A Freudian underpinning interacts with the strong emphasis by Piaget on affective schemata and raises the question of the specific relationship between emotions and cognitions. The issue arises as to the specific cognitive categories that might be formulated to correspond to basic emotions.

In the following section, such categories will be proposed as a first approximation of the relation of emotion and cognition within the epigenetic framework. These connections are speculative and at this point can only draw theoretical support from whatever synthesizing power can be generated by the construct validity of the entire emotion–personality theoretical structure.

## BASIC EMOTIONS AND THEIR PROPOSED
## COGNITIVE DISPOSITIONS

According to Piaget, cognitions, (actually values) are representations of the highest form of social development. Any theory that proposes cognitive correlates within an epigenetic framework should in some way consider this Piagetian axiom and, in addition, consider a new assumption concerning the relation between cognition and emotion; that is, because cognitive structures may be the most advanced form of development they will necessarily contain information on the entire personality system, including, of course, affective organization.

THE RELATION OF
EMOTION AND COGNITIVE DIMENSIONS:
AN EPIGENETIC STRUCTURE

Basic cognitive categories are proposed that are derived from the epigenetic emotion program. These categories have been formulated with respect to how each cognitive concept relates to corresponding basic emotion dimensions (including defenses, and diagnostic dispositions). In the following listing of cognitive elements, these connections will be further suggested. In addition, in Table 11.3, the entire proposed emotion substrate of the epigenetic program is portrayed with respect to the connection between basic emotions and traits, diagnostic dispositions, regulatory emotion defenses, intrapsychic elements, and cognitive dimensions of each of these basic emotions.

**Acceptance**

The cognitive dimension representing the emotion of acceptance and reflecting the diagnostic as well as defensive elements associated with this emotion is proposed as an *attention–distraction* dimension. Together, the emotion of acceptance and the cognitive element of attention reflect interest and positive focus on the object. The cognitive element of attention as a derivative form of acceptance represents one aspect of a behavioral sequence that results in incorporative or absorption behavior. That is, attention in the context of acceptance is here proposed as reflecting the incorporation behavioral prototype dimension described by Plutchik (1962, 1980a,b).

On the cognitive level, attention or positive focus on the object is a derivative form in a sequence of events that lead to acceptance or absorption of the object. This kind of focus on the object can also be characterized in cognitive terms as assimilating certain positive information about the object and in interpersonal terms as loving the object. Kellerman (1979, 1980) draws theoretical connections between the emotion dimension of acceptance and the dispositional diagnostic state of the hysteric along with its proposed denial defense mechanism. Kellerman points out that in the hysteric, denial mechanisms are invoked to prevent or minimize any critical view of the object. In a corollary sense the extent or success of the operation of such defense may be understood in terms of the extent of the subject's *distractability*. That is, denial acts to distract the subject from expressing a critical view. Correspondingly, the focus on the object (or *attention* on the object) in this context essentially means acceptance of the object. In denial, then, only positive acceptance experiences occur and potentially negative rejecting responses are avoided.

TABLE 11.3

A Proposed System of the Epigenetic Structure of the Substrate of Emotion

| Emotion | Intrapsychic component | Emotion defense | Defensive function | Diagnostic disposition | Trait element | Cognitive orientation | Cognitive theme | Psychosexual stage |
|---|---|---|---|---|---|---|---|---|
| Joy | Id | Reaction formation | To block impulse | Manic | Gregarious | Purposiveness–aimlessness | | |
| Sorrow | Superego | Compensation | To release impulse | Depressed | Depressed | Rumination–relinquishment | Loss | Oral |
| Expectation | Id | Intellectualization | To block impulse | Obsessive | Control | Analysis–scatteredness | | |
| Surprise | Superego | Regression | To release impulse | Psychopathic | Dyscontrol | Impatience–paralysis | Control | Anal |
| Anger | Id | Displacement | To block impulse | Aggressive | Aggressive | Condensing–reconstituting | | |
| Fear | Superego | Repression | To release impulse | Passive | Timid | Recalling–forgetting | Focus (remembering) | Phallic |
| Acceptance | Id | Denial | To block impulse | Hysteric | Trustful | Attention–distraction | | |
| Disgust | Superego | Projection | To release impulse | Paranoid | Distrustful | Certainty–uncertainty | Autonomy | Oedipal |

Hence it is proposed that the cognitive dimension here labeled *attention–distraction* corresponds to the diagnostic disposition of hysteric and defense of denial, and each of these are derivative aspects of the basic emotion of acceptance. The relation between the emotion of acceptance and the cognitive dimension of attention–distraction generally concerns the issue between subject and object of "taking-in."

## Disgust

It is further proposed that the cognitive dimension representing the emotion of disgust and reflecting the diagnostic as well as defensive elements of this emotion is designated as a *certainty–uncertainty* dimension. The cognitive quest for certainty is here defined as a need to reinforce distinctions between self and object. Together, the emotion of disgust and cognitive element of certainty reflect a negative focus on the object. The chief characteristic used to distinguish self from object is the critical stance toward the object that achieves the certainty that self and object are indeed different. The cognitive element of certainty as a derivative form of disgust also represents one aspect of a behavioral sequence that results in rejecting behavior. That is, certainty and criticalness in the context of disgust are here proposed as reflecting the rejection behavioral prototype dimension described in Plutchik (1962, 1980a,b).

On the cognitive level, achieving certainty in the distinction between self and object (largely through the critical attitude toward the object) is a derivative aspect of a sequence of events that leads to rejection of the object. This kind of focus on the object can also be characterized in cognitive terms as identifying certain negative information about the object, and in interpersonal terms as being suspicious of the object, feeling guarded toward the object, or even hating the object.

Kellerman (1979, 1980) suggest a basic personality correlation between the emotion of disgust and the paranoid diagnostic state along with its proposed projection defense. Kellerman proposes that in the paranoid, the projection mechanism is utilized to enhance a critical view of the object. The relative success of the operation of this defense may be understood in terms of the subject's degree of certainty or uncertainty with respect to self–object difference. Thus, the projective defense that reinforces a critical stance toward the object acts to generate certainty in the subject of the distinction between self and object and correspondingly minimizes whatever uncertainty may exist. In projection, then, only negative experiences occur, and potentially positive accepting responses are limited.

Hence it is proposed that the cognitive dimension here labeled *certainty–uncertainty* corresponds to the diagnostic disposition of paranoid and defense of projection and each of these are derivative aspects of the basic emotion of disgust. The relation between the emotion of disgust and the cognitive dimension of certainty–uncertainty generally concerns the issue between subject and object of maintaining separation.

Inspection of Table 11.3 shows that the emotion of acceptance and disgust can be conceived as opposites. So, too, it may be proposed, can the diagnoses of hysteric and paranoid and defenses of denial and projection be considered opposites. Furthermore, on a cognitive level, the attention–distraction element within the acceptance dimension is practically observed in the intuitive approach of the hysteric personality—one in which the object does not attend to details. Rather, the subject becomes concerned primarily with reinforcing positive feelings within an interpersonal context. Conversely, on a cognitive level, the certainty–uncertainty element of the disgust dimension is observed in the paranoid character with regard to this person's great attention to detail as a way of exercising critical judgment. Whereas the hysteric is highly suggestible and noncritical, the paranoid is highly critical and resists suggestion. The emotion–cognition theme of taking-in the object or separating from the object concerns the overall issue of *autonomy*.

## Joy

The cognitive dimension representing the emotion of joy and reflecting the diagnostic and defensive elements of this emotion is here labeled *purposiveness–aimlessness* (or *randomness*). The correspondence between the emotion of joy and the cognitive quality of purposiveness is suggested by the theoretical framework proposed by Kellerman (1979, 1980), which identifies the diagnostic state reflecting the emotion of joy as the manic state. The manic state becomes a bridge for understanding the relationship between the emotion of joy and cognitive quality of purposiveness because of the typical energized industriousness as well as apparent gregariousness of the manic person. Of course, as a clinical problem, mania is more than simply an example of industriousness in a person. In the manic state, industriousness and gregariousness are translated into the need to be involved in multitudes of projects, each ostensibly aiming toward a goal or containing a *purpose*. In this sense, the emotion of joy is proposed here to be related cognitively to the quality of purposiveness—a goal-oriented attitude. This purposiveness is one that seeks to accomplish enormous work aims. Although joy is a representative pleasure emotion that has its roots in sexuality, it is further proposed that through the reaction-formation defense and compensatory mechanisms, sexual energy is transformed into work energy. Inherent in the purposive cognitive orientation, therefore, is the drive involved in motivation and search for work.

Together, the emotion of joy, the defense of reaction-formation, and the cognitive element of purposiveness reflect a nonsexual focus on the object. Through goal-oriented aims, the object is possessed in a work frenzy (symbolically to accomplish the aim) and, therefore, the cognitive element of purposiveness as a derivative form of the emotion of joy also represents one aspect of a behavioral sequence that results in the possessing of the object in the form of accomplishment. Purposiveness in the context of the emotion of joy, therefore, is here proposed as reflecting the reproduction behavioral prototype dimension described in Plutchik (1962, 1980a,b) that has as its main characteristic possession of the object. The relationship between the emotion of joy and the cognitive dimension of purposiveness–aimlessness generally concerns the issue between subject and object of fusion with, or possession of, the object.

## Sorrow

It is proposed that the cognitive dimension representing the emotion of sorrow and reflecting the diagnostic as well as defensive elements of this emotion is designated as a *rumination–relinquishment* dimension. Together, the emotion of sorrow and cognitive element of rumination reflect a continuous focus on the lost object. The cognitive element of rumination as a derivative form of sorrow represents one aspect of a behavioral sequence resulting in a repetitive attempt to reintegrate the lost object. Thus, rumination in the context of sorrow is here proposed as reflecting the reintegration behavioral prototype dimension described by Plutchik (1980a,b).

On the cognitive level, rumination or the attempt by the subject to retain the object is actually an attempt not to acknowledge loss of the object; rather, attempts at reintegration of the object occur through rumination in memory and fantasy. Kellerman (1979) proposes certain theoretical connections between the dimension of the emotion of sorrow and the dispositional diagnostic state of depression—along with the corresponding defense of compensation. Kellerman suggests that in the depressive the compensation mechanism is invoked to minimize any acknowledgement of loss. Therefore, rumination represents a continuous compensatory focus ostensibly on the presence (or on the image) of the object. In the absence of the compensatory mechanism, a *relinquishment* of the object is experienced by the subject, along with the emotion of sorrow. The state of depression becomes a diagnostic expression for this entire syndrome.

In terms of this syndromal formulation, it is proposed that the cognitive dimension here labeled *rumination–relinquishment* corresponds to the diagnostic disposition of depression and defense of compensation, and each of these are derivative aspects of the basic emotion of sorrow. The relation between the emotion of sorrow and the cognitive dimension of rumination–relinquishment generally concerns the issue between subject and object of reintegration. The emotion–cognition theme of possessing the object and regaining the object concerns the overall issue of *loss*.

Inspection of Table 11.3 will show that the emotion of joy and sorrow can be conceived as opposites. So, too, are the diagnoses of manic and depressed and, therefore, the defenses of reaction-formation and compensation considered to be opposites. Furthermore, on a cognitive level, the purposiveness–aimlessness element within the joy dimension reflecting a possession of the object is opposite to the rumination–relinquishment element of the sorrow dimension that reflects a loss of the object and an attempt at repossession.

## Expectation

The cognitive dimension representing the emotion of expectation and reflecting the diagnostic as well as defense elements of this emotion is proposed here as an *analysis–scatteredness* dimension. Together, the emotion of expectation and the cognitive element of analysis reflect a process of scanning and control of the object in order to understand how subject and object can be related. The cognitive element of *analysis* as a derivative form of expectation represents one aspect of a behavioral sequence that can be applied to the behavioral prototype dimension of exploration described by Plutchik (1962, 1980a,b). In interpersonal terms, *analysis* of the object can be considered control of the object. Kellerman (1979) also draws theoretical connections between the dimension of the expectancy emotion and the dispositional diagnostic state of the obsessive, along with its proposed defense of intellectualization. That is, Kellerman points out that in the obsessive, intellectualization is utilized to examine, categorize, discover, or control the object. Intellectualization helps the subject maintain ties with the object rather than reinforce a scatteredness and dissolution of ties. The tie with the object, however, is characterized by the subject's need to control. Hence it is proposed that the cognitive dimension here labeled *analysis–scatteredness* corresponds to the diagnostic disposition of obsessive and defense of intellectualization, and each of these are derivative aspects of the basic emotion of expectation. The relation between the emotion of expectation and the cognitive dimension of analysis–scatteredness generally concerns the issue between subject and object of control.

## Surprise

It is proposed that the cognitive dimension representing the emotion of surprise and reflecting the diagnostic as well as defensive elements of this emotion is designated an *impatience–paralysis* dimension. As expectation is related to analysis and control of the object, surprise is related to a dyscontrol element, impulsivity, or impatience toward the object; that is, a state of dyscontrol in the subject prevents the object from controlling the subject. The relationship between the emotion of surprise and the dyscontrol element of personality is suggested by Kellerman (1979, 1980), who proposes a diagnostic syndrome consisting of the psychopathic disposition, the defense of regression, and the emotion of surprise. It is proposed that the regressive defense permits the subject to remain in a motoric state or a perpetual state of dyscontrol. In the absence of dyscontrol, the subject will experience a state of paralysis with respect to the object—akin to being controlled by the object. Kellerman points out that the disorientation response resulting from the emotion of surprise correspondingly permits a dyscontrolled state to exist in the subject. On a behavioral level, the dyscontrol is related to the prototype category of orientation (essentially disorientation) presented in Plutchik (1962, 1980a,b). On a cognitive level, the disorientation or dyscontrol is expressed as impatience (or short attention span). The relation between the emotion of surprise and the cognitive dimension of impatience–paralysis generally concerns the issue between subject and object of the subject remaining uncontrolled.

In Table 11.3, the emotions of expectation and surprise are listed as opposites. The diagnoses of obsessive and psychopathic are also seen as opposites, as are the defenses of intellectualization and regression. Correspondingly, on the cognitive level, the analysis–scatteredness element within the expectation dimension is utilized by the subject to control the object whereas the impatience–paralysis element within the surprise dimension is utilized by the subject to neutralize any control of the subject by the object. The emotion–cognition theme of controlling the object or undermining control by the object concerns the overall issue of *control*.

## Anger

It is proposed that the cognitive dimension representing the emotion of anger and reflecting the diagnostic as well as defensive elements associated with this emotion be designated a *condensing–reconstituting* dimension. Together, the emotion of anger and the cognitive element of condensing reflect displaced negative expression toward the object. Kellerman (1979, 1980) attempts to draw the connection between the emotion of anger and its associated defense of displacement by indicating that the displacement acts to block the destructive impulse toward the object and direct it to a substitute, yet less threatening, object. In this sense, on a cognitive level, such displacement is transposed as a condensing or coding capacity. The emotion of anger is also associated with the aggressive diagnostic disposition and corresponds to the destruction behavioral prototype category defined by Plutchik (1962, 1980a,b).

This kind of focus on the object dilutes negative feelings, thereby minimizing a direct expostulation or reconstitution of anger toward the object. In interpersonal terms, the displacement of anger permits the relationship between subject and object to remain relatively undisturbed. Hence it is proposed that the cognitive dimension here labeled *condensing–reconstituting* corresponds to the diagnostic disposition of aggressive and defense of displacement, and that each of these are derivative aspects of the basic emotion of anger. The relation between the emotion of anger and the cognitive dimension of condensing–reconstituting generally concerns the issue between subject and object of attenuating the expression of dissatisfaction.

## Fear

It is proposed that the cognitive dimension representing the emotion of fear and reflecting the diagnostic as well as defensive elements associated with this emotion be designated a *recalling–forgetting* dimension. Generally, the relation between fear and recall concerns the idea of remembering a threatening event. In this sense, Kellerman (1979, 1980) proposes the connection between the emotion of fear and the passive diagnostic disposition. In the passive syndrome, repression as a major defensive orientation facilitates forgetting of the event. On a cognitive level, recalling is a response by the subject to the ever-present conflict of suppression of memory through repressive defense versus the ever-present possibility of remembering the event; that is, the operation of repression creates a conflict between hiding or losing the memory and the tendency to retain or find the memory. The emotion of fear, diagnosis of passivity, defense of repression, and cognitive element of recalling are proposed here to be essentially related to the behavioral prototype dimension described by Plutchik (1962, 1980a,b) as the protection category. The relation between the emotion of fear and the cognitive dimension of recalling–forgetting generally concerns the issue between subject and object of remembering or focusing.

Again, in Table 11.3, the emotions of anger and fear are considered to be opposites. So, too, are the diagnoses of aggressive and passive seen as opposite dispositions, along with the respective defenses of displacement and repression. Correspondingly, on the cognitive level, the condensing–reconstituting element within the anger dimension is considered opposite to the recalling–forgetting element within the fear dimension. The emotion–cognition theme of alternating and recalling dissatisfaction concerns the overall issue of asserting consciousness or *remembering,* or focusing.

These basic emotions, defenses, and diagnostic dispositions are related in a number of publications that spell out in considerable detail the various connections of the epigenetic emotion program; from specific emotion-diagnostic connections to corresponding defense and trait elements of each emotion (Kellerman, 1976, 1977, 1979, 1980, 1981; Kellerman & Burry, 1981; Kellerman & Plutchik, 1968, 1977, 1978; Plutchik, Kellerman, & Conte, 1979). The analysis of the emotion system itself within a psychoevolutionary context is thoroughly explicated by Plutchik also in a number of publications (1955, 1958, 1960, 1962, 1980a, 1980b). The personality system and its internal theoretical correlations are similarly spelled out in greater detail by Kellerman (1979, 1980). Therefore, although the presentation of the relations of basic emotions with corresponding cognitive orientations has been considered in this section as a first tentative organization of ideas and concepts, nevertheless this presentation is guided in its formulations by a larger theoretical matrix containing a measure of construct validity derived from theoretical as well as empirical studies.

## CONCLUSION

The emphasis in this chapter has been to underscore the point that the personality of the individual contains a deep structure at the root of which are emotions. A series of hypotheses have been advanced to indicate that these emotions are marked with important dispositional information concerning personality and cognitive elements. In the infant, this epigenetic program expresses its imperatives so that the program is influenced by and also influences external experience. Accordingly, the nature of emotions in early development suggests a highly complex epigenetic program. Further interest in this epigenetic framework perhaps can inspire more theoretical investigation as well as research into the nature of the emotion program, its effect on the individual as well as its effect on personality.

## REFERENCES

Ainsworth, M. D. S., Blehar, M. C., Waters, E., & Wall, S. *Patterns of attachment*. Hillsdale, New Jersey: Erlbaum, 1978.

Ames, L. B. The child's emotions: A developmental approach. In *Conference on emotions and feelings*. Philadelphia, Pennsylvania: American Psychological Association, 1963.

Arlow, J. A., Freud, A., Lampl-de-Groot, J., & Beres, D. Panel discussion. *International Journal of Psychoanalysis*, 1968, *49*, 506–512.

Balint, M. *Primary love and psychoanalytic technique*. London: Hogarth, 1952.

Bell, S. M., & Ainsworth, M. D. S. Infant crying and maternal responsiveness. *Child Development*, 1972, *43*, 1171–1190.

Blum, G. S. *Psychoanalytic theories of personality*. New York: McGraw Hill, 1953.

Bowlby, J. *Attachment and loss* (Vol. 1). New York: Basic Books, 1969.

Brenner, C. Affects and psychic conflict. *The Psychoanalytic Quarterly,* 1975, *44*(1), 5–28.

Chess, S. Psychiatry of the first three years of life. In S. Arieti (Ed.), *American handbook of psychiatry* (Vol. 3). Basic Books, 1966.

Emde, R. N., Gaensbauer, T. J., & Harmon, R. J. *Emotional expression in infancy: A biobehavioral study.* New York: International Universities Press, 1976.

Fairbairn, W. R. D. *Psychoanalytic studies of the personality.* New York: Basic Books, 1952.

Freud, S. Three essays on the theory of sexuality: infantile sexuality. In J. Strachey (Ed.), *The complete psychological works of Sigmund Freud* (19th ed.). London: Hogarth Press, 1961. (Originally published, 1905)

Freud, S. Character and anal eroticism. In J. Strachey (Ed.), *The complete psychological works of Sigmund Freud* London: Hogarth Press, 1959. (Originally published, 1908)

Freud, S. Instincts and their vicissitudes. In J. Strachey (Ed.), *The complete psychological works of Sigmund Freud* (14th ed.). London: Hogarth Press, 1957. (Originally published, 1915)

Freud, S. Libidinal types. In J. Strachey (Ed.), *The complete psychological works of Sigmund Freud* (21st ed.). London: Hogarth Press, 1961. (Originally published, 1931)

Freud, S. An outline of psychoanalysis. In J. Strachey (Ed.), *The complete psychological works of Sigmund Freud* (23rd ed.). London: Hogarth Press, 1964. (Originally published, 1940)

Greenspan, S. I. *Intelligence and adaptation.* New York: International Universities Press, 1979.

Guntrip, H. *Personality structure and human interaction.* New York: International Universities Press, 1961.

Izard, C. E. On the ontogenesis of emotions and emotion–cognition relationship in infancy. In M. Lewis & L. A. Rosenblum (Eds.), *The development of affect.* New York: Plenum, 1978.

Kagan, J. Family experience and the child's development. *American Psychologist,* 1979, *34*(10), 886–891.

Kanner, L. Problems of nosology and psychodynamics of early infantile autism. *American Journal of Orthopsychiatry,* 1949, *19,* 416–426.

Kaywin, L. An epigenetic approach to the psychoanalytic theory of instincts and affects. *Journal of the American Psychoanalytic Association,* 1960, *8*(4), 613–658.

Kellerman, H. The emotional behavior of dolphins, *Tursiops truncatus:* Implications for psychoanalysis. *International Mental Health Research Newsletter,* 1966, *8*(1), 1–7.

Kellerman, H. *The sociobiology of group psychotherapy and the physics of group boundary structure.* Paper presented at a meeting of the Association of Science, Psychotherapy, and Ethics, New York, November 1976.

Kellerman, H. *Communication and emotion.* Paper presented at the Postgraduate Center for Mental Health Professional Meeting on Lacan and Psychoanalysis, New York, 1977.

Kellerman, H. *Group psychotherapy and personality: Intersecting structures.* New York: Grune & Stratton, 1979.

Kellerman, H. A structural model of emotion and personality: Psychoanalytic and sociobiological implications. In R. Plutchik & H. Kellerman (Eds.), *Emotion: theory, research, and experience* (Vol. 1). *Theories of emotion.* New York: Academic Press, 1980.

Kellerman, H. *Sleep disorders: Insomnia and narcolepsy.* New York: Brunner/Mazel, 1981.

Kellerman, H., Buirski, P., & Plutchik, R. Group behavior in a baboon troop: Implications for human group process. In L. R. Wolberg & M. L. Aronson (Eds.). *Group therapy 1974: An overview.* New York: Stratton Intercontinental Medical, 1974.

Kellerman, H., & Burry, A. *Handbook of psychodiagnostic testing: Personality analysis and report writing.* New York: Grune & Stratton, 1981.

Kellerman, H., & Plutchik, R. Emotion–trait interrelations and the measurement of personality. *Psychological Reports,* 1968, *23,* 1107–1114.

Kellerman, H., & Plutchik, R. The meaning of tension in group therapy. In L. R. Wolberg, M. L. Aronson, & A. R. Wolberg (Eds.), *Group therapy 1977—An overview.* New York: Stratton Intercontinental Medical, 1977.

Kellerman, H., & Plutchik, R. Personality patterns of drug addicts in a therapy group: A similarity structure analysis. *Group,* 1978, *2*(1), 14–21.

Kernberg, O. *Object relations theory and clinical psychoanalysis.* New York: Jason Aronson, 1976.

Kessen, W. Early cognitive development: Hot or cold? In T. Mischel (Ed.), *Cognitive development and epistemology.* New York: Academic Press, 1971.

Klein, M. *Contributions to psychoanalysis: 1921–1945.* London: Hogarth, 1948.

Klein, M. *New directions in psychoanalysis.* New York: Basic Books, 1955.

Klein, M., & Tribich, D. Kernberg's object relations theory: A critical evaluation. *International Journal of Psychoanalysis,* 1981, *62,* 27–44.

Lacan, J. *Ecrits.* New York: Norton, 1968.

McDougall, W. *An introduction to social psychology.* Boston: Luce, 1921.

Needles, W. Comments on the pleasure–unpleasure experience: The role of biological factors. *Journal of the American Psychoanalytic Association,* 1964, *12*(2), 300–314.

Piaget, J. *Play, dreams, and imitation in childhood.* New York: Norton, 1945.

Piaget, J. The relation of affectivity to intelligence in the mental development of the child. In S. I. Harrison & J. F. McDermott (Eds.), *Childhood psychopathology.* New York: International Universities Press, 1972.

Plutchik, R. Some problems for a theory of emotion. *Psychosomatic Medicine,* 1955, *17,* 306–310.

Plutchik, R. Outlines of a new theory of emotion. *Transactions of the New York Academy of Science,* 1958, *20,* 394–403.

Plutchik, R. The multifactor analytic theory of emotion. *Journal of Psychology,* 1960, *50,* 153–171.

Plutchik, R. *The emotions: Theories, facts, and a new model.* New York: Random House, 1962.

Plutchik, R. *Emotion: A psychoevolutionary synthesis.* New York: Harper & Row, 1980. (a)

Plutchik, R. A general psychoevolutionary theory of emotion. In R. Plutchik & H. Kellerman, (Eds.), *Emotion: Theory, research, and experience.* (Vol. 1). *Theories of emotion.* New York: Academic Press, 1980. (b)

Plutchik, R., & Kellerman, H. *The emotions profile index: Test and manual.* San Francisco, California: Western Psychological Services, 1974.

Plutchik, R., Kellerman, H., & Conte, H. A structural theory of ego defenses. In C. E. Izard (Ed.), *Emotions, personality, and psychopathology.* New York: Plenum, 1979.

Rado, S. *Psychoanalysis of behavior.* New York: Grune & Stratton, 1956.

Rapaport, D., & Gill, M. M. The points of view and assumptions of metapsychology. *International Journal of Psychoanalysis,* 1959, *40,* 153–162.

Schwarz, J. C. Childhood origins of psychopathology. *American Psychologist,* 1979, *34,*(10), 879–885.

Scott, J. P. *Animal behavior.* Chicago, Illinois: Univ. of Chicago Press, 1958.

Sroufe, L. A. Socioemotional development. In J. Osofsky (Ed.), *Handbook of infant development.* New York: Wiley, 1979.

Stern, G. G., Caldwell, B. M., Hersher, L., Lipton, E. L. and Richmond, J. B. A factor analytic study of the mother–infant dyad. *Child Development,* 169, *40,* 163–181.

Suttie, I. *The origins of love and hate.* London: Keegan Paul, 1935.

Tennes, K. H., & Lampl, E. E. Stranger and separation anxiety in infancy. *Journal of Nervous and Mental Disease,* 1964, *139,* 247–254.

Watson, J. B. *Psychology from the standpoint of a behaviorist.* Philadelphia, Pennsylvania: Lippincott, 1929.

Winnicott, D. W. *The maturnational processes and the facilitating environment.* New York: International Universities Press, 1965.

Yarrow, L. J. Emotional development. *American Psychologist,* 1979, *34*(10), 951–957.

# Subject Index

## A

A-not-B error, 135
Acceptance
  and cognition, 339, 341
  in Oedipal stage, 333–334
Accessibility, of emotional response, 263,
    270–275, 285, 286
  definition of, 270
  and education of attention, 275–277
  and expressive behavior, 272, 273, 275, 276
  and instrumental behavior, 271, 273, 275
  and physiological responding, 273, 275
  and self-reports, 271–272, 273, 275
  and subjective experience, 271–272, 273,
    275
Accomodation, 282–283, 285, 337
Achievement
  motor, satisfaction with, 2, 13–14
  parents' approval of, 37–38
  sense of, 37–38
Achievement motivation, 286
Action anticipation, 74–75

Activation, 27, 28
Adaptation, and primary motivational/emo-
    tional systems, 261–263, 267, 269
Adaptive behavior, 222–223
Adaptive value
  of emotions, 7–8, 15–16, 296, 299, 300,
    306
  of facial expressions, 62–63
  of prolonged infancy, 40
Addition sequence, 150, 151, 165
Adultomorphising, 6, 37
Affect(s)
  beginnings or precursors of, 12–19
  covert, approaches to, 9–10
  definition of, 5
  function of, 238
  and motor achievements, 2, 13–14
  problems in labeling, 6–7
  topics in research on, 8
Affect development
  impaired, 38
  individual differences in, 2
Affectional systems, 278–280